HOUGHTON MIFFLIN

Vocabulary for Achievement

Second Course

Margaret Ann Richek
Arlin T. McRae
Susan K. Weiler

Houghton Mifflin Company · Boston

Atlanta · Dallas · Geneva, Illinois · Lawrenceville, New Jersey · Palo Alto · Toronto

Authors

Margaret Ann Richek
Professor of Education, Northeastern Illinois University; consultant in reading and vocabulary study; author of *The World of Words*

Arlin T. McRae
Supervisor of English, Evansville-Vanderburgh School Corporation, Evansville, Indiana; Adjunct Instructor in English, University of Evansville

Susan K. Weiler
Teacher of Latin, Beaumont School for Girls, Cleveland Heights, Ohio

Classroom Consultants

Jack Pelletier
Teacher of English, Mira Loma High School, Sacramento, California

Valerie M. Webster
Teacher of English, Walnut Hill School, Natick, Massachusetts

Acknowledgments
Definitions for the three hundred words taught in this textbook are based on Houghton Mifflin dictionaries—in particular, the *Houghton Mifflin Student Dictionary*—but have been abbreviated and adapted for instructional purposes. In the skill lessons, dictionary entries from the *Houghton Mifflin Student Dictionary*, copyright © 1986, appear on pages 20 and 40; dictionary entries from the *Houghton Mifflin College Dictionary*, copyright © 1986, appear on pages 19–20, 39–40, and 59–60. Some of the entries have been abridged. The pronunciation key on the inside front cover is adapted from *The American Heritage Dictionary of the English Language, Third Edition*, copyright © 1992.

Credits
Design and art production: Design Office, San Francisco

Illustration
Alex Bloch: pages 185, 197; Dick Cole: pages 65, 77, 145, 151, 177; Simon Galkin: pages 31, 57, 117, 125; Charles Scogins: pages 11, 45, 71, 171.

Printed in the U.S.A.

ISBN: 0-395-67513-8

123456789-SM-97 96 95 94 93

Contents

Complete Word List

— abet, 81
— abide, 133
— abode, 53
— abrupt, 181
— accent, 1
— accessible, 173
— accompanist, 13
— accomplice, 13
— acquit, 107
— administer, 141
— admonish, 187
— adversary, 87
— aggression, 87
— alienate, 187
— alloy, 41
— altruistic, 193
— amenable, 133
— amicable, 33
— amiss, 113
— anarchy, 101
— anguish, 33
— animate, 141
— annex, 53
— antiquated, 61
— aqueduct, 73
— arson, 107
— articulate, 1
— authoritarian, 101

— belated, 67
— benefactor, 193
— beneficial, 193
— benevolent, 193
— benign, 193
— bewilder, 113
— bias, 133
— blithe, 33
— blockade, 47
— blunder, 113
— boisterous, 153
— bountiful, 193
— buoyant, 41

— cache, 173
— celestial, 41
— censure, 187
— centenarian, 61
— chaos, 153
— claimant, 93
— clamor, 93
— coagulate, 41
— coalition, 13
— combustible, 41
— communal, 13
— compel, 167
— complacent, 153
— complement, 13
— comport, 147
— compulsion, 167
— concoct, 141
— conduct, 73
— conduit, 73

— confines, 161
— conflagration, 41
— congenial, 27
— congregate, 13
— consensus, 13
— conservative, 101
— conspicuous, 173
— contemporary, 61
— contradict, 87
— controversy, 87
— corrupt, 107
— counterfeit, 107
— culprit, 107

— declaim, 93
— deduce, 73
— defiant, 33
— degenerate, 27
— delegate, 101
— delineate, 161
— deliverance, 81
— demarcation, 161
— denounce, 187
— deportment, 147
— descendant, 21
— desolate, 33
— despondent, 33
— detriment, 187
— devise, 141
— dialect, 1
— diction, 1
— disclaim, 93
— disclosure, 173
— discord, 87
— discrimination, 133
— disgruntled, 33
— disillusion, 33
— disport, 147
— disrupt, 181
— dissection, 41
— distend, 161
— distill, 41
— distinct, 161
— distress, 33
— dominion, 101
— duration, 67
— dynamic, 153

— edifice, 53
— embellish, 121
— embody, 161
— embroil, 87
— eminent, 127
— endeavor, 141
— ennoble, 81
— enunciate, 1
— erroneous, 113
— eruption, 181
— evocative, 93
— excavate, 53
— exceed, 121
— execute, 141

— expedite, 81
— expire, 67
— exuberant, 33

— fallible, 113
— faux pas, 113
— felony, 107
— fledgling, 61
— fluster, 113
— forbearance, 133
— foregone, 67
— fractious, 181
— fragment, 181
— frail, 61
— fundamental, 1

— gender, 27
— genealogy, 27
— generation, 21
— generic, 27
— genesis, 27
— gentry, 27
— gerontology, 61
— glut, 121
— gratify, 193

— haggle, 87
— hijack, 107
— humanitarian, 193

— immoderate, 121
— impeach, 101
— impel, 167
— imperil, 187
— implement, 141
— impulsive, 167
— inaugurate, 101
— incapacitate, 187
— incessant, 67
— incriminate, 107
— indestructible, 47
— indispensable, 127
— induce, 73
— inductee, 13
— induction, 73
— indulge, 193
— infraction, 181
— infringe, 181
— inheritance, 21
— injurious, 187
— insular, 7
— insupportable, 147
— intelligible, 1
— intense, 121
— inter, 173
— intercede, 81
— intrigue, 173
— invoke, 93

— latitude, 7
— lavish, 121
— liberal, 101
— lineage, 21
— longevity, 61
— longitude, 7

— luxurious, 121
— malign, 187
— marginal, 161
— martial, 47
— mason, 53
— maternal, 21
— matriarch, 21
— medieval, 67
— meridian, 7
— meteorology, 41
— miscalculate, 113
— miscellaneous, 13
— misinterpret, 113
— momentous, 127
— monotonous, 153

— nascent, 61

— objective, 133
— obscure, 173
— offset, 81
— omnipotent, 47
— omnipresent, 161
— outrageous, 121
— overestimate, 113

— pacify, 81
— panorama, 7
— paramount, 127
— parental, 21
— partisan, 133
— patriarch, 21
— peal, 167
— peer, 1
— penetration, 161
— peninsula, 7
— petty, 127
— philanthropic, 193
— portable, 147
— portage, 147
— porter, 147
— portfolio, 147
— posterity, 21
— precipice, 7
— preconceived, 133
— prefabricate, 53
— prejudice, 133
— premature, 67
— prestige, 127
— primogeniture, 27
— priority, 127
— productivity, 73
— profuse, 121
— progeny, 27
— prominence, 127
— propulsion, 167
— puerile, 61
— pulsate, 167
— purport, 147

— quagmire, 7

— reactivate, 141
— reclaim, 93
— reduction, 73

— refractory, 181
— refurbish, 81
— regenerate, 27
— reinforce, 81
— render, 141
— repeal, 167
— repellent, 167
— repent, 107
— repulse, 167
— respite, 67
— restive, 153
— revoke, 93
— robust, 47
— rotunda, 53
— rout, 181
— rupture, 181

— sanctuary, 81
— saturate, 41
— scoff, 187
— secluded, 173
— sibling, 21
— simultaneous, 67
— skirmish, 87
— solar, 53
— Spartan, 101
— spendthrift, 121
— sportive, 147
— stability, 47
— stalemate, 87
— static, 153
— status, 1
— staunch, 47
— steadfast, 153
— stress, 1
— strife, 87
— subdue, 73
— subsequent, 67
— substantial, 161
— superficial, 127
— swindle, 107

— terrestrial, 7
— throng, 13
— tolerance, 133
— topography, 7
— tranquil, 153
— trellis, 53
— trivial, 127
— turret, 53
— tyrant, 101

— unavailable, 173
— undertaking, 141
— unearth, 173

— valiant, 47
— velocity, 153
— venerable, 61
— viaduct, 73
— vocation, 93
— vouch, 93
— vulnerable, 47

— withstand, 47

HOUGHTON MIFFLIN VOCABULARY FOR ACHIEVEMENT, SECOND COURSE

Classroom Insights

Why Study Vocabulary Systematically?

Teachers generally agree on the importance of vocabulary development in the refining of language skills. The greater the store of words we have at our disposal, the better equipped we are to comprehend what we read and to express what we think.

A systematic approach to vocabulary building helps students to understand and use words effectively. By studying words in depth and in a variety of contexts, students can not only recognize new words but also retain and apply them. Furthermore, a methodical program of vocabulary development provides students with strategies for unlocking the meanings of unfamiliar words and promotes ongoing, independent learning.

The results of the systematic study of vocabulary are noteworthy. The number of words that we know is a reliable indicator of our ability to understand what we read. Therefore, as students increase their supply of words, their reading comprehension improves across all areas of the curriculum. Their performance on standardized tests is likewise dependent upon their available vocabulary and their word-attack skills. Because language skills permit the effective expression of ideas, students with vocabulary proficiency are more likely to select and use words forcefully in speaking and writing. Finally, by increasing their overall sensitivity to language, students develop a curiosity about words that encourages them continually to assimilate new words into their vocabularies. A systematic program ensures the development of the large storehouse of words that is important to achievement, both in and out of the classroom.

The Major Thrust of the Program

Houghton Mifflin Vocabulary for Achievement is a systematic program of vocabulary development that provides comprehensive instruction and practice. In devising the seven-book program, the authors have followed four major principles.

1. *Structured lessons teach best.*

Each book consists of 30 six-page lessons. Each lesson covers ten words chosen for their usefulness and appropriateness to the grade level. To provide the conceptual links that help students master the definitions, each word list is based on a topic or theme or on a word root or roots.

Based on information from the authoritative Houghton Mifflin dictionaries, each word is presented in considerable detail. Pronunciations, part-of-speech labels, multiple definitions, etymologies, and examples provide students with the information necessary for understanding, learning, and using each word.

The planned progression of the four follow-up exercises in each lesson establishes a variety of contexts for each word and leads students through the recognition and recall stages of learning. Students first identify literal definitions, then decide whether words are used correctly in sentences, next choose the appropriate word for the context, and finally use different forms of the words.

2. *Application aids retention.*

In a culminating exercise, students work with a reading passage that incorporates the ten words from the lesson. The exercise challenges students' understanding of the words by restating the meaning of each original sentence; in each case, students must understand the word and the sentence in order to select the correct answer. In addition to providing a larger, natural context for the vocabulary words, the passages present interesting information and strengthen the vital link between vocabulary development and reading comprehension.

Students put their grasp of new words into practice in specially designed writing assignments that accompany each lesson. Related to the lesson theme or passage topic, the assignments require students to write for a given audience and fulfill a certain purpose. In addition to providing an opportunity to apply words from the lesson, each assignment also stresses effective writing. As they write, students acquire experience in using words smoothly and proficiently in the contexts that they create.

3. *Special vocabulary-acquisition skills promote independent learning.*

A **skill feature** on dictionary use, on test taking, or on reading appears after each cluster of three vocabulary lessons. Each of the ten skill features consists of two pages of explanation and practice. Students learn how to utilize dictionary information and how to approach and complete test items. In addition, they learn how to use context clues and how to analyze word parts to unlock the meanings of unfamiliar words encountered in reading.

4. *Vocabulary materials must be readily accessible and easily adaptable to classroom needs.*

The consistent structure of the program makes it ideal either for classroom instruction or for independent use. Complete presentation, abundant practice, numerous examples of context, and opportunities for application provide students with the information that they need in order to learn new words. **Skill features** furnish practical strategies for ongoing vocabulary acquisition, and **flash cards** are an effective tool for learning and review.

You can establish a consistent schedule and monitor student progress with the materials included in the **Teacher's Edition.** The interleafing

of the facsimiles of **Tests** and **Bonuses** among the vocabulary lessons provides a built-in reminder of the special resources that accompany the program. Answers printed in color on full-size student exercise pages and on Test and Bonus pages enable you to correct student work quickly and easily. The **Teaching Suggestions** section provides concrete ideas to help you adapt these materials for special classroom needs and to extend the range and usefulness of the materials. Finally, the *Teacher's Resource Masters* booklet contains reproducible masters of the Tests and Bonuses with answers on the front sides. The systematic approach and comprehensive resources of *Houghton Mifflin Vocabulary for Achievement* allow you to direct a sound and successful vocabulary program.

The Anatomy of a Lesson

Lessons are **theme-centered** or **root-centered** to provide a context in which students can learn new words.

Introductions are motivational.

Pronunciations, definitions, and **etymologies** are from Houghton Mifflin dictionaries.

Word entries are presented **dictionary-style.**

Related words were chosen for their usefulness and appropriateness to grade level.

The **Word List** is a convenient reference for both students and teacher.

Writing new words on word blanks reinforces correct **spelling.**

Example sentences illustrate the primary definition of each word.

Usage notes or **memory cues** provide tips for using the words correctly or remembering them.

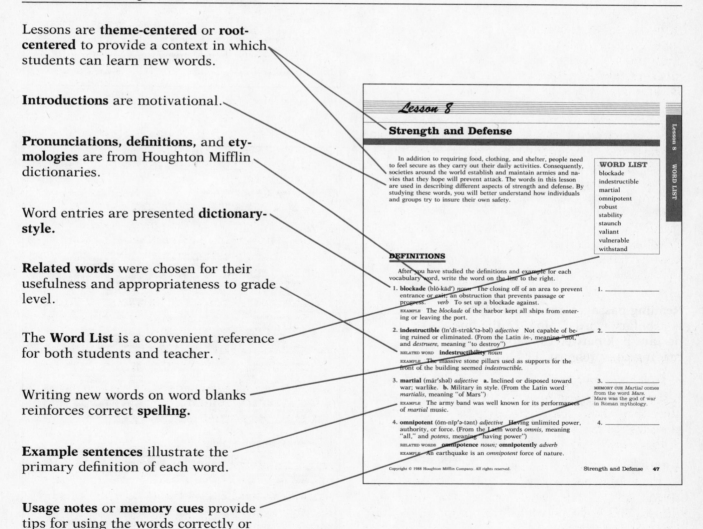

HOUGHTON MIFFLIN VOCABULARY FOR ACHIEVEMENT, SECOND COURSE

A variety of **exercise formats** provides practice and aids in **recognition, recall,** and **application** of the words.

Reading passages, incorporating the vocabulary words, reinforce the important link between vocabulary and reading comprehension.

Name _____ Date _____

Exercise 1   Completing Definitions

On the answer line, write the word from the vocabulary list that best completes each definition.

1. To be sturdy, strong, and healthy is to be ___?___ .
2. To endure or to resist something successfully is to ___?___ it.
3. The closing off of an area to prevent movement in or out is a ___?___ .
4. A person who displays great courage or boldness is considered ___?___ .
5. Behavior that is warlike or military in style is ___?___ .
6. Firmness of character or resistance to change is ___?___ .
7. A position that can be easily attacked is ___?___ .
8. When something cannot be ruined or eliminated, it is ___?___ .
9. A person or thing that is firm, strong, and loyal is ___?___ .
10. To have unlimited power is to be ___?___ .

1. _____robust_____
2. _____withstand_____
3. _____blockade_____
4. _____valiant_____
5. _____martial_____
6. _____stability_____
7. _____vulnerable_____
8. _____indestructible_____
9. _____staunch_____
10. _____omnipotent_____

Exercise 2   Using Words Correctly

Each of the following questions contains an italicized vocabulary word. Decide the answer to the question, and write *Yes* or *No* on the answer line.

1. Would a *martial* nation be known for its peace-loving nature?
2. Would a *valiant* person face danger in order to help a friend?
3. Is a sleeping deer *vulnerable* prey for a hungry wolf?
4. Would a weak, foolish king be an *omnipotent* ruler?
5. Would a *robust* person have difficulty walking one mile?
6. Would a *staunch* friend refuse to talk about you behind your back?
7. In the event of a naval *blockade*, would ships be allowed to pass freely in and out of a harbor?
8. Can penguins *withstand* the cold air and water of Antarctica?
9. Would a tool shed made of flattened tin cans and plywood be *indestructible* during a tornado?
10. Does a bridge that rocks back and forth when you walk on it have *stability*?

1. _____No_____
2. _____Yes_____
3. _____Yes_____
4. _____No_____
5. _____No_____
6. _____Yes_____
7. _____No_____
8. _____Yes_____
9. _____No_____
10. _____No_____

Exercise 3   Choosing the Best Word

Decide which vocabulary word or related form best completes the sentence, and write the letter of your choice on the answer line.

1. The ship was able to ___?___ the strong winds and heavy rain.
   a. blockade **b.** stabilize **c.** staunch **d.** withstand

1. _____d_____

Strength and Defense **49**

Name _____ Date _____

Reading Comprehension

Each numbered sentence in the following passage contains an italicized vocabulary word or related form. After you have read the passage, you will complete an exercise.

The Spanish Armada

Conflict had existed between Spain and England since the 1570s. England wanted a share of the wealth that Spain had been taking from the lands it had claimed in the Americas. (1)Elizabeth I, Queen of England, encouraged her *staunch* admiral of the navy, Sir Francis Drake, to raid Spanish ships and towns. (2)Though these raids were on a small scale, Drake achieved dramatic success, adding gold and silver to England's treasury and diminishing Spain's *omnipotence.*

Religious differences also caused conflict between the two countries. Whereas Spain was Roman Catholic, most of England had become Protestant. King Philip II of Spain wanted to claim the throne and make England a Catholic country again. To satisfy his ambition and also to retaliate against England's theft of his gold and silver, King Philip began to build his fleet of warships, the Armada, in January 1586. (3)Philip intended his fleet to be *indestructible.* (4)In addition to building new warships, he marshaled 130 sailing vessels of all types and recruited more than 19,000 *robust* soldiers and 8,000 sailors. (5)Although some of his ships lacked guns and others lacked ammunition, Philip was convinced that his Armada could *withstand* any battle with England.

(6)The *martial* Armada set sail from Lisbon, Portugal, on May 9, 1588, but bad weather forced it back to port. (7)The voyage resumed on July 22 after the weather became more *stable.* The Spanish fleet met the smaller, faster, and more maneuverable English ships in battle off the coast of Plymouth, England, first on July 31 and again on August 2. (8)The two battles left Spain *vulnerable,* having lost several ships and with its ammunition depleted.

On August 7, while the Armada lay at anchor on the French side of the Strait of Dover, England sent eight burning ships into the midst of the Spanish fleet to set it on fire. (9)*Blockaded* on one side, the Spanish ships could only drift away, their crews in panic and disorder. Before the Armada could regroup, the English attacked again on August 8.

(10)Although the Spaniards made a *valiant* effort to fight back, the fleet suffered extensive damage. During the eight hours of battle, the Armada drifted perilously close to the rocky coastline. At the moment when it seemed that the Spanish ships would be driven onto the English shore, the wind shifted, and the Armada drifted out into the North Sea. The Spaniards recognized the superiority of the English fleet and returned home, defeated.

Reading Comprehension Exercise

Each of the following statements corresponds to a numbered sentence in the passage. Each statement contains a blank and is followed by four answer choices. Decide which choice fits best in the blank. The word or phrase that you choose must express roughly the same meaning as the italicized word in the passage. Write the letter of your choice on the answer line.

1. Elizabeth I encouraged her ___?___ admiral of the navy to raid Spanish ships and towns.
   a. wise **b.** crafty **c.** loyal **d.** precise

1. _____c_____

Strength and Defense **51**

HOUGHTON MIFFLIN VOCABULARY FOR ACHIEVEMENT, SECOND COURSE

A **follow-up exercise** on the passage tests student understanding of the vocabulary words in context.

A **Writing Assignment,** related to the lesson theme or passage topic, lets students apply new words. Assignments are designed to stimulate interest, enthusiasm, and creativity.

Vocabulary Enrichment(s) provide interesting and unusual word histories.

The **Activity** encourages students to investigate the origins of several related words.

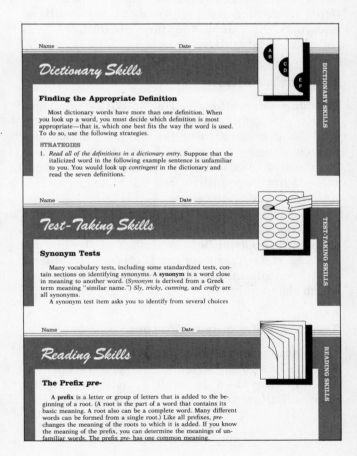

2. Drake added wealth to the treasury and diminished Spain's ___?___ .
   a. unlimited power   c. reputation
   b. unrestricted growth   d. territory

3. Philip intended his fleet to be ___?___ .
   a. respected   c. incapable of being copied
   b. incapable of being eliminated   d. special

4. Philip recruited many ___?___ soldiers and sailors.
   a. warlike   b. strong   c. accomplished   d. creative

5. Philip was convinced that the Armada could ___?___ any battle with England.
   a. engage   b. arrange   c. break   d. endure

6. The ___?___ Armada set sail on May 9, 1588.
   a. complete   b. warlike   c. independent   d. luxurious

7. The voyage resumed after the weather became more ___?___ .
   a. reliable   b. idle   c. serious   d. restless

8. The two battles left the Spanish fleet ___?___ .
   a. open to change   c. open to attack
   b. triumphant   d. hopeful

9. The Armada was ___?___ on one side.
   a. closed off   b. damaged   c. dependable   d. alone

10. The Spaniards made a ___?___ attempt to fight back.
    a. slight   b. ridiculous   c. huge   d. courageous

2. ___a___
3. ___b___
4. ___b___
5. ___d___
6. ___b___
7. ___a___
8. ___c___
9. ___a___
10. ___d___

Writing Assignment

Write a letter to your local or school newspaper in which you take a position on an issue of importance in your school or community. For example, you might write a letter defending the quality of the food served in the school cafeteria. Use at least five of the words from this lesson and underline them.

Vocabulary Enrichment

The word *martial* comes from the name of a Roman god, Mars. Mars was originally the Roman god of agriculture, and the early Romans paid tribute to him for good harvests.

After the Romans captured Greece, they adopted the Greek gods and myths into their own culture. Because the Greeks believed that a goddess was responsible for growing crops, the Romans removed this function from Mars, who was a male. Instead, they gave him the characteristics and responsibilities of Ares, the Greek god of war. Thus, the word *martial*, derived from the name of Mars, describes military activities.

ACTIVITY Other words besides *martial* come from the names of gods or goddesses. Use your dictionary and an encyclopedia to find the origin of each of the words that follow. Write a definition of each word as well as a brief description of the origin.

1. jovial 2. titanic 3. iridescent 4. psyche 5. narcissistic

Skill Features

A skill feature on dictionary use, on test taking, or on reading appears after each group of three vocabulary lessons. These ten special features provide students with the practical techniques that they need for building and using their pool of words independently. Concise teaching includes appropriate examples, tables of information, and strategies and procedures for learning and using new words effectively. An accompanying exercise allows students to practice each skill.

Dictionary Skills   In learning to use the dictionary, students are often unsure about selecting the single definition that best fits the way a word is used. Students receive pointers on determining the part of speech, distinguishing between homographs, and testing the definition in the context of a sentence. In a follow-up exercise, students use dictionary extracts to choose appropriate definitions and then apply their understanding of the definitions by writing original sentences.

The emphasis in the remaining dictionary features is on using the dictionary as a source of information. Students learn how to locate the inflected forms of words and to use biographical and geographical entries. Exercises allow students to

Name _____ Date _____

Dictionary Skills

Finding the Appropriate Definition

Most dictionary words have more than one definition. When you look up a word, you must decide which definition is most appropriate—that is, which one best fits the way the word is used. To do so, use the following strategies.

STRATEGIES
1. *Read all of the definitions in a dictionary entry.* Suppose that the italicized word in the following example sentence is unfamiliar to you. You would look up *contingent* in the dictionary and read the seven definitions.

DICTIONARY SKILLS

Name _____ Date _____

Test-Taking Skills

Synonym Tests

Many vocabulary tests, including some standardized tests, contain sections on identifying synonyms. A **synonym** is a word close in meaning to another word. (*Synonym* is derived from a Greek term meaning "similar name.") *Sly, tricky, cunning,* and *crafty* are all synonyms.

A synonym test item asks you to identify from several choices

TEST-TAKING SKILLS

Name _____ Date _____

Reading Skills

The Prefix *pre-*

A **prefix** is a letter or group of letters that is added to the beginning of a root. (A root is the part of a word that contains its basic meaning. A root also can be a complete word.) Like all prefixes, *pre-* changes the meaning of the roots to which it is added. Many different words can be formed from a single root. If you know the meaning of the prefix, you can determine the meanings of unfamiliar words. The prefix *pre-* has one common meaning.

READING SKILLS

HOUGHTON MIFFLIN VOCABULARY FOR ACHIEVEMENT, SECOND COURSE

practice their skills by answering questions about the number, tense, and degree of the parts of speech of words and about notable people and places.

Test-Taking Skills In these features students are given pointers for completing three types of standardized-test items—synonyms, sentence completions, and analogies. Examples are provided so that students can understand the thought processes required to eliminate inappropriate answer choices and to select the correct answer.

Reading Skills These features address two separate areas of vocabulary proficiency. In the first of the reading-skill lessons, students learn to use context clues containing synonyms to determine the meaning of an unfamiliar word. Methods of reasoning are illustrated so that students can see how information in a sentence can be utilized. As a check of their understanding, students then use the dictionary to compare their ''working'' definitions against the actual meanings.

The remaining reading-skill lessons acquaint students with a method of determining the meaning of unfamiliar words by analyzing word parts. At this grade level, students learn two prefixes and two suffixes that are added to familiar words and roots. Because word analysis is a cumulative process, students are reminded that the more prefixes, suffixes, and roots they know, the more unfamiliar words they will be able to figure out.

Teacher's Edition

Teaching Suggestions The activities on pages x–xiii will help you to incorporate vocabulary study into every area of the English curriculum. Exercises, assignments, and discussion topics have been provided for work in vocabulary review, spelling, reading, word histories, grammar and usage, literature, and composition.

Resources To help you plan testing and enrichment opportunities, facsimiles of the accompanying resource materials (**Tests** and **Bonuses**) have been placed after the vocabulary lessons to which they apply.

Teacher's Resource Masters

For your convenience, reproducible **Tests** and **Bonuses** have been included in a separate booklet. Answers printed on the front of each reproducible page will allow you to check results easily.

Tests There are ten reproducible multiple-choice tests, each covering three consecutive lessons. This format ensures that students can discriminate within a wider context of definition choices than is found in a single lesson.

Test formats resemble those of the lesson exercises. Each test is divided into two parts of fifteen items each, allowing for the testing of all words in the three lessons. Part A focuses on recognizing and recalling definitions, while Part B emphasizes placing words within the context of sentences or discriminating among a choice of synonyms.

Answers to the tests are located on the front sides of the reproducible masters and on the resource pages located after the appropriate lessons in the Teacher's Edition.

Bonuses Fifteen Bonus activities, each covering two consecutive lessons, offer students further opportunities for reinforcement and enrichment. In crossword puzzles, word searches, sentence completions, scrambled words, and other word games, students review their knowledge of words, definitions, synonyms, and etymologies.

Answers to the Bonuses are located on the front sides of the reproducible masters and on resource pages in the Teacher's Edition, following the related vocabulary lessons.

Depending on classroom needs, use these activities as added practice, as reviews of already-mastered words, or as extra-credit assignments.

Teaching Suggestions

Review and Retention

Frequent review helps students retain the meanings of new words. Use any or all of the following practices to help students learn and apply new words.

1. Have students use the **flash cards,** located on pages 201–220 of the student books, for individual drill or game-style classroom practice.

2. Assign the **Bonuses** as follow-up activities for the vocabulary lessons.

3. Provide extra-credit points for those students who use new words correctly in classroom discussion or in written assignments.

4. As you cover new lessons, ask students how particular words relate to ones already studied.
   EXAMPLES In what situations could you use *congenial* (Lesson 5), *amicable* (Lesson 6), and *amenable* (Lesson 21) interchangeably?
   How do *accomplice* (Lesson 3) and *culprit* (Lesson 17) differ?

How are *exuberant* (Lesson 6), *blithe* (Lesson 6), and *buoyant* (Lesson 7) similar, and how are they different?

Can the same behavior be described as both *staunch* (Lesson 8) and *steadfast* (Lesson 24)?

Refer to the **Complete Word List** on page v to aid in making similarly related word groups.

5. Have students periodically review their own or others' compositions for word choice. Encourage them to replace overused words or phrases with new vocabulary words. For example, in the sentence "Jack and Lou argued over the bicycle," they might rewrite the sentence as "The argument between Jack and Lou *imperiled* their friendship" (Lesson 29), or "Jack and Lou reached a *stalemate* on the topic of the bicycle" (Lesson 14), or "The discussion between Jack and Lou *degenerated* into an argument" (Lesson 5).

Vocabulary and Spelling

Vocabulary study and spelling are complementary. Students cannot completely understand a word until they can say and write it as well as cite its definition. Make use of the numerous opportunities provided in *Houghton Mifflin Vocabulary for Achievement* in order to reinforce spelling skills.

1. Once students have studied the definitions and examples for each vocabulary word, have them write the word in the blank provided for this purpose. Writing the word reinforces the visual-graphic patterns of letters, aids in sight recognition, and helps students to apply the word.

2. Encourage students to pay close attention to the listing of related forms and the use of these, along with the inflected forms of words, throughout the exercises. Point out to them how different endings can change the spelling of a word.

3. Have students pay special heed to lessons based on word roots, since these show how similar word elements contribute to the similarity of meaning and spelling. In the same way, have them study the **skill features** treating prefixes and suffixes. Point out how the addition of the word element can change the part of speech, the meaning, and the spelling of the new word that is formed.

4. When students apply their understanding of new words by using them in the writing assignments, remind them that checking spelling, as well as other aspects of mechanics, is a final step in the revising process.

5. Remind students that **Bonus** features highlight correct spelling. Emphasize that in order for crossword puzzles, word searches, scrambled words, and word-clue games to work, students must write the letters in the correct sequence.

Vocabulary and Reading

1. To help students realize how they naturally make use of context clues as they read, review with them some of the more common and obvious ways that words are defined in context.

Formal definition: A *micrometer* is a device that measures minute distances, as gauged by the rotations of a finely threaded screw in a microscope.

Definition by appositive: *Lichen*, or plants consisting of a fungus in close combination with certain green or blue-green algae, covered every surface of the fallen log.

The *metric system*, that is, a decimal system of weights and measures, is widely accepted in manufacturing, international trade, and science. The *croissant*—a crescent-shaped roll made of dough or puff pastry—was created by bakers in Vienna to commemorate their city's successful stand against an army of Turks in 1863.

Definition by example: Mosses and liverworts are examples of *Bryophyta*, one of the oldest living groups of plants on earth.

Point out to students that words like *is*, *that is*, and *or*, as well as typographical aids like parentheses, commas, and dashes, may signal the presence of a definition in context.

2. To show students how their awareness of the order and function of words in sentences helps them to eliminate improbable meanings of unfamiliar words, give them a passage like the following.

EXAMPLE Primitive, *kanless* insects found their *lumwat* by *nusing* tree ferns in search of *fidals* and vegetable debris. The *sopsa* was *meresuny*, but getting down proved more *pandart*, involving detours over fingered leaf formations and shoots. At some point they started to *delp* to the ground, extending their "arms" or *kranning* in order to *bing* downward. This is one *planesis* for the development of *kans*.

Have students make a number of guesses for each nonsense word. While they may not be able to determine that *kanless* is actually *wingless* and *lumwat* is actually *food*, they will be able to reduce uncertainty and to approximate the meaning by looking at the position of the nonsense word in the sentence.

Vocabulary and Word Histories

To help students appreciate language as dynamic, use the following as discussion or assignment topics.

Words that have undergone changes in meaning: *cloud* (rock or hill), *guest* (stranger or enemy), *puny* (born later), *slim* (crafty, bad, or crooked), *branch* (paw or claw), *bugle* (young ox), *nice* (ignorant), *pretty* (clever), and so forth.

Shortened forms of words: *bus/omnibus, pants/ pantaloons, taxicab/taxi-meter cabriolet, airlines/ airplane lines, gyp/gypsy, mend/amend, extra/extraordinary,* and so forth.

Compound words: *salesclerk, blackbird, shortcake, lightweight, threadbare, airtight, outlaw, underdog, self-control, law-abiding, heart-to-heart, hide-and-seek,* and so forth.

Special interest words, such as those from architecture, that have been adopted for more general use: *arch, column, gable, belfry, tower, porch, spire, pendant, vault, girder, dormer, flamboyant, arcade, capital, lattice, lantern, canopy,* and so forth.

Portmanteau words, in which the sounds and meanings of two or more words are merged to form a new word: *squawk* (squall + squeak), *broasted* (broiled + roasted), *splatter* (splash + spatter), *flounder* (founder + blunder), *Eurasia* (Europe + Asia), *flabbergast* (flabby or flap + aghast), and so forth.

Words borrowed directly from other languages, such as Greek: *metropolis, phenomenon, cinema, drama, electron, oasis, parenthesis, plasma, logic, cosmic, protein, chronic, criterion,* and so forth.

Vocabulary, Grammar, and Usage

1. Remind students that a word may be several parts of speech depending on its use. Then have them examine the multiple meanings of such words as *progress, absent, produce, project, torment, use, contest, perfect,* and so forth. Have students write sentences like the following to illustrate the different meanings.
   EXAMPLE   Jeremy got a *perfect* score on his last math test. (adjective)
   EXAMPLE   Monica has *perfected* her swan dive. (verb)

2. Have students write original sentences that both illustrate particular principles of grammar or usage and incorporate vocabulary words. For example, when covering independent clauses, ask students to write sentences like the following.
   EXAMPLE   Rowena is difficult to be with when she is in a *refractory* mood.
   EXAMPLE   Before we left the meeting, we had reached an *amicable* settlement.

3. Give students sentences containing malapropisms, or humorously misused words. To make certain that students can distinguish the problematic word, underline the malapropism in each sentence.
   EXAMPLE   The management requested a *conjunction* against the union.
   EXAMPLE   Mayor Dale's speech made a great *oppression* on the audience.
   EXAMPLE   Sam, an honest and truthful young man, *virtually* turned in the money he found.

   Students should be able to reword the malapropism and explain the humor that results from the misuse of the word. If not, have them use the dictionary to get definitions of both the malapropism and the correct replacement.

4. When discussing usage problems, have the students examine the likelihood of confusion between pairs of homophones like the following: *coarse/course, horse/hoarse, bear/bare, foul/ fowl, fair/fare, wear/ware/where, peer/pier,* and so forth. Then have them look up the definitions of each word and write a sentence for each illustrating its use.

Vocabulary and Composition

1. You can help students become more aware of word choice by emphasizing the importance of revision. Remind them that revising a rough draft gives them the opportunity to choose the appropriate words and to use concrete or figurative words, depending on the purpose of the assignment.

2. To help students distinguish between literal and figurative language, give them pairs of sentences like the following.
   EXAMPLE   The attorney presents facts as if they were rare and valuable gemstones.
   Ann's favorite gemstone is the amethyst.
   EXAMPLE   The carpenter repaired the two broken stairsteps.
   Charles treats his friends as if they are stairsteps to success.

   After students have successfully identified which sentence uses a literal noun and which uses a figurative one, give them a list of nouns and verbs and have them write their own pairs of sentences.

3. When choosing a synonym from the dictionary or thesaurus, some students may have difficulty selecting the one with connotations appropriate to the topic and purpose of their composition. To help them learn to discriminate between positive and negative connotations, give them pairs of words like the following: *house/hovel, brief/*

curt, firm/stubborn, reserved/aloof, relaxed/lazy, mature/old, and so forth. If students cannot identify the word in each pair that has negative connotations, have them look up the definitions in a dictionary.

4. To help students distinguish shades of meaning, give them a list of synonyms and ask them to rank them according to intensity, degree, or amount.
   EXAMPLE *disorderly, chaotic, disrupted, disorganized*
   EXAMPLE *enjoyable, amusing, convivial, propitious*

5. For students who use inflated language, provide them with proverbs that have been overwritten. By extracting the ideas hidden behind the verbiage, students can gain practice in expressing simple ideas clearly.
   EXAMPLE Individuals who perforce are constrained to be domiciled in vitreous structures of patent frangibility should on no account employ petrous formations as projectiles. (People who live in glass houses should never throw stones.)

Vocabulary and Literature

1. In discussing literature selections, reinforce vocabulary study by pointing out authors' literary techniques. Ask students questions like the following.
   EXAMPLES Which words or phrases indicate that a certain character believes himself or herself to be superior to others?
   Which words or phrases does the author use to evoke the reader's sympathy for a particular character?

2. When covering Norse tales, Celtic legends (King Arthur), or Old and Middle English poems or ballads (*Lord Randal, Sir Patrick Spens, Barbara Allen,* and so forth), provide students with both the original and the translation of the work if possible. Have students draw conclusions about the changes in vocabulary, grammar, and mechanics by comparing the earlier and later forms.

3. To help students understand the rich nature of idioms, ask them to explain the difference between "Bury the hatchet" and "Stop fighting with each other." Help students to locate and explain the literal and figurative meanings of other expressions like the following used in short stories and novels.
   EXAMPLES *According to Hoyle, know the ropes, play second fiddle, pull strings, face the music, straight from the horse's mouth,* and so forth.

4. As an alternative, have students explore proverbs as a rich source of figurative language.
   EXAMPLE Better have an egg today than a hen tomorrow. (Italian)
   EXAMPLE Without going, you can get nowhere. (Chinese)
   EXAMPLE The best cloth has uneven threads. (Spanish)
   EXAMPLE The sweetest grapes hang the highest. (English)

As a follow-up, have students look for literal expressions with figurative meanings in the total content of stories, poems, plays, novels, and essays.

Scope and Sequence of Skills

Course	Dictionary Skills	Test-Taking Skills	Reading Skills
Sixth Course	Using a Dictionary and a Thesaurus to Find Synonyms (pp. 19–20)	ACT Reading-Comprehension Tests (pp. 39–40); Tests of Standard Written English (pp. 59–60)	Context Clues and the Reading of Primary Sources (pp. 79–80); Context Clues and the Reading of British Literature (pp. 99–100); The Prefixes bi-, semi- (pp. 119–120); Prefixes Indicating Number (pp. 139–140); The Prefixes counter-, contra-, anti- (pp. 159–160); The Prefixes circum-, peri- (pp. 179–180); The Prefixes extra-, super-, ultra- (pp. 199–200)
Fifth Course	Using a Thesaurus (pp. 19–20)	Antonym Test Items (pp. 39–40); SAT Sentence-Completion Test Items (pp. 59–60); SAT Analogy Test Items (pp. 79–80); SAT Reading-Comprehension Test Items (pp. 99–100)	Context Clues and the Reading of American History (pp. 119–120); Context Clues and the Reading of American Literature (pp. 139–140); The Prefixes bene-, mal- (pp. 159–160); The Prefixes inter-, intra-, intro- (pp. 179–180); The Prefixes ante-, post- (pp. 199–200)
Fourth Course	Synonym Paragraphs (pp. 19–20)	Antonym Test Items (pp. 39–40); Sentence-Completion Test Items (pp. 59–60); Analogy Test Items (pp. 79–80); Reading-Comprehension Test Items (pp. 99–100)	Context Clues: Examples and Appositives (pp. 119–120); Context Clues: Contrast (pp. 139–140); The Prefix ad- (pp. 159–160); Com- and Related Prefixes (pp. 179–180); Five Adjective Suffixes (pp. 199–200)
Third Course	Finding the Appropriate Definition (pp. 19–20); Usage Notes (pp. 39–40)	Antonym Tests (pp. 59–60); Analogy Tests (pp. 79–80); Reading-Comprehension Tests (pp. 99–100)	Context Clues: Substitution (pp. 119–120); The Prefixes ex-, e- (pp. 139–140); The Prefixes ab-, a-, abs- (pp. 159–160); The Suffixes -ful, -ous (pp. 179–180); Four Verb Suffixes (pp. 199–200)
Second Course	Finding the Appropriate Definition (pp. 19–20); Inflected Forms of Words (pp. 39–40); Biographical and Geographical Entries (pp. 59–60)	Sentence-Completion Tests (pp. 79–80); Synonym Tests (pp. 99–100); Analogy Tests (pp. 119–120)	Context Clues: Synonyms (pp. 139–140); The Prefix pre- (pp. 159–160); The Prefix in- (pp. 179–180); The Suffixes -ion, -ness (pp. 199–200)
First Course	Finding the Appropriate Definition (pp. 19–20); Part-of-Speech Labels (pp. 39–40); Understanding Etymologies (pp. 59–60)	Sentence-Completion Tests (pp. 79–80)	Context Clues: Definition in the Sentence (pp. 99–100); The Prefix dis- (pp. 119–120); The Prefix re- (pp. 139–140); The Prefix sub- (pp. 159–160); The Suffixes -ance, -ence, -ancy (pp. 179–180); The Suffix -able (pp. 199–200)
Introductory Course	Parts of a Dictionary Entry (pp. 19–20); Finding the Right Definition (pp. 39–40)	Synonym Tests (pp. 59–60); Antonym Tests (pp. 79–80)	Context Clues (pp. 99–100); Dividing Words into Parts (pp. 119–120); The Prefixes non-, un- (pp. 139–140); The Prefix trans- (pp. 159–160); The Prefix de- (pp. 179–180); The Suffixes -ity, -hood (pp. 199–200)

HOUGHTON MIFFLIN VOCABULARY FOR ACHIEVEMENT, SECOND COURSE

Lesson 1

Dialect

Suppose that someone said, "My car stalled, so I raised the *bonnet* and looked at the engine." This sentence would make perfect sense to a person who had grown up in England. Someone raised in the United States, however, would express the same thought by saying, "My car stalled, so I raised the *hood* and looked at the engine." Americans use the word *hood*, but the English say *bonnet* because of differences in the dialects of the English language.

Dialects are systematic variations in the pronunciation, vocabulary, and grammar of a language that distinguish one group from another. This lesson contains words that are used to discuss dialects and the variety of ways in which people talk to one another.

> **WORD LIST**
> accent
> articulate
> dialect
> diction
> enunciate
> fundamental
> intelligible
> peer
> status
> stress

DEFINITIONS

After you have studied the definitions and example for each vocabulary word, write the word on the line to the right.

1. **accent** (ăk′sĕnt′) *noun* A style of speech or pronunciation that is characteristic of a certain region or country.   *verb* To emphasize in speech or in music. (From the Latin *ad-*, meaning "to," and *cantus*, meaning "song")

   RELATED WORD **accentuate** *verb*

   EXAMPLE When Hans speaks English, he has a slight German *accent*.

1. _____

2. **articulate** (är-tĭk′yə-lĭt) *adjective* **a.** Expressed in a clear and effective manner. **b.** Able to speak effectively.   *verb* (är-tĭk′yə-lāt′) To express in words.

   RELATED WORDS **articulately** *adverb;* **articulation** *noun*

   EXAMPLE In an *articulate* speech, the student council president talked about the exciting opportunities open to the graduates.

2. _____

3. **dialect** (dī′ə-lĕkt′) *noun* The form or version of a language that is spoken in a country or region or by a particular social group; a dialect has characteristic differences in pronunciation, vocabulary, and grammar. (From the Greek word *dialektos*, meaning "language")

   RELATED WORD **dialectal** *adjective*

   EXAMPLE In the United States, people who speak northern *dialects* refer to "corn on the cob"; those who speak southern *dialects* refer to "roasting ears."

3. _____

4. **diction** (dĭk′shən) *noun*   **a.** The choice and use of words in speaking or writing.   **b.** Distinctness of pronunciation. (From the Latin word *dicere*, meaning "to say")

EXAMPLE   The *diction* of an encyclopedia article is more difficult than that of a comic book.

4. _____

5. **enunciate** (ĭ-nŭn′sē-āt′) *verb*   **a.** To pronounce, especially in a clear manner.   **b.** To state or set forth clearly. (From the Latin *ex-*, meaning "out," and *nuntiare*, meaning "to announce")

RELATED WORD   **enunciation** *noun*

EXAMPLE   The candidate carefully *enunciated* his words so that the huge audience would understand him.

5. _____

6. **fundamental** (fŭn′də-mĕn′tl) *adjective*   **a.** Basic; primary; essential.   **b.** Of major significance.   *noun*   A basic or necessary part: *the fundamentals of science.* (From the Latin word *fundamentum*, meaning "foundation")

RELATED WORD   **fundamentally** *adverb*

EXAMPLE   Plumbers must master the *fundamental* techniques of their trade.

6. _____

7. **intelligible** (ĭn-tĕl′ĭ-jə-bəl) *adjective*   Able to be understood. (From the Latin word *intellegere*, meaning "to perceive")

RELATED WORDS   **intelligibility** *noun;* **intelligibly** *adverb*

EXAMPLE   The telegram written in code was not *intelligible* to Eleanor.

7. _____

8. **peer** (pîr) *noun*   **a.** A person who is equal to another in age, class, or rank.   **b.** A member of the British nobility. (From the Latin word *par,* meaning "equal")

EXAMPLE   Five-year-old Scott avoided his *peers* because he preferred to play with older children.

8. _____

9. **status** (stăt′əs) *noun*   **a.** Position in society; condition.   **b.** A stage of progress or development. (From the Latin word *status,* meaning "position" or "standing")

EXAMPLE   Owning a carriage was once considered a symbol of high social *status.*

9. _____

10. **stress** (strĕs) *verb*   To emphasize, particularly when speaking. *noun*   **a.** Emphasis, particularly when speaking.   **b.** Importance; significance.

EXAMPLE   People learning some foreign languages may *stress* the wrong syllables in words.

10. _____

Exercise 1   Matching Words and Definitions

Match the definition in Column B with the word in Column A. Write the letter of the correct definition on the answer line.

		1. ___a___
		2. ___d___
		3. ___h___

Column A   *Column B*

1. enunciate   a. To pronounce, especially in a clear manner
2. peer   b. Choice of words in speaking or writing
3. stress   c. Expressed in a clear and effective way
4. fundamental   d. A person who is equal to another
5. intelligible   e. A form of a language spoken in a region
6. articulate   or by a group
7. status   f. Position in society; stage of progress
8. dialect   g. A style of speech or pronunciation that is
9. accent   characteristic of a certain region
10. diction   h. To emphasize, particularly when speaking
     i. Able to be understood
     j. Basic or essential; of major significance

Answer lines:
4. ___j___
5. ___i___
6. ___c___
7. ___f___
8. ___e___
9. ___g___
10. ___b___

Exercise 2   Using Words Correctly

Decide whether the italicized vocabulary word has been used correctly in the sentence. On the answer line, write *Correct* for correct use and *Incorrect* for incorrect use.

1. The Franklin family has enjoyed high *status* in this city for many years.   1. ___Correct___

2. People should *enunciate* clearly when writing letters.   2. ___Incorrect___

3. The director told the actors and actresses to work on perfecting their English *accents*.   3. ___Correct___

4. People stopped listening to the speech because it was so *articulate*.   4. ___Incorrect___

5. Army officers and their *peers*, the enlisted men, must cooperate on the battlefield.   5. ___Incorrect___

6. If your teacher *stresses* a certain subject, you would be wise to study that subject carefully.   6. ___Correct___

7. The *dialect* is an important part of the telephone.   7. ___Incorrect___

8. Drivers today need a *fundamental* understanding of automobiles in case their cars break down.   8. ___Correct___

9. Dana could not figure out what the note said because it was *intelligible*.   9. ___Incorrect___

10. People can improve their *diction* by using electronic calculators.   10. ___Incorrect___

Exercise 3   Choosing the Best Word

Decide which vocabulary word or related form best completes the sentence, and write the letter of your choice on the answer line.

1. Paula, who grew up in Maine, still speaks with a New England __?__ .
   a. status   b. accent   c. fundamental   d. peer

   1. ___b___

2. The actors' __?__ improved so that they could be heard in the last row of the auditorium.
   a. peer   b. status   c. dialect   d. enunciation

   2. ___d___

3. My brother muttered a comment that was barely __?__ .
   a. intelligible   b. fundamental   c. dialect   d. diction

   3. ___a___

4. Buddy enjoyed his __?__ as class president.
   a. diction   b. dialect   c. status   d. stress

   4. ___c___

5. The politician's remarks were so __?__ that the crowd cheered.
   a. articulate   b. accented   c. dialectal   d. enunciated

   5. ___a___

6. Instead of always pleasing their __?__ , people should also please themselves.
   a. status   b. diction   c. dialects   d. peers

   6. ___d___

7. A(n) __?__ requirement for the job is the ability to type fifty words per minute.
   a. accented   b. fundamental   c. intelligible   d. status

   7. ___b___

8. What makes Lincoln's Gettysburg Address so great is its simple but eloquent __?__ .
   a. dialect   b. status   c. diction   d. accent

   8. ___c___

9. The __?__ of the magazine article was on the importance of exercising regularly.
   a. enunciation   b. stress   c. peer   d. fundamental

   9. ___b___

10. When Roger spoke, his __?__ indicated that he had grown up in our part of the country.
    a. fundamental   b. status   c. peer   d. dialect

    10. ___d___

Exercise 4   Using Different Forms of Words

Decide which form of the vocabulary word in parentheses best completes the sentence. The form given may be correct. Write your answer on the answer line.

1. The board of directors was __?__ opposed to major advertising expenditures. *(fundamental)*

   1. ___fundamentally___

2. The comedian is a master of many foreign __?__ . *(accent)*

   2. ___accents___

3. Gloria seemed much older than her __?__ in high school. *(peer)*

   3. ___peers___

4. Yesterday Mr. Chang __?__ that the final examination would cover ten chapters. *(stress)*

   4. ___stressed___

5. The coach of the debate team spent an hour discussing __?__ . *(enunciate)*.

   5. ___enunciation___

6. If you do not speak __?__ , people may misunderstand you. *(intelligible)*

   6. ___intelligibly___

7. I could not determine where Joni lived from hearing her __?__ . *(dialect)*

7. _____dialect_____

8. The poem's __?__ was both formal and ornate. *(diction)*

8. _____diction_____

9. Some people are better than others at __?__ their feelings. *(articulate)*

9. _____articulating_____

10. Each committee member reported on the __?__ of his or her project. *(status)*

10. _____status_____

Reading Comprehension

Each numbered sentence in the following passage contains an italicized vocabulary word. After you read the passage, you will complete an exercise.

Dialects of the English Language

(1) When people from Canada, the United States, Great Britain, and Australia gather in the same room, they speak with a wide variety of **accents.** **(2)** In spite of this variety, however, they are able to make themselves **intelligible** to one another. **(3)** This is because they all speak **dialects** of the English language.

A dialect is a version of a language that distinguishes one group of speakers from another. **(4)** People learn the dialects they speak from their families and from adults and **peers** in the areas in which they grow up. **(5)** Usually there is not a **fundamental** difference between the dialect of one region or country and that of another. There are minor differences, though, in pronunciation, vocabulary, and grammar.

The first difference that most people notice between dialects is in pronunciation. For example, when Americans say *garage*, they emphasize the second syllable.

(6) In Britain, though, people put the **stress** on the first syllable.

Even within a country, there are regional differences in pronunciation. To take just one example, when many Americans say the word *aunt*, they pronounce it in the same way that they pronounce *ant*. Many others, though, pronounce the word so that it rhymes with *font*.

(7) Another major difference among dialects is in **diction.** In the United States, people say *gasoline* and *truck*. In Britain they say *petrol* and *lorry*. In some parts of the United States, people refer to the *basement*; in other areas, *cellar* is the more common word.

(8) No dialect in itself is better than another; a person speaking one dialect can be just as **articulate** as a person speaking another. **(9)** Dialect, however, may indicate a person's social **status.** This fact was the basis of the Irish playwright George Bernard Shaw's play *Pygmalion*,

which was later adapted into the successful musical *My Fair Lady*.

In both the play and the musical, the main character is a young Englishwoman, Eliza Doolittle, who speaks the dialect of one of London's poor districts. Professor Henry Higgins teaches her to speak — and act — like a woman of the nobility. **(10)** In one famous scene, Eliza practices **enunciating** the sentence "The rain in Spain stays mainly in the plain." Once she does so successfully, she rapidly acquires the dialect that Higgins has been attempting to teach her.

The best way to learn about dialects is to listen closely to other people. Do they pronounce words differently? Do they use expressions with which you are not familiar? Do they use some grammatical constructions that are different from the ones that you use? By listening closely, you will add to your understanding of the English language.

Please turn to the next page.

Reading Comprehension Exercise

Each of the following statements corresponds to a numbered sentence in the passage. Each statement contains a blank and is followed by four answer choices. Decide which choice fits best in the blank. The word or phrase that you choose must express roughly the same meaning as the italicized word in the passage. Write the letter of your choice on the answer line.

1. People from Canada, the United States, Britain, and Australia display a variety of __?__ .
   a. ways of spelling words   c. fashions in dressing
   b. ways of behaving   d. ways of pronouncing words

   1. ____d____

2. People from these countries make themselves __?__ .
   a. suspicious   b. understood   c. helpful   d. at home

   2. ____b____

3. The people from these countries speak __?__ of English.
   a. well   b. versions   c. fondly   d. the rules

   3. ____b____

4. People learn dialects from their families and __?__ .
   a. people their age   c. television announcers
   b. teachers   d. language records

   4. ____a____

5. Usually no __?__ differences in dialect exist between regions.
   a. noticeable   b. minor   c. special   d. basic

   5. ____d____

6. The British __?__ the first syllable in *garage*.
   a. drop   b. almost drop   c. emphasize   d. mispronounce

   6. ____c____

7. Another difference among dialects is in __?__ .
   a. spelling   c. word choices
   b. handwriting methods d. dictionaries

   7. ____c____

8. A person speaking one dialect can be as __?__ as a person speaking another dialect.
   a. confusing   b. clear   c. fancy   d. artistic

   8. ____b____

9. Dialect may indicate one's __?__ .
   a. profession   c. popularity
   b. self-confidence d. social position

   9. ____d____

10. In one scene of *Pygmalion*, Eliza Doolittle practices __?__ a particular sentence.
    a. pronouncing clearly   c. memorizing
    b. singing   d. explaining briefly

    10. ____a____

Writing Assignment

This lesson refers to differences among the English dialects spoken in Britain, the United States, Canada, and Australia. Find a book or an encyclopedia article in the library about the English language, and read about the differences between the English spoken in the United States and that spoken in one of the other countries. Then write a report in which you explain to other students what some of those differences are. In your report use at least five of the words from this lesson and underline them.

Lesson 2

Geography

The study of geography is far more than just learning the names and locations of countries. Geography, or "earth description," is the investigation of facts about the earth's surface, which differs from place to place. This study includes both natural features and those that result from human occupation of an area. The geographer, who is also interested in climate, vegetation, population, and degree of use of land by animals and people, brings together information from many sciences — physical, biological, and social. In this lesson you will learn words that will aid you in your study of this complex science.

WORD LIST
insular
latitude
longitude
meridian
panorama
peninsula
precipice
quagmire
terrestrial
topography

DEFINITIONS

After you have studied the definitions and example for each vocabulary word, write the word on the line to the right.

1. **insular** (ĭn'sə-lər) *adjective* **a.** Relating to an island. **b.** Characteristic of the isolated life of an island people. **c.** Narrow-minded. (From the Latin word *insula*, meaning "island")

   RELATED WORD **insularity** *noun*

   EXAMPLE The *insular* life of Nantucket Island is relaxed except during the summer tourist season.

   1. _____

2. **latitude** (lăt'ĭ-tood') *noun* **a.** The distance north or south of the equator, measured in degrees. **b.** Freedom from usual restraint. (From the Latin word *latitude,* meaning "width" or "breadth")

   RELATED WORD **latitudinal** *adjective*

   EXAMPLE *Latitude* is indicated on a map by horizontal lines.

   2. _____

3. **longitude** (lŏn'jĭ-tood') *noun* The distance east or west of Greenwich (pronounced GRENN-itch), England, and measured in degrees. (From the Latin word *longitude,* meaning "length")

   RELATED WORD **longitudinal** *adjective*

   EXAMPLE *Longitude* is indicated on a map by vertical lines.

   3. _____

4. **meridian** (mə-rĭd'ē-ən) *noun* Any of the imaginary circles around the earth that pass through the North Pole and South Pole. (From the Latin word *meridies,* meaning "midday")

   EXAMPLE Although a *meridian* is an imaginary line, navigators use it to determine location.

   4. _____

5. **panorama** (păn′ə-răm′ə) *noun* **a.** A wide-ranging view over a large area. **b.** A comprehensive picture of a specific subject; an overview. (From the Greek *pan-*, meaning "all," and *horama*, meaning "sight")

RELATED WORD **panoramic** *adjective*

EXAMPLE From the hills of Los Angeles, one sees a spectacular *panorama* of the coast to the downtown area.

5. _____

6. **peninsula** (pə-nĭn′syə-lə) *noun* A strip of land with water on three sides. (From the Latin words *paene*, meaning "almost," and *insula*, meaning "island")

RELATED WORD **peninsular** *adjective*

EXAMPLE The scout troop camped out on a small *peninsula* that jutted into the ocean.

6. _____

7. **precipice** (prĕs′ə-pĭs) *noun* A steep cliff or overhanging rock. (From the Latin word *praeceps*, meaning "headlong")

RELATED WORD **precipitous** *adjective*

EXAMPLE The horse stumbled and nearly fell from the *precipice*.

7. _____

8. **quagmire** (kwăg′mīr′) *noun* **a.** Muddy land into which one can easily sink. **b.** A difficult situation in which one can get caught; entanglement.

EXAMPLE David and Christina got caught in a *quagmire* while photographing ducks.

8. _____

9. **terrestrial** (tə-rĕs′trē-əl) *adjective* **a.** Having to do with the earth. **b.** Of or consisting of land in contrast to water or air. (From the Latin word *terra*, meaning "earth")

EXAMPLE *Terrestrial* upheavals such as earthquakes and volcanoes can endanger people living nearby.

9. _____

10. **topography** (tə-pŏg′rə-fē) *noun* The physical features of a region, such as mountains, plains, and rivers. (From the Greek words *topos*, meaning "place," and *graphein*, meaning "to write")

RELATED WORD **topographical** *adjective*

EXAMPLE The *topography* of Switzerland is mountainous.

10. _____
MEMORY CUE *Topography* refers to the *top* of the land — the features that are visible.

Name _____ Date _____

Exercise 1   Writing Correct Words

On the answer line, write the word from the vocabulary list that fits each definition.

1. Relating to the earth

2. A steep cliff or overhanging rock

3. The distance east and west of Greenwich, England, measured in degrees

4. Any of the imaginary circles around the earth that pass through the poles

5. An area of land with water on three sides

6. The physical features of a region

7. Pertaining to an island

8. Wet, soft ground in which one can get caught

9. The distance north or south of the equator, measured in degrees

10. A wide-ranging view over an area; an overview

1. _____ terrestrial
2. _____ precipice
3. _____ longitude
4. _____ meridian
5. _____ peninsula
6. _____ topography
7. _____ insular
8. _____ quagmire
9. _____ latitude
10. _____ panorama

Exercise 2   Using Words Correctly

Decide whether the italicized vocabulary word or related form has been used correctly in the sentence. On the answer line, write *Correct* for correct use and *Incorrect* for incorrect use.

1. Someone with a fear of heights would be comfortable walking near a *precipice*.

2. Marblehead Neck in Massachusetts is a *peninsula* because it is surrounded on three sides by water.

3. A *meridian* is parallel to the equator.

4. The inhabitants of the island of Barbados are *insular* people.

5. You can figure out the *latitude* of an island by measuring east of Greenwich.

6. When geographers examine the *topography* of a region, they are studying the elements in the earth's core.

7. Whales are *terrestrial* mammals.

8. In geography class Christopher found the *longitude* of Vancouver by measuring west of the meridian at Greenwich, England.

9. When his mother learned that he had lied to her, Joseph found himself in a *quagmire*.

10. A convict in a cell with a small window near the ceiling would probably have a *panoramic* view of the outside.

1. _____ Incorrect
2. _____ Correct
3. _____ Incorrect
4. _____ Correct
5. _____ Incorrect
6. _____ Incorrect
7. _____ Incorrect
8. _____ Correct
9. _____ Correct
10. _____ Incorrect

Exercise 3   Choosing the Best Word

Decide which vocabulary word or related form best completes the sentence, and write the letter of your choice on the answer line.

1. As the chair lift reached the peak, we saw a spectacular __?__ of the snow-covered landscape.
   a. meridian   **b.** quagmire   **c.** peninsula   **d.** panorama

1. _____d_____

2. The ape is a(n) __?__ mammal.
   a. precipitous   **b.** insular   **c.** terrestrial   **d.** topographical

2. _____c_____

3. The French artist Paul Gauguin painted the __?__ peoples of the South Pacific.
   a. insular   **b.** quagmire   **c.** peninsula   **d.** terrestrial

3. _____a_____

4. When the Calkins drove through Manitoba, they noticed that the __?__ was very flat.
   a. quagmire   **b.** topography   **c.** peninsula   **d.** longitude

4. _____b_____

5. Sir Francis Drake determined the __?__ of his ship to find out how far he was from the equator.
   a. topography   **b.** meridian   **c.** latitude   **d.** panorama

5. _____c_____

6. Fred could not pull his boot free when it got stuck in the __?__ .
   a. precipice   **b.** peninsula   **c.** panorama   **d.** quagmire

6. _____d_____

7. At 112° __?__ east of Greenwich, the captain of the steamship noticed some huge rocks that were not shown on the charts.
   a. panorama   **b.** longitude   **c.** latitude   **d.** meridian

7. _____b_____

8. The Pritzlaffs' house on the __?__ has a beautiful view of the water to the east, north, and west.
   a. panorama   **b.** meridian   **c.** quagmire   **d.** peninsula

8. _____d_____

9. To reach the South Pole, the captain steered a course parallel to a __?__ .
   a. latitude   **b.** precipice   **c.** meridian   **d.** peninsula

9. _____c_____

10. Our guide warned us not to get too close to the dangerous __?__ because we might lose our balance and fall off.
    a. precipice   **b.** panorama   **c.** quagmire   **d.** peninsula

10. _____a_____

Exercise 4   Using Different Forms of Words

Decide which form of the vocabulary word in parentheses best completes the sentence. The form given may be correct. Write your answer on the answer line.

1. __?__ navigation involves the use of a map and compass. *(terrestrial)*

1. _____Terrestrial_____

2. The __?__ position of the lighthouse is 145° E. *(longitude)*

2. _____longitudinal_____

3. The __?__ form of the jetty protects the harbor from high seas and rough weather. *(peninsula)*

3. _____peninsular_____

4. It is hard for Hawaiians to get some goods from the mainland because of their __?__ . *(insular)*

4. _____insularity_____

5. The book provides a __?__ history of the sports and games people have played since the earliest times. *(panorama)*

5. _____panoramic_____

6. The geologists checked the __?__ map to determine the shape of the mesa. *(topography)*

6. _____ topographical

7. Mrs. Gunn asked the class to determine the __?__ distance between Miami and Minneapolis. *(latitude)*

7. _____ latitudinal

8. The novice skier found himself at the top of a __?__ expert slope. *(precipice)*

8. _____ precipitous

9. Denise plotted several __?__ on the map of the world. *(meridian)*

9. _____ meridians

10. Can you tell me if a fen and a marsh and a bog and a __?__ are different? *(quagmire)*

10. _____ quagmire

Reading Comprehension

Each numbered sentence in the following passage contains an italicized vocabulary word. After you read the passage, you will complete an exercise.

Magellan: Portuguese Navigator

(1) In the sixteenth century, an age of great marine and *terrestrial* exploration, Ferdinand Magellan led the first expedition to sail around the world. (2) As a young Portuguese noble, he served the king of Portugal, but he became involved in the *quagmire* of political intrigue at court and lost the king's favor. After he was dismissed from service to the king of Portugal, he offered to serve the future Emperor Charles V of Spain.

(3) A papal decree of 1493 had assigned all land in the New World west of 50° W *longitude* to Spain and all the land east of that line to Portugal. Magellan offered to prove that the East Indies fell under Spanish authority.

On September 20, 1519, Magellan set sail from Spain with five ships. (4) More than a year later, one of these ships was exploring the *topography* of South America in search of a water route across the continent. (5) This ship sank, but the remaining four ships searched along the southern *peninsula* of South America. (6) Finally, they found the passage they sought near a *latitude* of 50° S. Magellan named this passage the Strait of All Saints, but today we know it as the Strait of Magellan.

(7) One ship deserted while in this passage and returned to Spain, so fewer sailors were privileged to gaze at that first *panorama* of the Pacific Ocean. (8) Those who remained crossed the *meridian* we now call the International Date Line in the early spring of 1521

after ninety-eight days on the Pacific Ocean. During those long days at sea, many of Magellan's men died of starvation and disease.

(9) Later Magellan became involved in an *insular* conflict in the Philippines and was killed in a tribal battle. (10) Only one ship and seventeen sailors under the command of the Basque navigator Elcano survived to complete the westward journey to Spain and thus prove once and for all that the world is round, with no *precipice* at the edge.

Please turn to the next page.

Reading Comprehension Exercise

Each of the following statements corresponds to a numbered sentence in the passage. Each statement contains a blank and is followed by four answer choices. Decide which choice fits best in the blank. The word or phrase that you choose must express roughly the same meaning as the italicized word in the passage. Write the letter of your choice on the answer line.

1. The sixteenth century was an age of great __?__ exploration.
   a. cosmic   **b.** land   **c.** scientific   **d.** seafaring

   1. _____b_____

2. Magellan lost the favor of the king of Portugal when he became involved in a political __?__ .
   a. entanglement   **c.** discussion
   b. assassination   **d.** negotiation

   2. _____a_____

3. The Pope divided New World lands between Spain and Portugal according to their location on one side or the other of an imaginary geographical line 50° west of Greenwich that extends in a __?__ direction.
   a. north-and-south   **b.** crosswise   **c.** easterly   **d.** westerly

   3. _____a_____

4. One of Magellan's ships explored the __?__ of South America for a passage across the continent.
   a. coastline   **c.** mountain range
   b. horizon   **d.** physical features

   4. _____d_____

5. Four of the ships sought a passage along a southern __?__ .
   a. coast   **c.** body of land with water on three sides
   b. island   **d.** body of land surrounded by water

   5. _____c_____

6. The passage was found near 50° S of __?__ .
   a. Greenwich   **b.** Spain   **c.** Portugal   **d.** the equator

   6. _____d_____

7. Few sailors gazed at the __?__ of the Pacific.
   a. view   **b.** horizon   **c.** ocean   **d.** picture

   7. _____a_____

8. In the spring of 1521, the ships crossed the __?__ now called the International Date Line.
   a. ocean   **c.** imaginary circle passing through the poles
   b. area   **d.** imaginary line parallel to the equator

   8. _____c_____

9. Magellan was killed in a(n) __?__ conflict.
   a. violent   **b.** island   **c.** Spanish   **d.** naval

   9. _____b_____

10. There is no __?__ at the edge of the world.
    a. sea monster   **b.** tortoise   **c.** cliff   **d.** water

    10. _____c_____

Writing Assignment

Using a map, select a place such as a country, state, or city. Consult an encyclopedia for additional information about that place. Then, using five words from this lesson and underlining them, give its location and tell about its natural features. Assume that you are preparing this assignment as a presentation to be given to your classmates as a geography lesson.

Bonus: Lessons 1 and 2

(pages 1–12)

Use the clues to complete the crossword puzzle.

Across

1. Describes a clear and effective speaker
6. Life on a(n) __?__ may be INSULAR.
8. People from other countries may speak English with a foreign __?__ .
9. Indicated on a map by horizontal lines
11. Distance east or west of Greenwich is indicated by __?__ lines.
12. Synonym for FUNDAMENTAL
16. Muddy land, or an entanglement
17. To pronounce in a clear manner
19. Synonym for STRESS
20. From a Latin word meaning "position" or "standing"

Down

2. Having to do with the earth or land
3. Synonym for PRECIPICE
4. Understandable
5. A MERIDIAN is a(n) __?__ circle.
7. The choice and use of words in speaking and writing
10. Almost an island
13. An equal in age, class, or rank
14. The version of a language that is spoken in a country or region
15. A PANORAMA is a wide-ranging __?__ .
18. TOPOGRAPHY charts the '__?__' of the land.

HOUGHTON MIFFLIN VOCABULARY FOR ACHIEVEMENT, SECOND COURSE

Notes

The following lists of words are from the preceding two lessons. You may wish to use these lists to pinpoint words for ongoing review or for mid-term or final exams.

Lesson 1

accent
articulate
dialect
diction
enunciate

fundamental
intelligible
peer
status
stress

Lesson 2

insular
latitude
longitude
meridian
panorama

peninsula
precipice
quagmire
terrestrial
topography

Cooperation and Groups

Members of the Elmsville High School Drama Club spent more time debating than they did acting.

"We've got four weeks to put on a production, and we still haven't decided on a play," Ron, the drama club president, informed the group.

"I'm not finding costumes for anything written in another century," Emily announced.

"That's not fair. I want to play a historical role!" John insisted.

"I want to do a musical!" Susan demanded.

"This is getting us nowhere," Ron concluded.

When you work in a group like a drama club, it is very important for group members to cooperate with one another. Individuals must respect and work with others who have different points of view. In this lesson, you will learn words that refer to people working in groups.

WORD LIST
accompanist
accomplice
coalition
communal
complement
congregate
consensus
inductee
miscellaneous
throng

DEFINITIONS

After you have studied the definitions and example for each vocabulary word, write the word on the line to the right.

1. **accompanist** (ə-kŭm′pə-nĭst) *noun* A musician, such as a pianist, who plays along with a performer or performers. (From the Old French word *compaignon*, meaning "companion")

   RELATED WORDS **accompaniment** *noun;* **accompany** *verb*

   EXAMPLE The opera singer asked Alan to be her *accompanist* on the piano.

   1. _____

2. **accomplice** (ə-kŏm′plĭs) *noun* One who knowingly aids or helps another person break a law but is not necessarily present at the time of the crime. (From the Middle English word *complice,* meaning "companion.")

   EXAMPLE Bobby was Cindy's willing *accomplice* in the plot to raid the refrigerator.

   2. _____

3. **coalition** (kō′ə-lĭsh′ən) *noun* An alliance, usually temporary, of a group of people with a common cause. (From the Latin word *coalescere,* meaning "to grow together")

   EXAMPLE A *coalition* of groups favored increased support for national parks.

   3. _____

4. **communal** (kə-my$\overline{oo}$′nəl) *adjective* Belonging to a community, group, or society; public. (From the Latin word *communis*, meaning "common")

   RELATED WORDS **communally** *adverb;* **commune** *noun*

   EXAMPLE The *communal* recreation room was a popular feature provided by the company.

4. _____

5. **complement** (kŏm′plə-mənt) *noun* Something that completes, makes up a whole, or brings to perfection. *verb* To make complete; add to the effect of. (From the Latin word *complere*, meaning "to fill out")

   RELATED WORD **complementary** *adjective*

   EXAMPLE An attractive table setting is a *complement* to a well-prepared meal.

5. _____

   USAGE NOTE Do not confuse *complement*, which refers to completing something, with *compliment*, an expression of praise.

6. **congregate** (kŏng′grĭ-gāt′) *verb* To bring or come together in a crowd or assembly. (From the Latin *com-*, meaning "together," and *gregare*, meaning "to assemble")

   RELATED WORDS **congregation** *noun;* **congregational** *adjective*

   EXAMPLE The geese *congregated* in a large group in front of the pond.

6. _____

7. **consensus** (kən-sĕn′səs) *noun* General agreement among a group of people. (From the Latin *com-*, meaning "together," and *sentire*, meaning "to feel")

   EXAMPLE The board of directors reached a *consensus* that the company should have a new headquarters constructed.

7. _____

8. **inductee** (ĭn′-dŭk-tē′) *noun* A new member of a club or organization; a person being placed formally in an office, a society, or the armed forces. (From the Latin *in-*, meaning "in," and *ducere*, meaning "to lead")

   RELATED WORDS **induct** *verb;* **induction** *noun*

   EXAMPLE The army *inductees* were outfitted in uniforms for their first field exercise.

8. _____

9. **miscellaneous** (mĭs′ə-lā′nē-əs) *adjective* **a.** Made up of a variety of different elements or ingredients. **b.** Not falling into a particular category. (From the Latin word *miscere*, meaning "to mix")

   RELATED WORD **miscellany** *noun*

   EXAMPLE In the cluttered attic, Meg found old toys, books, and other *miscellaneous* objects.

9. _____

10. **throng** (thrông) *noun* A large group of people or things gathered or packed closely together; a crowd. *verb* **a.** To crowd into; gather. **b.** To move in a throng.

    EXAMPLE *Throngs* of shoppers filled the aisles of the department store.

10. _____

14 Cooperation and Groups

Exercise 1 Matching Words and Definitions

Match the definition in Column B with the word in Column A. Write the letter of the correct definition on the answer line.

Column A

1. inductee
2. congregate
3. communal
4. coalition
5. accompanist
6. complement
7. miscellaneous
8. consensus
9. accomplice
10. throng

Column B

a. A person who helps another to commit a crime
b. A crowd of people packed tightly together
c. Someone who plays music in support of a singer or other musician
d. Belonging to a community; public
e. A new member of an organization
f. To assemble in a large group
g. General agreement or opinion
h. Temporary alliance of people sharing a common cause
i. Something that completes a whole
j. Made up of a variety of items

1. ____e____
2. ____f____
3. ____d____
4. ____h____
5. ____c____
6. ____i____
7. ____j____
8. ____g____
9. ____a____
10. ____b____

Exercise 2 Using Words Correctly

Decide whether the italicized vocabulary word has been used correctly in the sentence. On the answer line, write *Correct* for correct use and *Incorrect* for incorrect use.

1. Everyone applauded the *accompanist's* solo performance.

1. ____Incorrect____

2. A *consensus* in favor of the proposal was reached when five of the thirty club members voted for it.

2. ____Incorrect____

3. An *accomplice* watched for security guards while the criminal opened the bank safe.

3. ____Correct____

4. Cucumbers and tomatoes are *complements* in salads.

4. ____Correct____

5. A new arrival at a school dance is an *inductee*.

5. ____Incorrect____

6. A group of politicians formed a *coalition* for educational reform.

6. ____Correct____

7. The *communal* garden was used by families in the neighborhood.

7. ____Correct____

8. A *throng* of people left the crowded stadium.

8. ____Correct____

9. Tanya *congregated* alone outside the building.

9. ____Incorrect____

10. The garage contained two *miscellaneous* objects, a lawn mower and an old air conditioner.

10. ____Incorrect____

Exercise 3 Choosing the Best Word

Decide which vocabulary word or related form best expresses the meaning of the italicized word or phrase in the sentence. On the answer line, write the letter of that word.

1. Many children *gathered* around the ice-cream truck.
   a. inducted   c. congregated
   b. were accompanists   d. were accomplices

1. ____c____

2. A *new member of the army* must complete a basic training program.
   a. accomplice   **b.** accompanist   **c.** throng   **d.** inductee

2. _____d_____

3. The *person who aided the criminal* forged company records.
   a. accompanist   **b.** inductee   **c.** throng   **d.** accomplice

3. _____d_____

4. The four seasons are *related parts that work together to make up a whole.*
   a. complements   **c.** miscellanies
   b. congregations   **d.** accomplices

4. _____a_____

5. A *closely packed group* of spectators admired the museum exhibit.
   a. coalition   **b.** commune   **c.** throng   **d.** consensus

5. _____c_____

6. The *musician who played along with the singer* also took a bow.
   a. consensus   **b.** accomplice   **c.** accompanist   **d.** inductee

6. _____c_____

7. The class reached a *general agreement* and voted to visit the aquarium.
   a. consensus   **b.** throng   **c.** congregation   **d.** accomplice

7. _____a_____

8. The factory workers formed a *temporary alliance* on the issue of safety.
   a. induction   **b.** throng   **c.** coalition   **d.** complement

8. _____c_____

9. The neighborhood pool is a *public* facility.
   a. congregational   **c.** miscellaneous
   b. complementary   **d.** communal

9. _____d_____

10. While looking through the back of the catalogue, Jenny discovered *various* items.
    a. communal   **c.** accomplice
    b. congregational   **d.** miscellaneous

10. _____d_____

Exercise 4   Using Different Forms of Words

Decide which form of the vocabulary word in parentheses best completes the sentence. The form given may be correct. Write your answer on the answer line.

1. The pastor gave a sermon before a large __?__ . (*congregate*)

1. ____congregation____

2. Janet was an __?__ in the prank played on her little brother. (*accomplice*)

2. ____accomplice____

3. Mr. Newhall accumulated __?__ in his barn. (*miscellaneous*)

3. ____miscellany____

4. Roger __?__ Violet on the long walk home. (*accompanist*)

4. ____accompanied____

5. After hours of debate, the Senate committee reached a __?__ . (*consensus*)

5. ____consensus____

6. We worked __?__ to clean up the school playground. (*communal*)

6. ____communally____

7. The __?__ of new club members took place at a special ceremony. (*inductee*)

7. ____induction____

8. The cover nicely __?__ the contents of the yearbook. (*complement*)

8. ____complements____

9. A __?__ of people filled the convention center. (*throng*)

9. ____throng____

10. At least three __?__ are working for improved social services. (*coalition*)

10. ____coalitions____

Reading Comprehension

Each numbered sentence in the following passage contains an italicized vocabulary word. After you read the passage, you will complete an exercise.

The Talent Show

Excitement ran high at Sam Houston Junior High School, for plans were well under way for the annual Spring Carnival. **(1)** In the past, students had planned such *miscellaneous* activities as a dunking booth, a chili-cooking contest, and an armadillo-racing competition. The class or club that came up with the most original activity won a trophy. This year, the eighth grade class was determined to win.

(2) Billy Ray Johnson, the class president, called a planning session, and a *throng* of students gathered around his desk. **(3)** As they *congregated,* they talked excitedly among themselves.

Mrs. Harris, the class sponsor, cleared her throat loudly, gaining their attention. **(4)** "For the first time that I can remember," she explained, "you eighth graders have reached a *consensus* about the kind of show you want to put on. For the Spring Carnival, we'll do a talent show!"

Loud cheers greeted her announcement.

(5) "Remember," she warned, "the carnival is a *communal* event. Everyone should join in planning the skits and routines. **(6)** In addition, the acts ought to *complement* one another. Debbie, how is the show shaping up?"

"There's still a great deal of work to be done," explained Debbie, the director. **(7)** "Does anyone know a good *accompanist* for the musical numbers?" Debbie was greeted by silence and turned quickly to a new topic. "Joleen, were you able to find uniforms for the military routine?" Debbie took in Joleen's enthusiastic nod.

(8) "All of you army *inductees* are going to look terrific in uniforms." Debbie paused. "How about the rest of you? Have you decided on your skits?"

(9) "We can't think of anything!" complained Jeff, the outspoken member of a *coalition* of discouraged students. "What can people do if they can't sing or dance?"

"How about a takeoff of a movie?" Billy Ray suggested.

"That's a great idea!" Debbie was enthusiastic. "How about a James Bond picture? **(10)** Some of you can play fumbling enemy agents while others can be their mixed-up *accomplices.* You try to eliminate Bond, but he outsmarts you in his usual smooth way."

"Fine with me," Billy Ray said. Casually, he flashed his most sophisticated smile. "As long as I play James Bond."

Reading Comprehension Exercise

Each of the following statements corresponds to a numbered sentence in the passage. Each statement contains a blank and is followed by four answer choices. Decide which choice fits best in the blank. The word or phrase that you choose must express roughly the same meaning as the italicized word in the passage. Write the letter of your choice on the answer line.

1. In previous carnivals students had planned __?__ projects.
   a. few   **b.** special   **c.** interesting   **d.** varied

   1. _____d_____

2. A __?__ of eighth grade students filled the room for the planning session.
   a. group   **b.** crowd   **c.** handful   **d.** small number

   2. _____b_____

3. As they __?__ , they talked excitedly.
   a. planned   **b.** sat down   **c.** assembled   **d.** looked around

   3. _____c_____

4. The __?__ of the eighth grade was to put on a talent show.
   a. constant complaint   **c.** general decision
   b. dream   **d.** demand

   4. ___c___

5. Because the carnival was a(n) __?__ event, Mrs. Harris wanted everyone to join in planning it.
   a. large   **b.** individual   **c.** special   **d.** group

   5. ___d___

6. She also wanted the acts to __?__ one another.
   a. follow   **c.** go well with
   b. be similar to   **d.** interrupt

   6. ___c___

7. The musical numbers required a __?__ .
   a. person to direct   **c.** person to coach
   b. person to help   **d.** person to play an instrument

   7. ___d___

8. The __?__ in the army were told to wear uniforms.
   a. new soldiers   **c.** higher officers
   b. special forces   **d.** student officers

   8. ___a___

9. A(n) __?__ of students complained that they could think of nothing to do.
   a. series   **b.** alliance   **c.** society   **d.** party

   9. ___b___

10. They finally decided to do a spy-movie takeoff, complete with enemy agents and their __?__ .
    a. partners in crime   **c.** friends
    b. victims   **d.** disguises

    10. ___a___

Writing Assignment

Imagine that you are a reporter for a local television station. Your assignment is to cover a town meeting that promises to be controversial. Invent and write a news story that explains what went on at the meeting. Follow news-writing format by making sure that your story answers the questions who, what, where, when, why, and how. Use five words from the lesson and underline each one.

Vocabulary Enrichment

The word *accompanist*, which appears in this lesson, comes from the Latin word *panis*, meaning "bread," and is related to the words *accompany*, *company*, and *companion*. In ancient times the sharing of bread with another person symbolized the making of friends. Today the words *accompanist*, *accompany*, *company*, and *companion* all refer to activities involving friendship or sharing. For example, an *accompanist* who plays the piano shares his or her talent by performing with another person, such as a singer.

ACTIVITY In a high school or college dictionary, look up the following words and write their meanings and Latin roots. In each case, explain the connection between the root and the definition.

1. pantry 2. herbivore 3. carnivore 4. vineyard

Test: Lessons 1, 2, and 3
(pages 1–18)

Part A Choosing the Best Definition

On the answer line, write the letter of the best definition of the italicized word.

1. Not many two-year-olds can engage in *intelligible* conversation.
   a. scholarly   **b.** understandable   **c.** adult   **d.** literary

   1. _____ b

2. The movie star was greeted by a *throng* of admirers.
   a. crowd   **b.** scarcity   **c.** couple   **d.** unruly mob

   2. _____ a

3. Recording the *topography* of a mountainous region can be difficult.
   a. physical features   **b.** snowfall   **c.** customs   **d.** plant life

   3. _____ a

4. Citizens of Grenchen, Switzerland, speak a *dialect* of German.
   a. unrelated form   **c.** regional version
   b. few words   **d.** elevated style

   4. _____ c

5. One of Dale's *miscellaneous* talents is wood carving.
   a. varied   **b.** promising   **c.** obvious   **d.** expert

   5. _____ a

6. The Fourth of July celebration will include a *panorama* of the United States' struggle for independence.
   a. overview   **b.** criticism   **c.** definition   **d.** record

   6. _____ a

7. Arthur denied having a New England *accent*.
   a. regional pronunciation   **c.** sense of humor
   b. prejudice   **d.** philosophy

   7. _____ a

8. The *inductees* to the Hall of Fame will soon be announced.
   a. perfect examples   **c.** visitors
   b. new members   **d.** employees

   8. _____ b

9. Troy is studying *terrestrial* and aquatic life forms.
   a. ancient   **b.** strange   **c.** land   **d.** winged

   9. _____ c

10. Carmen learned the *fundamental* moves of the chess pieces.
    a. limited   **b.** complicated   **c.** basic   **d.** many

    10. _____ c

11. The *consensus* of the committee was to delay voting on the bond issue.
    a. decision   **b.** intent   **c.** agreement   **d.** desire

    11. _____ c

12. There is no *meridian* that does not pass through water at some point.
    a. imaginary circle   **c.** geographical point
    b. time zone   **d.** border of a country

    12. _____ a

13. Connie gave an *articulate* speech about robots.
    a. fascinating   **b.** scientific   **c.** long   **d.** clearly expressed

    13. _____ d

14. Ants quickly *congregated* around the dropped sandwich.
    a. scurried   **b.** swallowed up   **c.** danced   **d.** gathered

    14. _____ d

15. The ground surrounding the barn has turned into a *quagmire*.
    a. maze   **b.** muddy land   **c.** pond   **d.** fertile ground

    15. _____ b

Test: Lessons 1, 2, and 3

Part B Choosing the Best Word

On the answer line, write the letter of the word that best expresses the meaning of the italicized word or phrase.

16. Sal joined a conservation *alliance of people with a common cause*.
    a. coalition   **b.** throng   **c.** accomplice   **d.** meridian
    16. _____ a

17. Mr. Juarez *emphasized when speaking* our need for recreation areas.
    a. enunciated   **b.** accented   **c.** stressed   **d.** articulated
    17. _____ c

18. The fishing boat radioed its location as 115° *the distance west of Greenwich, England*.
    a. latitude   **b.** longitude   **c.** peninsula   **d.** topography
    18. _____ b

19. New Year's Eve celebrations are *public* rituals in many cities.
    a. intelligible   **b.** communal   **c.** fundamental   **d.** insular
    19. _____ b

20. Classical Greek actors, who wore masks, had to *pronounce clearly* their words when performing.
    a. enunciate   **b.** complement   **c.** accent   **d.** accompany
    20. _____ a

21. Certain breeds of sheep and goats can easily climb *steep cliffs*.
    a. precipices   **b.** peninsulas   **c.** meridians   **d.** quagmires
    21. _____ a

22. This striped tie *adds to the effect of* my suit.
    a. complements   **b.** accompanies   **c.** enunciates   **d.** articulates
    22. _____ a

23. Lucinda wrote a report on the *position in society* that women had in Renaissance England.
    a. diction   **b.** stress   **c.** latitude   **d.** status
    23. _____ d

24. This unique location is an island at high tide and a *strip of land with water on three sides* at low tide.
    a. consensus   **b.** longitude   **c.** peninsula   **d.** meridian
    24. _____ c

25. Francesca asked Paco to be her *musician who plays along with a performer* while she danced a flamenco.
    a. peer   **b.** complement   **c.** accomplice   **d.** accompanist
    25. _____ d

26. The class analyzed the *choice and use of words* in the poem.
    a. topography   **b.** diction   **c.** accent   **d.** congregation
    26. _____ b

27. Do you have the *freedom from usual restraints* to determine the hour at which you go to bed?
    a. longitude   **b.** latitude   **c.** status   **d.** consensus
    27. _____ b

28. Who was Jeff's *helper in breaking the law?*
    a. accompanist   **b.** complement   **c.** peer   **d.** accomplice
    28. _____ d

29. The Constitution provides an accused person with the right to be tried by a jury made up of his or her *equals in age, class, or rank*.
    a. accompanists   **b.** throngs   **c.** peers   **d.** accomplices
    29. _____ c

30. Alison went to St. John to study *pertaining to island* weather patterns.
    a. miscellaneous   **b.** fundamental   **c.** communal   **d.** insular
    30. _____ d

HOUGHTON MIFFLIN VOCABULARY FOR ACHIEVEMENT, SECOND COURSE

Dictionary Skills

Finding the Appropriate Definition

Most dictionary words have more than one definition. When you look up a word, you must decide which definition is most appropriate—that is, which one best fits the way the word is used. To do so, use the following strategies.

STRATEGIES

1. *Read all of the definitions in a dictionary entry.* Suppose that the italicized word in the following example sentence is unfamiliar to you. You would look up *contingent* in the dictionary and read the seven definitions.

    The launching of the space shuttle is *contingent* on the weather.

    con·tin·gent (kən-tĭn′jənt) *adj.* [ME < Lat. *contingens*, pr. part. of *contingere*, to touch. —see CONTACT.] **1.** Likely but not certain to occur: POSSIBLE. **2.** Dependent on conditions or events not yet established: CONDITIONAL. **3.** Happening by accident or chance: FORTUITOUS. **4.** *Logic*. Possessing a truth value derived from facts apart from the proposition itself: not necessarily true or false. —*n.* **1.** A contingent event: CONTINGENCY. **2.** A share or quota, as of troops, contributed to a general effort. **3.** A representative group forming part of an assemblage. **—con·tin′gent·ly** *adv.*

2. *If the word can be more than one part of speech, decide which part of speech the word is in the sentence. Then concentrate on the definitions for that part of speech.* In a dictionary entry, the part-of-speech label is italicized and comes before the definitions. In the sentence above, *contingent* is an adjective modifying the noun *launching.* Of the four adjective definitions in the entry, only one is appropriate.

3. *Read the sentence to yourself, substituting each correct part-of-speech definition for the word. Decide which one best fits the sentence.* The appropriate definition of *contingent* as it is used in the sentence is the second:

    The launching of the space shuttle is *dependent on conditions not yet established* (the weather).

4. *If there is more than one entry for a word, read each entry completely.* Some words are **homographs**—they are spelled alike but have different origins and meanings. For example, the words *fly* meaning "to move through the air" and *fly* meaning "an insect" are homographs. Homographs are given separate entries in the dictionary. Be sure to choose the correct one.

Please turn to the next page.

Finding the Appropriate Definition **19**

Using the dictionary entries provided, find the appropriate definition of the italicized word in each of the following sentences. *Step 1:* Write the appropriate dictionary definition. *Step 2:* Write a sentence of your own using the word with this definition.

1. Desperate to get a laugh, Steven *resorted* to slapstick comedy.

   DEFINITION To turn for help or as a means of achieving something

   SENTENCE Their food gone, the stranded explorers resorted to eating roots, berries, and nuts.

2. The aircraft carrier was accompanied by seven destroyer *escorts*.

   DEFINITION A ship accompanying another to provide protection

   SENTENCE The Coast Guard escort stayed close to the disabled sailboat.

3. Before the ceremony an usher *escorted* the bride's mother to her seat.

   DEFINITION To accompany as an escort

   SENTENCE I escorted Ms. Duarte to the auditorium stage.

4. The potter painted a design on the jar before applying the *glaze*.

   DEFINITION A coating of material applied to ceramics before firing

   SENTENCE This glaze is very hard and resists chipping.

5. Last summer my parents were finally able to take a vacation at a *resort* in Wisconsin.

   DEFINITION A place where people go for relaxation or recreation

   SENTENCE I have a summer job this year at a lake resort.

6. The workers removed a panel from the door and *glazed* the opening.

   DEFINITION To furnish or fit with glass

   SENTENCE I did not have enough material to glaze all the windows.

es·cort (ĕs′kôrt′) *n.* **1.** One or more persons accompanying another to give protection or guidance or to pay honor. **2.** One or more planes, ships, etc., accompanying another or others to provide protection. **3.** A man who acts as the companion of a woman in public. —*v.* (ĭ-skôrt′). To accompany as an escort: *Police escorted the President during the parade. I escorted her home.*

glaze (glāz) *n.* [ME *glasen* < *glas*, glass < OE *glæs*.] **1.** A smooth, thin, shiny coating. **2.** A thin, glassy ice coating. **3. a.** A coating of colored, opaque, or transparent material applied to ceramics before firing. **b.** A coating, as of syrup, applied to food. **c.** A transparent coating applied to the surface of a painting to modify color tones. **4.** A glassy film, as over the eyes. —*v.* **glazed, glaz·ing, glaz·es. 1.** To furnish or fit with glass <*glaze* the broken windows> **2.** To apply a *glaze* to <*glazing* a dozen doughnuts> <*glaze* a set of pottery dishes> **3.** To give a smooth, lustrous surface to. **4.** To be or become glazed or glassy <eyes *glazing* over with fatigue> **5.** To form a glaze. —**glaz′er** *n.*

re·sort (rĭ-zôrt′) *v.* To go or turn for help or as a means of achieving something: *resort to violence.* —*n.* **1.** A place where people go for relaxation or recreation: *a ski resort.* **2.** A person or thing to which one turns for help: *I would ask him only as a last resort.* **3.** The act of turning for help in a certain situation: *raising money without resort to borrowing.*

Lesson 4

Families

Years ago, families were much larger than they are today. There were more children in the average family, and grandparents often lived with their children and grandchildren. Other relatives sometimes lived with the family or in the same neighborhood. This was known as the "extended family."

Today we speak of the modern family as a "nuclear family" because single households now usually contain only the nucleus of parents and children. It is also common for families to be separated geographically from grandparents and other relatives. In this lesson you will learn words that refer to the family.

DEFINITIONS

After you have studied the definitions and example for each vocabulary word, write the word on the line to the right.

1. **descendant** (dĭ-sĕn′dənt) *noun* An individual or animal coming from a specific ancestor; offspring of a certain family or group. (From the Latin *de-*, meaning "down," and *scandere*, meaning "to climb")

   RELATED WORDS **descend** *verb;* **descent** *noun*

   EXAMPLE John claims to be a *descendant* of George Washington.

   1. _____

2. **generation** (jĕn′ə-rā′shən) *noun* **a.** All of the offspring that are at the same stage of descent from a common ancestor. **b.** A group of people who grow up at the same time and are thought to have similar ideas. (From the Latin word *genus*, meaning "birth")

   RELATED WORDS **generate** *verb;* **generational** *adjective*

   EXAMPLE Three *generations* of McCleary women were represented at the party — Alice, Alice's mother, and Alice's grandmother.

   2. _____

3. **inheritance** (ĭn-hĕr′ĭ-təns) *noun* **a.** The act of receiving property or money after the death of a relative or friend. **b.** The property or money received at such a time. **c.** A characteristic, such as red hair, that is received genetically from a parent, grandparent, etc. (From the Latin *in-*, meaning "in," and *heres*, meaning "heir")

   RELATED WORDS **inherit** *verb;* **inheritor** *noun*

   EXAMPLE Esther received a large *inheritance* after her grandmother's death.

   3. _____

4. lineage (lĭn′ē-ĭj) *noun*   **a.** Direct descent from a particular ancestor; ancestry.   **b.** All of the descendants of a common ancestor. (From the Old French word *ligne,* meaning "line")

RELATED WORD   **lineal** *adjective*

EXAMPLE   The horse had an impressive *lineage,* which began with the Thoroughbred champion Thunder.

5. maternal (mə-tûr′nəl) *adjective*   **a.** Referring to a mother or motherhood: *maternal concern.*   **b.** Inherited from one's mother: *maternal trait.*   **c.** Related to one's mother. (From the Latin word *mater,* meaning "mother")

RELATED WORD   **maternally** *adverb*

EXAMPLE   Baby-sitting brought out the *maternal* side of Joan's personality.

6. matriarch (mā′trē-ärk′) *noun*   A woman who rules a family or clan. (From the Latin word *mater,* meaning "mother," and the Greek word *arkhos,* meaning "ruler")

RELATED WORDS   **matriarchal** *adjective;* **matriarchy** *noun*

EXAMPLE   Because she is a strong leader, Grandma Jessie is the *matriarch* of the Hobart family.

7. parental (pə-rĕn′tl) *adjective*   Characteristic of a mother or father. (From the Latin word *parere,* meaning "to give birth")

RELATED WORDS   **parent** *noun;* **parentally** *adverb*

EXAMPLE   Small children require a great deal of *parental* guidance.

8. patriarch (pā′trē-ärk′) *noun*   **a.** The male leader of a family or clan.   **b.** A very old and respected man. (From the Greek word *pater,* meaning "father," and *arkhos,* meaning "ruler")

RELATED WORDS   **patriarchal** *adjective;* **patriarchy** *noun*

EXAMPLE   At family reunions, Uncle Charlie is the acknowledged *patriarch.*

9. posterity (pŏ-stĕr′ĭ-tē) *noun*   **a.** Future generations.   **b.** All of a person's descendants. (From the Latin word *posterus,* meaning "coming after")

EXAMPLE   The famous artist will leave many paintings to *posterity.*

10. sibling (sĭb′lĭng) *noun*   One of two or more children of the same parents; a brother or a sister. (From the Old English word *sibb,* meaning "kinsman")

EXAMPLE   *Siblings* often resemble one another physically.

4. _____

5. _____

6. _____

7. _____

8. _____

9. _____

10. _____

Exercise 1   Completing Definitions

On the answer line, write the word from the vocabulary list that best completes each definition.

1. Something that relates to a mother or father is __?__ .
2. The male ruler of a clan or family is called a(n) __?__ .
3. If something is left to future generations, it is given to __?__ .
4. Something that refers to a mother or motherhood is __?__ .
5. The offspring of a specific ancestor is a(n) __?__ .
6. Property or a characteristic received from a parent or ancestor is a(n) __?__ .
7. A __?__ consists of people who are at the same stage of descent.
8. Two or more individuals having the same parents are __?__ .
9. A female ruler of a clan or family is a(n) __?__ .
10. One's __?__ is one's descent from a particular ancestor.

1. ____parental____
2. ____patriarch____
3. ____posterity____
4. ____maternal____
5. ____descendant____
6. ____inheritance____
7. ____generation____
8. ____siblings____
9. ____matriarch____
10. ____lineage____

Exercise 2   Using Words Correctly

Each of the following questions contains an italicized vocabulary word. Decide the answer to the question, and write *Yes* or *No* on the answer line.

1. Would a *matriarch* lack power within a family?
2. Are you a member of the same *generation* as your grandfather?
3. Is an older brother a *sibling?*
4. Would a male ruler of a Scottish clan be a *patriarch?*
5. If a poet destroyed his or her work, could it still be left to *posterity?*
6. Would a direct ancestor of a king be of royal *lineage?*
7. Would your father's uncle be a *maternal* relative?
8. Would a *descendant* be born before an ancestor?
9. Is a five-dollar loan an *inheritance?*
10. Might a father sign a *parental* permission form?

1. ____No____
2. ____No____
3. ____Yes____
4. ____Yes____
5. ____No____
6. ____Yes____
7. ____No____
8. ____No____
9. ____No____
10. ____Yes____

Exercise 3   Choosing the Best Word

Decide which vocabulary word or related form best completes the sentence, and write the letter of your choice on the answer line.

1. The devoted mother of five has strong __?__ instincts.
   a. descendant   **b.** patriarchal   **c.** lineage   **d.** maternal

2. As the great-granddaughter of homesteaders, Judy is proud of her __?__ .
   a. lineage   **b.** posterity   **c.** sibling   **d.** generation

1. ____d____
2. ____a____

3. "Introduce your younger ___?___ ," Mrs. Henderson instructed Lynn, the older of the two sisters.
   a. generation **b.** patriarch **c.** sibling **d.** matriarch

3. _____c_____

4. The graduates of the class of 1980 are members of the same ___?___ .
   a. inheritance **b.** patriarch **c.** matriarch **d.** generation

4. _____d_____

5. City officials left a time capsule for ___?___ .
   a. posterity **b.** lineage **c.** siblings **d.** descendants

5. _____a_____

6. The beautiful antique furniture is part of Mrs. Cavendish's ___?___ .
   a. posterity **b.** inheritance **c.** sibling **d.** descendant

6. _____b_____

7. Lady Agatha Ashcroft is a powerful ___?___ who controls a large family.
   a. patriarch **b.** descendant **c.** sibling **d.** matriarch

7. _____d_____

8. " ___?___ intervention is sometimes unavoidable," the counselor told the mothers and fathers.
   a. Descendant **b.** Posterity **c.** Parental **d.** Lineal

8. _____c_____

9. Lisa thinks that she is a ___?___ of the poet Henry Wadsworth Longfellow.
   a. matriarch **b.** descendant **c.** sibling **d.** patriarch

9. _____b_____

10. The members of the village looked to their ___?___ for advice because he was a great leader.
    a. patriarch **b.** descendant **c.** lineage **d.** matriarch

10. _____a_____

Exercise 4   Using Different Forms of Words

Each sentence contains an italicized vocabulary word in a form that does not fit the sentence. On the answer line, write the form of that word that does fit the sentence.

1. Donald *inheritance* eight hundred dollars.

1. _____inherited_____

2. Before going on a class field trip, Steve had to get permission from his *parental*.

2. _____parents_____

3. Blair discovered that she was *descendant* from Thomas Jefferson.

3. _____descended_____

4. The explorers found a *matriarch* family group while exploring the islands.

4. _____matriarchal_____

5. Gerald's *lineage* history includes famous painters and writers.

5. _____lineal_____

6. Although they do not look alike, Martha and Rachel are *sibling*.

6. _____siblings_____

7. In early Scottish history, clans ruled the land through a *patriarch* system.

7. _____patriarchal_____

8. The park system was created not just for present residents of the city but for *posterity*.

8. _____posterity_____

9. Claude wrote a composition about the *generation* differences between his views and those of his grandparents.

9. _____generational_____

10. The young girl cradled the doll *maternal* in her arms.

10. _____maternally_____

Reading Comprehension

Each numbered sentence in the following passage contains an italicized vocabulary word. After you read the passage, you will complete an exercise.

The Family Game

ANNOUNCER: Welcome to another round of the Family Game. I'm your announcer and host, Eddie Hull. Now let's meet our competing families, the McCormacks and the Westovers. (1) To my right, we have Team One, which includes three *generations* of McCormack men. Audience, say hello to Grandpa Horace, son Michael, and grandson Robby. *(There is a pause.)* Folks, Robby told me that Grandpa Horace was the one who insisted that the family audition for the show.

GRANDPA HORACE: That's right, Ed. The rules in our family are simple. After everyone voices an opinion, I make the final decision. (2) You might call me the *patriarch* of the family.

GRANDMA AMELIA WESTOVER: Say, Ed, aren't you forgetting about the Westovers? (3) My girls and I are sure to give answers that will be recorded for *posterity.*

ANNOUNCER: Team number one, say hello to Team Two, the Westovers: Grandma Amelia, daughter Rebecca, and granddaughter Tracey.

AMY: Hey, how about me?

ANNOUNCER: Whoops! Tracey, please introduce your sister.

TRACEY: Do I have to?

ANNOUNCER: (4) Now, now, don't let *sibling* rivalry get in the way.

TRACEY: This is my sister, Amy, everyone.

ANNOUNCER: Very nice. Now let's play the Family Game! Remember the rules. I'll begin by asking Team One a question about a well-known head of a family. You McCormack men will have thirty seconds to give the right answer. If you can't answer the question in time, Team Two, the Westovers, will have a chance. Get ready, McCormacks! Here's your question. (5) Queen Victoria was considered one of the greatest *matriarchs* in the history of England. (6) In addition to being an impressive leader, Queen Victoria raised many children and had a strong *maternal* side. For one hundred dollars and a chance for our jackpot, whom was Queen Victoria married to?

GRANDPA HORACE: That's easy. I'll let Robby tell you.

ROBBY: Queen Victoria's husband was —

GRANDMA AMELIA *(interrupting Robby):* (7) You know, Ed, Queen Victoria is not the only one with an impressive *lineage.* (8) It just so happens that I am a direct *descendant* of Henry Harold Horton III.

ROBBY *(in a loud voice):* Queen Victoria's husband was —

ANNOUNCER *(interrupting Robby):* Tell me more about your fascinating family history, Amelia. Charting family trees is my favorite hobby. *(joking)* It's no accident that I'm the host of the Family Game.

GRANDMA AMELIA: And a wonderful one at that. Now, where was I? (9) Oh, yes, from Henry Harold's line our family has received its *inheritance* of strength and discipline. Henry Harold was one of the original settlers who came over on the *Mayflower.*

ANNOUNCER: Imagine that! *(He checks the clock.)* Oops! Time's running out, McCormacks!

ROBBY *(angry):* Well, if you and Mrs. Westover would quit interrupting, I could answer the question.

GRANDMA AMELIA: Interrupting! How dare you? Mr. McCormack, I demand that you do something about your son's bad manners. (10) Where is your *parental* authority?

ANNOUNCER: Time's up! Do you have an answer, Westovers?

GRANDMA AMELIA: Well, Ed, everyone knows Queen Victoria was married to —

ROBBY *(interrupting):* Prince Albert!

(For once, Grandma Amelia is speechless.)

ANNOUNCER: You are right, Robby! You are absolutely right for one hundred dollars and a chance to compete against another family for our super jackpot! Time's up, but thanks for a terrific Family Game.

Please turn to the next page.

Reading Comprehension Exercise

Each of the following statements corresponds to a numbered sentence in the passage. Each statement contains a blank and is followed by four answer choices. Decide which choice fits best in the blank. The word or phrase that you choose must express roughly the same meaning as the italicized word in the passage. Write the letter of your choice on the answer line.

1. The game show announcer introduces three __?__ of the McCormack family.
   a. close relatives   **c.** next-door neighbors
   b. different stages of descent   **d.** men who are related

   1. _____ b _____

2. Grandpa Horace is the __?__ of the family.
   a. scholar   **c.** male leader
   b. devoted grandfather   **d.** financial adviser

   2. _____ c _____

3. Grandma Amelia thinks that her family's answers will be recorded for __?__ .
   a. future generations   **c.** television cameras
   b. her grandchildren   **d.** good friends

   3. _____ a _____

4. The announcer warns about the conflict between __?__ .
   a. family   **b.** mothers and daughters   **c.** friends   **d.** sisters

   4. _____ d _____

5. He points out that Queen Victoria was a great __?__ .
   a. wife and mother   **c.** antique collector
   b. female leader   **d.** devoted grandmother

   5. _____ b _____

6. Furthermore, Queen Victoria also had a strong __?__ side.
   a. motherly   **b.** historical   **c.** intellectual   **d.** fatherly

   6. _____ a _____

7. Grandma Amelia talks about her own impressive __?__ .
   a. party   **b.** history   **c.** ancestry   **d.** society

   7. _____ c _____

8. She is a(n) __?__ of Henry Harold Horton III.
   a. daughter   **b.** admirer   **c.** friend   **d.** offspring

   8. _____ d _____

9. The __?__ from Henry Harold include(s) strength and discipline.
   a. characteristics passed down   **c.** large fortune
   b. ancient letters   **d.** descriptions

   9. _____ a _____

10. Grandma Amelia questions Michael McCormack's __?__ authority.
    a. personal   **b.** social   **c.** fatherly   **d.** political

    10. _____ c _____

Practice with Analogies

An analogy compares word pairs that are related in some way. For example, in "Package is to parcel as lariat is to lasso," both pairs are synonyms.

See page 119 for some strategies to use with analogies.

DIRECTIONS On the answer line, write the vocabulary word that completes each analogy.

1. Father is to paternal as mother is to __?__ .

   1. _____ maternal _____

2. Male is to patriarch as female is to __?__ .

   2. _____ matriarch _____

3. Father is to parent as brother is to __?__ .

   3. _____ sibling _____

4. Bride is to dowry as heir is to __?__ .

   4. _____ inheritance _____

5. Grandmother is to granddaughter as ancestor is to __?__ .

   5. _____ descendant _____

Bonus: Lessons 3 and 4
(pages 13–18, 21–26)

Use the following clues to identify the words, and write the words on the lines to the right. Then circle each word in the word-search box below. The words may overlap and may read in any direction.

1. Made up of a variety of different elements (13 letters)
2. COMMUNAL comes from the Latin word meaning "__?__." (6 letters)
3. A COMPLEMENT is something that __?__. (9 letters)
4. A MATRIARCH belongs to the __?__ gender. (6 letters)
5. General agreement among the members of a group (9 letters)
6. An ACCOMPLICE helps another person break a(n) __?__. (3 letters)
7. MATERNAL refers to a(n) __?__. (6 letters)
8. An ACCOMPANIST is a(n) __?__. (8 letters)
9. A DESCENDANT is a(n) __?__ of a certain family. (9 letters)
10. To come together in a crowd (10 letters)
11. A male leader of a family (9 letters)
12. Refers to all descendants of a common ancestor (7 letters)
13. A COALITION is a(n) __?__ of those sharing a cause. (8 letters)
14. A crowd (6 letters)
15. Future generations (9 letters)

1. miscellaneous
2. common
3. completes
4. female
5. consensus
6. law
7. mother
8. musician
9. offspring
10. congregate
11. patriarch
12. lineage
13. alliance
14. throng
15. posterity

BONUS

Lessons 3 and 4

```
C O N M I S C E L L A N E O U S S
G R E G A T E C O M M O N A T U E
A C E C O M P L S E N S U G S S T
C L T P A T R I A R C H R N E N E
E A A N N A I C I S U M E L C O L
C T G E G A E N I L Y S G E N I P
N N E T N H G R E G N N A N A T M
A E R M O T H E R O I C E W T A O
I R G P R A E N C L T E A L I R C
L A N C H N S E B N S L U S R E O
L P O S T E R I T Y F A F S E N I
A E C D U C S T E H E M R O H E T
N C E P A I N D U C T E E T N G R
I A R C G N I R P S F F O H I M A
```

CHALLENGE
Locate and circle the five additional vocabulary words in the word-search box

generation
inductee
inheritance
parental
sibling

Notes

The following lists of words are from the preceding two lessons. You may wish to use these lists to pinpoint words for ongoing review or for mid-term or final exams.

Lesson 3

accompanist	congregate	
accomplice	consensus	
coalition	inductee	
communal	miscellaneous	
complement	throng	

Lesson 4

descendant	matriarch
generation	parental
inheritance	patriarch
lineage	posterity
maternal	sibling

Lesson 5

The Root -*gen*-

The root -*gen*- has ancient origins and can be found in various forms in many Indo-European languages. As you will learn in this lesson, -*gen*- conveys many meanings, such as kind, type, class, family, race, origin, birth, or source. When it is combined with prefixes or suffixes, it produces many words that you will find useful when speaking or writing about the origins of things or about their classifications and types.

DEFINITIONS

After you have studied the definitions and example for each vocabulary word, write the word on the line to the right.

1. **congenial** (kən-jēn′yəl) *adjective* **a.** Having the same tastes, habits: *congenial friends*. **b.** Sociable; agreeable; amiable. (From the Latin *com-*, meaning "together" and *genialis*, meaning "festive")

   RELATED WORD **congeniality** *noun*

   EXAMPLE Adrian and Anastasia are very *congenial* and spend most of their spare time together.

   1. _____

2. **degenerate** (dĭ-jĕn′ə-rāt′) *verb* To sink into a much worse or lower condition; deteriorate. *adjective* (dĭ-jĕn′ər-ĭt) Having deteriorated from a previous state. (From the Latin *de-*, meaning "down," and *genus*, meaning "family" or "ancestry")

   RELATED WORDS **degeneration** *noun;* **degenerative** *adjective*

   EXAMPLE Houses often *degenerate* after decades of exposure to the elements.

   2. _____

3. **gender** (jĕn′dər) *noun* One of the categories — masculine, feminine, or neuter — into which words and the people, animals, or objects they denote are divided.

   EXAMPLE A deer, rabbit, or kangaroo of the female *gender* is called a doe.

   3. _____

4. **genealogy** (jē'nē-ŏl'ə-jē) *noun* **a.** A record of the descent of a family or person from an ancestor or ancestors. **b.** Direct descent from an ancestor; lineage. **c.** The study of ancestry and family histories. (From the Greek words *genea*, meaning "family," and *logos*, meaning "speech")

RELATED WORDS **genealogical** *adjective*; **genealogist** *noun*

EXAMPLE David traced his *genealogy* back to Charlemagne, the ninth-century Frankish ruler.

4. _____

5. **generic** (jə-nĕr'ĭk) *adjective* **a.** Of, including, or indicating an entire group, class, category; general rather than specific. **b.** Not protected by a trademark: *generic aspirin*. (From the Latin word *genera*, meaning "kinds")

RELATED WORD **generically** *adverb*

EXAMPLE The word "cats" is a *generic* term for tigers, jaguars, and house cats.

5. _____

6. **genesis** (jĕn'ĭ-sĭs) *noun* The coming into being of anything; origin. (From the Greek word *genesis*, meaning "birth")

EXAMPLE The *genesis* of Paul's short story was an experience that he had when he was ten.

6. _____

7. **gentry** (jĕn'trē) *noun* **a.** Well-bred people of good family and high social standing. **b.** A social class ranking next below the nobility. (From the Latin word *gens*, meaning "race" or "clan")

EXAMPLE In that country the *gentry* has large holdings of private property.

7. _____

8. **primogeniture** (prī'mō-jĕn'ĭ-chŏŏr') *noun* **a.** The condition of being the first-born child in a family. **b.** In law, the right of the eldest child — especially the eldest son — to inherit all of his parents' estates. (From the Latin words *primus*, meaning "first," and *genitura*, meaning "birth")

EXAMPLE Because of Jonathan's *primogeniture*, he assumed many responsibilities for his younger brothers.

8. _____

9. **progeny** (prŏj'ə-nē) *noun* Children; descendants; offspring. (From the Latin *pro-*, meaning "forward," and *gignere*, meaning "to beget")

RELATED WORD **progenitor** *noun*

EXAMPLE Several of the *progeny* of the great composer Johann Sebastian Bach were also composers.

9. _____

10. **regenerate** (rĭ-jĕn'ə-rāt') *verb* **a.** To give new life to; revive. **b.** To reform spiritually or morally. **c.** To replace (a damaged or lost part or organ) by growing new tissue. (From the Latin *re-*, meaning "again," and *generare*, meaning "produce")

RELATED WORDS **regeneration** *noun*; **regenerative** *adjective*

EXAMPLE The astonishing success of the Alamo High School football team has *regenerated* interest in the game.

10. _____

Name _____ Date _____

Exercise 1   Writing Correct Words

On the answer line, write the word from the vocabulary list that fits each definition.

1. Agreeable; sociable; having the same tastes

2. Classification as male or female

3. To create anew or revive

4. Descendants; offspring

5. General; relating to an entire class or group

6. Origin, source, or birth

7. To deteriorate or decline

8. People of high social position and good breeding

9. A record of ancestry

10. The condition of being first-born; the custom or law by which the eldest child receives property or inheritance

1. _____congenial_____

2. _____gender_____

3. _____regenerate_____

4. _____progeny_____

5. _____generic_____

6. _____genesis_____

7. _____degenerate_____

8. _____gentry_____

9. _____genealogy_____

10. _____primogeniture_____

Exercise 2   Using Words Correctly

Decide whether the italicized vocabulary word or related form has been used correctly in the sentence. On the answer line, write *Correct* for correct use and *Incorrect* for incorrect use.

1. My grandmother's *progeny* include her sisters, Mary and Martha, and her cousin Simeon.

2. Most plant life *degenerates* during a drought.

3. The Earl of Wessex, following the law of *primogeniture*, left his estate to his eldest son.

4. Christina looked in the family *genealogy* and learned that her great-grandfather had nine brothers and sisters.

5. The *gender* of a cardinal is red.

6. The *genesis* of a novel may lie in the author's imagination.

7. Our *congenial* neighbor offered to help me with the heavy suitcases.

8. In the supermarket the paper towels with specific brand names are *generic*.

9. Weakened muscles can be *regenerated* through exercise.

10. A story about the *gentry* would be about poor people with no education.

1. _____Incorrect_____

2. _____Correct_____

3. _____Correct_____

4. _____Correct_____

5. _____Incorrect_____

6. _____Correct_____

7. _____Correct_____

8. _____Incorrect_____

9. _____Correct_____

10. _____Incorrect_____

Exercise 3　Choosing the Best Word

Decide which vocabulary word or related form best expresses the meaning of the italicized word or phrase in the sentence. On the answer line, write the letter of that word.

1. Some scientists think that the *origin* of nuclear theory lay in the philosophy of Aristotle.
   a. progeny   **b.** degeneration   **c.** genesis   **d.** primogeniture

2. The diplomats believe that relations will *deteriorate* between the two countries.
   a. gender   **b.** degenerate   **c.** regenerate   **d.** gentry

3. Some people do not consider the *classification as male or female* of the President to be an important issue.
   a. gender   **b.** progeny   **c.** genealogy   **d.** primogeniture

4. The *descendants* of the famous author helped to restore his estate.
   a. primogeniture   **b.** regeneration   **c.** gender   **d.** progeny

5. As a result of his *moral reformation,* my friend Tyrone has become very thoughtful.
   a. congeniality   **b.** regeneration   **c.** genealogy   **d.** degeneration

6. Some of the *well-bred, upper-middle class* maintain estates in Virginia.
   a. primogeniture   **b.** progeny   **c.** gender   **d.** gentry

7. While looking at our *record of ancestry,* I discovered names like Ezekiel and Ebenezer.
   a. genealogy   **b.** primogeniture   **c.** progeny   **d.** gentry

8. When the king died, his throne was to be taken over by his eldest son according to the law of *inheritance by the eldest child.*
   a. genesis   **b.** regeneration   **c.** primogeniture   **d.** gender

9. The *unnamed, general type of* canned tomatoes are cheaper.
   a. degenerate   **b.** generic   **c.** regenerative   **d.** congenial

10. My friend James is so *sociable and friendly* that most people like him.
    a. generic   **b.** degenerate   **c.** regenerative   **d.** congenial

1. _____c_____
2. _____b_____
3. _____a_____
4. _____d_____
5. _____b_____
6. _____d_____
7. _____a_____
8. _____c_____
9. _____b_____
10. _____d_____

Exercise 4　Using Different Forms of Words

Decide which form of the vocabulary word in parentheses best completes the sentence. The form given may be correct. Write your answer on the answer line.

1. Only peafowl of the male __?__ have beautiful tail feathers. *(gender)*

2. The healing of a wound is an example of the __?__ power of the human body. *(regenerate)*

3. The biologist gave a lecture on the __?__ of amphibians. *(genesis)*

4. The term *gentrification,* which refers to the upgrading of urban neighborhoods, comes from the word __?__ . *(gentry)*

5. *Cheaper by the Dozen* tells the story of the crusty but lovable __?__ of twelve children. *(progeny)*

6. Our neighbors were known for their __?__ . *(congenial)*

1. _____gender_____
2. _____regenerative_____
3. _____genesis_____
4. _____gentry_____
5. _____progenitor_____
6. _____congeniality_____

7. Carmen is a __?__ and is an authority on the ancestry of early settlers in Arizona. (*genealogy*)

8. Mr. Van Allen was concerned about the __?__ of the muscles in his right arm. (*degenerate*)

9. By right of __?__ , the title of Prince of Wales falls to the eldest son of the British sovereign. (*primogeniture*)

10. In ancient Greece, the __?__ term for people who did not speak Greek was *barbarians*. (*generic*)

7. __genealogist__

8. __degeneration__

9. __primogeniture__

10. __generic__

Reading Comprehension

Each numbered sentence in the following passage contains an italicized vocabulary word or related form. After you read the passage, you will complete an exercise.

A Nineteenth-Century Romance

Imagine for a moment what life must have been like for a younger son of the gentry in nineteenth-century England. The future must not have seemed bright. Even his chances for marriage could have been affected by the laws of primogeniture, as you will see in the following fictional letter.

My dear Cecily,

I wish to thank you for your kind and sympathetic words when last we met. **(1)** You, more than anyone, dear cousin, are aware of the **genesis** of my current difficulties. I love Emily deeply and genuinely, and she loves me, yet I think it unlikely that we shall be wed. **(2)** I shan't inherit any property because by **primogeniture** my eldest brother, Sir Stephen, will inherit everything.

Emily likewise has little of her own. **(3)** Her father, Lord Plumsole, is a **congenial** fellow, but he has managed his estates neither wisely nor well. **(4)** He has allowed Plumsole Abbey to **degenerate** to such a point that it is no longer fit hab-

itation for such as Emily and me. 'Tis more the pity, for it was once the fairest house in the eastern part of northwest central Shropshire.

(5) The Plumsole **genealogy** is distinguished, to be sure. **(6)** It is nonetheless unlikely that any present members of the Plumsole family will witness the **regeneration** of its glorious past. **(7)** The Plumsoles suffer from that **generic** problem of the lower nobility, an inability to organize their lives properly.

At present, Cecily, I am

saddened. **(8)** Emily and I ask only to be simple members of the local **gentry,** free to ride to the hounds, read novels, and play the pianoforte. **(9)** Is this asking too much for ourselves and our **progeny? (10)** Whatever **gender** our children turn out to be, are they not entitled to lives even happier than ours?

These questions I leave to you, dear Cecily, to consider. I have at present neither joy nor contentment save for your kind and comforting words.

Your loving cousin,
Reginald

Please turn to the next page.

Reading Comprehension Exercise

Each of the following statements corresponds to a numbered sentence in the passage. Each statement contains a blank and is followed by four answer choices. Decide which choice fits best in the blank. The word or phrase that you choose must express roughly the same meaning as the italicized word in the passage. Write the letter of your choice on the answer line.

1. Cecily knows something about the ___?___ of Reginald's difficulties.
   a. reason   **b.** quality   **c.** origin   **d.** importance

1. _____c_____

2. Reginald will not inherit anything because of the law of inheritance by the ___?___ .
   a. richest   **b.** noblest   **c.** eldest   **d.** nicest

2. _____c_____

3. Lord Plumsole is ___?___ .
   a. plump   **b.** likable   **c.** stingy   **d.** thoughtful

3. _____b_____

4. He has allowed Plumsole Abbey to ___?___ .
   a. deteriorate   **b.** prosper   **c.** be sold   **d.** be painted

4. _____a_____

5. The Plumsole record of ___?___ is distinguished.
   a. land holdings   **b.** ancestors   **c.** diplomas   **d.** birthdays

5. _____b_____

6. No Plumsole living is likely to see the ___?___ of the glorious past.
   a. record   **b.** honor   **c.** glory   **d.** revival

6. _____d_____

7. The lower nobility has a ___?___ problem.
   a. minor   **b.** serious   **c.** general   **d.** difficult

7. _____c_____

8. Reginald wishes only to be a member of ___?___ .
   a. the nobility
   b. the well-bred upper-middle class
   c. the downtrodden lower-middle class
   d. no class at all

8. _____b_____

9. Does Reginald ask too much for his ___?___ ?
   a. offspring   **b.** ancestors   **c.** fiancée   **d.** parents

9. _____a_____

10. Reginald wants his children to be happy, whether they are ___?___ .
    a. rich or poor   **c.** English or Scottish
    b. male or female   **d.** friendly or shy

10. _____b_____

Writing Assignment

Everyone has ancestors, and some people are familiar with the lives of their parents, grandparents, and even great-grandparents. For presentation to members of a genealogical society, write a paragraph about an ancestor, real or imaginary. Use at least five words from this lesson and underline each one.

Lesson 6

Happiness and Unhappiness

When you are happy, you feel pleasure and joy. When you are sad, you feel just the opposite. Perhaps completing a difficult task makes you happy while the illness of a close friend makes you sad. Every individual is unique in his or her experience of joy and sorrow. In this lesson you will learn words that refer to happiness and unhappiness.

WORD LIST
amicable
anguish
blithe
defiant
desolate
despondent
disgruntled
disillusion
distress
exuberant

DEFINITIONS

After you have studied the definitions and example for each vocabulary word, write the word on the line to the right.

1. **amicable** (ăm′ĭ-kə-bəl) *adjective* Friendly in tone: *an amicable discussion.* (From the Latin word *amicus,* meaning "friend")

   RELATED WORDS **amicability** *noun;* **amicably** *adverb*

   EXAMPLE The carefree members of the soccer team are an *amicable* group.

   1. _____

2. **anguish** (ăng′gwĭsh) *noun* Great physical or mental pain; torment; torture.   *verb* To suffer greatly. (From the Latin word *angustia,* meaning "narrowness")

   RELATED WORD **anguished** *adjective*

   EXAMPLE Paul suffered *anguish* when his grandfather died.

   2. _____
   SEE *distress.*

3. **blithe** (blīth) *adjective* Cheerful; carefree; lighthearted.

   RELATED WORD **blithely** *adverb*

   EXAMPLE That *blithe* fellow can't keep from smiling as he walks down the street.

   3. _____

4. **defiant** (dĭ-fī′ənt) *adjective* Openly or boldly resisting authority. (From the Old French word *desfier,* meaning "to challenge")

   RELATED WORDS **defiance** *noun;* **defiantly** *adverb;* **defy** *verb*

   EXAMPLE The *defiant* workers refused to return to the factory until they received fairer treatment.

   4. _____

Happiness and Unhappiness   **33**

5. desolate (dĕs′ə-lĭt) *adjective* **a.** Lonely and sad; wretched; forlorn. **b.** Having little or no vegetation; barren. **c.** Having few or no inhabitants; deserted. *verb* (dĕs′ə-lāt′) To make desolate. (From the Latin word *desolare*, meaning "to leave all alone")

RELATED WORD **desolation** *noun*

EXAMPLE The earthquake left many people homeless and *desolate*.

5. _____

6. despondent (dĭ-spŏn′dənt) *adjective* In low spirits; depressed; dejected. (From the Latin word *despondere*, meaning "to give up")

RELATED WORDS **despondency** *noun;* **despondently** *adverb*

EXAMPLE . The artist Vincent van Gogh became *despondent* when people rejected his paintings.

6. _____

7. disgruntled (dĭs-grŭn′tld) *adjective* Discontented or cross.

EXAMPLE The longer they were stuck in traffic, the more *disgruntled* the motorists became.

7. _____

8. disillusion (dĭs′ĭ-lōō′zhən) *verb* To free or deprive of an idea or belief that proves false or in error; disenchant.

RELATED WORD **disillusionment** *noun*

EXAMPLE The magazine article *disillusioned* Ted because he hadn't realized that traveling in Japan was so expensive.

8. _____

9. distress (dĭ-strĕs′) *noun* Anxiety, discomfort, or suffering; worry. *verb* To cause suffering or discomfort. (From the Latin *dis-*, meaning "apart," and *stringere*, meaning "to draw tight")

RELATED WORD **distressingly** *adverb*

EXAMPLE Because the teen-agers were late coming home from the dance, their parents were *distressed*.

9. _____

Distress is physical or mental discomfort. *Anguish* is physical or mental torment.

10. exuberant (ĭg-zōō′bər-ənt) *adjective* Lively and joyous; enthusiastic; high-spirited. (From the Latin word *exuberare*, meaning "to abound")

RELATED WORDS **exuberance** *noun;* **exuberantly** *adverb*

EXAMPLE The *exuberant* child skipped into the room and shook hands with all present.

10. _____

Name _____ Date _____

Exercise 1 Writing Correct Words

On the answer line, write the word from the vocabulary list that fits each definition.

1. Challenging authority

2. High-spirited; joyous; lively

3. Dejected; depressed

4. Great pain; to suffer greatly

5. Worry; discomfort; anxiety; to cause suffering

6. Cross or discontented

7. Friendly

8. Carefree or cheerful

9. To disenchant or deprive of a false idea

10. Forlorn; sad and lonely

1. _____defiant_____

2. ____exuberant____

3. ___despondent___

4. ____anguish____

5. ____distress____

6. ___disgruntled___

7. ____amicable____

8. _____blithe_____

9. ___disillusion___

10. ____desolate____

Exercise 2 Using Words Correctly

Each of the following questions contains an italicized vocabulary word. Decide the answer to the question, and write *Yes* or *No* on the answer line.

1. Might an actor's fans become *disillusioned* upon learning that their idol is very conceited?

2. Would a *despondent* laborer look forward to her work each day?

3. Would a *blithe* person tend to complain constantly?

4. Would the death of a greatly loved pet be likely to *distress* someone?

5. Is *anguish* a pleasant feeling?

6. Would a gardener be *disgruntled* to find that someone had ridden a bicycle through the flower beds?

7. Would an *amicable* person make a new student feel welcome at a school?

8. Would *exuberant* basketball fans cheer loudly at a game?

9. Would a *defiant* person be likely to obey rules happily?

10. Might a person feel *desolate* after her closest friend had moved far away?

1. ____Yes____

2. ____No____

3. ____No____

4. ____Yes____

5. ____No____

6. ____Yes____

7. ____Yes____

8. ____Yes____

9. ____No____

10. ____Yes____

Exercise 3 Choosing the Best Word

Decide which vocabulary word or related form best completes the sentence, and write the letter of your choice on the answer line.

1. Peggy felt __?__ after receiving a low grade on the test.
   a. amicable   **b.** despondent   **c.** exuberant   **d.** blithe

1. ____b____

Happiness and Unhappiness   **35**

2. Although Constantine was quite ___?___ as a teen-ager, in adulthood he became fairly obedient.
   a. exuberant   **b.** amicable   **c.** desolate   **d.** defiant

2. _____d_____

3. Gail felt great ___?___ because she lost the fifty dollars her father had entrusted to her.
   a. distress   **b.** exuberance   **c.** defiance   **d.** amicability

3. _____a_____

4. Having received a scholarship to his favorite college, Jim was ___?___ .
   a. disillusioned   **b.** disgruntled   **c.** amicable   **d.** exuberant

4. _____d_____

5. After visiting her hometown, Ellen was ___?___ because it was so dull.
   a. amicable   **b.** blithe   **c.** disillusioned   **d.** defiant

5. _____c_____

6. Our new neighbors were so ___?___ that I felt at ease immediately.
   a. disgruntled   **b.** amicable   **c.** despondent   **d.** desolate

6. _____b_____

7. Juliana felt ___?___ when she moved to New York City, where she knew no one.
   a. desolate   **b.** disillusioned   **c.** blithe   **d.** exuberant

7. _____a_____

8. George becomes ___?___ whenever he makes a typing error.
   a. exuberant   **b.** desolate   **c.** disgruntled   **d.** blithe

8. _____c_____

9. In contrast to nasty Captain Hook, Peter Pan is ___?___ .
   a. disillusioned   **b.** despondent   **c.** desolate   **d.** blithe

9. _____d_____

10. Have you ever experienced the ___?___ of a broken bone?
    a. disillusionment   **b.** anguish   **c.** defiance   **d.** exuberance

10. _____b_____

Exercise 4   Using Different Forms of Words

Decide which form of the vocabulary word in parentheses best completes the sentence. The form given may be correct. Write your answer on the answer line.

1. Sally skipped ___?___ into the room. (*blithe*)

1. _____blithely_____

2. A pang of ___?___ struck Miguel as he watched his son drive away. (*desolate*)

2. _____desolation_____

3. Filled with ___?___ after winning the race, Terry leaped into the air. (*exuberant*)

3. _____exuberance_____

4. Irwin was ___?___ when he found that he had made several careless errors on his exam. (*disgruntled*)

4. _____disgruntled_____

5. Mrs. Rutherford ___?___ invited my sister and me to dinner when our parents had to go out. (*amicable*)

5. _____amicably_____

6. Leonora watched ___?___ as her best friend moved to another city. (*despondent*)

6. _____despondently_____

7. Katherine strode ___?___ out of the room. (*defiant*)

7. _____defiantly_____

8. "It ___?___ me to see you so unhappy," Carol told Monique. (*distress*)

8. _____distresses_____

9. For three hours the Robinsons suffered the ___?___ of not knowing whether their pet had survived the auto accident. (*anguish*)

9. _____anguish_____

10. A sense of ___?___ overwhelmed young Sidney when he discovered that there was no tooth fairy. (*disillusion*)

10. _____disillusionment_____

Name _____ Date _____

Reading Comprehension

Each numbered sentence in the following passage contains an italicized vocabulary word or related form. After you read the passage, you will complete an exercise.

Marie Curie: Discoverer of Radium

Marie Curie was one of the most accomplished scientists in history. Together with her husband, Pierre, she discovered radium, an element widely used for treating cancer, and studied uranium and other radioactive substances. **(1)** Pierre and Marie's **amicable** collaboration later helped to unlock the secrets of the atom.

Marie was born in 1867 in Warsaw, Poland, where her father was a professor of physics. **(2)** At an early age, she displayed a brilliant mind and a **blithe** personality. **(3)** Her great **exuberance** for learning prompted her to continue with her studies after high school. **(4)** She became **disgruntled,** however, when she learned that the university in Warsaw was closed to women. **(5)** Deter-mined to receive a higher education, she **defiantly** left Poland and in 1891 entered the Sorbonne, a French university, where she earned her master's degree and doctorate in physics.

Marie was fortunate to have studied at the Sorbonne with some of the greatest scientists of her day, one of whom was Pierre Curie. Marie and Pierre were married in 1895 and spent many productive years working together in the physics laboratory. In 1906, a short time after they discovered radium, Pierre was killed by a horse-drawn wagon. **(6)** Marie was stunned by this horrible misfortune and endured heartbreaking **anguish.** **(7)** **Despondently** she recalled their close relationship and the joy that they had shared in scientific research. **(8)** The fact that she had two young daughters to raise by herself greatly increased her **distress.**

(9) Curie's feeling of **desolation** finally began to fade when she was asked to succeed her husband as a physics professor at the Sorbonne. She was the first woman to be given a professorship at the world-famous university. In 1911 she received the Nobel Prize in chemistry for isolating radium. **(10)** Although Marie Curie eventually suffered a fatal illness from her long exposure to radium, she never became **disillusioned** about her work. Regardless of the consequences, she had dedicated herself to science and to revealing the mysteries of the physical world.

Reading Comprehension Exercise

Each of the following statements corresponds to a numbered sentence in the passage. Each statement contains a blank and is followed by four answer choices. Decide which choice fits best in the blank. The word or phrase that you choose must express roughly the same meaning as the italicized word in the passage. Write the letter of your choice on the answer line.

1. The Curies' __?__ collaboration helped to unlock the secrets of the atom.
   a. competitive   **b.** courteous   **c.** cold   **d.** friendly

   1. _____d_____

2. Marie had a bright mind and a __?__ personality.
   a. lighthearted   **b.** humorous   **c.** strong   **d.** depressed

   2. _____a_____

3. Her __?__ for learning did not end with her high school education.
   a. enthusiasm   **b.** aptitude   **c.** desire   **d.** talent

   3. _____a_____

4. When she learned that she could not attend the university in Warsaw, she felt __?__.
   a. hopeless   **b.** sad   **c.** annoyed   **d.** depressed

   4. _____c_____

5. Marie __?__ by leaving Poland and traveling to France to enter the Sorbonne.
   a. challenged authority   **c.** showed intelligence
   b. made a mistake   **d.** behaved well

   5. _____a_____

6. Marie's __?__ over Pierre's accidental death was great.
   a. pity   **b.** emptiness   **c.** pain   **d.** loneliness

   6. _____c_____

7. __?__ she remembered their joy together.
   a. Joyously   **b.** Dejectedly   **c.** Worriedly   **d.** Tearfully

   7. _____b_____

8. Her __?__ increased because she had two children to raise all alone.
   a. anxiety   **b.** loss   **c.** work   **d.** problem

   8. _____a_____

9. Her __?__ began to fade when she returned to the Sorbonne to succeed her husband.
   a. misfortune   **b.** bad luck   **c.** wretchedness   **d.** anger

   9. _____c_____

10. Even though she became fatally ill from working with radium, Marie was never __?__.
    a. troubled   **b.** worried   **c.** bored   **d.** disappointed

    10. _____d_____

Writing Assignment

Jane is a wonderful athlete and has been involved in gymnastics since she was very young. Often Jane participates in competitions. Sometimes she wins, and other times she loses. Write a story for a sports magazine that tells about Jane's most recent competition. If necessary, research the topic at the library before writing your story. Use at least five words from this lesson and underline each one.

Vocabulary Enrichment

In French the word for "friend" is *ami*. In Spanish it is *amigo;* in Italian, *amico*. All three are derived from *amicus*, the Latin word for "friend." Although the English word *friend* does not come from *amicus*, there are many English words about friends and friendship that are derived from *amicus*.

In this lesson you learned the word *amicable*, meaning "friendly." There is also the word *amiable* (without a *c*), which means "likable" or "good-natured." In other words, *amiable* implies having the qualities one would wish for in a friend. The word *amity*, a noun, means friendship in the special sense of peaceful relations between nations.

ACTIVITY   The word *amicus* also has a negative form in Latin, *inimicus*, which means "not friendly." The English word *enemy* is derived from *inimicus*, as are the two words that follow. Using a dictionary, look up these two words, write a definition for each one, and use each in a sentence.

1. enmity   2. inimical

Bonus: Lessons 5 and 6

(pages 27–38)

Use the clues to complete the crossword puzzle.

The completed crossword grid contains:

- 3 Across: ORIGIN
- 4 Across: GENTRY
- 5 Across: DESOLATE
- 7 Across: CONGENIAL
- 9 Across: REGENERATE
- 12 Across: DEGENERATE
- 14 Across: KIND
- 16 Across: DEFIANT
- 18 Across: DESPONDENT
- 19 Across: ANGUISH
- 20 Across: DISENCHANT
- 21 Across: WORRY
- 1 Down: FIRST
- 2 Down: GENERIC
- 6 Down: ANNOYED
- 8 Down: DESCENDANCY
- 10 Down: BLITHE
- 11 Down: MALE
- 13 Down: EXUBERANT
- 15 Down: ANCESTR
- 17 Down: FRIEND

Across

3. Synonym for GENESIS
4. People of high social position
5. Lonely and sad
7. Sociable
9. Revive, or replace by growing new tissue
12. To deteriorate
14. One of the meanings of the root -gen-
16. A ___?___ person may resist authority.
18. In low spirits
19. Great physical or mental pain
20. Synonym for DISILLUSION
21. Synonym for DISTRESS

Down

1. PRIMOGENITURE is the condition of being the ___?___-born child in a family.
2. Often less expensive than brand-name products
6. Synonym for DISGRUNTLED
8. PROGENY
10. Lighthearted
11. GENDER refers to both ___?___ and female.
13. Full of enthusiasm
15. GENEALOGY
17. AMICABLE comes from a Latin word meaning "___?___."

HOUGHTON MIFFLIN VOCABULARY FOR ACHIEVEMENT, SECOND COURSE

BONUS
Lessons 5 and 6

Notes

The following lists of words are from the preceding two lessons. You may wish to use these lists to pinpoint words for ongoing review or for midterm or final exams.

Lesson 5

congenial
degenerate
gender
genealogy
generic

genesis
gentry
primogeniture
progeny
regenerate

Lesson 6

amicable
anguish
blithe
defiant
desolate

despondent
disgruntled
disillusion
distress
exuberant

Test: Lessons 4, 5, and 6

(pages 21–38)

Part A   Completing the Definition

On the answer line, write the letter of the word or phrase that correctly completes each sentence.

1. A *sibling* is a(n) __?__ .
   a. ancestor   **b.** utensil   **c.** cousin   **d.** brother or sister

   1. ____d____

2. If Sheila is researching her *genealogy*, she is working on her __?__ .
   a. needlepoint   **b.** ancestry   **c.** career   **d.** special project

   2. ____b____

3. Anything that __?__ can be described as *parental*.
   a. includes men and women   **c.** applies to a mother or father
   b. pertains to birth   **d.** is cautious

   3. ____c____

4. Someone who feels *despondent* is __?__ .
   a. lucky   **b.** successful   **c.** wicked   **d.** dejected

   4. ____d____

5. *Generic* products are __?__ .
   a. general   **b.** specific   **c.** store-bought   **d.** handmade

   5. ____a____

6. A *matriarch* is a __?__ .
   a. type of butterfly   **c.** tool used to bale hay
   b. female leader of a family   **d.** type of Greek column

   6. ____b____

7. A member of the *gentry* __?__ .
   a. is a peasant   **c.** is a person of high social standing
   b. lives in the country   **d.** is involved in business

   7. ____c____

8. *Primogeniture* refers to __?__ .
   a. the first-born child   **c.** the color of hair and eyes
   b. groups of ancestors   **d.** the ability to dance

   8. ____a____

9. Something __?__ is called an *inheritance*.
   a. received after the owner dies   **c.** sacrificed for another
   b. tax deductible   **d.** donated to charity

   9. ____a____

10. If you are *disillusioned*, you feel __?__ .
    a. cheated   **b.** surrounded   **c.** disenchanted   **d.** foolish

    10. ____c____

11. *Gender* refers to __?__ categories of objects or people.
    a. age   **b.** strength   **c.** sex   **d.** origin

    11. ____c____

12. Tracing one's *lineage* involves tracing __?__ .
    a. ancestors   **b.** shapes   **c.** nationalities   **d.** personal progress

    12. ____a____

13. A person who feels __?__ is in *distress*.
    a. energetic   **b.** eager   **c.** inquisitive   **d.** anxious

    13. ____d____

14. When we refer to the __?__ of something, we refer to its *genesis*.
    a. complexity   **b.** origin   **c.** movement   **d.** strength

    14. ____b____

15. If offspring from a common ancestor are __?__ , they are called a *generation*.
    a. at odds with each other   **c.** restricted in number
    b. still living   **d.** at the same level of descent

    15. ____d____

HOUGHTON MIFFLIN VOCABULARY FOR ACHIEVEMENT, SECOND COURSE

Test: Lessons 4, 5, and 6

Part B Identifying Synonyms

On the answer line, write the letter of the word or phrase that has the meaning that is the same as that of the capitalized vocabulary word.

16. DESOLATE :
    a. guilty   **b.** respectful   **c.** helpful   **d.** lonely

17. ANGUISH :
    a. joy   **b.** suffering   **c.** confusion   **d.** satisfaction

18. AMICABLE :
    a. friendly   **b.** shy   **c.** curious   **d.** sensitive

19. PATRIARCH :
    a. coach   **b.** president   **c.** boss   **d.** male leader of a family

20. REGENERATE :
    a. deteriorate   **b.** manipulate   **c.** illuminate   **d.** revive

21. BLITHE :
    a. sorrowful   **b.** bitter   **c.** cheerful   **d.** limited

22. DESCENDANT :
    a. lawyer   **b.** son-in-low   **c.** underling   **d.** offspring

23. DEGENERATE :
    a. deteriorate   **b.** volunteer   **c.** propel   **d.** ignore

24. DISGRUNTLED :
    a. agreeable   **b.** cross   **c.** respectful   **d.** tired

25. MATERNAL :
    a. kindly   **b.** instructive   **c.** motherly   **d.** long-lived

26. PROGENY :
    a. descendants   **b.** families   **c.** liquids   **d.** colleagues

27. EXUBERANT :
    a. wrinkled   **b.** noisy   **c.** enthusiastic   **d.** listless

28. POSTERITY :
    a. future generations   **c.** predecessors
    b. hosts   **d.** previous neighbors

29. CONGENIAL :
    a. foolish   **b.** shameless   **c.** talkative   **d.** sociable

30. DEFIANT :
    a. yielding   **b.** resistant   **c.** destructive   **d.** loud

16. _____d_____

17. _____b_____

18. _____a_____

19. _____d_____

20. _____d_____

21. _____c_____

22. _____d_____

23. _____a_____

24. _____b_____

25. _____c_____

26. _____a_____

27. _____c_____

28. _____a_____

29. _____d_____

30. _____b_____

HOUGHTON MIFFLIN VOCABULARY FOR ACHIEVEMENT, SECOND COURSE

A
B
C
D
E
F

Dictionary Skills

Inflected Forms of Words

The spelling of words changes to indicate things such as number, tense, and degree. Dictionaries include these different forms of words, called **inflected forms.** This lesson explains the way in which inflected forms are listed in dictionaries.

1. *Noun plurals.* Some noun plurals present a spelling problem or are formed in irregular ways. For example, the dictionary entry for *penny* gives the plural (often abbreviated *pl.*), *pennies.*

2. *Verb forms.* Irregular forms of a verb or forms that involve a spelling change are also given in dictionary entries. The forms are usually listed in this order: past tense, past participle, present participle, third-person singular present tense. *Show* is an example of a verb entry that lists each of these inflected forms. Notice that *show* has both regular *(showed, showing, shows)* and irregular *(shown)* forms. All the inflected forms of a verb may be given if any one is irregular.

   show (shō) *v.* **showed, shown** (shōn) or **showed,**
   show·ing, shows.

3. *Comparatives and superlatives of modifiers.* Dictionary entries give both regular and irregular comparison forms of modifiers. The following entries show the inflected forms of a regular adjective, *slow,* and an irregular adjective, *good.*

   slow (slō) *adj.* **slow·er, slow·est.**

   good (go͝od) *adj.* **bet·ter** (bĕt′ər), **best** (bĕst).

A dictionary will not show comparatives and superlatives when they are formed with *more* and *most,* as for example, *more pitiful* and *most pitiful.*

Exercise   Finding Inflected Forms of Words

Using the dictionary entries at the end of this exercise, write the inflected form asked for in each item. Then write a sentence of your own in which you use this form.

1. Write the present participle form of *delete.* deleting
   SENTENCE   Rodney is deleting the incorrect figures from the club minutes.

2. Write the comparative form of *oily.* oilier
   SENTENCE   My hair is oilier than yours.

Please turn to the next page.

3. Write the plural form of *parenthesis.* parentheses

SENTENCE Michael put parentheses around the shopping list items that he couldn't find.

4. Write the superlative form of *expressive.* most expressive

SENTENCE She has the most expressive face I've ever seen.

5. Write the past tense form of *throw.* threw

SENTENCE Before we moved to Brownsville, we threw away everything that was no longer usable.

6. Write the past participle form of *throw.* thrown

SENTENCE Although my sister has ridden a horse almost all her life, she has never been thrown.

7. Write the plural form of *bacterium.* bacteria

SENTENCE Canned food is cooked at high temperatures to kill bacteria.

8. Write the third-person singular present form of *belie.* belies

SENTENCE His enormous size belies a gentle spirit.

9. Write the past tense form of *delete.* deleted

SENTENCE The student deleted the unnecessary words from her rough draft.

10. Write the superlative form of *oily.* oiliest

SENTENCE This is the oiliest salad dressing that I have ever eaten.

bac·te·ri·um (băk-tîr′ē-əm) *n. pl.* **-ri·a** (ē-ə) [NLat. < Gk. *baktērion,* little rod, dim. of *baktron,* rod.] Any of numerous unicellular microorganisms of the class Schizomycetes, occurring in many forms, existing either as free-living organisms or as parasites, and having a broad range of biochemical, often pathogenic properties. **—bac·te′ri·al** *adj.* **—bac· te′ri·al·ly** *adv.*

be·lie (bĭ-lī′) *v.* **be·lied, be·ly·ing, be·lies. 1.** To give a wrong or false idea of: *His cheerful tone belied his feelings of anger and frustration.* **2.** To be inconsistent with; contradict: *Nineteenth-century America went on a pleasure-seeking binge that belied its puritanical past.*

de·lete (dĭ-lēt′) *v.* **de·let·ed, de·let·ing.** To strike out; remove; eliminate: *delete a name from a list; delete the last sentence of a paragraph.*

ex·pres·sive (ĭk-sprěs′ĭv) *adj.* **1.** Of, relating to, or marked by expression. **2.** Serving to indicate or express <a tone of voice *expressive* of anger> **3.** Full of expression: SIGNIFICANT <an *expressive* smile> **—ex·pres′sive·ly** *adv.* **—ex·pres′sive· ness** *n.*

oil·y (oi′lē) *adj.* **oil·i·er, oil·i·est. 1.** Of or like oil: *an oily liquid.* **2.** Covered with, soaked with, or containing much oil: *oily rags; an oily complexion.* **3.** Unpleasantly smooth, as in manner or behavior: *his oily, insincere compliments.* **—oil′i·ness** *n.*

pa·ren·the·sis (pə-rĕn′thĭ-sĭs) *n., pl.* **pa·ren·the· ses** (pə-rĕn′thĭ-sēz′). **1.** Either or both of the upright curved lines, ( ), used to mark off additional remarks in printing or writing. **2.** An additional phrase, explanation, etc., enclosed within such marks. **3.** A qualifying phrase placed within a sentence in such a way that the sentence is grammatically complete without it. **4.** Any comment departing from the main topic.

throw (thrō) *v.* **threw** (thrōō), **thrown** (thrōn), **throw·ing. 1.** To propel through the air with a swift motion of the arm; fling: *throw a ball.* **2.** To hurl with great force, as in anger: *He threw himself at his opponent.* **3.** To cast: *throw a glance at the window displays; throw a shadow.* **4.** To put on or off casually: *hurriedly throwing a cape over her shoulders.* **5.** To hurl to the ground or floor: *The wrestler threw his opponent with a swift blow.* **6.** *Informal.* To arrange or give: *throw a party.* **7.** *Informal.* To lose (a fight, race, etc.) purposely. **8.** To put into a specified condition: *new regulations that threw the players into confusion.* **9.** To actuate (a switch or control lever). **—***n.* **1.** The act of throwing; a cast. **2.** The distance, height, or direction of something thrown. **3.** A scarf, shawl, or light coverlet. **4.** The distance or region through which a mechanical part moves. **—throw′er** *n.*

Lesson 7

Science and Technology

Throughout history, scientific research has led to new inventions. For example, Ben Franklin's kite experiments helped later scientists to harness electricity. Today bionicists study anatomy in order to create devices such as artificial hearts. Many technical developments like these have altered and enriched our lives.

The words in this lesson will help you to understand some of the vocabulary used by scientists and technologists. Studying these words may also help you to understand how scientific knowledge leads to technological progress.

WORD LIST

alloy
buoyant
celestial
coagulate
combustible
conflagration
dissection
distill
meteorology
saturate

DEFINITIONS

After you have studied the definitions and example for each vocabulary word, write the word on the line to the right.

1. **alloy** (ăl′oi′) *noun*   A metal that is formed by mixing two or more other metals, or by combining a metal and a nonmetal. *verb* (ə-loi′)   To combine metals to form an alloy. (From the Latin word *alligare,* meaning "to bind to")

   EXAMPLE   Candlesticks are frequently made of brass, which is an *alloy* of zinc and copper.

   1. _____

2. **buoyant** (boi′ənt) *adjective*   **a.** Capable of floating in a liquid; able to keep other things afloat.   **b.** Not easily depressed; cheerful.

   RELATED WORD   **buoyancy** *noun*

   EXAMPLE   The *buoyant* raft bounced over the swirling rapids.

   2. _____

3. **celestial** (sə-lĕs′chəl) *adjective*   **a.** Of or related to the sky or heavens.   **b.** Heavenly or divine. (From the Latin word *caelum,* meaning "sky")

   EXAMPLE   The astronomers tracked the *celestial* object carefully with their high-powered telescopes.

   3. _____

4. **coagulate** (kō-ăg′yə-lāt′) *verb*   **a.** To change a liquid into a solid or nearly solid mass; clot.   **b.** To become coagulated. (From the Latin *com-,* meaning "together," and *agere,* meaning "to bring")

   EXAMPLE   Egg whites *coagulate* when they are cooked.

   4. _____

5. **combustible** (kəm-bŭs′tə-bəl) *adjective* **a.** Capable of catching fire and burning; inflammable. **b.** Easily excited; quick to anger. (From the Latin word *combustus,* meaning "burnt up")

   RELATED WORD **combustion** *noun*

   EXAMPLE Rags that have been soaked in turpentine are highly *combustible.*

5. _____

6. **conflagration** (kŏn′flə-grā′shən) *noun* A large and destructive fire. (From the Latin word *conflagrare,* meaning "to burn up")

   EXAMPLE In 1906 many blocks of buildings were destroyed by the *conflagration* that followed the San Francisco earthquake.

6. _____

7. **dissection** (dĭ-sĕk′shən) *noun* **a.** The process of cutting apart an animal or plant to examine its internal structure. **b.** A detailed analysis or examination. (From the Latin *dis-,* meaning "apart," and *secare,* meaning "to cut")

   RELATED WORD **dissect** *verb*

   EXAMPLE After our *dissection* of the worm, we studied its primitive circulatory system.

7. _____

8. **distill** (dĭ-stĭl′) *verb* To treat or purify a liquid by heating it until it forms a vapor and then cooling it so that it returns to liquid form. (From the Latin *de-,* meaning "down," and *stillare,* meaning "to drip")

   RELATED WORD **distillation** *noun*

   EXAMPLE The engineers *distilled* gasoline from crude oil in their small laboratory.

8. _____

9. **meteorology** (mē′tē-ə-rŏl′ə-jē) *noun* The science dealing with atmospheric conditions, especially weather conditions. (From the Greek word *meteōron,* meaning "astronomical phenomenon," and *logos,* meaning "speech")

   RELATED WORDS **meteorological** *adjective;* **meteorologist** *noun*

   EXAMPLE People who do research in *meteorology* believe that volcanic eruptions affect the weather.

9. _____

10. **saturate** (săch′ə-rāt′) *verb* To cause to be thoroughly soaked; fill to capacity. (From the Latin word *satur,* meaning "full")

    RELATED WORDS **saturated** *adjective;* **saturation** *noun*

    EXAMPLE Rain had *saturated* the garden and killed all of the seedlings.

10. _____

Name _____ Date _____

Exercise 1 Writing Correct Words

On the answer line, write the word from the vocabulary list that fits each definition.

1. Tending to float in a liquid; not easily depressed
2. Located in the sky or heavens
3. To treat or purify a liquid
4. The study of atmospheric conditions
5. To soak thoroughly or fill to capacity
6. A large, destructive fire
7. A mixture of two or more metals
8. To change a liquid into a solid mass; clot
9. The process of cutting apart to examine and study
10. Inflammable; easily excited

1. _____buoyant_____
2. _____celestial_____
3. _____distill_____
4. _____meteorology_____
5. _____saturate_____
6. _____conflagration_____
7. _____alloy_____
8. _____coagulate_____
9. _____dissection_____
10. _____combustible_____

Exercise 2 Using Words Correctly

Decide whether the italicized vocabulary word has been used correctly in the sentence. On the answer line, write *Correct* for correct use and *Incorrect* for incorrect use.

1. Doug was fascinated by the *celestial* creatures of the sea.
2. *Dissection* of the maps in geography class made them easier to study.
3. The towel was *saturated* before I had dried all the dishes.
4. In order to gain a better understanding of *meteorology*, Betty read a book on weaving.
5. A handshake confirmed the *alloy* between the boys.
6. The children were upset that their toy boat was not *buoyant*.
7. Grandfather *distills* tap water to make it purer for cleaning his contact lenses.
8. If *combustible* materials collect in a storage area, they may become a fire hazard.
9. Lucinda's *conflagration* was interrupted by her brother's singing.
10. The sauce has to be stirred constantly so that it will not *coagulate*.

1. _____Incorrect_____
2. _____Incorrect_____
3. _____Correct_____
4. _____Incorrect_____
5. _____Incorrect_____
6. _____Correct_____
7. _____Correct_____
8. _____Correct_____
9. _____Incorrect_____
10. _____Correct_____

Exercise 3 Choosing the Best Definition

For each italicized vocabulary word in the following sentences, write the letter of the best definition on the answer line.

1. The insurance agent photographed what remained of the beach houses after the *conflagration*.
   a. storm   **b.** large fire   **c.** loud party   **d.** earthquake

1. _____b_____

2. The jewelry designer displayed necklaces made of a new *alloy*.
   a. synthetic material   **c.** mixture of liquids
   b. mineral   **d.** mixture of metals

2. _____d_____

3. Roger is looking forward to the frog *dissection* scheduled for the final week of biology class.
   a. test   **c.** cutting and examining
   b. sketching and labeling   **d.** review

3. _____c_____

4. Margot's interest in *meteorology* began when a heat wave damaged her lettuce crop.
   a. agricultural study   **c.** weather study
   b. vegetable study   **d.** insect study

4. _____c_____

5. Jon has worked hard to control his *combustible* personality.
   a. easily angered   **c.** unpopular
   b. complex   **d.** easily influenced

5. _____a_____

6. As part of the experiment, the scientist tested the rate at which blood *coagulates*.
   a. flows   **b.** clots   **c.** burns   **d.** is created

6. _____b_____

7. Our spirits were *buoyant* even after the terrible weather.
   a. cheerful   **b.** soaked   **c.** confused   **d.** depressed

7. _____a_____

8. My family spent the evening discussing *celestial* phenomena.
   a. strange   **c.** ancient
   b. occurring on the earth   **d.** occurring in the sky

8. _____d_____

9. Rochelle *saturated* the sponge with soapy water before washing her car.
   a. dampened   **b.** covered   **c.** soaked   **d.** cleaned

9. _____c_____

10. The scientist could not obtain accurate results without *distilling* the liquids.
    a. purifying   **b.** removing   **c.** combining   **d.** stirring

10. _____a_____

Exercise 4 Using Different Forms of Words

Decide which form of the vocabulary word in parentheses best completes the sentence. The form given may be correct. Write your answer on the answer line.

1. In 1871 a major __?__ leveled much of the city of Chicago. *(conflagration)*

1. _____conflagration_____

2. Many students will __?__ snakes and frogs in biology class. *(dissection)*

2. _____dissect_____

3. Greg's gelatin failed to __?__ because he added too much water. *(coagulate)*

3. _____coagulate_____

4. To cultivate flowers, the Dutch use fresh water that has been __?__ from sea water. *(distill)*

4. _____distilled_____

5. My ring is not pure gold; it is made from an __?__. *(alloy)*

5. _____alloy_____

6. The room seemed to be __?__ with the spicy aroma of cinnamon and cloves. *(saturate)*

6. _____saturated_____

7. In a planetarium one can learn about __?__ occurrences. *(celestial)*

8. Under certain conditions __?__ takes place spontaneously — that is, it starts without a match or other external source. *(combustible)*

9. Janine is reading about unusual __?__ events. *(meteorology)*

10. When Helda scuba-dives in salt water, she adds ten pounds of weight to control her __?__ . *(buoyant)*

7. _____celestial_____

8. _____combustion_____

9. _____meteorological_____

10. _____buoyancy_____

Reading Comprehension

Each numbered sentence in the following passage contains an italicized vocabulary word or related form. After you read the passage, you will complete an exercise.

The Eruption of Mount Vesuvius

Mount Vesuvius, a volcano located between the ancient Italian cities of Pompeii and Herculaneum, has received much attention because of its frequent and destructive eruptions. The most famous of these eruptions occurred in A.D. 79.

The volcano had been inactive for centuries. **(1)** There was little warning of the coming eruption, although one account unearthed by archaeologists says that a hard rain and a strong wind had disturbed the **celestial** calm during the preceding night. **(2)** Early the next morning, the volcano poured a huge river of molten rock down upon Herculaneum, completely burying the city and filling in the harbor with **coagulated** lava.

Meanwhile, on the other side of the mountain, cinders, stone, and ash rained down on Pompeii. **(3)** Sparks from the burning ash ignited the **combustible** rooftops quickly. **(4)** Large portions of the city were destroyed in the **conflagration.** Fire, however, was not the only cause of destruction. **(5)** Poisonous sulphuric gases **saturated** the air. **(6)** These heavy

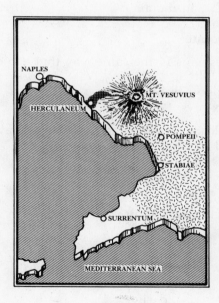

gases were not **buoyant** in the atmosphere and therefore sank toward the earth and suffocated people.

Over the years, excavations of Pompeii and Herculaneum have revealed a great deal about the behavior of the volcano. **(7)** By analyzing data, much as a zoologist **dissects** a specimen animal, scientists have concluded that the eruption changed large portions of the area's geography. For instance, it turned the Sarno

River from its course and raised the level of the beach along the Bay of Naples. **(8)** **Meteorologists** studying these events have also concluded that Vesuvius caused a huge tidal wave that affected the world's climate.

(9) In addition to making these investigations, archaeologists have been able to study the skeletons of victims by using **distilled** water to wash away the volcanic ash. By strengthening the brittle bones with acrylic paint, scientists have been able to examine the skeletons and draw conclusions about the diet and habits of the residents. **(10)** Finally, the excavations at both Pompeii and Herculaneum have yielded many examples of classical art, such as jewelry made of bronze, which is an **alloy** of copper and tin.

The eruption of Mount Vesuvius and its tragic consequences have provided us with a wealth of data about the effects that volcanoes can have on the surrounding area. Today volcanologists can locate and predict eruptions, saving lives and preventing the destruction of cities and cultures.

Please turn to the next page.

Reading Comprehension Exercise

Each of the following statements corresponds to a numbered sentence in the passage. Each statement contains a blank and is followed by four answer choices. Decide which choice fits best in the blank. The word or phrase that you choose must express roughly the same meaning as the italicized word in the passage. Write the letter of your choice on the answer line.

1. The night before the earthquake a storm disturbed the __?__ calm.
   a. heavenly   **b.** uneasy   **c.** residents'   **d.** ocean's

   1. _____ a

2. Herculaneum and its harbor were buried under __?__ lava.
   a. liquid   **b.** solid   **c.** hot   **d.** flowing

   2. _____ b

3. Sparks from burning ash ignited the __?__ rooftops.
   a. peaked   **b.** wooden   **c.** inflammable   **d.** flat

   3. _____ c

4. A __?__ destroyed major portions of the city.
   a. burning ash   **b.** strong wind   **c.** large fire   **d.** hot coal

   4. _____ c

5. Poisonous gases __?__ the air.
   a. half-filled   **b.** removed   **c.** diminished   **d.** filled

   5. _____ d

6. The poisonous gases were not __?__ in the air.
   a. able to float   **c.** present
   b. visible   **d.** able to evaporate

   6. _____ a

7. Scientists analyzed data about Vesuvius in the same way that a zoologist __?__ a specimen.
   a. describes in detail   **c.** photographs
   b. studies by cutting apart   **d.** x-rays

   7. _____ b

8. __?__ have concluded that the volcanic eruption caused a tidal wave.
   a. Scientists who study bones and teeth
   b. Scientists who study oceans
   c. Scientists who study atmospheric conditions
   d. Scientists who study metals

   8. _____ c

9. Scientists have used __?__ water to wash away volcanic ash from the skeletons of victims.
   a. warm   **b.** bottled   **c.** volcanic   **d.** purified

   9. _____ d

10. Archaeologists have found jewelry made of bronze, which is a(n) __?__ of copper and tin.
    a. layering   **b.** ore   **c.** mixture   **d.** design

    10. _____ c

Practice with Analogies

DIRECTIONS On the answer line, write the vocabulary word that completes each analogy.

See page 119 for some strategies to use with analogies.

1. Open is to close as liquefy is to __?__ .

   1. _____ coagulate

2. Earth is to terrestrial as sky is to __?__ .

   2. _____ celestial

3. Earth is to geology as weather is to __?__ .

   3. _____ meteorology

4. Puddle is to flood as campfire is to __?__ .

   4. _____ conflagration

5. Dense is to sink as __?__ is to float.

   5. _____ buoyant

Lesson 8

Strength and Defense

In addition to requiring food, clothing, and shelter, people need to feel secure as they carry out their daily activities. Consequently, societies around the world establish and maintain armies and navies that they hope will prevent attack. The words in this lesson are used in describing different aspects of strength and defense. By studying these words, you will better understand how individuals and groups try to insure their own safety.

WORD LIST
blockade
indestructible
martial
omnipotent
robust
stability
staunch
valiant
vulnerable
withstand

DEFINITIONS

After you have studied the definitions and example for each vocabulary word, write the word on the line to the right.

1. **blockade** (blŏ-kād′) *noun* The closing off of an area to prevent entrance or exit; an obstruction that prevents passage or progress.   *verb* To set up a blockade against.

   EXAMPLE   The *blockade* of the harbor kept all ships from entering or leaving the port.

   1. _____

2. **indestructible** (ĭn′dĭ-strŭk′tə-bəl) *adjective* Not capable of being ruined or eliminated. (From the Latin *in-*, meaning "not," and *destruere*, meaning "to destroy")

   RELATED WORD   **indestructibility** *noun*

   EXAMPLE   The massive stone pillars used as supports for the front of the building seemed *indestructible*.

   2. _____

3. **martial** (mär′shəl) *adjective* **a.** Inclined or disposed toward war; warlike. **b.** Military in style. (From the Latin word *martialis*, meaning "of Mars")

   EXAMPLE   The army band was well known for its performances of *martial* music.

   3. _____

   MEMORY CUE *Martial* comes from the word *Mars*. Mars was the god of war in Roman mythology.

4. **omnipotent** (ŏm-nĭp′ə-tənt) *adjective* Having unlimited power, authority, or force. (From the Latin words *omnis*, meaning "all," and *potens*, meaning "having power")

   RELATED WORDS   **omnipotence** *noun;* **omnipotently** *adverb*

   EXAMPLE   An earthquake is an *omnipotent* force of nature.

   4. _____

5. robust (rō-bŭst′) *adjective* Full of strength and health; sturdy; powerfully built. (From the Latin word *robustus*, meaning "of oak")

RELATED WORDS **robustly** *adverb;* **robustness** *noun*

EXAMPLE A summer of exercise and healthful food transformed Arnie into a *robust* athlete.

5. _____

MEMORY CUE The adjective *robust* comes from the Latin word for *oak*, an extremely strong and hard wood.

6. stability (stə-bĭl′ĭ-tē) *noun* **a.** Firmness of character or purpose. **b.** Resistance to change; changelessness. **c.** Reliability and dependability. (From the Latin word *stabilis*, meaning "standing firm")

RELATED WORDS **stabilize** *verb;* **stable** *adjective*

EXAMPLE The company wanted evidence of *stability* in its new president.

6. _____

7. staunch (stônch) *adjective* **a.** Characterized by firmness, steadfastness, or loyalty. **b.** Strong and substantial.

RELATED WORDS **staunchly** *adverb;* **staunchness** *noun*

EXAMPLE The judge was a *staunch* defender of equal rights.

7. _____

USAGE NOTE The verb *staunch* (or *stanch*) means "to check the flow of (blood)" — by pressing *firmly*.

8. valiant (văl′yənt) *adjective* Displaying bravery, courage, and boldness. (From the Latin word *valere*, meaning "to be strong")

RELATED WORDS **valiantly** *adverb;* **valor** *noun*

EXAMPLE The soldier was rewarded for his *valiant* actions in the battle.

8. _____

9. vulnerable (vŭl′nər-ə-bəl) *adjective* Capable of being wounded or hurt; open to attack or difficult to defend. (From the Latin word *vulnerare*, meaning "to wound")

RELATED WORDS **vulnerability** *noun;* **vulnerably** *adverb*

EXAMPLE In football, running backs are particularly *vulnerable* to injury.

9. _____

10. withstand (wĭth-stănd′) *verb* To resist something successfully by using force; endure. (From the Old English words *with*, meaning "against," and *standan*, meaning "to stand")

EXAMPLE The sand castle could not *withstand* the force of the powerful waves.

10. _____

Exercise 1   Completing Definitions

On the answer line, write the word from the vocabulary list that best completes each definition.

1. To be sturdy, strong, and healthy is to be __?__ .
2. To endure or to resist something successfully is to __?__ it.
3. The closing off of an area to prevent movement in or out is a __?__ .
4. A person who displays great courage or boldness is considered __?__ .
5. Behavior that is warlike or military in style is __?__ .
6. Firmness of character or resistance to change is __?__ .
7. A position that can be easily attacked is __?__ .
8. When something cannot be ruined or eliminated, it is __?__ .
9. A person or thing that is firm, strong, and loyal is __?__ .
10. To have unlimited power is to be __?__ .

1. _____ robust _____
2. _____ withstand _____
3. _____ blockade _____
4. _____ valiant _____
5. _____ martial _____
6. _____ stability _____
7. _____ vulnerable _____
8. _____ indestructible _____
9. _____ staunch _____
10. _____ omnipotent _____

Exercise 2   Using Words Correctly

Each of the following questions contains an italicized vocabulary word. Decide the answer to the question, and write *Yes* or *No* on the answer line.

1. Would a *martial* nation be known for its peace-loving nature?
2. Would a *valiant* person face danger in order to help a friend?
3. Is a sleeping deer *vulnerable* prey for a hungry wolf?
4. Would a weak, foolish king be an *omnipotent* ruler?
5. Would a *robust* person have difficulty walking one mile?
6. Would a *staunch* friend refuse to talk about you behind your back?
7. In the event of a naval *blockade*, would ships be allowed to pass freely in and out of a harbor?
8. Can penguins *withstand* the cold air and water of Antarctica?
9. Would a tool shed made of flattened tin cans and plywood be *indestructible* during a tornado?
10. Does a bridge that rocks back and forth when you walk on it have *stability?*

1. _____ No _____
2. _____ Yes _____
3. _____ Yes _____
4. _____ No _____
5. _____ No _____
6. _____ Yes _____
7. _____ No _____
8. _____ Yes _____
9. _____ No _____
10. _____ No _____

Exercise 3   Choosing the Best Word

Decide which vocabulary word or related form best completes the sentence, and write the letter of your choice on the answer line.

1. The ship was able to __?__ the strong winds and heavy rain.
   a. blockade   **b.** stabilize   **c.** staunch   **d.** withstand

1. _____ d _____

2. A table with four legs has greater __?__ than one with only three legs.
   a. valor   **b.** stability   **c.** vulnerability   **d.** omnipotence

2. ____b____

3. __?__ seafaring people called Vikings invaded many countries in northern and western Europe.
   a. Martial   **b.** Stable   **c.** Blockading   **d.** Vulnerable

3. ____a____

4. The __?__ camper chopped wood for a campfire.
   a. martial   **b.** valiant   **c.** vulnerable   **d.** robust

4. ____d____

5. The trainer said that the boxer was __?__ because he had won every fight.
   a. indestructible   **b.** vulnerable   **c.** martial   **d.** blockaded

5. ____a____

6. Kate received a standing ovation for her __?__ attempts to win the basketball game.
   a. vulnerable   **b.** stable   **c.** valiant   **d.** martial

6. ____c____

7. No one could leave or enter the town because of the enemy's __?__ .
   a. stability   **b.** staunchness   **c.** blockade   **d.** vulnerability

7. ____c____

8. Carlisle has several __?__ friends who support her effort to become an artist.
   a. omnipotent   **b.** staunch   **c.** robust   **d.** martial

8. ____b____

9. The old house was __?__ to the winds that blew off the ocean.
   a. valiant   **b.** robust   **c.** staunch   **d.** vulnerable

9. ____d____

10. As ruler of the Roman Empire, Julius Caesar was very nearly __?__ .
    a. omnipotent   **b.** vulnerable   **c.** stable   **d.** withstanding

10. ____a____

Exercise 4   Using Different Forms of Words

Decide which form of the vocabulary word in parentheses best completes the sentence. The form given may be correct. Write your answer on the answer line.

1. Hannah __?__ risked her life to save the kittens from the burning house. *(valiant)*

1. ____valiantly____

2. Flying in the hot-air balloon gave Andrea a feeling of __?__ . *(omnipotent)*

2. ____omnipotence____

3. The falcon could sense the mouse's __?__ . *(vulnerable)*

3. ____vulnerability____

4. The police are __?__ the avenue so that the ambassadors can leave their meeting safely. *(blockade)*

4. ____blockading____

5. The __?__ of the sea wall assured the residents that large waves would not destroy their houses. *(indestructible)*

5. ____indestructibility____

6. Lynn's family __?__ supported her decision to go to law school. *(staunch)*

6. ____staunchly____

7. __?__ is an essential quality in a furniture mover. *(Robust)*

7. ____Robustness____

8. Before the painter climbed the ladder, he made sure that it was __?__ . *(stability)*

8. ____stable____

9. The army doctor received a medal for his __?__ at the front. *(valiant)*

9. ____valor____

10. In Greek mythology, Zeus ruled __?__ over all other gods and goddesses. *(omnipotent)*

10. ____omnipotently____

Reading Comprehension

Each numbered sentence in the following passage contains an italicized vocabulary word or related form. After you have read the passage, you will complete an exercise.

The Spanish Armada

Conflict had existed between Spain and England since the 1570s. England wanted a share of the wealth that Spain had been taking from the lands it had claimed in the Americas. (1) Elizabeth I, Queen of England, encouraged her *staunch* admiral of the navy, Sir Francis Drake, to raid Spanish ships and towns. (2) Though these raids were on a small scale, Drake achieved dramatic success, adding gold and silver to England's treasury and diminishing Spain's *omnipotence.*

Religious differences also caused conflict between the two countries. Whereas Spain was Roman Catholic, most of England had become Protestant. King Philip II of Spain wanted to claim the throne and make England a Catholic country again. To satisfy his ambition and also to retaliate against England's theft of his gold and silver, King Philip began to build his fleet of warships, the Armada, in January 1586.

(3) Philip intended his fleet to be *indestructible.* (4) In addition to building new warships, he marshaled 130 sailing vessels of all types and recruited more than 19,000 *robust* soldiers and 8,000 sailors. (5) Although some of his ships lacked guns and others lacked ammunition, Philip was convinced that his Armada could *withstand* any battle with England.

(6) The *martial* Armada set sail from Lisbon, Portugal, on May 9, 1588, but bad weather forced it back to port. (7) The voyage resumed on July 22 after the weather had become *stable.*

The Spanish fleet met the smaller, faster, and more maneuverable English ships in battle off the coast of Plymouth, England, first on July 31 and again on August 2. (8) The two battles left Spain *vulnerable,* costing it several ships and depleting its ammunition.

On August 7, while the Armada lay at anchor on the French side of the Strait of Dover, England sent eight burning ships into the midst of the Spanish fleet to set it on fire. (9) *Blockaded* on one side, the Spanish ships could only drift away, their crews in panic and disorder. Before the Armada could regroup, the English attacked again on August 8.

(10) Although the Spaniards made a *valiant* effort to fight back, the fleet suffered extensive damage. During the eight hours of battle, the Armada drifted perilously close to the rocky coastline. At the moment when it seemed that the Spanish ships would be driven onto the English shore, the wind shifted, and the Armada drifted out into the North Sea. The Spaniards recognized the superiority of the English fleet and returned home, defeated.

Reading Comprehension Exercise

Each of the following statements corresponds to a numbered sentence in the passage. Each statement contains a blank and is followed by four answer choices. Decide which choice fits best in the blank. The word or phrase that you choose must express roughly the same meaning as the italicized word in the passage. Write the letter of your choice on the answer line.

1. Elizabeth I encouraged her __?__ admiral of the navy to raid Spanish ships and towns.
   a. wise   **b.** crafty   **c.** loyal   **d.** precise

1. _____ c

2. Drake added wealth to the treasury and diminished Spain's __?__ .
   a. unlimited power **c.** reputation
   b. unrestricted growth **d.** territory

2. ___a___

3. Philip intended his fleet to be __?__ .
   a. respected **c.** incapable of being copied
   b. incapable of being eliminated **d.** special

3. ___b___

4. Philip recruited many __?__ soldiers and sailors.
   a. warlike **b.** strong **c.** accomplished **d.** creative

4. ___b___

5. Philip was convinced that the Armada could __?__ any battle with England.
   a. engage **b.** arrange **c.** break **d.** endure

5. ___d___

6. The __?__ Armada set sail on May 9, 1588.
   a. complete **b.** warlike **c.** independent **d.** luxurious

6. ___b___

7. The voyage resumed after the weather became more __?__ .
   a. reliable **b.** idle **c.** serious **d.** restless

7. ___a___

8. The two battles left the Spanish fleet __?__ .
   a. open to change **c.** open to attack
   b. triumphant **d.** hopeful

8. ___c___

9. The Armada was __?__ on one side.
   a. closed off **b.** damaged **c.** dependable **d.** alone

9. ___a___

10. The Spaniards made a __?__ attempt to fight back.
    a. slight **b.** ridiculous **c.** huge **d.** courageous

10. ___d___

Writing Assignment

Write a letter to your local or school newspaper in which you take a position on an issue of importance in your school or community. For example, you might write a letter defending the quality of the food served in the school cafeteria. Use at least five of the words from this lesson and underline them.

Vocabulary Enrichment

The word *martial* comes from the name of a Roman god, Mars. Mars was originally the Roman god of agriculture, and the early Romans paid tribute to him for good harvests.

After the Romans captured Greece, they adopted the Greek gods and myths into their own culture. Because the Greeks believed that a goddess was responsible for growing crops, the Romans removed this function from Mars, who was a male. Instead, they gave him the characteristics and responsibilities of Ares, the Greek god of war. Thus, the word *martial*, derived from the name of Mars, describes military activities.

ACTIVITY Other words besides *martial* come from the names of gods or goddesses. Use your dictionary and an encyclopedia to find the origin of each of the words that follow. Write a definition of each word as well as a brief description of the origin.

1. jovial 2. titanic 3. iridescent 4. psyche 5. narcissistic

Bonus: Lessons 7 and 8

(pages 41–52)

Use the clues to spell out the words on the answer blanks. Then identify the mystery person at the bottom of the page by writing the numbered letters on the lines with the corresponding numbers.

1. A CONFLAGRATION is a large and destructive ___?___ .

2. Brass is a(n) ___?___ of zinc and copper.

3. The ___?___ arts include karate and judo.

4. A hearty, vigorous person is ___?___ .

5. Having unlimited power or authority

6. Ships cannot enter a harbor when there is a(n) ___?___ .

7. The process of cutting apart and examining internal structure

8. The planets are ___?___ bodies.

9. To clot

10. Firm, steadfast, or loyal

11. Opposite of timid or fearful

12. To soak thoroughly

13. Firmness of character or purpose

14. DISTILLING a liquid makes it ___?___ .

15. To resist by force

1. F I R E
    13

2. A L L O Y
       14

3. M A R T I A L
              5

4. R O B U S T
       3

5. O M N I P O T E N T
       4   9

6. B L O C K A D E
   16   7   8

7. D I S S E C T I O N
          6

8. C E L E S T I A L
       7

9. C O A G U L A T E
            15

10. S T A U N C H
            10

11. V A L I A N T
    11

12. S A T U R A T E
              12

13. S T A B I L I T Y
        1

14. P U R E
    17

15. W I T H S T A N D
        2

T H O M A S   E D I S O N ,   I N V E N T O R
1 2 3 4 5 6   7 8 9 6 3 10   9 10 11 7 10 1 3 12

O F   T H E   L I G H T   B U L B
3 13 1 2 7   14 9 15 2 1 16 17 14 16

HOUGHTON MIFFLIN VOCABULARY FOR ACHIEVEMENT, SECOND COURSE

T8

BONUS

Lessons 7 and 8

Notes

The following lists of words are from the preceding two lessons. You may wish to use these lists to pinpoint words for ongoing review or for mid-term or final exams.

Lesson 7

alloy	conflagration
buoyant	dissection
celestial	distill
coagulate	meteorology
combustible	saturate

Lesson 8

blockade	stability
indestructible	staunch
martial	valiant
omnipotent	vulnerable
robust	withstand

Buildings and Structures

Architecture is one of the oldest art forms. Unlike other creative arts, such as painting, sculpture, and music, architecture must satisfy practical considerations. Someone may design an office building that looks beautiful, but if people cannot work comfortably and efficiently in it, the building does not serve its purpose. The words in this lesson will introduce you to some of the terminology used by architects to describe aspects of buildings and other structures.

WORD LIST
abode
annex
edifice
excavate
mason
prefabricate
rotunda
solar
trellis
turret

DEFINITIONS

After you have studied the definitions and example for each vocabulary word, write the word on the line to the right.

1. **abode** (ə-bōd') *noun* A dwelling place or home. (From the Old English word *abidan,* meaning "to wait")

   EXAMPLE   Mt. Olympus was the *abode* of the ancient Greek gods and goddesses.

   1. _____

   USAGE NOTE   One meaning of the related verb *abide* is "to dwell." One *abides* in an *abode.*

2. **annex** (ăn'ĕks') *noun* A wing or building added to or located close to a larger building and used for the same purpose. *verb* (ə-nĕks') To join or attach. (From the Latin *ad-,* meaning "to," and *nectere,* meaning "to bind")

   RELATED WORD   **annexation** *noun*

   EXAMPLE   The Library of Congress has an *annex* to house additional books.

   2. _____

   MEMORY CUE An *annex* is usually *next* to the original structure.

3. **edifice** (ĕd'ə-fĭs) *noun* A building, especially one of great size or elegant appearance. (From the Latin words *aedis,* meaning "a building," and *facere,* meaning "to make")

   EXAMPLE   The Doge's Palace in Venice is a colorful marble *edifice* perched on the side of a canal.

   3. _____

4. **excavate** (ĕk'skə-vāt') *verb* **a.** To dig or hollow out. **b.** To expose or uncover by digging. (From the Latin *ex-,* meaning "out," and *cavare,* meaning "to hollow")

   RELATED WORD   **excavation** *noun*

   EXAMPLE   The construction crew *excavated* the basement of the building in three days.

   4. _____

5. **mason** (mā'sən) *noun*   A person who works with stone and brick.

    RELATED WORD   **masonry** *noun*

    EXAMPLE   The Ghilardis hired a *mason* to build their patio.

5. ————————
USAGE NOTE   *Masonry* means "the trade of a mason" and also the finished product: "stone- or brickwork."

6. **prefabricate** (prē-făb'rĭ-kāt') *verb*   To produce or build in advance; make in sections that can be shipped easily and assembled quickly. (From the Latin *prae-*, meaning "before," and *fabricari*, meaning "to make")

    RELATED WORD   **prefabrication** *noun*

    EXAMPLE   Today, many companies *prefabricate* houses.

6. ————————

7. **rotunda** (rō-tŭn'də) *noun*   A circular building or room, especially one with a domed ceiling. (From the Latin word *rotunda*, meaning "round")

    EXAMPLE   Tourists who visit the Capitol are fascinated by the high ceiling of the *rotunda*.

7. ————————

8. **solar** (sō'lər) *adjective*   Having to do with the sun; using energy from the sun. (From the Latin word *sol*, meaning "sun")

    EXAMPLE   Our *solar* heating system has helped to decrease our electricity bill.

8. ————————

9. **trellis** (trĕl'ĭs) *noun*   A framework of crossed strips of wood on which vines or climbing plants are trained to grow. (From the Latin word *trilix*, meaning "woven with three threads")

    EXAMPLE   Masses of pink roses covered the *trellis* on the side of the house.

9. ————————

10. **turret** (tûr'ĭt) *noun*   **a.** A small ornamental tower projecting from a building, usually at a corner.   **b.** A dome or tower, usually rotating, that contains the mounted guns of a tank, warship, or warplane. (From the Latin word *turris*, meaning "tower")

    EXAMPLE   We stood in the castle's *turret* and looked down at the drawbridge and moat.

10. ————————

Exercise 1 Writing Correct Words

On the answer line, write the word from the vocabulary list that fits each definition.

1. To uncover by digging; hollow out or remove

2. A round building or room

3. A person who works with stone or brick

4. An addition to a building; to join or attach

5. A framework for climbing plants

6. To construct in advance; make in sections that can be shipped and assembled

7. Relating to the sun; using energy from the sun

8. A building, often of great size or elegant appearance

9. A small tower on the roof of a building; a rotating dome that contains the mounted guns of a tank or warship

10. A dwelling place

1. _____excavate_____

2. _____rotunda_____

3. _____mason_____

4. _____annex_____

5. _____trellis_____

6. _____prefabricate_____

7. _____solar_____

8. _____edifice_____

9. _____turret_____

10. _____abode_____

Exercise 2 Using Words Correctly

Decide whether the italicized vocabulary word or related form has been used correctly in the sentence. On the answer line, write *Correct* for correct use and *Incorrect* for incorrect use.

1. Daily use of an *edifice* will keep your teeth healthy.

2. A greenhouse can use *solar* energy on bright winter days.

3. *Masons* must know the qualities of different types of stone used in construction.

4. Donna looked for an appropriate *trellis* to wear for the wedding.

5. If you do not like your *abode*, you can buy another at a hardware store.

6. A *rotunda* has four corners.

7. If a business wishes to expand, it may add an *annex* to its original store.

8. The company will send a *turret* repairperson to fix the washing machine.

9. Workers might have to *excavate* part of a lawn to build a fishpond.

10. Builders can put up a structure quickly with *prefabricated* parts.

1. _____Incorrect_____

2. _____Correct_____

3. _____Correct_____

4. _____Incorrect_____

5. _____Incorrect_____

6. _____Incorrect_____

7. _____Correct_____

8. _____Incorrect_____

9. _____Correct_____

10. _____Correct_____

Exercise 3   Choosing the Best Definition

For each italicized vocabulary word in the following sentences, write the letter of the best definition on the answer line.

1. When Diane could not find what she wanted in the main store, she walked over to the *annex.*
   a. addition   **b.** station   **c.** shed   **d.** basement

   1. _____a_____

2. It was easy to put together the doghouse once we had the *prefabricated* parts.
   a. separate   **c.** constructed in advance
   b. produced by machine   **d.** necessary

   2. _____c_____

3. The stairway to the *turret* was blocked during the renovation of the castle.
   a. prison   **b.** cellar   **c.** attic   **d.** tower

   3. _____d_____

4. Firefighters put out the blaze before it severely damaged the *edifice.*
   a. large building   **b.** thatched roof   **c.** window   **d.** addition

   4. _____a_____

5. Many buildings have large windows facing south to collect *solar* energy.
   a. atomic   **b.** from the sun   **c.** isolated   **d.** from the south

   5. _____b_____

6. Miners began to *excavate* the area, hoping to find valuable minerals.
   a. survey   **b.** dig out   **c.** claim   **d.** map out

   6. _____b_____

7. The dome of the *rotunda* provided a landmark for travelers several miles from the city.
   a. rotating building   **c.** arena
   b. state capitol   **d.** round building

   7. _____d_____

8. The Geralds sold their mansion and built a new *abode* by the sea.
   a. apartment   **b.** garage   **c.** home   **d.** castle

   8. _____c_____

9. The *mason* repaired the wall quickly and skillfully.
   a. stoneworker   **b.** bulldozer   **c.** painter   **d.** carpenter

   9. _____a_____

10. Covered with dried vines and a few brown leaves, the *trellis* looked dismal in the winter.
    a. porch   **b.** wooden frame   **c.** garden   **d.** view

   10. _____b_____

Exercise 4   Using Different Forms of Words

Decide which form of the vocabulary word in parentheses best completes the sentence. The form given may be correct. Write your answer on the answer line.

1. At the beach, the children built a __?__ of sand. *(rotunda)*

   1. _____rotunda_____

2. When the store next to them became vacant, the Corderos __?__ it. *(annex)*

   2. _____annexed_____

3. The __?__ of parts makes the assembly of a jungle gym quite simple. *(prefabricate)*

   3. _____prefabrication_____

4. The children recognized the castle and its many __?__ from the photograph. *(turret)*

   4. _____turrets_____

5. During the archaeological __?__, scientists uncovered a number of ancient relics. *(excavate)*

   5. _____excavation_____

6. Lila learned __?__ in order to join her father's company. *(mason)*

7. Carl settled himself at the gate and sketched the front of the __?__ . *(edifice)*

8. The city's __?__ of several suburbs created some problems at first. *(annex)*

9. Delia moaned that she would find her missing ring only by __?__ the entire field. *(excavate)*

10. The __?__ was not strong enough to support the heavy vine. *(trellis)*

6. _____masonry_____

7. _____edifice_____

8. _____annexation_____

9. _____excavating_____

10. _____trellis_____

Reading Comprehension

Each numbered sentence in the following passage contains an italicized vocabulary word or related form. After you read the passage, you will complete an exercise.

Casa Loma: A Canadian Castle

(1) Some houses, assembled from **prefabricated** sections, look ultramodern because of their sleek exteriors and lack of architectural detail. **(2)** Other **edifices,** inspired by designs of the past, are built purposely to appear old. **(3)** One such place, located in Toronto, Canada, is Casa Loma, a grand **abode** that resembles a castle of the Middle Ages.

(4) The **excavation** for this ninety-eight-room castle started in 1911, and the home was completed, at a cost of three million dollars, in 1914. Its owner, Sir Henry Pellatt, a financier and industrialist, had a life-long interest in medieval architecture. **(5)** Casa Loma reflects that interest with its numerous **turrets,** hidden passageways, and winding staircases.

Sir Henry spared no expense to create his architectural fantasy. **(6)** He hired special **masons** from Scotland to build the huge wall that surrounds the six-acre site. Other artisans worked for three years to carve the French paneling for the Oak

Room. Pellatt even imported glass, marble, and bronze from Europe and Asia for the interior of the castle.

Built to show Sir Henry's collection of massive furniture and art, the castle is dramatic and magnificent in every way. **(7)** The spacious **rotunda** is filled with large plants placed in front of arched Gothic windows. **(8)** With light streaming through the windows and stained-glass panels, the rotunda becomes a **solar** room where orchids thrive. The large library has a marble floor and shelves for a hundred thousand books. **(9)** An eight-hundred-foot underground tunnel connects the house with the stable **annex.** Even the horses lived luxuriously at Casa Loma, for Spanish tiled floors and mahogany-paneled walls decorate the stalls.

A view from either of the two stable towers reveals the handsome grounds. **(10)** Roses climbing on **trellises,** carefully clipped hedges, sculpted flower beds, and manicured lawns contribute to the atmosphere of medieval elegance.

Unfortunately, Sir Henry Pellatt lived in his castle for only ten years. In the early 1920s he found the cost of the castle's upkeep beyond even his ample means. The castle fell into disrepair until the Kiwanis Club purchased it in 1937. Since then, Casa Loma has been a Toronto landmark and an attraction for tourists.

Please turn to the next page.

Reading Comprehension Exercise

Each of the following statements corresponds to a numbered sentence in the passage. Each statement contains a blank and is followed by four answer choices. Decide which choice fits best in the blank. The word or phrase that you choose must express roughly the same meaning as the italicized word in the passage. Write the letter of your choice on the answer line.

1. Some modern houses are constructed from sections that are __?__ .
   a. fabric   c. recycled lumber
   b. produced in advance   d. unique

   1. ____b____

2. Many __?__ are based on past designs and are built to look old.
   a. large buildings   c. churches
   b. small structures   d. castles

   2. ____a____

3. Casa Loma is a __?__ that resembles a castle from the Middle Ages.
   a. dwelling   b. stable   c. monument   d. symbol

   3. ____a____

4. The __?__ for the castle began in 1911.
   a. framework   b. plans   c. digging   d. contracts

   4. ____c____

5. The castle has many hidden passageways and __?__ .
   a. cannons   b. towers   c. rotating windows   d. stairways

   5. ____b____

6. Scottish __?__ built a huge wall to surround the castle and its grounds.
   a. architects   c. researchers
   b. sculptors   d. stoneworkers

   6. ____d____

7. The spacious __?__ has Gothic windows and many plants.
   a. circular room   b. arch   c. garden   d. castle

   7. ____a____

8. The rotunda becomes a(n) __?__ room where orchids thrive.
   a. operating   b. spacious   c. sunny   d. successful

   8. ____c____

9. The stable __?__ is connected to the house by an underground passage.
   a. door   b. addition   c. yard   d. room

   9. ____b____

10. Sculpted flower beds and __?__ of climbing roses create an atmosphere of elegance.
    a. additions   c. clay pots
    b. creations   d. wooden frameworks

    10. ____d____

Writing Assignment

Your local newspaper is sponsoring a contest for essays about the most attractive or impressive example of architecture in your city. Winning entries will be published in the paper. For the contest you wish to nominate a skyscraper, the wing of a museum, a school, or a restored house. Write a description of your choice, and explain why it is attractive or impressive. Use at least five of the vocabulary words from this lesson in your contest entry and underline each word that you use.

Test: Lessons 7, 8, and 9

(pages 41–58)

Part A Choosing the Best Definition

On the answer line, write the letter of the best definition of the italicized word.

1. Marian made sure that no *combustible* substances were near the furnace.
   a. inflammable   **b.** ancient   **c.** poisonous   **d.** fireproof

   1. _____a_____

2. The ancient Greek gods were considered *omnipotent*.
   a. make-believe   **b.** clever   **c.** all-knowing   **d.** all-powerful

   2. _____d_____

3. Anne Frank wrote her diary while hiding in a secret *annex*.
   a. added building   **b.** storage area   **c.** passage   **d.** dungeon

   3. _____a_____

4. The human body uses vitamin K to help blood *coagulate*.
   a. use oxygen   **b.** clot   **c.** flow   **d.** appear red

   4. _____b_____

5. Although its form can be altered, physical matter is *indestructible*.
   a. poorly organized   **c.** not capable of being eliminated
   b. easily saved   **d.** the product of heat and light

   5. _____c_____

6. Talented *masons* completed the exterior of the cathedral.
   a. woodworkers   **c.** stone workers
   b. architects   **d.** mural painters

   6. _____c_____

7. Ancient mariners depended on *celestial* navigation to chart their courses.
   a. referring to instruments   **c.** common-sense
   b. related to the sky   **d.** symbolic

   7. _____b_____

8. The border guards removed the *blockade* and let us pass through.
   a. obstruction   **b.** traffic   **c.** old restriction   **d.** flag

   8. _____a_____

9. The Old Manse was the *abode* of Nathaniel Hawthorne.
   a. birthplace   **b.** publisher   **c.** home   **d.** garden

   9. _____c_____

10. Pumice is a *buoyant* type of rock produced by volcanic activity.
    a. delicate   **b.** superior   **c.** artificial   **d.** capable of floating

    10. _____d_____

11. Although he has turned ninety, Doctor Orwell is still *robust*.
    a. reliable   **b.** strong and healthy   **c.** dedicated   **d.** pleasant

    11. _____b_____

12. The Erechtheum is a magnificent *edifice* on the Acropolis.
    a. statue   **b.** playing field   **c.** large building   **d.** cavern

    12. _____c_____

13. The weightless environment of space is ideal for producing certain *alloys* that cannot be made on earth.
    a. combinations of metals   **c.** chemical solutions
    b. crystals   **d.** forms of life

    13. _____a_____

14. Okinawa is the home of karate, the most famous of all *martial* arts.
    a. military   **b.** oriental   **c.** punishing   **d.** peaceful

    14. _____a_____

15. It took many years to *excavate* the ruins of ancient Carthage.
    a. investigate   **b.** uncover   **c.** predict   **d.** conceal

    15. _____b_____

Test: Lessons 7, 8, and 9

Part B Choosing the Best Word

On the answer line, write the letter of the word that best completes the sentence.

16. The Spartans made a __?__ effort to protect their homeland.
    a. celestial   **b.** valiant   **c.** stable   **d.** buoyant   16. ____b____

17. When you __?__ sea water, you separate the water from the salt.
    a. excavate   **b.** prefabricate   **c.** saturate   **d.** distill   17. ____d____

18. The sun shining through the __?__ cast crisscrossed shadows.
    a. trellis   **b.** rotunda   **c.** turret   **d.** edifice   18. ____a____

19. Many temples in Egypt have __?__ the ravages of time.
    a. distilled   **b.** saturated   **c.** withstood   **d.** coagulated   19. ____c____

20. We watched the __?__ of the frog to learn about its digestive system.
    a. dissection   **b.** blockade   **c.** annex   **d.** rotunda   20. ____a____

21. Thomas Jefferson liked the round design of the Pantheon so well that he used the __?__ as the central feature of Monticello.
    a. abode   **b.** alloy   **c.** annex   **d.** rotunda   21. ____d____

22. The security of a nation depends on the __?__ of its leadership.
    a. alloy   **b.** stability   **c.** conflagration   **d.** abode   22. ____b____

23. Nero played his violin by firelight during the __?__ of Rome.
    a. stability   **b.** blockade   **c.** dissection   **d.** conflagration 23. ____d____

24. Randall Jarrell wrote a sad poem about a man who died in the __?__ of a World War II airplane.
    a. rotunda   **b.** blockade   **c.** turret   **d.** conflagration   24. ____c____

25. The way to stop the Greek hero Achilles was to hit the only __?__ spot on his body—his heel.
    a. celestial   **b.** omnipotent   **c.** vulnerable   **d.** indestructible 25. ____c____

26. The paramedic __?__ the bandages with antiseptic.
    a. saturated   **b.** prefabricated   **c.** coagulated   **d.** distilled 26. ____a____

27. The company __?__ tool sheds that you can easily assemble.
    a. excavates   **b.** prefabricates   **c.** withstands   **d.** distills 27. ____b____

28. An early civil rights leader, John Brown was a __?__ advocate of universal freedom.
    a. vulnerable   **b.** staunch   **c.** martial   **d.** coagulated   28. ____b____

29. The science of __?__ has improved greatly since satellites began taking pictures of our atmosphere.
    a. conflagration   **b.** stability   **c.** dissection   **d.** meteorology 29. ____d____

30. The photoelectric cells on some satellites are aimed toward the sun in order to convert __?__ energy into electrical energy.
    a. solar   **b.** omnipotent   **c.** distilled   **d.** indestructible   30. ____a____

HOUGHTON MIFFLIN VOCABULARY FOR ACHIEVEMENT, SECOND COURSE

Dictionary Skills

Biographical and Geographical Entries

Dictionaries do more than define words. Many also contain biographical entries about notable people and geographical entries about important places and geographical features. In some dictionaries the entries are contained in the body of the dictionary. In others they are grouped in special sections at the back. The entries are usually very short. The primary information that they contain is how the name is spelled, how it is divided into syllables, and how it is pronounced. They also give a few basic facts about each person or place. The following information is typical.

1. *Biographical entries give the years of a person's birth and death.* Suppose that you need to know when Grover Cleveland was born. The following entry tells you that he was born in 1837.

    Cleve•land (klēv′lənd), **(Stephen) Grover.** 1837–1908. 22nd & 24th U.S. President (1885–89, 1893–97).

2. *Biographical entries note the individual's historical importance.* Biographical entries briefly state the field or the accomplishment of a famous person. The entry above tells you that Grover Cleveland was President of the United States twice.

3. *Geographical entries give facts about political divisions.* The following entry lists three cities named Paris, with their locations and populations. Paris, Texas, for example, is located in northeast Texas and has a population of 25,498.

    Par•is (păr′ĭs). **1.** Cap. of France in the N central part on the Seine. Pop. 2,291,554. **2.** City of NW Tenn. WNW of Nashville. Pop. 10,728. **3.** City of NE Tex. NE of Dallas. Pop. 25,498. —**Pa•ri′sian** (pə-rē′zhən, -rĭzh′ən) *adj. & n.*

4. *Geographical entries give information about natural geographical features.* Entries on oceans and seas, important lakes and waterways, mountain ranges and peaks, and deserts are included in geographical listings. The entries give such facts as the lengths of rivers and the heights of mountain peaks.

Exercise   Using Biographical and Geographical Entries

Use the dictionary entries at the end of this exercise to answer each of the following questions.

1. What are the dates of Franklin Delano Roosevelt's birth and death?
   1882 and 1945

Please turn to the next page.

Biographical and Geographical Entries   **59**

2. Who was President of the United States longer, Franklin Delano Roosevelt or Theodore Roosevelt?

   Franklin Delano Roosevelt

3. What were Eleanor Roosevelt's achievements?

   American diplomat, author, and wife of President Franklin Delano Roosevelt

4. What else was Theodore Roosevelt besides President of the United States?

   A soldier and an author

5. What are the locations and populations of the two American cities named Miami?

   Miami, Florida, pop. 346,931; and Miami, Ohio, pop. 14,237

6. In which American state is the Great Miami River located, and how long is the river?

   Ohio; 160 miles long

7. Which of the following is *not* named Victoria: a waterfall, a river, a city, or a desert?

   A desert

8. In which country is Victoria Island located?

   Canada

9. In which country or countries is Lake Victoria located?

   Uganda, Kenya, and Tanzania

10. What is the Namib?

    A desert in Africa

Mi·am·i (mī-ăm′ē). **1.** *also* **Great Miami.** River, c. 160 mi (257 km), of W Ohio flowing c. 160 mi (257 km) into the Ohio R. **2.** City of SE Fla. on Biscayne Bay S of West Palm Beach. Pop. 346,931. **3.** City of extreme NW Ohio WSW of Joplin, Mo. Pop. 14,237.

Na·mib (nä′mĭb′). Desert of SW Africa extending c. 800 mi (1,290 km) along the coast of Namibia.

Roo·se·velt (rō′zə-vĕlt′, rōz′vĕlt′, rōō′zə-), **(Anna) Eleanor.** 1884–1962. Amer. diplomat, author, & wife of Franklin Delano Roosevelt.

Roosevelt, Franklin Delano ("FDR"). 1882–1945. 32nd U.S. President (1933–45).

Roosevelt, Theodore. 1858–1919. 26th U.S. President (1901–9; Nobel, 1906), soldier, & author.

Vic·to·ri·a (vĭk-tôr′ē-ə, -tōr′-). **1. Lake.** *also* **Victoria Ny·an·za** (nē-ăn′zə, nī-). Lake, c. 26,830 sq mi (69,490 sq km), of E central Africa in Uganda, Kenya, & Tanzania. **2.** River, c. 240 mi (386 km), of N Australia. **3.** Falls, c. 420 ft (128 m) high & 1.1 mi (1.7 km) wide, in the Zambesi R. on the Zambia-Zimbabwe border. **4.** Island of N.W.T., Canada, in the Arctic Ocean N of the mainland & S of Parry Channel. **5. Land.** Region of E Antarctica S of New Zealand, bordering the Ross Sea. **6.** Cap. of B.C., Canada, on SE Vancouver Is. & Juan de Fuca Strait. Pop. 62,551. **7.** Cap. of Hong Kong colony on the NW coast of Hong Kong Is. Pop. 1,026,870. **8.** Cap. of the Seychelles on the NE coast of Mahé Is. Pop. 15,559. **9.** City of SE Tex. SE of San Antonio. Pop. 50,695.

Maturity

Nearly all children have been asked, "What do you want to be when you grow up?" For most of these children, a response is simple to make. As they grow older, however, they learn that there are many options and possibilities available that they did not consider earlier. Life grows richer and much more complex as one matures, and the experience that leads to adulthood makes one more confident and also more competent to deal with these complexities. Maturity is the triumph of experience. In this lesson you will study words concerning the process of maturing.

WORD LIST
antiquated
centenarian
contemporary
fledgling
frail
gerontology
longevity
nascent
puerile
venerable

DEFINITIONS

After you have studied the definitions and example for each vocabulary word, write the word on the line to the right.

1. **antiquated** (ăn′tĭ-kwā′tĭd) *adjective* Old and no longer useful or suitable; outmoded.

   RELATED WORDS **antique** *noun;* **antique** *adjective*

   EXAMPLE At the car museum, Maureen and I learned about the *antiquated* practice of starting an automobile by hand-cranking it.

   1. _____

   USAGE NOTE *Antique* means "made in an earlier period." Unlike *antiquated, antique* suggests great value in age.

2. **centenarian** (sĕn′tə-nâr′ē-ən) *noun* One who lives one hundred or more years. (From the Latin word *centum,* meaning "hundred")

   RELATED WORDS **centenary** *noun;* **centenary** *adjective*

   EXAMPLE In our little town of Scarborough Falls, we are fortunate to have three *centenarians.*

   2. _____

   MEMORY CUE There are one hundred years in a *century.*

3. **contemporary** (kən-tĕm′pə-rĕr′ē) *adjective* **a.** Living or happening during the same period of time. **b.** Current; modern: *contemporary history.* *noun* Someone of the same age or living at the same time as another or others. (From the Latin *con-,* meaning "together," and *tempus,* meaning "time")

   RELATED WORD **contemporaneous** *adjective*

   EXAMPLE Michelangelo and Leonardo were *contemporary* artists.

   3. _____

   USAGE NOTE The adjective *contemporaneous* means the same as *contemporary* but applies most often to things.

4. **fledgling** (flĕj'lĭng) *noun* **a.** A young or inexperienced person. **b.** A young bird that has just grown feathers needed for flying. *adjective* Inexperienced.

EXAMPLE As a reporter Moses was only a *fledgling*, but he was given many different assignments.

4. _____
ETYMOLOGY NOTE *Fledgling* probably comes from the obsolete word *fledge*, meaning "feathered."

5. **frail** (frāl) *adjective* **a.** Flimsy; not strong or substantial; fragile. **b.** Physically weak. (From the Latin word *fragilis,* meaning "fragile")

RELATED WORD **frailty** *noun*

EXAMPLE The staircase was so *frail* that it was roped off.

5. _____

6. **gerontology** (jĕr'ən-tŏl'ə-jē) *noun* The scientific study of the process and effects of aging. (From the Greek words *gerōn,* meaning "old man," and *logos,* meaning "word")

RELATED WORDS **gerontological** *adjective;* **gerontologist** *noun*

EXAMPLE As the average life span increases, *gerontology* is becoming an increasingly important field of study.

6. _____

7. **longevity** (lŏn-jĕv'ĭ-tē) *noun* **a.** Length of life. **b.** Long duration, as in an occupation. (From the Latin words *longa,* meaning "long," and *aevitas,* meaning "age")

EXAMPLE *Longevity* is increasing because of better nutrition and medical treatment.

7. _____

8. **nascent** (nā'sənt) *adjective* Coming into existence; emerging. (From the Latin word *nasci,* meaning "to be born")

EXAMPLE The students' *nascent* interest in the stock market prompted the school library to buy books on investment planning.

8. _____

9. **puerile** (pyŏŏr'ĭl') *adjective* **a.** Childish; immature; silly. **b.** Belonging to childhood; youthful. (From the Latin word *puer,* meaning "boy")

RELATED WORD **puerility** *noun*

EXAMPLE When her brother was born, Sara exhibited *puerile* behavior for several weeks.

9. _____

10. **venerable** (vĕn'ər-ə-bəl) *adjective* Worthy of respect or reverence, particularly because of position or age.

RELATED WORDS **venerably** *adverb;* **venerate** *verb;* **veneration** *noun*

EXAMPLE Charles de Gaulle remained a *venerable* statesman in France even after his retirement from active political life.

10. _____
USAGE NOTE Don't confuse *venerable* with *vulnerable,* which means "capable of being wounded or hurt."

Exercise 1   Completing Definitions

On the answer line, write the word from the vocabulary list that best completes each definition.

1. Someone with little experience is a __?__ .
2. __?__ refers to the length of life.
3. Something that is current or modern is __?__ .
4. One who is worthy of respect because of age is __?__ .
5. Anything useless or outmoded is __?__ .
6. A person who is physically weak is __?__ .
7. A __?__ is a person who is at least one hundred years old.
8. Someone whose behavior is childish or silly can be said to be __?__ .
9. Something just emerging is __?__ .
10. __?__ refers to the scientific study of aging.

1. _____ fledgling
2. _____ Longevity
3. _____ contemporary
4. _____ venerable
5. _____ antiquated
6. _____ frail
7. _____ centenarian
8. _____ puerile
9. _____ nascent
10. _____ Gerontology

Exercise 2   Using Words Correctly

Each of the following questions contains an italicized vocabulary word. Decide the answer to the question, and write *Yes* or *No* on the answer line.

1. Is a *frail* person usually very strong?
2. Is a student likely to be a *contemporary* of another student in the same grade?
3. Is a withering flower *nascent?*
4. Is a *fledgling* old and wise?
5. Are practical jokes sometimes *puerile?*
6. Is an *antiquated* tool the most efficient one available?
7. Would people be likely to seek advice from a *venerable* leader?
8. Does a dog have greater *longevity* than a fly?
9. Would *gerontology* teach you about caring for a baby's skin?
10. Has a *centenarian* lived for a whole century?

1. _____ No
2. _____ Yes
3. _____ No
4. _____ No
5. _____ Yes
6. _____ No
7. _____ Yes
8. _____ Yes
9. _____ No
10. _____ Yes

Exercise 3   Choosing the Best Word

Decide which vocabulary word or related form best completes the sentence, and write the letter of your choice on the answer line.

1. Born in 1885, Prince Igor became a __?__ in 1985.
   a. puerility   **b.** fledgling   **c.** centenarian   **d.** frailty

2. Grandmother enjoys telling about the __?__ technology of her youth.
   a. frail   **b.** nascent   **c.** puerile   **d.** centenary

1. _____ c

2. _____ b

3. I enjoy ___?___ music more than traditional music.
   a. frail **b.** venerable **c.** antiquated **d.** contemporary

3. _____d_____

4. For decades we have respected the noble words of this ___?___ poet.
   a. nascent **b.** fledgling **c.** venerable **d.** puerile

4. _____c_____

5. ___?___ behavior, such as pushing and shoving, will not be tolerated on the field trip.
   a. Puerile **b.** Contemporary **c.** Frail **d.** Antiquated

5. _____a_____

6. Dr. Crane's talk on ___?___ included a discussion of the effects of aging on human bones.
   a. puerility **b.** fledglings **c.** veneration **d.** gerontology

6. _____d_____

7. Although she was an experienced swimmer, Anna was a ___?___ diver.
   a. centenary **b.** fledgling **c.** gerontological **d.** contemporary

7. _____b_____

8. Because the textile factory had only ___?___ machinery, it was less productive than its competitors.
   a. venerable **b.** contemporary **c.** antiquated **d.** nascent

8. _____c_____

9. Although Julio appeared ___?___, he was quite strong.
   a. antiquated **b.** venerable **c.** puerile **d.** frail

9. _____d_____

10. Human ___?___ varies from nation to nation and is generally greater in Europe than in Asia.
    a. longevity **b.** frailty **c.** puerility **d.** fledgling

10. _____a_____

Exercise 4 Using Different Forms of Words

Decide which form of the vocabulary word in parentheses best completes the sentence. The form given may be correct. Write your answer on the answer line.

1. A flash of the dragon's eyes warned Sir Geoffrey of the beast's ___?___ anger. *(nascent)*

1. _____nascent_____

2. The mother bird watched as her three ___?___ left the nest. *(fledgling)*

2. _____fledglings_____

3. The teen-agers continued to ___?___ their teacher years after they had graduated. *(venerable)*

3. _____venerate_____

4. The inventions of the phonograph and motion pictures were ___?___. *(contemporary)*

4. _____contemporaneous_____

5. Dr. Wong's specialty is ___?___. *(gerontology)*

5. _____gerontology_____

6. The ___?___ of redwood trees is amazing. *(longevity)*

6. _____longevity_____

7. Brooks and Felicia will celebrate August Partridge's ___?___ next month in Bedminster. *(centenarian)*

7. _____centenary_____

8. The ___?___ of the play offended the audience. *(puerile)*

8. _____puerility_____

9. My grandmother's house is full of fine ___?___ furniture that her grandparents brought from France. *(antiquated)*

9. _____antique_____

10. Mary's outward appearance of ___?___ was deceptive. *(frail)*

10. _____frailty_____

Reading Comprehension

Each numbered sentence in the following passage contains an italicized vocabulary word. After you read the passage, you will complete an exercise.

The Centenarians of the Caucasus Mountains

(1) Around the upper reaches of the Caspian Sea in the Caucasus Mountains live the Georgians, a people known for their *longevity*. (2) Many of these Soviet people are *centenarians* leading active lives. (3) There are, in fact, so many people who have lived to the age of one hundred or more that a sixty-year-old in Georgia might seem to be a mere *fledgling*.

What accounts for such long lives? (4) Research in *gerontology* has not been able to provide any definite answers. Nevertheless, the Georgians do have, and have historically had, a high level of physical activity. (5) Their society, while not *antiquated*, relies much less on labor-saving devices than many other societies do. (6) Even in *contemporary* Georgia, automobiles and tractors are less common than in western Europe. Every day presents many opportunities for vigorous exercise, and this fact may contribute to longevity. One must keep in mind, however, that other nations with high levels of physical activity do not necessarily have the same extreme longevity.

(7) One can build only a *frail* argument for the accuracy of the ages claimed by older Georgians, because the evidence is so limited. In the last century, Georgians were not issued birth certificates, and the baptismal certificates for most of them are no longer available. (8) It would be *puerile* to quibble over whether an elderly person is one hundred ten or one hundred twenty. Whatever the case, Georgians are exceptionally long-lived.

(9) A *nascent* interest in the process of aging has developed during the twentieth century into a large-scale scientific concern. The more we learn about how people age, the more likely we are to improve life expectancy among all people. (10) The *venerable* centenarians of Georgia may yet teach us much about long life.

Please turn to the next page.

Reading Comprehension Exercise

Each of the following statements corresponds to a numbered sentence in the passage. Each statement contains a blank and is followed by four answer choices. Decide which choice fits best in the blank. The word or phrase that you choose must express roughly the same meaning as the italicized word in the passage. Write the letter of your choice on the answer line.

1. The Georgians are renowned for their __?__ .
   a. wisdom   **b.** health   **c.** length of life   **d.** seclusion

1. _____c_____

2. Many of these Soviet people are __?__ .
   a. more than one hundred years old
   b. fun to be with
   c. healthy and happy
   d. living alone in the mountains

2. _____a_____

3. A sixty-year-old in Georgia might seem to be a __?__ .
   a. healthy person   **c.** fortunate person
   b. young person   **d.** retired person

3. _____b_____

4. Research in the __?__ has provided no firm answers.
   a. field of public health   **c.** study of aging
   b. study of nutrition   **d.** usefulness of exercise

4. _____c_____

5. Georgian society is not __?__ .
   a. valuable   **b.** civilized   **c.** out-of-date   **d.** quaint

5. _____c_____

6. In __?__ Georgia, automobiles are not common.
   a. unpolluted   **b.** urban   **c.** fashionable   **d.** modern

6. _____d_____

7. One can build only a __?__ case for the accuracy of the ages claimed by older Georgians.
   a. weak   **b.** serious   **c.** natural   **d.** reasonable

7. _____a_____

8. Quibbling over ages would be __?__ .
   a. wise   **b.** unscientific   **c.** difficult   **d.** silly

8. _____d_____

9. There is __?__ interest in the process of aging.
   a. medical   **b.** emerging   **c.** valuable   **d.** scholarly

9. _____b_____

10. The __?__ centenarians may yet teach us much.
    a. honorable   **b.** old   **c.** clever   **d.** wise

10. _____a_____

Practice with Analogies

DIRECTIONS On the answer line, write the vocabulary word that completes each analogy.

See page 119 for some strategies to use with analogies.

1. Weak is to strong as __?__ is to robust.

1. _____frail_____

2. Present is to past as modern is to __?__ .

2. _____antiquated_____

3. Eighty is to octogenarian as hundred is to __?__ .

3. _____centenarian_____

4. Cheerful is to cranky as mature is to __?__ .

4. _____fledgling_____

5. Short is to brevity as long is to __?__ .

5. _____longevity_____

6. Newborn is to neonatology as aged is to __?__ .

6. _____gerontology_____

Name _____ Date _____

Unscramble the letters of each italicized vocabulary word, and write the word on the answer line to the right.

1. The *utrdona* had a circular stained-glass window.

   1. _____ rotunda

2. A(n) *nxean* is located close to the original structure.

   2. _____ annex

3. Today we would consider it a(n) *uiaaettdqn* practice to churn butter by hand.

   3. _____ antiquated

4. A *eeaainnntcr* has lived one hundred years or longer.

   4. _____ centenarian

5. Although Maureen is just a *llgfdgnei* cook, she attempts some difficult recipes.

   5. _____ fledgling

6. George Washington and Thomas Jefferson were *pryrmncooeat* political leaders.

   6. _____ contemporary

7. The first step in building the house was the *oncvxtaaei* of the basement.

   7. _____ excavation

8. A *rosla* heating system depends upon the sun for energy.

   8. _____ solar

9. Climbing roses and clematis grew on the *slerilt* that bordered the garage.

   9. _____ trellis

10. The poet lived in a pleasant *oeadb* by the sea.

    10. _____ abode

11. In spite of his age, Geoffrey is often guilty of *lupeier* behavior.

    11. _____ puerile

12. The storm destroyed many *tcnaesn* spring flowers.

    12. _____ nascent

13. That railing is so *iarfl* that it may give way if you lean on it.

    13. _____ frail

14. Good nutrition and medical care increase your *ivylgntoe*.

    14. _____ longevity

15. Colorful banners flew above the *seuttrr* of the castle.

    15. _____ turrets

16. Buckingham Palace in England is an impressive *iieefcd* that attracts thousands of tourists every year.

    16. _____ edifice

17. Since people are living longer, doctors have become more interested in the field of *ytlroooengg*.

    17. _____ gerontology

18. The welcoming committee treated the *baveerenl* statesman with great respect.

    18. _____ venerable

19. The city planners hired a *oansm* to add a brick front to the courthouse.

    19. _____ mason

20. The *dcerapefiatrb* doghouse took only minutes to assemble.

    20. _____ prefabricated

HOUGHTON MIFFLIN VOCABULARY FOR ACHIEVEMENT, SECOND COURSE

Notes

The following lists of words are from the preceding two lessons. You may wish to use these lists to pinpoint words for ongoing review or for midterm or final exams.

Lesson 9

abode	prefabricate
annex	rotunda
edifice	solar
excavate	trellis
mason	turret

Lesson 10

antiquated	gerontology
centenarian	longevity
contemporary	nascent
fledgling	puerile
frail	venerable

Time and Sequence

How big a role does time play in your life?

To find out, read the following list of time-related statements, and ask yourself which ones apply to you.

I check a clock or wristwatch every fifteen minutes.
I frequently remind myself to stop wasting time.
I constantly ask others what time it is.
I often use expressions like "Procrastination is the thief of time" or "Time waits for no one."
I create elaborate time schedules and actually stick to them.

If three or more of the statements apply to you, then time plays an important part in your life. Whether time is important to you or not, the words in this lesson will give you new ways to express yourself on this subject.

> **WORD LIST**
> belated
> duration
> expire
> foregone
> incessant
> medieval
> premature
> respite
> simultaneous
> subsequent

DEFINITIONS

After you have studied the definitions and example for each vocabulary word, write the word on the line to the right.

1. **belated** (bĭ-lā′tĭd) *adjective*   Tardy; too late.

   RELATED WORD   **belatedly** *adverb*

   EXAMPLE   Lorraine sent a *belated* birthday card to a friend whose birthday had already passed.

   1. _____

2. **duration** (do͞o-rā′shən) *noun*   The period of time during which something exists or persists. (From the Latin word *durare,* meaning "to last")

   EXAMPLE   An average movie is about two hours in *duration*.

   2. _____

3. **expire** (ĭk-spīr′) *verb*   **a.** To come to an end; terminate; die. **b.** To exhale or breathe out. (From the Latin *ex-*, meaning "out," and *spirare,* meaning "to breathe")

   RELATED WORD   **expiration** *noun*

   EXAMPLE   Harold hurried to renew his magazine subscription before it *expired*.

   3. _____

   USAGE NOTE   One meaning of *inspire* is "to inhale"; in that sense it is an antonym of *expire*.

4. **foregone** (fôr′gôn′) *adjective*   Having gone before; past; previous.
   foregone conclusion   An end or result regarded as inevitable.

   RELATED WORD   **forego** *verb*

   EXAMPLE   The nomination of the popular politician was considered a *foregone* conclusion.

   4. _____

   USAGE NOTE   Don't confuse *forego* ("to precede in time or place") with *forgo* ("to abstain from; relinquish").

5. incessant (ĭn-sĕs′ənt) *adjective* Continuing without interruption; constant. (From the Latin *in-*, meaning "not," and *cessare*, meaning "to stop")

RELATED WORD **incessantly** *adverb*

EXAMPLE The *incessant* rain upset the picnickers.

5. _____

6. medieval (mē′dē-ē′vəl) *adjective* Characteristic of or referring to the Middle Ages, the period in European history from the fall of the western Roman Empire (about A.D. 476) to the rise of the Renaissance (about 1453). (From the Latin words *medius*, meaning "middle," and *aevum*, meaning "age")

EXAMPLE Numerous castles were built during the *medieval* period of history.

6. _____

7. premature (prē′mə-tyo͞or′) *adjective* Appearing or occurring before the usual time; unexpectedly early; happening too soon. (From the Latin *prae-*, meaning "before," and *maturus*, meaning "ripe")

RELATED WORDS **prematurely** *adverb;* **prematureness** *noun*

EXAMPLE Arthur's congratulations were *premature* because Lisa's birthday was still one week away.

7. _____

8. respite (rĕs′pĭt) *noun* A short time of rest or relief; a postponement or delay. (From the Latin word *respectus,* meaning "a refuge")

EXAMPLE A half-hour break provided a welcome *respite* from studying.

8. _____

9. simultaneous (sī′məl-tā′nē-əs) *adjective* Happening, existing, or done at the same time. (From the Latin word *simul*, meaning "at the same time")

RELATED WORD **simultaneously** *adverb*

EXAMPLE Because they were *simultaneous,* we could not attend both Judy's basketball game and Ben's play.

9. _____

10. subsequent (sŭb′sĭ-kwĕnt′) *adjective* Following in time or order; succeeding. (From the Latin word *subsequi*, meaning "to follow close after")

RELATED WORD **subsequently** *adverb*

EXAMPLE Heavy rains and *subsequent* floods caused a great deal of damage to the town.

10. _____

Exercise 1 Completing Definitions

On the answer line, write the word from the vocabulary list that best completes each definition.

1. Time __?__ at the end of an event.

2. We refer to events that took place in the Middle Ages as __?__ .

3. If an event happens before its expected or usual time, it is __?__ .

4. When an event is delayed or late, it is __?__ .

5. When events occur at the same time, they are __?__ .

6. An action that continues without interruption is __?__ .

7. The amount of time that an event lasts is its __?__ .

8. One event that follows another is __?__ to the first event.

9. A brief period of rest or relaxation is called a __?__ .

10. When a conclusion is inevitable or unavoidable, it is __?__ .

1. _____ expires
2. _____ medieval
3. _____ premature
4. _____ belated
5. _____ simultaneous
6. _____ incessant
7. _____ duration
8. _____ subsequent
9. _____ respite
10. _____ foregone

Exercise 2 Using Words Correctly

Decide whether the italicized vocabulary word has been used correctly in the sentence. On the answer line, write *Correct* for correct use and *Incorrect* for incorrect use.

1. The bus driver could not hear Peter's shouts because he was already too *foregone*.

2. The *premature* baby had to stay in the hospital for three extra weeks.

3. Ted silently forgave Marcella but still hoped for a *belated* apology.

4. *Subsequent* to its retirement, the horse won three more races.

5. A good exercise instructor is able to *expire* students to do more.

6. Vanessa plans to be an artist *respite* the fact that she knows very little about art.

7. The *medieval* castle was recently built.

8. Glen opened the *duration* of his briefcase and took out a writing pad.

9. Running neck and neck, two runners had *simultaneous* bursts of speed and tied for first place at the finish line.

10. The *incessant* noise from the party next door kept Penny awake.

1. _____ Incorrect
2. _____ Correct
3. _____ Correct
4. _____ Incorrect
5. _____ Incorrect
6. _____ Incorrect
7. _____ Incorrect
8. _____ Incorrect
9. _____ Correct
10. _____ Correct

Exercise 3 Choosing the Best Word

Decide which vocabulary word or related form best completes the sentence, and write the letter of your choice on the answer line.

1. __?__ to his fall from the tree, Tommy was afraid of heights.
   a. Respite **b.** Subsequent **c.** Belated **d.** Foregone

1. _____ b

2. Millie received a parking ticket when the time on the meter __?__ .
   a. was subsequent   c. expired
   b. was foregone   d. was premature

2. ____c____

3. Troy continued weeding the garden after a brief __?__ .
   a. respite   b. duration   c. expiration   d. subsequent

3. ____a____

4. To turn the machine on, you must push both buttons __?__ .
   a. incessantly   b. prematurely   c. belatedly   d. simultaneously

4. ____d____

5. Gretchen was fully recovered by the time she received Terry's __?__ get-well card.
   a. belated   b. premature   c. incessant   d. medieval

5. ____a____

6. The __?__ chatter of the small child annoyed the baby sitter.
   a. premature   b. subsequent   c. incessant   d. simultaneous

6. ____c____

7. Robert's football gear resembled a __?__ suit of armor.
   a. foregone   b. belated   c. medieval   d. premature

7. ____c____

8. When they began their study, the committee's __?__ conclusion was that the company should build a new main office.
   a. foregone   b. simultaneous   c. incessant   d. belated

8. ____a____

9. Mr. Lowell assigned seats for the __?__ of the semester.
   a. foregone   b. expiration   c. duration   d. respite

9. ____c____

10. Instead of making __?__ decisions, you should first weigh all the facts.
    a. medieval   b. belated   c. premature   d. simultaneous

10. ____c____

Exercise 4   Using Different Forms of Words

Decide which form of the vocabulary word in parentheses best completes the sentence. The form given may be correct. Write your answer on the answer line.

1. The Millers are angry at Rover because he barks __?__ . (incessant)

1. ____incessantly____

2. The stories of King Arthur and the Knights of the Round Table take place in a __?__ setting. (medieval)

2. ____medieval____

3. I spoke __?__ when I predicted that Carl would win the tennis match. (premature)

3. ____prematurely____

4. The orchestra will be leaving the city upon the __?__ of its contract. (expire)

4. ____expiration____

5. Alan and Trudy left the movie theater; __?__ they went to a restaurant. (subsequent)

5. ____subsequently____

6. Because of Celeste's __?__ opinion that the play was dull, she did not attend. (foregone)

6. ____foregone____

7. Walter __?__ warned Betty about the detour on Route 3. (belated)

7. ____belatedly____

8. Jimmy spent the __?__ of his vacation visiting new places. (duration)

8. ____duration____

9. The actors walked onstage __?__ . (simultaneous)

9. ____simultaneously____

10. Drinking a glass of water was a welcome __?__ for the speaker. (respite)

10. ____respite____

70   Time and Sequence

Reading Comprehension

Each numbered sentence in the following passage contains an italicized vocabulary word or related form. After you read the passage, you will complete an exercise.

Americans on the Moon

For centuries people wondered about the moon. Was its surface like the earth's? Could anyone actually live there? **(1)** Greek, Roman, and *medieval* authors wrote that walking on the moon was an impossible dream. On July 20, 1969, though, that dream became a reality for two American astronauts.

President John F. Kennedy did much to bring this reality about when he launched the Apollo program, the United States mission to the moon, in 1961. **(2)** For nine years, scientists worked *incessantly* on this project. **(3)** When they started, the possibility of a successful moon landing was by no means a *foregone* conclusion. Flights into space were considered very dangerous.

The most depressing setback in the Apollo program occurred in 1967. **(4)** Scientists hoped to put a spacecraft with three astronauts into orbit, but this attempt turned out to be tragically *premature.* During a practice takeoff, fire broke out inside the spacecraft, and three astronauts lost their lives. **(5)** Saddened by this disaster, Apollo scientists *belatedly* planned improvements in fire-prevention equipment.

Two years later, scientists launched another spacecraft, with astronauts Neil Armstrong, Edwin "Buzz" Aldrin, and Michael Collins aboard. The launch was successful.

Once their craft was in orbit around the moon, Collins remained in the command module. Meanwhile, Aldrin and Armstrong boarded the lunar module and descended to the moon's surface. **(6)** Via a worldwide television broadcast transmitted by satellite, millions of people watched *simultaneously* as Neil Armstrong took the first step onto the moon. Eighteen minutes later, Aldrin joined him. **(7)** This first moon landing was almost twenty-two hours in *duration.* **(8)** When the scheduled time for the excursion on the moon *expired,* Armstrong and Aldrin returned to the command module.

(9) Even after the astronauts had landed safely on Earth, there was no *respite* from duty. The men remained in isolation for almost three weeks before scientists were satisfied that the three men were free from contamination by harmful germs or chemicals.

(10) Since 1969 Americans have made *subsequent* moon landings, but the first voyage will always be remembered. As Armstrong said as he took his first step on the moon, "That's one small step for a man and one giant leap for mankind."

Please turn to the next page.

Reading Comprehension Exercise

Each of the following statements corresponds to a numbered sentence in the passage. Each statement contains a blank and is followed by four answer choices. Decide which choice fits best in the blank. The word or phrase that you choose must express roughly the same meaning as the italicized word in the passage. Write the letter of your choice on the answer line.

1. Authors in ancient times and in ___?___ considered reaching the moon to be an impossible dream.
   a. the Victorian era   **c.** prehistoric times
   b. modern days   **d.** the Middle Ages

   1. _____ d _____

2. Scientists worked ___?___ on the Apollo moon mission.
   a. without stopping   **c.** without knowledge
   b. without success   **d.** without leadership

   2. _____ a _____

3. The possibility of a successful moon landing was not a(n) ___?___ conclusion.
   a. inevitable   **b.** true   **c.** negative   **d.** worrisome

   3. _____ a _____

4. The 1967 attempt to put a manned spacecraft into orbit was ___?___ .
   a. successful   **c.** poorly executed
   b. unwise   **d.** too early

   4. _____ d _____

5. The planners of the Apollo program designed improvements ___?___ in fire-prevention equipment.
   a. too late   **b.** previously   **c.** efficiently   **d.** reluctantly

   5. _____ a _____

6. Television viewers ___?___ watched a broadcast of Armstrong's walk on the moon.
   a. breathlessly   **c.** at different times
   b. listlessly   **d.** at the same time

   6. _____ d _____

7. The first moon landing was almost twenty-two hours in ___?___ .
   a. length   **b.** space   **c.** danger   **d.** miles

   7. _____ a _____

8. When the astronauts' time on the moon ___?___ , they returned to the spacecraft.
   a. continued   **c.** was renewed
   b. ended   **d.** was determined

   8. _____ b _____

9. The astronauts landed safely on Earth, but there was no ___?___ from duty.
   a. satisfaction   **b.** reward   **c.** break   **d.** fun

   9. _____ c _____

10. Since 1969 the United States has made ___?___ landings on the moon.
    a. additional   **c.** energetic
    b. more spectacular   **d.** unsuccessful

    10. _____ a _____

Writing Assignment

People sometimes have trouble budgeting their time well in order to meet deadlines. In a paragraph or two of advice to younger students, tell about a situation in which you had trouble managing your time. Explain how you resolved this problem. Include five words from the lesson and underline them.

The Root *-duce-*

All of the words in this lesson are formed from the Latin root *-duce-*. This root comes from the Latin word *ducere*, meaning "to lead," and also takes the form *-duc-*, *-duct-*, *-duit-*, or *-due-*. More than fifty English words are derived from this useful root. You may already be familiar with some of them, such as *introduction*, *producer*, and *product*. Studying the vocabulary words in this lesson will increase your understanding of other words derived from *-duce-* and their related forms.

WORD LIST

aqueduct
conduct
conduit
deduce
induce
induction
productivity
reduction
subdue
viaduct

DEFINITIONS

After you have studied the definitions and example for each vocabulary word, write the word on the line to the right.

1. **aqueduct** (ăk′wĭ-dŭkt′) *noun* **a.** A large pipe or channel made to carry water from a distant source. **b.** A bridgelike structure designed to carry such a pipe or channel across low ground or a river. (From the Latin words *aqua*, meaning "water," and *ducere*, meaning "to lead")

   EXAMPLE   The ancient Romans built *aqueducts* to transport water into Rome.

1. _____
SEE *conduit.*

2. **conduct** (kən-dŭkt′) *verb* **a.** To lead or guide. **b.** To direct the course of something such as an experiment. **c.** To lead or direct musicians or a musical work. **d.** To act as a medium through which a form of energy such as electricity can travel.   *noun* (kŏn′dŭkt) The way a person acts or behaves. (From the Latin *com-*, meaning "together," and *ducere*)

   RELATED WORDS   **conducive** *adjective;* **conductor** *noun*

   EXAMPLE   The guide *conducted* a tour of the museum.

2. _____

3. **conduit** (kŏn′dōō-ĭt) *noun* **a.** A channel or pipe for carrying water or other fluids. **b.** A tube or pipe through which electrical wires or cables pass. (From the Medieval Latin word *conductus*, meaning "transportation")

   EXAMPLE   The plumber installed *conduits* in the new house.

3. _____
USAGE NOTE A *conduit* is a channel for fluids such as water. An *aqueduct* also carries water but is much larger.

4. **deduce** (dĭ-dōōs′) *verb* To reach a conclusion by logical reasoning. (From the Latin *de-*, meaning "away," and *ducere*)

   RELATED WORDS **deduction** *noun;* **deductive** *adjective*

   EXAMPLE When Susan saw that the picnic table was filled with food, she *deduced* that the campers were nearby.

4. _____

5. **induce** (ĭn-dōōs′) *verb* **a.** To persuade or influence. **b.** To cause or bring about the occurrence of. **c.** In reasoning, to reach a general principle from particular facts or instances. (From the Latin *in-*, meaning "in," and *ducere*)

   RELATED WORDS **inducement** *noun;* **inductive** *adjective*

   EXAMPLE The promise of better working conditions *induced* Charles to change jobs.

5. _____

6. **induction** (ĭn-dŭk′shən) *noun* The act of being formally admitted to the armed forces or placed in office. (From the Latin *in-*, meaning "in," and *ductus*, meaning "the act of drawing or pulling")

   RELATED WORDS **induct** *verb;* **inductee** *noun*

   EXAMPLE A large crowd attended the *induction* of the newly elected public officials.

6. _____

7. **productivity** (prō′dŭk-tĭv′ĭ-tē) *noun* **a.** The ability to produce or manufacture food or goods. **b.** Abundance of output; output. (From the Latin *pro-*, meaning "forth," and *ducere*)

   RELATED WORDS **product** *noun;* **productive** *adjective*

   EXAMPLE Farmers increase their *productivity* by using new tractors.

7. _____

8. **reduction** (rĭ-dŭk′shən) *noun* The act or process of making something smaller. (From the Latin *re-*, meaning "back," and *ducere*)

   RELATED WORD **reduce** *verb*

   EXAMPLE Price *reductions* on all merchandise attracted many people to the sale.

8. _____

9. **subdue** (səb-dōō′) *verb* **a.** To conquer, quiet, or bring under control. **b.** To make less intense; tone down. (From the Latin *sub-*, meaning "away," and *ducere*)

   EXAMPLE With soothing words the speaker *subdued* the noisy audience.

9. _____

10. **viaduct** (vī′ə-dŭkt′) *noun* A series of spans or arches used to carry a road or railroad over a wide valley or over other roads. (A blend of the Latin word *via*, meaning "road," and the English word *aqueduct*)

    EXAMPLE The *viaduct* enabled trains to cross the river.

10. _____

Exercise 1   Writing Correct Words

On the answer line, write the word from the vocabulary list that fits each definition.

1. The ability to manufacture or produce goods
2. To conquer or to quiet
3. A bridge with arches that supports a road or a railroad
4. To guide or direct
5. The process of decreasing in size or amount
6. To come to a logical conclusion
7. A means of transporting water over long distances
8. To persuade; bring about or cause something to happen
9. A formal installation in office or admittance to the armed forces
10. A channel for transporting liquid or carrying electrical cables

1. _____productivity_____
2. _____subdue_____
3. _____viaduct_____
4. _____conduct_____
5. _____reduction_____
6. _____deduce_____
7. _____aqueduct_____
8. _____induce_____
9. _____induction_____
10. _____conduit_____

Exercise 2   Using Words Correctly

Each of the following statements contains an italicized vocabulary word. Decide whether the sentence is true or false, and write *True* or *False* on the answer line.

1. The type of furniture in a farmhouse affects the farm's *productivity*.
2. To *conduct* people through the zoo, you should walk away from them.
3. Plumbers and electricians work with *conduits*.
4. People often ride underwater in a *viaduct*.
5. You could reasonably *deduce* that a person walking with the aid of a guide dog is blind.
6. *Induction* occurs when a person resigns from a public office.
7. A mother might *subdue* her son if he fell asleep at a play.
8. An *aqueduct* could make farming possible in a dry region.
9. A *reduction* in food intake helps people to lose weight.
10. Trainers *induce* seals to perform tricks by offering them fish.

1. _____False_____
2. _____False_____
3. _____True_____
4. _____False_____
5. _____True_____
6. _____False_____
7. _____False_____
8. _____True_____
9. _____True_____
10. _____True_____

Exercise 3   Choosing the Best Word

Decide which vocabulary word or related form best expresses the meaning of the italicized word or phrase in the sentence. On the answer line, write the letter of the correct choice.

1. The workers needed two weeks to repair the sagging *bridge*.
   a. reduction   **b.** viaduct   **c.** deduction   **d.** induction

1. _____b_____

2. The children could not *persuade* their busy father to drive them to the beach.
   a. subdue   **b.** conduct   **c.** deduce   **d.** induce

   2. _____d_____

3. The company's *making of goods* slowed down after many employees became ill with the flu.
   a. productivity   **b.** conduit   **c.** reduction   **d.** induction

   3. _____a_____

4. Was John able to *conclude by reasoning* that school closed early because of the snow?
   a. conduit   **b.** subdue   **c.** deduce   **d.** conduct

   4. _____c_____

5. The *channel for transporting water* in the area had sprung a leak.
   a. reduction   **b.** induction   **c.** aqueduct   **d.** viaduct

   5. _____c_____

6. The *formal installation* of the president took place yesterday.
   a. conduit   **b.** induction   **c.** reduction   **d.** productivity

   6. _____b_____

7. The politician *directed* the discussion in a loud manner.
   a. conducted   **b.** subdued   **c.** induced   **d.** deduced

   7. _____a_____

8. Janet was delighted about the *decrease* in homework.
   a. viaduct   **b.** reduction   **c.** productivity   **d.** conduit

   8. _____b_____

9. The baby sitter was unable to *quiet* the noisy five-year-old.
   a. induct   **b.** conduct   **c.** deduce   **d.** subdue

   9. _____d_____

10. The *pipe for transporting water* through the park is very convenient for campers.
    a. induction   **b.** viaduct   **c.** conduit   **d.** reduction

    10. _____c_____

Exercise 4   Using Different Forms of Words

Decide which form of the vocabulary word in parentheses best completes the sentence. The form given may be correct. Write your answer on the answer line.

1. Viewing a frightening movie is not __?__ to getting a good night's sleep. *(conduct)*

   1. _____conducive_____

2. During the ceremony, the club will __?__ five new members. *(induction)*

   2. _____induct_____

3. The frantic robbery victim was not easily __?__ . *(subdue)*

   3. _____subdued_____

4. To meet deadlines, newspaper reporters must be __?__ . *(productivity)*

   4. _____productive_____

5. Susan built a miniature __?__ for her school project. *(viaduct)*

   5. _____viaduct_____

6. The detective made a __?__ concerning the crime. *(deduce)*

   6. _____deduction_____

7. The builder ordered a new supply of __?__ . *(conduit)*

   7. _____conduits_____

8. The Winslows hoped to __?__ the amount of clutter in their cellar. *(reduction)*

   8. _____reduce_____

9. The promise of a picnic was an effective __?__ . *(induce)*

   9. _____inducement_____

10. The ancient __?__ were of great interest to the tourists. *(aqueduct)*

    10. _____aqueducts_____

Reading Comprehension

Each numbered sentence in the following passage contains an italicized vocabulary word. After you read the passage, you will complete an exercise.

The Baby Sitter

My friends tried to caution me about baby-sitting for nine-year-old Elizabeth Meyers. **(1)** "No matter how much money Mrs. Meyers offers to pay, don't let her *induce* you to watch Elizabeth!" they warned.

I didn't tell them that Mrs. Meyers had already offered me double my usual rate, which I had gratefully accepted. After all, how noisy and out-of-control could one nine-year-old be? **(2)** Plenty of times in the past, I had *subdued* several screaming children and still gotten my homework done.

I was ready for anything when I arrived. **(3)** Elizabeth opened the door and *conducted* me into the living room. She looked like a pleasant, well-behaved little girl until her critical eyes studied me from head to toe.

"Well, Amanda," she said, wearing a look of superiority, "it's pretty obvious why you took this job. **(4)** I can *deduce* from your appearance that you need the money for new clothes."

I was speechless as Mrs. Meyers appeared, dressed to go out. "I'm off to the library," Elizabeth's mother explained. **(5)** "I'm working on my master's degree, and I'm eager to increase my *productivity.* It's sometimes difficult to concentrate at home." Her eyes wandered to Elizabeth.

"Just call me if you get stuck, Mom," Elizabeth advised.

"Elizabeth is quite advanced for her age," Mrs. Meyers whispered to me before making a hasty exit.

After Mrs. Meyers closed the door behind her, Elizabeth smiled slyly. "I've had many baby sitters," she said.

"Oh, really?"

"Mm-hm. **(6)** But in my opinion, most of them had experienced a severe *reduction* in intelligence somewhere along the line. I hope you're not like that."

I felt the need to defend myself. "I'm smart. I get good grades."

"If you say so." Elizabeth smiled her infuriating smile. "Well, what plans do you have to entertain me?"

"I could read you a story, but I guess you don't read children's books. How about a game?"

"Yes, let's play something on my computer. **(7)** As far as I'm concerned, the computer is the best *conduit* to all kinds of interesting information. Fascinating Facts is my favorite game." Elizabeth led me to the den and turned on the computer. "Pick a field that you know something about."

"History," I said, with some degree of confidence.

(8) "What year was Vice President Daniel D. Tompkins *inducted* into office?" Elizabeth asked.

"Uh, who was President that year?"

Elizabeth shook her head. "We'd better go down to the beginner's level. How did Roman engineers transport water to Rome?"

I was silent.

Elizabeth couldn't believe my ignorance. **(9)** "The Romans transported water through a system of *aqueducts.* **(10)** These structures are similar to *viaducts,* except that viaducts support roads and train tracks, not channels of water." Elizabeth sighed. "I knew this would be hopeless. What grade did you say you were in?" Elizabeth switched off her computer. "Never mind." Having totally humiliated me, she was unexpectedly sympathetic. "I'll help you with your homework until Mom comes home."

Please turn to the next page.

Reading Comprehension Exercise

Each of the following statements corresponds to a numbered sentence in the passage. Each statement contains a blank and is followed by four answer choices. Decide which choice fits best in the blank. The word or phrase that you choose must express roughly the same meaning as the italicized word in the passage. Write the letter of your choice on the answer line.

1. Amanda's friends warned her not to be __?__ to baby-sit Elizabeth.
   a. offended   **b.** limited   **c.** persuaded   **d.** expected

1. _____ c

2. However, Amanda felt that she could __?__ noisy children.
   a. control   **b.** entertain   **c.** ignore   **d.** separate

2. _____ a

3. Elizabeth __?__ the baby sitter into the living room.
   a. followed   **b.** led   **c.** helped   **d.** pushed

3. _____ b

4. Elizabeth __?__ that Amanda needed money for new clothes.
   a. disagreed   **b.** hoped   **c.** reasoned   **d.** argued

4. _____ c

5. Mrs. Meyers went to the library to increase her work __?__ .
   a. knowledge   **b.** reading   **c.** interest   **d.** output

5. _____ d

6. Elizabeth believed that most baby sitters had suffered a __?__ in intelligence.
   a. decrease   **b.** increase   **c.** change   **d.** advancement

6. _____ a

7. She felt that the computer was a(n) __?__ for interesting information.
   a. example   **b.** channel   **c.** helper   **d.** storehouse

7. _____ b

8. Elizabeth asked Amanda in what year Daniel Tompkins was __?__ as Vice President.
   a. impeached   **b.** elected   **c.** installed   **d.** overruled

8. _____ c

9. Amanda didn't know that the Romans transported water through __?__ .
   a. tunnels   **b.** large channels   **c.** sprinklers   **d.** dams

9. _____ b

10. Elizabeth pointed out that __?__ are similar to aqueducts in design.
    a. governments   **c.** stone sculptures
    b. irrigation systems   **d.** bridges with arches

10. _____ d

Practice with Analogies

DIRECTIONS   On the answer line, write the vocabulary word that completes each analogy.

See page 119 for some strategies to use with analogies.

1. Fight is to struggle as conquer is to __?__ .

1. _____ subdue

2. Caution is to encourage as dissuade is to __?__ .

2. _____ induce

3. Think is to cogitate as conclude is to __?__ .

3. _____ deduce

4. Film is to direct as music is to __?__ .

4. _____ conduct

5. Add is to enlargement as subtract is to __?__ .

5. _____ reduction

6. Presidency is to inauguration as army is to __?__ .

6. _____ induction

Bonus: Lessons 11 and 12

(pages 67–78)

Use the following clues to identify the words, and write the words on the lines to the right. Then circle each word in the word-search box below. The words may overlap and may read in any direction.

1. An AQUEDUCT carries ___?___ from a distant source. (5 letters)

2. Sherlock Holmes could ___?___ the solution to crimes. (6 letters)

3. The Latin root *-duce-* means "to ___?___." (4 letters)

4. Synonym for INCESSANT (8 letters)

5. A SUBSEQUENT action ___?___ a former one. (7 letters)

6. A(n) ___?___ conclusion is accepted ahead of time. (8 letters)

7. REDUCTION involves making something ___?___. (7 letters)

8. Synonym for BELATED (5 letters)

9. A(n) ___?___ baby is born earlier than expected. (9 letters)

10. A VIADUCT carries a(n) ___?___ over a wide valley. (4 letters)

11. Synonym for INDUCE (8 letters)

12. A CONDUIT is a(n) ___?___ that transports fluids. (4 letters)

13. The vacation provided a welcome ___?___ from their jobs. (7 letters)

14. SIMULTANEOUS events occur at the ___?___ time. (4 letters)

15. The art museum has guides who ___?___ visitor tours. (7 letters)

1. _____ water
2. _____ deduce
3. _____ lead
4. _____ constant
5. _____ follows
6. _____ foregone
7. _____ smaller
8. _____ tardy
9. _____ premature
10. _____ road
11. _____ persuade
12. _____ pipe
13. _____ respite
14. _____ same
15. _____ conduct

BONUS

Lessons 11 and 12

```
P R O D U C T I V I T Y D U C T L R U
C I N D U C T I O N E C U D E D E D E
M R P D C A T I O N M E D I S L U B R
A E E D A U S R E P S T A L N T S U
T M E A D U R A T I O N L A W L E R T
M I T D A D L E T A G S M B E A L A M
T E I D E N L N S U B S S E O U T E M
N T P T L L A V E I D E M N M E C E E
S E S Q U T E N C E M D U O F O U R R
G O E N S C O N C A T E M G P O D R P
R E R N S P I T S U B D U E C O N D U
I T O I D U C E A Q U Y D R A T O E V
I C A C C I C S H E R L R O A D C R E
M A T C O N C S W O L L O F S U B D L
```

CHALLENGE

Locate and circle the five additional vocabulary words in the word-search box.

duration
induction
medieval
productivity
subdue

Notes

The following lists of words are from the preceding two lessons. You may wish to use these lists to pinpoint words for ongoing review or for mid-term or final exams.

Lesson 11

belated	medieval
duration	premature
expire	respite
foregone	simultaneous
incessant	subsequent

Lesson 12

aqueduct	induction
conduct	productivity
conduit	reduction
deduce	subdue
induce	viaduct

Test: Lessons 10, 11, and 12

(pages 61–78)

Part A Completing the Definition

On the answer line, write the letter of the word or phrase that correctly completes each sentence.

1. *Reduction* is a process of ___?___ .
   a. removing irritants　　　c. twisting things
   b. making something smaller　　d. multiplication

2. The study of ___?___ is called *gerontology.*
   a. castles　b. classical music　c. aging　d. ancient ruins

3. A *premature* celebration is one that occurs ___?___ .
   a. too soon　b. periodically　c. abruptly　d. conveniently

4. The act of ___?___ is called *induction.*
   a. conducting business　　c. formally placing someone in office
   b. surrendering　　　　　d. leading others

5. An object's *longevity* is its ___?___ .
   a. depth　b. price　c. composition　d. length of life

6. Things that are ___?___ are said to be *medieval.*
   a. forbidden　　　　　　　c. old before their time
   b. characteristic of the Middle Ages　　d. made of cast iron

7. When you *subdue* something, you ___?___ it.
   a. ignore　b. control　c. sell　d. visit

8. Something that is *nascent* is ___?___ .
   a. emerging　　　　c. breathing
   b. already accomplished　　d. destroyed

9. A *respite* is a(n) ___?___ .
   a. authority　b. resolution　c. rest period　d. difficult task

10. *Productivity* is an abundance of ___?___ .
    a. ideas　b. output　c. resources　d. concentration

11. Something that is ___?___ is *puerile.*
    a. childish　b. delicate　c. very easy　d. innovative

12. *Simultaneous* events ___?___ .
    a. happened long ago　c. occur at different times
    b. have importance　　d. occur at the same time

13. A *viaduct* is a series of ___?___ .
    a. vaccinations　c. arches carrying a road
    b. copper pipes　d. competitive games

14. Something is *venerable* if it is ___?___ .
    a. valuable　　c. borrowed
    b. easily broken　d. worthy of respect

15. ___?___ events are said to be *subsequent.*
    a. Frustrating　b. Succeeding　c. Exciting　d. Uncertain

1. _____b_____
2. _____c_____
3. _____a_____
4. _____c_____
5. _____d_____
6. _____b_____
7. _____b_____
8. _____a_____
9. _____c_____
10. _____b_____
11. _____a_____
12. _____d_____
13. _____c_____
14. _____d_____
15. _____b_____

TEST Lessons 10, 11, and 12

HOUGHTON MIFFLIN VOCABULARY FOR ACHIEVEMENT, SECOND COURSE

Test: Lessons 10, 11, and 12

Part B   Choosing the Best Word

On the answer line, write the letter of the word that best expresses the meaning of the italicized word or phrase.

16. A well-preserved *channel that carries water from a distant source* runs through Segovia.
   a. aqueduct   **b.** centenarian   **c.** fledgling   **d.** viaduct

16. _____ a

17. Mrs. Gutierrez is one of several *persons who live 100 years or more* in our town.
   a. durations   **b.** fledglings   **c.** conduits   **d.** centenarians

17. _____ d

18. The *constant* howl of the puppy unnerved Jared.
   a. puerile   **b.** incessant   **c.** belated   **d.** nascent

18. _____ b

19. Gold is an excellent metal for *acting as a medium through which travels* electricity.
   a. deducing   **b.** conducting   **c.** subduing   **d.** inducing

19. _____ b

20. Though she was new at her job, Candy didn't like being called a *young and inexperienced person.*
   a. contemporary   **b.** centenarian   **c.** fledgling   **d.** conduit

20. _____ c

21. The possibility of failure in this endeavor was a *previously accepted* conclusion.
   a. incessant   **b.** contemporary   **c.** foregone   **d.** belated

21. _____ c

22. The Toltecs built *channels for carrying water* between their buildings.
   a. conduits   **b.** viaducts   **c.** centenarians   **d.** contemporaries

22. _____ a

23. Richard moved into a house with an *outmoded* heating system.
   a. contemporary   **b.** foregone   **c.** belated   **d.** antiquated

23. _____ d

24. This offer will *come to an end* in thirty days.
   a. conduct   **b.** expire   **c.** deduce   **d.** subdue

24. _____ b

25. One can *conclude by logical reasoning* that Gerald is upset.
   a. conduct   **b.** induce   **c.** expire   **d.** deduce

25. _____ d

26. Egg shells are very *flimsy.*
   a. frail   **b.** antiquated   **c.** puerile   **d.** nascent

26. _____ a

27. Salina used Max's car for the *existing period of time* of his visit.
   a. duration   **b.** respite   **c.** induction   **d.** longevity

27. _____ a

28. Paul thought of a way to *influence* his brothers to sing at the party.
   a. deduce   **b.** expire   **c.** induce   **d.** subdue

28. _____ c

29. Aleta particularly enjoys *modern* American literature.
   a. premature   **b.** contemporary   **c.** foregone   **d.** subsequent

29. _____ b

30. "Please accept my *tardy* apology," said Ben.
   a. belated   **b.** contemporary   **c.** foregone   **d.** frail

30. _____ a

Test-Taking Skills

Sentence-Completion Tests

Standardized tests often contain sentence-completion items. These items require you to choose a word or phrase. Use the following strategies to answer sentence-completion test items.

STRATEGIES

1. *Read the directions carefully.* You can lose credit for answers if you fail to follow the directions for answering sentence-completion items.

2. *Read the entire sentence and analyze its structure and probable meaning.* The sentence you are asked to complete may contain clues to the correct answer.

   The flame of the candle ___?___ in the faint breeze.
   a. went out   **b.** blazed   **c.** smoked   **d.** flickered

   In this test item, the words *faint breeze* are a clue. You can ask yourself what effect a light breeze has on a candle flame.

3. *Read all of the answer choices and eliminate as many wrong answers as you can.* In the test item above, you can use the sentence clue to eliminate *went out*. Since a candle usually smokes when it goes out, you can also eliminate choice *c*. The second choice, *blazed*, does not make sense. Notice that all answer choices are verbs; any other part of speech would be incorrect. A correct answer must sound right in the sentence.

4. *Insert your choice in the blank and read the sentence to make sure your answer makes sense.* The last choice in the test item, *flickered*, means "gave off light that burned unsteadily." If you insert the word in the blank, the sentence does make sense.

5. *Be alert for words that look or sound much like the right answer.* An answer choice like *snickered* or *bickered*, which readers could confuse with *flickered*, is sometimes put in to make the test more challenging.

Exercise   Answering Sentence-Completion Test Items

Choose the word that best completes each of the following sentences. Write the letter of your choice on the answer line. Use your dictionary as needed.

1. John walks to school every day, ___?___ of the weather.
   a. despite   **b.** regardless   **c.** anxious   **d.** inattentive

   1. ____b____

Please turn to the next page.

2. The simple furniture contrasted with the complex design of the __?__ floor.
   a. parquet   **b.** durable   **c.** cement   **d.** croquet

2. _____a_____

3. Alice's __?__ performance on stage had me believing she really was the Queen of England.
   a. poor   **b.** credible   **c.** incredulous   **d.** inept

3. _____b_____

4. To deposit a check in the bank, you must __?__ it by writing your name on the back.
   a. endorse   **b.** spend   **c.** guarantee   **d.** cash

4. _____a_____

5. Brookville has a(n) __?__ against parking on the streets.
   a. ordinal   **b.** municipal   **c.** ordinance   **d.** ordnance

5. _____c_____

6. My only __?__ about your suggestion is the large amount of money it will require.
   a. worrisome   **b.** preservation   **c.** reservation   **d.** drawback

6. _____c_____

7. __?__ in poetry, Melanie mostly read novels and short stories.
   a. Enthusiastic   **b.** Disinterested   **c.** Indifferent   **d.** Uninterested

7. _____d_____

8. Dr. Helena Ward is a specialist in __?__ , the scientific study of the heart.
   a. neurology   **b.** geriatrics   **c.** cardiology   **d.** pediatrics

8. _____c_____

9. Daniel works as a steamfitter, but painting is his __?__ .
   a. work   **b.** avocation   **c.** occupation   **d.** labor

9. _____b_____

10. Not wishing to ask directions, the tourist __?__ down the street.
    a. bantered   **b.** daunted   **c.** cantered   **d.** sauntered

10. _____d_____

11. According to __?__ Queen Nefertiti was the most beautiful woman in ancient Egypt.
    a. tradition   **b.** intuition   **c.** fiction   **d.** traction

11. _____a_____

12. The museum will be __?__ with proceeds from its traveling exhibition.
    a. nominated   **b.** renovated   **c.** inaugurated   **d.** fated

12. _____b_____

13. In this resort city, tourists seem to be __?__ .
    a. unconscious   **b.** perilous   **c.** ubiquitous   **d.** miraculous

13. _____c_____

14. Both scientist and artist, Leonardo da Vinci was one of the most __?__ artists of all time.
    a. versatile   **b.** vertical   **c.** veteran   **d.** vehicular

14. _____a_____

15. A __?__ helped the two opposing groups to reach a settlement.
    a. medicine   **b.** median   **c.** medium   **d.** mediator

15. _____d_____

Help and Improvement

People are constantly trying to improve their lives and abilities. Even as adults, many people learn to speak a new language, to cook, or to play a sport. Improvement is a lifelong process.

When people give help, they try to improve something. For example, one might help a friend with mathematics, and then that friend might get an improved score on the next math test.

The words in this lesson are about improving and helping. These words will increase your ability to communicate about ways of making things better.

WORD LIST
abet
deliverance
ennoble
expedite
intercede
offset
pacify
refurbish
reinforce
sanctuary

DEFINITIONS

After you have studied the definitions and example for each vocabulary word, write the word on the line to the right.

1. **abet** (ə-bĕt′) *verb*   To encourage or assist, particularly in doing something wrong.

   RELATED WORD   **abettor, abetter** *noun*

   EXAMPLE   One who *abets* the criminal actions of another may also be found guilty of a crime.

   1. _____

2. **deliverance** (dĭ-lĭv′ər-əns) *noun*   **a.** Rescue from danger. **b.** Liberation. (From the Latin word *liber,* meaning "free")

   RELATED WORD   **deliver** *verb*

   EXAMPLE   Farmers hoped for rain to bring them *deliverance* from the dry weather.

   2. _____

3. **ennoble** (ĕn-nō′bəl) *verb*   To add to the honor of; make finer or more noble in nature. (From the Latin word *nobilis,* meaning "noble")

   EXAMPLE   Good deeds *ennoble* those who perform them.

   3. _____

4. **expedite** (ĕk′spĭ-dīt′) *verb*   **a.** To speed or ease the progress of; assist. **b.** To perform quickly and efficiently. (From the Latin word *expedire,* meaning "to set free")

   RELATED WORDS   **expeditious** *adjective;* **expeditiously** *adverb*

   EXAMPLE   We shall *expedite* the delivery of the package by sending it through a special mail service.

   4. _____

5. **intercede** (ĭn′tər-sēd′) *verb* To ask for help for or plead for another person. (From the Latin *inter-*, meaning "between," and *cedere*, meaning "to go")

RELATED WORD   **intercession** *noun*

EXAMPLE   Dominic *interceded* with his parents on behalf of his younger brother, who wanted to go to the carnival with him.

6. **offset** (ôf′sĕt′) *verb* To make up for; compensate for; counteract.   *noun* (ôf′sĕt′) Something that balances, compensates, or counteracts.

EXAMPLE   The runner *offset* her slow time on the first lap by speeding up the pace on the second lap.

7. **pacify** (păs′ə-fī′) *verb*   **a.** To ease the anger or agitation of; calm. **b.** To establish peace in; end fighting or violence in. (From the Latin words *pax*, meaning "peace," and *facere*, meaning "to make")

RELATED WORDS   **pacification** *noun;* **pacifier** *noun*

EXAMPLE   When the singer failed to perform at the concert, the management issued refunds to *pacify* the crowd.

8. **refurbish** (rē-fûr′bĭsh) *verb* To clean, renew, repair, or refresh.

EXAMPLE   We wanted to *refurbish* the apartment before we moved in, so we hired someone to paint it.

9. **reinforce** (rē′ĭn-fôrs′) *verb* To strengthen; give more effectiveness to; support.

RELATED WORD   **reinforcement** *noun*

EXAMPLE   The citizens' requests for a new hospital were *reinforced* by the mayor's speech.

10. **sanctuary** (săngk′chōō-ĕr′ē) *noun*   **a.** Any place of safety or protection. **b.** A holy place; a house of worship. (From the Latin word *sanctus*, meaning "sacred")

EXAMPLE   Many different kinds of animals roam freely in the wildlife *sanctuary*.

5. _____

6. _____

7. _____

8. _____

9. _____

10. _____

Exercise 1 Matching Words and Definitions

Match the definition in Column B with the word in Column A. Write the letter of the correct definition on the answer line.

Column A	Column B
1. deliverance	a. To ask for help for another person
2. refurbish	b. To encourage in doing wrong
3. expedite	c. Rescue from danger
4. sanctuary	d. To calm; establish peace in
5. ennoble	e. To clean, renew, or refresh
6. reinforce	f. To make up for; counteract
7. pacify	g. To add to the honor of
8. intercede	h. To speed the progress of; perform efficiently
9. abet	i. To strengthen; support
10. offset	j. A place of safety or protection

1. _____c_____
2. _____e_____
3. _____h_____
4. _____j_____
5. _____g_____
6. _____i_____
7. _____d_____
8. _____a_____
9. _____b_____
10. _____f_____

Exercise 2 Using Words Correctly

Each of the following statements contains an italicized vocabulary word. Decide whether the sentence is true or false, and write *True* or *False* on the answer line.

1. Sometimes only food will *pacify* a crying baby.

1. _____True_____

2. When someone *abets* a prank, that person helps another to commit it.

2. _____True_____

3. People often send important mail by special *deliverance*.

3. _____False_____

4. An employer can always *expedite* work by sending the workers on vacation.

4. _____False_____

5. In construction, steel is often used to *reinforce* concrete blocks.

5. _____True_____

6. A *sanctuary* is usually a safe place to hide.

6. _____True_____

7. Weather, time, and neglect will gradually *refurbish* the exterior of a house.

7. _____False_____

8. If you *intercede* your flower bed, you will have flowers in bloom all summer long.

8. _____False_____

9. Spending money will help *offset* one's debts.

9. _____False_____

10. Helping others can *ennoble* a person's life.

10. _____True_____

Exercise 3 Choosing the Best Definition

For each italicized vocabulary word in the following sentences, write the letter of the best definition on the answer line.

1. Those who *abet* criminals are liable to be prosecuted.
   a. please   **b.** assist   **c.** defend   **d.** trick

1. _____b_____

2. All the students were asking for *deliverance* from the final examination.
   a. surrender   **b.** transfer   **c.** rescue   **d.** security

2. _____c_____

3. After his defeat by English forces at Culloden Moor in 1746, Bonnie Prince Charlie found *sanctuary* in Scotland.
   a. direction   **c.** peace
   b. a place of safety   **d.** a new place to live

3. _____b_____

4. Genevieve will *refurbish* her old coat by cleaning and shortening it and adding new buttons.
   a. renew   **b.** retain   **c.** resell   **d.** trade

4. _____a_____

5. Treating his tenant farmers badly did not *ennoble* the squire.
   a. enliven   **c.** harm the reputation of
   b. enrich   **d.** add to the honor of

5. _____d_____

6. The tide turned against Napoleon at the Battle of Waterloo when the Prussians arrived to *reinforce* the British troops under Wellington.
   a. rout   **b.** strengthen   **c.** restrict   **d.** lead

6. _____b_____

7. Groups often try to *expedite* the passage of bills by lobbying members of Congress.
   a. slow   **b.** speed   **c.** influence   **d.** block

7. _____b_____

8. To *pacify* her mother, Simone promised to write twice a week while traveling.
   a. rouse   **b.** help   **c.** calm   **d.** please

8. _____c_____

9. The team's early losses were *offset* by wins later in the season.
   a. counteracted   **b.** overcome   **c.** excused   **d.** worsened

9. _____a_____

10. The princess *interceded* with her father to free the prisoner.
    a. argued   **b.** conspired   **c.** agreed   **d.** pleaded

10. _____d_____

Exercise 4   Using Different Forms of Words

Decide which form of the vocabulary word in parentheses best completes the sentence. The form given may be correct. Write your answer on the answer line.

1. The most __?__ sea route between the Atlantic and the Pacific is the Panama Canal. *(expedite)*

1. _____expeditious_____

2. In ancient times Moses __?__ his people out of bondage in Egypt. *(deliverance)*

2. _____delivered_____

3. Archie was charged as an __?__ of the criminal. *(abet)*

3. _____abettor_____

4. Dogs can be trained through __?__ of good behavior. *(reinforce)*

4. _____reinforcement_____

5. __?__ the library was a challenging task. *(refurbish)*

5. _____Refurbishing_____

6. Some people feel that great art __?__ human character. *(ennoble)*

6. _____ennobles_____

7. Not even the __?__ of the President could save the bill from defeat. *(intercede)*

7. _____intercession_____

8. The diplomats brought about the __?__ of the two nations involved in a dispute. *(pacify)*

8. _____pacification_____

9. The __?__ was a quiet refuge from the noise and bustle of the city. *(sanctuary)*

9. _____sanctuary_____

10. The small company had to raise prices as a means of __?__ its losses. *(offset)*

10. _____offsetting_____

Reading Comprehension

Each numbered sentence in the following passage contains an italicized vocabulary word. After you read the passage, you will complete an exercise.

Victory at Marathon

The victory of the small Greek democracy of Athens over the mighty Persian empire in 490 B.C. is one of the most famous events in history. **(1)** Darius, king of the Persian empire, was furious because Athens had **interceded** for the other Greek city-states in revolt against Persian domination. In anger the king sent an enormous army to defeat Athens. **(2)** He thought it would take drastic steps to **pacify** the rebellious part of the empire.

Persia was ruled by one man. In Athens, however, all citizens helped to rule. **(3)** **Ennobled** by this participation, Athenians were prepared to die for their city-state. Perhaps this was the secret of the remarkable victory at Marathon, which freed them from Persian rule.

On their way to Marathon, the Persians tried to fool some Greek city-states by claiming to have come in peace. The frightened citizens of Delos refused to believe this. **(4)** Not wanting to **abet** the conquest of Greece, they fled from their city and did not return until the Persians had left. They were wise, for the Persians next conquered the city of Etria and captured its people.

Tiny Athens stood alone against Persia. **(5)** The Athenian people went to their **sanctuaries.** **(6)** There they prayed for **deliverance.** **(7)** They asked their gods to **expedite** their victory.

(8) The Athenians **refurbished** their weapons and moved to the plain of Marathon, where their little band would meet the Persians. **(9)** At the last moment, soldiers from Plataea **reinforced** the Athenian troops.

The Athenian army attacked, and Greek citizens fought bravely. **(10)** The power of the mighty Persians was **offset** by the love that the Athenians had for their city. Athenians defeated the Persians in archery and hand combat. Greek soldiers seized Persian ships and burned them, and the Persians fled in terror. Herodotus, a famous historian, reports that 6400 Persians died, compared with only 192 Athenians.

Reading Comprehension Exercise

Each of the following statements corresponds to a numbered sentence in the passage. Each statement contains a blank and is followed by four answer choices. Decide which choice fits best in the blank. The word or phrase that you choose must express roughly the same meaning as the italicized word in the passage. Write the letter of your choice on the answer line.

1. Athens had __?__ the other Greek city-states against the Persians.
   a. wanted to fight   **c.** provided reasons for
   b. intervened on behalf of   **d.** refused help to

   1. ___b___

2. Darius took drastic steps to __?__ the rebellious Athenians.
   a. weaken   **b.** destroy   **c.** calm   **d.** raise

   2. ___c___

3. Their participation __?__ to the Athenians.
   a. gave comfort   **c.** gave strength
   b. gave honor   **d.** gave safety

   3. ___b___

4. The people of Delos did not want to __?__ the conquest of Greece.
   a. end **b.** encourage **c.** allow **d.** think about

4. _____b_____

5. The Athenian people went to their __?__ and prayed.
   a. homes **b.** priests **c.** gatherings **d.** holy places

5. _____d_____

6. They prayed for __?__ .
   a. rain **b.** rescue **c.** defeat **d.** riches

6. _____b_____

7. The Athenians asked their gods to __?__ their victory.
   a. join **b.** encourage **c.** speed **d.** watch

7. _____c_____

8. The Athenians __?__ their weapons and moved to the plain of Marathon.
   a. repaired **b.** threw out **c.** replaced **d.** grabbed

8. _____a_____

9. The Athenians were __?__ by some soldiers who arrived from Plataea.
   a. welcomed **b.** strengthened **c.** held **d.** awaited

9. _____b_____

10. The power of the Persians was __?__ by the love that the Athenians had for Athens.
    a. made stronger **b.** increased **c.** required **d.** counteracted

10. _____d_____

Writing Assignment

Government and businesses have often tried to improve the quality of people's lives. Choose one example of a government agency or a business renovating a historic building, protecting parkland, helping the disabled, or making any similar improvement. Write a paragraph explaining the program. Use at least five words from this lesson in your paragraph and underline them.

Vocabulary Enrichment

The term *marathon,* widely used to describe any difficult task or contest requiring great effort and endurance, is derived from the plain of Marathon, where the Athenians defeated the Persians. After the battle of Marathon, an Athenian soldier ran from Marathon to Athens, a distance of approximately twenty-six miles, to announce to the citizens of Athens the victory over the Persians. Today races of this length are run in many cities throughout the world and are known as *marathons.*

ACTIVITY *Marathon* is one of many words in English derived from the names of places. Using a dictionary that includes etymologies, identify the origin of the following words, write a definition for each word, and use each word in a sentence.

1. cashmere 2. dollar 3. meander 4. tuxedo 5. wiener

Lesson 14

Disagreement

Mark Twain, in his novel *Pudd'nhead Wilson,* comments, "It were not best that we should all think alike; it is difference of opinion that makes horse races." Twain seems to indicate that differences of opinion keep life interesting.

Sometimes disagreement may lead to a better understanding or a changed attitude. At other times, disagreement may result in hurt feelings or a stubborn refusal to listen to another's point of view. The words in this lesson describe different aspects and different outcomes of disputes.

DEFINITIONS

After you have studied the definitions and example for each vocabulary word, write the word on the line to the right.

1. **adversary** (ăd′vər-sĕr′ē) *noun*   An opponent; enemy. (From the Latin word *adversus,* meaning "against")

   EXAMPLE   The *adversaries* had a spirited debate on television.

   1. _____

2. **aggression** (ə-grĕsh′ən) *noun*   **a.** The act of beginning an invasion; a bold, unprovoked attack.   **b.** Hostile action or behavior. (From the Latin *ad-,* meaning "toward," and *gradi,* meaning "to advance")

   RELATED WORDS   **aggressive** *adjective;* **aggressively** *adverb*

   EXAMPLE   The defenseless country was not prepared for the *aggression* of its warlike neighbor.

   2. _____

3. **contradict** (kŏn′trə-dĭkt′) *verb*   **a.** To express the opposite of.   **b.** To deny the statement of.   **c.** To be inconsistent with; be contrary to. (From the Latin *contra-,* meaning "against," and *dicere,* meaning "to say")

   RELATED WORDS   **contradiction** *noun;* **contradictory** *adjective*

   EXAMPLE   On the radio show, the caller *contradicted* several of the guest's ideas.

   3. _____
   SEE *controversy.*

4. controversy (kŏn'trə-vûr'sē) *noun*   **a.** A public dispute between sides holding opposing views.   **b.** Argument or debate. (From the Latin *contra-*, meaning "against," and *vertere*, meaning "to turn")

RELATED WORD   **controversial** *adjective*

EXAMPLE   The *controversy* between the communities was featured on the front page of the newspaper.

4. _____
MEMORY CUE In a *controversy*, people *contradict* one another.

5. discord (dĭs'kôrd') *noun*   **a.** A lack of agreement among persons or groups.   **b.** A combination of harsh or unpleasant sounds or musical tones; dissonance. (From the Latin *dis-*, meaning "apart," and *cor*, meaning "heart")

RELATED WORD   **discordant** *adjective*

EXAMPLE   The *discord* among the committee members was noticeable as soon as the meeting began.

5. _____
SEE *skirmish*.

6. embroil (ĕm-broil') *verb*   **a.** To involve in an argument or conflict.   **b.** To throw into confusion or disorder; entangle. (From the French word *embrouiller*, meaning "to tangle")

RELATED WORD   **embroilment** *noun*

EXAMPLE   The traffic accident *embroiled* the drivers of the two cars in an argument.

6. _____

7. haggle (hăg'əl) *verb*   **a.** To bargain, as over the price of something.   **b.** To argue in an attempt to come to terms.

RELATED WORD   **haggler** *noun*

EXAMPLE   Many people enjoy shopping at flea markets because they can *haggle* over prices.

7. _____

8. skirmish (skûr'mĭsh) *noun*   **a.** A minor battle between small groups of troops, often as part of a larger battle.   **b.** A minor or preliminary conflict or disagreement.   *verb*   To engage in a skirmish. (From the Old French word *eskermir*, meaning "to fight with a sword")

EXAMPLE   The first battle at Bull Run was a *skirmish* between Union and Confederate troops.

8. _____
USAGE NOTE A *skirmish* is a fight, whereas *discord* is lack of agreement.

9. stalemate (stāl'māt') *noun*   **a.** A situation in which action or progress has come to a halt; a deadlock.   **b.** A situation in chess in which neither player can win.

EXAMPLE   Union and management reached a *stalemate* in their negotiations.

9. _____

10. strife (strīf) *noun*   **a.** Bitter conflict; heated and often violent disagreement.   **b.** A struggle between rivals.

EXAMPLE   The *strife* between the two countries has continued for many years.

10. _____

Name _____ Date _____

Exercise 1   Completing Definitions

On the answer line, write the word from the vocabulary list that best completes each definition.

1. A dispute between sides holding opposing views is called a(n) __?__ .

2. People who like to bargain over the price of something like to __?__ .

3. A bold, unprovoked attack is an act of __?__ .

4. When progress in a situation has stopped, there is a(n) __?__ .

5. An opponent or enemy is a(n) __?__ .

6. Bitter conflict or violent disagreement is __?__ .

7. A minor battle or a preliminary conflict is a(n) __?__ .

8. To involve someone in an argument is to __?__ that person.

9. If you deny or oppose an idea, you __?__ it.

10. A lack of agreement between people is called __?__ .

1. _____ controversy _____

2. _____ haggle _____

3. _____ aggression _____

4. _____ stalemate _____

5. _____ adversary _____

6. _____ strife _____

7. _____ skirmish _____

8. _____ embroil _____

9. _____ contradict _____

10. _____ discord _____

Exercise 2   Using Words Correctly

Decide whether the italicized vocabulary word has been used correctly in the sentence. On the answer line, write *Correct* for correct use and *Incorrect* for incorrect use.

1. Before the football season starts, the coach divides our team for practice *skirmishes*.

2. Loretta enjoys the *strife* of sleep after a hard day's work.

3. The town is *embroiled* in a disagreement about cable television.

4. Proud Dancer is the *stalemate* of the famous thoroughbred Citation.

5. Judge Smith is an *adversary* of injustice.

6. The witness *contradicted* his earlier testimony.

7. The *controversy* over who could run faster ended when Leah beat Ray.

8. "If you want to open those curtains, Jessica, pull the *discord* on the left," said Grandmother.

9. Because of his *aggressive* behavior, Marty had to sit in the penalty box during the hockey game.

10. Terry had to *haggle* behind the other hikers because of a sprained ankle.

1. _____ Incorrect _____

2. _____ Incorrect _____

3. _____ Correct _____

4. _____ Incorrect _____

5. _____ Correct _____

6. _____ Correct _____

7. _____ Correct _____

8. _____ Incorrect _____

9. _____ Correct _____

10. _____ Incorrect _____

Exercise 3   Choosing the Best Word

Decide which vocabulary word or related form best completes the sentence, and write the letter of your choice on the answer line.

1. Emma and Josie become __?__ on the tennis court.
   a. stalemates   **b.** hagglers   **c.** adversaries   **d.** contradictions

1. _____ c _____

2. My dad __?__ with the dealer until he gets a good price on a car.
   a. haggles   **b.** contradicts   **c.** embroils   **d.** discords

2. _____a_____

3. The governor expected that no one on his staff would __?__ him.
   a. haggle   **b.** contradict   **c.** discord   **d.** embroil

3. _____b_____

4. Garth's resignation ended the __?__ with his boss.
   a. strife   **b.** aggression   **c.** adversary   **d.** contradiction

4. _____a_____

5. The principal refused to state her opinion on the __?__ concerning the school dance.
   a. aggression   **b.** adversary   **c.** haggle   **d.** controversy

5. _____d_____

6. The crowd just wants to __?__ you in a dispute.
   a. haggle   **b.** embroil   **c.** contradict   **d.** discord

6. _____b_____

7. The __?__ between the fans of the two teams reached a peak at last night's game.
   a. contradiction   **b.** adversary   **c.** discord   **d.** stalemate

7. _____c_____

8. The referee warned Cindy that she would be penalized if she could not control her __?__ .
   a. skirmish   **b.** adversary   **c.** discord   **d.** aggression

8. _____d_____

9. The newspaper misrepresented the __?__ by calling it a battle.
   a. skirmish   **b.** adversary   **c.** contradiction   **d.** stalemate

9. _____a_____

10. Contract negotiations between management and players reached a __?__ .
    a. contradiction   **b.** skirmish   **c.** stalemate   **d.** strife

10. _____c_____

Exercise 4   Using Different Forms of Words

Decide which form of the vocabulary word in parentheses best completes the sentence. The form given may be correct. Write your answer on the answer line.

1. Senator Matthews tried to ease the __?__ caused by his statements. *(embroil)*

1. _____embroilment_____

2. The teacher was concerned about the child's __?__ behavior on the playground. *(aggression)*

2. _____aggressive_____

3. The __?__ between his two children caused Mr. Hooper much sorrow. *(strife)*

3. _____strife_____

4. Professor Bevilaqua and Professor Strate have __?__ political views. *(discord)*

4. _____discordant_____

5. Jon learned to be a successful __?__ by watching his boss. *(haggle)*

5. _____haggler_____

6. The outcome of the final __?__ will determine which team wins Capture-the-Flag. *(skirmish)*

6. _____skirmish_____

7. The Senate reached a __?__ on the new tax bill. *(stalemate)*

7. _____stalemate_____

8. The Bulldogs won on a __?__ call by the umpire. *(controversy)*

8. _____controversial_____

9. Although the two attorneys were __?__ , they managed to work out a solution. *(adversary)*

9. _____adversaries_____

10. Celina's __?__ statements about where she had been aroused our suspicion. *(contradict)*

10. _____contradictory_____

Reading Comprehension

Each numbered sentence in the following passage contains an italicized vocabulary word or related form. After you read the passage, you will complete an exercise.

The Apple of Discord

The Trojan War is one of the most famous wars in history. It is well known for its ten-year duration, for the heroism of a number of legendary characters, and for the Trojan horse. What may not be familiar, however, is the story of how the war began.

(1) According to Greek myth, the **strife** between the Trojans and the Greeks started at the wedding of Peleus, King of Thessaly, and Thetis, a sea nymph. (2) All of the gods and goddesses had been invited to the wedding celebration in Troy except Eris, goddess of **discord.** (3) She had been omitted from the guest list because her presence always **embroiled** mortals and immortals alike in conflict. (4) To take revenge on those who had slighted her,

Eris decided to cause a **skirmish.** Into the middle of the banquet hall, she threw a golden apple marked "for the most beautiful." (5) All of the goddesses began to **haggle** over who should possess it. (6) The gods and goddesses reached a **stalemate** when the choice was narrowed to Hera, Athena, and Aphrodite. (7) Someone was needed to settle the **controversy** by picking a winner. The job eventually fell to Paris, son of King Priam of Troy, who was said to be a good judge of beauty.

Paris did not have an easy job. (8) Each goddess, eager to win the golden apple, tried **aggressively** to bribe him.

"I'll grant you vast kingdoms to rule," promised Hera.

(9) "Vast kingdoms are

nothing in comparison with my gift," **contradicted** Athena. "Choose me and I'll see that you win victory and fame in war."

(10) Aphrodite outdid her **adversaries,** however. She won the golden apple by offering Helen, Zeus' daughter and the most beautiful mortal, to Paris.

Paris, anxious to claim Helen, set off for Sparta in Greece. Although Paris learned that Helen was married, he accepted the hospitality of her husband, King Menelaus of Sparta, anyway. Therefore, Menelaus was outraged for a number of reasons when Paris departed, taking Helen and much of the king's wealth back to Troy. Menelaus collected his loyal forces and set sail for Troy to begin the war to reclaim Helen.

Reading Comprehension Exercise

Each of the following statements corresponds to a numbered sentence in the passage. Each statement contains a blank and is followed by four answer choices. Decide which choice fits best in the blank. The word or phrase that you choose must express roughly the same meaning as the italicized word in the passage. Write the letter of your choice on the answer line.

1. The __?__ between the Greeks and the Trojans began at a wedding.
   a. game   **b.** conflict   **c.** history   **d.** debate
   1. ___b___

2. Eris, the goddess of __?__ , was not invited to the wedding.
   a. love   **b.** war   **c.** music   **d.** disagreement
   2. ___d___

3. Eris was known for __?__ both mortals and immortals.
   a. scheming against   **c.** keeping aloof from
   b. involving in conflict   **d.** feeling hostile toward
   3. ___b___

Disagreement   **91**

4. To get revenge, Eris caused a __?__ .
   a. minor battle   **b.** hurricane   **c.** problem   **d.** major mistake

   4. _____ a _____

5. The goddesses __?__ who should win the apple.
   a. argued about   **b.** decided on   **c.** voted for   **d.** ignored

   5. _____ a _____

6. They reached a __?__ when the choice was narrowed to three of the goddesses.
   a. decision   **b.** majority   **c.** deadlock   **d.** conclusion

   6. _____ c _____

7. Someone was needed to settle the __?__ .
   a. debt   **b.** group   **c.** dispute   **d.** problem

   7. _____ c _____

8. Each goddess tried __?__ to bribe Paris.
   a. boldly   **b.** quietly   **c.** secretly   **d.** effectively

   8. _____ a _____

9. Athena __?__ Hera, promising Paris victory and fame in war.
   a. denied the statement of   **c.** agreed with
   b. defeated   **d.** laughed at

   9. _____ a _____

10. Aphrodite outdid her __?__ .
    a. friends   **b.** sisters   **c.** students   **d.** opponents

   10. _____ d _____

Writing Assignment

Imagine that your class is working on a debate unit. In preparation for your debate, your teacher has asked you to write a practice dialogue between two student debaters. Choose a topic that is appropriate for a debate, such as the pros and cons of a law requiring drivers and passengers to wear seat belts. Show how each student would present his or her side of the issue. In your dialogue use at least four vocabulary words from this lesson and underline them.

Vocabulary Enrichment

Discord, as you have already learned, comes from the Latin *dis-*, meaning "apart," and *cor*, meaning "heart." The word *discord* has an interesting connection with the heart. People once associated the heart with certain characteristics and capabilities, such as memory, bravery, and friendliness. We have preserved this association in modern expressions such as *to learn by heart, to have heart*, and *kindhearted*.

In *discord* the prefix *dis-* gives the major clue to the meaning of the word. If you are "apart" from the heart, you are "apart from friendliness," or ready for an argument. Consequently, for us *discord* has taken on its current meaning — "disagreement."

ACTIVITY   In a high school or college dictionary, look up the following words, all of which are derived from the root *-cor-*. Write the meaning and Latin etymology of each word. Then write an explanation of the connection between the etymology and the definition.

1. concord   2. cordial   3. discourage   4. encourage   5. record

Name ______________________________ Date ______________

Bonus: Lessons 13 and 14

(pages 81–92)

Use the clues to complete the crossword puzzle.

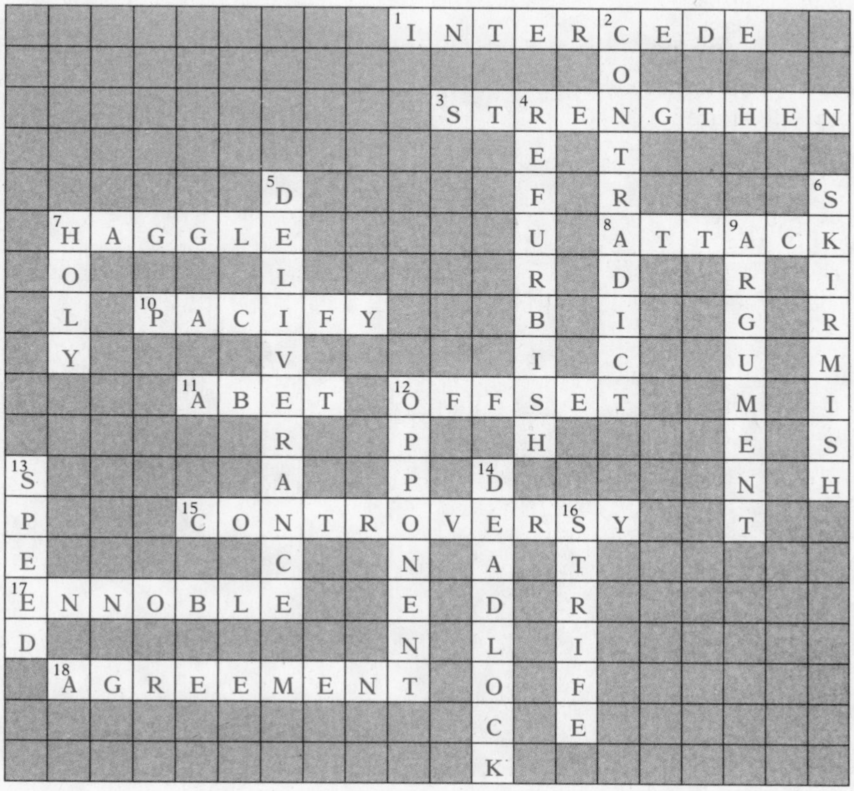

1 INTERCEDE
3 STRENGTHEN
7 HAGGLE
8 ATTACK
10 PACIFY
11 ABET
12 OFFSET
15 CONTROVERSY
17 ENNOBLE
18 AGREEMENT
2 CONTRADICT
4 REFURBISH
5 DELIVERANCE
6 SKIRMISH
7 HOLY
9 ARGUMENT
12 OPPONENT
13 SPEED
14 DEADLOCK
16 STRIFE

Across

1. To plead for another person
3. Synonym for REINFORCE
7. To argue in an attempt to come to terms
8. AGGRESSION is a bold, unprovoked __?__.
10. Derived from the Latin word meaning "peace"
11. To encourage or assist in doing something wrong
12. To compensate for or counteract
15. A dispute between opposing sides
17. To add to the honor of
18. DISCORD is a lack of __?__.

Down

2. To express the opposite of
4. Renew or repair
5. When people are in danger, they hope for __?__.
6. A minor battle
7. A SANCTUARY is a(n) __?__ place.
9. To EMBROIL is to involve in a(n) __?__.
12. Synonym for ADVERSARY
13. To EXPEDITE a matter is to __?__ its progress.
14. Synonym for STALEMATE
16. Bitter conflict

Notes

The following lists of words are from the preceding two lessons. You may wish to use these lists to pinpoint words for ongoing review or for midterm or final exams.

Lesson 13

abet	offset
deliverance	pacify
ennoble	refurbish
expedite	reinforce
intercede	sanctuary

Lesson 14

adversary	embroil
aggression	haggle
contradict	skirmish
controversy	stalemate
discord	strife

Lesson 15

The Roots -*clam*- and -*voc*-

The Latin roots -*clam*- and -*voc*- are the foundations of many of our English words. In Latin the word *clamare* means "to cry or call out." Therefore, if you *proclaim* something, you call it out officially and publicly. If you *exclaim*, you cry out from surprise or emotion. A second Latin word, *vocare*, means "to call." If you *convoke* a meeting, you call together or assemble a group. If you make an *irrevocable* decision, you make a decision that cannot be called back. In this lesson you will study words that are derived from the roots -*clam*- and -*voc*- as well as from their related forms, -*claim*- and -*voke*-.

DEFINITIONS

After you have studied the definitions and example for each vocabulary word, write the word on the line to the right.

1. **claimant** (klā′mənt) *noun* One who makes a claim or asks for something that he or she believes rightfully belongs to him or her. (From the Latin word *clamare*, meaning "to call out")

   RELATED WORDS **claim** *verb*; **claimable** *adjective*

   EXAMPLE During the conquest of the New World, both Spain and Portugal were *claimants* to all of South America.

   1. _____

2. **clamor** (klăm′ər) *noun* **a.** A loud, continuous noise. **b.** A strong expression of discontent or protest; public outcry. *verb* To make insistent demands or complaints. (From the Latin word *clamare*)

   RELATED WORDS **clamorous** *adjective*; **clamorously** *adverb*

   EXAMPLE The *clamor* of rush-hour traffic prevented Gary from concentrating on his book.

   2. _____

3. **declaim** (dĭ-klām′) *verb* **a.** To speak loudly and forcefully. **b.** To deliver a formal speech. (From the Latin word *declamare*, meaning "to make speeches")

   RELATED WORDS **declamation** *noun*; **declamatory** *adjective*

   EXAMPLE Patrick Henry *declaimed* for liberty.

   3. _____

4. **disclaim** (dĭs-klām′) *verb* **a.** To deny or give up any claim to or connection with; disown. **b.** To reject as untrue. (From the Latin *dis-*, meaning "reversal of," and *clamare*)

RELATED WORD **disclaimer** *noun*

EXAMPLE The senator *disclaimed* any involvement with the scandal.

5. **evocative** (ĭ-vŏk′ə-tĭv) *adjective* **a.** Tending to call to mind or memory. **b.** Tending to create anew through the power of the memory or imagination: *an evocative poem.* (From the Latin *ex-*, meaning "out," and *vocare*, meaning "to call")

RELATED WORD **evoke** *verb*

EXAMPLE Driving down the street where she had grown up was an *evocative* experience for Sheila.

6. **invoke** (ĭn-vōk′) *verb* **a.** To call upon for assistance, support, or inspiration. **b.** To use or apply: *The President invoked his veto power.* (From the Latin *in-*, meaning "in," and *vocare*)

RELATED WORD **invocation** *noun*

EXAMPLE The family *invoked* the help of their friends.

7. **reclaim** (rē-klām′) *verb* **a.** To ask for the return of something; recover. **b.** To convert to something better; reform: *to reclaim land.* (From the Latin *re-*, meaning "back" or "again," and *clamare*)

RELATED WORDS **reclaimable** *adjective;* **reclamation** *noun*

EXAMPLE Alicia *reclaimed* her runaway dog from the pound.

8. **revoke** (rĭ-vōk′) *verb* To cancel or make void by reversing, recalling, or withdrawing. (From the Latin *re-*, meaning "back" or "again," and *vocare*)

RELATED WORDS **revocable** *adjective;* **revocation** *noun*

EXAMPLE Ms. Slocum *revoked* Nat's library privileges.

9. **vocation** (vō-kā′shən) *noun* **a.** An occupation or profession, especially one for which a person is specially suited or trained. **b.** A strong desire to do a particular type of work, especially one of a religious nature; a calling. (From the Latin word *vocare*)

RELATED WORD **vocational** *adjective*

EXAMPLE After seven summers as a camp counselor, Anita decided that teaching was her *vocation.*

MEMORY CUE A *vocational* school is one that offers training in specific trades or occupations.

10. **vouch** (vouch) *verb* **a.** To give personal assurance. **b.** To furnish or serve as a guarantee; supply supporting evidence. (From the Old French word *voucher*, meaning "to summon to court")

EXAMPLE Ms. Gordon *vouched* for Morgan's dependability.

USAGE NOTE *Vouch* is usually followed by a phrase beginning with *for* or a clause beginning with *that.*

Exercise 1 Writing Correct Words

On the answer line, write the word from the vocabulary list that fits each definition.

1. To deliver a formal speech; speak forcefully about a subject

2. To ask for the return of something; convert to something better

3. To give personal assurance; supply supporting evidence

4. Tending to call to mind or memory

5. To cancel by reversing or withdrawing

6. One who makes a claim or asks for something that he or she believes rightfully belongs to him or her

7. An occupation or profession for which one is specially suited or trained

8. To call upon for assistance; use or apply

9. A loud noise; a strong expression of discontent or protest

10. To deny or give up any claim to; reject as untrue

1. _____ declaim _____

2. _____ reclaim _____

3. _____ vouch _____

4. _____ evocative _____

5. _____ revoke _____

6. _____ claimant _____

7. _____ vocation _____

8. _____ invoke _____

9. _____ clamor _____

10. _____ disclaim _____

Exercise 2 Using Words Correctly

Decide whether the italicized vocabulary word has been used correctly in the sentence. On the answer line, write *Correct* for correct use and *Incorrect* for incorrect use.

1. Jim is a fine sculptor: his style is *evocative* of Michelangelo's.

2. A baby kangaroo spends much time in its mother's *vouch*.

3. The *clamor* of hoofs on the cobblestones startled the innkeeper.

4. The Dutch *reclaim* much of their land from the sea.

5. Dolores spent her three weeks of *vocation* water-skiing on Lake Powell.

6. By using ropes, Edmund can *declaim* the mountain faster than anyone else.

7. Hal was the only *claimant* to the reward money.

8. Connie must learn to *revoke* direction several times to complete a perfect figure eight on ice skates.

9. Before Homer created any poetry, he *invoked* the aid of a muse, or guiding spirit.

10. Corinne *disclaimed* any knowledge of who might have broken the window.

1. _____ Correct _____

2. _____ Incorrect _____

3. _____ Correct _____

4. _____ Correct _____

5. _____ Incorrect _____

6. _____ Incorrect _____

7. _____ Correct _____

8. _____ Incorrect _____

9. _____ Correct _____

10. _____ Correct _____

Exercise 3 Choosing the Best Definition

For each italicized vocabulary word in the following sentences, write the letter of the best definition on the answer line.

1. Galileo is one of several *claimants to* the title "Father of Modern Astronomy."
   a. undeserving seekers of   **c.** designators of
   b. candidates for   **d.** originators of
      1. _____b_____

2. For thousands of years, most astronomers had *vouched* that the earth was the center of the solar system.
   a. asserted as true **b.** hoped **c.** guessed **d.** required proof
      2. _____a_____

3. Galileo *revoked* traditional assumptions of science.
   a. canceled **b.** strengthened **c.** proved **d.** questioned
      3. _____a_____

4. Galileo's ideas raised a *clamor* among scientists and philosophers.
   a. eyebrow **b.** question **c.** plea **d.** outcry
      4. _____d_____

5. In *declaiming* his beliefs Galileo caused controversy.
   a. whispering   **c.** forcefully expressing
   b. nervously stuttering   **d.** guessing
      5. _____c_____

6. Although Galileo *invoked* proof that his theory was true, he could not convince others.
   a. criticized **b.** used **c.** forgot **d.** rejected
      6. _____b_____

7. Certain leaders wanted Galileo to *disclaim* his theories.
   a. present **b.** prove **c.** deny **d.** burn
      7. _____c_____

8. These leaders wanted to *reclaim* the reputation of the traditional theories of astronomy.
   a. destroy **b.** discover **c.** restore **d.** irrigate
      8. _____c_____

9. In Germany Johannes Kepler proposed a theory of the solar system that was *evocative of* Galileo's.
   a. tending to call to mind   **c.** the opposite of
   b. more concentrated than   **d.** easier than
      9. _____a_____

10. Today the study of astronomy is as acceptable to us as any other *vocation*.
   a. hobby **b.** idea **c.** science **d.** occupation
      10. _____d_____

Exercise 4 Using Different Forms of Words

Decide which form of the vocabulary word in parentheses best completes the sentence. The form given may be correct. Write your answer on the answer line.

1. In Greek myths mortals often made __?__ to gods and goddesses. (*invoke*)
      1. _____invocations_____

2. Rosy __?__ that she had won the race. (*claimant*)
      2. _____claimed_____

3. Joshua wanted to go to a __?__ school. (*vocation*)
      3. _____vocational_____

4. On the editorial page is a __?__ stating that views expressed in letters to the editor are not necessarily those of the newspaper. (*disclaim*)
      4. _____disclaimer_____

5. Vanessa's driver's license can be __?__ if she gets another speeding ticket. (*revoke*)
      5. _____revoked_____

6. The crowd gathered __?__ on the Capitol steps. *(clamor)*

7. Each applicant must have a sponsor who will __?__ for the applicant's experience. *(vouch)*

8. Uncle Jared's barn is in such a state of disrepair that it is barely __?__ . *(reclaim)*

9. Senator Moore's __?__ did not impress the convention delegates. *(declaim)*

10. When I see Genevieve, her smile __?__ the image of her grandfather. *(evocative)*

6. _____clamorously_____

7. _____vouch_____

8. _____reclaimable_____

9. _____declamation_____

10. _____evokes_____

Reading Comprehension

Each numbered sentence in the following passage contains an italicized vocabulary word. After you read the passage, you will complete an exercise.

The Mystery of Anastasia

One of the most intriguing stories of the Russian Revolution concerns the identity of Anastasia, the youngest daughter of Czar Nicholas II. **(1)** During his reign over Russia, the Czar had planned to **revoke** many of the harsh laws established by previous czars. **(2)** Some workers and peasants, however, **clamored** for more rapid social reform. In 1918 a group of these people, known as Bolsheviks, overthrew the government. On July 17 or 18, they murdered the Czar and what was thought to be his entire family.

(3) Although witnesses **vouched** that all the members of the Czar's family had been executed, there were rumors suggesting that Anastasia had survived. Over the years, a number of women claimed to be Grand Duchess Anastasia. **(4)** Perhaps the best-known **claimant** was Anastasia Tschaikovsky, who was also known as Anna Anderson.

In 1920, eighteen months after the Czar's execution, this terrified young woman was rescued from drowning in a Berlin river. **(5)** She spent two years in a hospital, where she attempted to **reclaim** her health and shattered mind. The doctors and nurses thought that she resembled Anastasia and questioned her about her background. **(6)** She **disclaimed** any connection with the Czar's family.

Eight years later, though, she claimed that she *was* Anastasia. She said that she had been rescued by two Russian soldiers after the Czar and the rest of her family had been killed. Two brothers named Tschaikovsky had carried her into Romania. **(7)** She had married one of the brothers, who had taken her to Berlin and left her there, penniless and without a **vocation**. **(8)** Unable to **invoke** the aid of her mother's family in Germany, she had tried to drown herself.

During the next few years, scores of the Czar's relatives, ex-servants, and acquaintances interviewed her. **(9)** Many of these people said that her looks and mannerisms were **evocative** of the Anastasia that they had known. Her grandmother and other relatives denied that she was the real Anastasia, however.

Tired of being accused of fraud, Anastasia immigrated to the United States in 1928 and took the name Anna Anderson. She still wished to prove that she was Anastasia, though, and returned to Germany in 1933 to bring suit against her mother's family. **(10)** There she **declaimed** to the court, asserting that she was indeed Anastasia and deserved her inheritance.

In 1957, the court decided that it could neither confirm nor deny Anastasia's identity. Although we will probably never know whether this woman was the Grand Duchess Anastasia, her search to establish her identity has been the subject of numerous books, plays, and movies.

Please turn to the next page.

Reading Comprehension Exercise

Each of the following statements corresponds to a numbered sentence in the passage. Each statement contains a blank and is followed by four answer choices. Decide which choice fits best in the blank. The word or phrase that you choose must express roughly the same meaning as the italicized word in the passage. Write the letter of your choice on the answer line.

1. Czar Nicholas II planned to __?__ the harsh laws.
   a. enforce   **b.** announce   **c.** cancel   **d.** think about

   1. _____c_____

2. Some Russian peasants and workers __?__ for social reform.
   a. longed   **b.** cried out   **c.** begged   **d.** worked

   2. _____b_____

3. Witnesses __?__ that all members of the Czar's family had been executed.
   a. gave assurance   **b.** thought   **c.** hoped   **d.** should have known

   3. _____a_____

4. Anastasia Tschaikovsky was __?__ the title of Grand Duchess Anastasia.
   a. one who makes a rightful demand for   **c.** holder of
   b. a celebrator of   **d.** named after

   4. _____a_____

5. Two years in a hospital helped her to __?__ her health.
   a. destroy   **b.** moderate   **c.** deny   **d.** recover

   5. _____d_____

6. She __?__ any connection with the Czar's family.
   a. denied   **b.** stopped   **c.** whispered   **d.** noted

   6. _____a_____

7. Anastasia was without __?__ after her husband abandoned her.
   a. friends   **b.** an occupation   **c.** hope   **d.** a home

   7. _____b_____

8. She was unable to __?__ the aid of her relatives.
   a. locate   **b.** speak about   **c.** call upon   **d.** force

   8. _____c_____

9. Many people said that her looks and mannerisms were __?__ of Anastasia.
   a. unlike those   **c.** poor imitations
   b. signs of the insanity   **d.** suggestive

   9. _____d_____

10. In court she __?__, maintaining that she was Anastasia and deserved her inheritance.
    a. finally appeared   **c.** acted as a witness
    b. spoke forcefully   **d.** testified

    10. _____b_____

Practice with Analogies

DIRECTIONS On the answer line, write the vocabulary word that completes each analogy.

See page 119 for some strategies to use with analogies.

1. Defend is to defendant as claim is to __?__ .

   1. _____claimant_____

2. Start is to begin as cancel is to __?__ .

   2. _____revoke_____

3. Admit is to acknowledge as deny is to __?__ .

   3. _____disclaim_____

4. Event is to occurrence as occupation is to __?__ .

   4. _____vocation_____

5. Soft is to murmur as loud is to __?__ .

   5. _____clamor_____

6. Admire is to idolize as say is to __?__ .

   6. _____declaim_____

Test: Lessons 13, 14, and 15

(pages 81–98)

Part A   Choosing the Best Definition

On the answer line, write the letter of the best definition of the italicized word.

1. Spain won the *deliverance* of Granada from the Moors.
   a. liberation   **b.** return   **c.** recognition   **d.** control

   1. _____a_____

2. No one has yet been able to *disclaim* the merits of my plan.
   a. verify   **b.** comprehend   **c.** employ   **d.** reject as untrue

   2. _____d_____

3. There is natural *aggression* between baboons and lions.
   a. friendly feeling   **c.** tendency to be shy
   b. hostile behavior   **d.** barrier

   3. _____b_____

4. Chase asked his father to *intercede* with his teachers on his behalf.
   a. bargain   **b.** prophesy   **c.** plead   **d.** debate

   4. _____c_____

5. Mother's work is *evocative* of that of some impressionist painters.
   a. a duplicate   **c.** a demonstration
   b. tending to call to mind   **d.** little-known proof

   5. _____b_____

6. The accident *embroiled* the motorists in a heated argument.
   a. surrounded   **b.** subdued   **c.** united   **d.** involved

   6. _____d_____

7. The Panthers *offset* their scoreless first half with a dramatic comeback.
   a. explained   **b.** changed   **c.** displayed   **d.** made up for

   7. _____d_____

8. Venus often *invoked* the aid of Cupid.
   a. rewarded   **c.** called upon
   b. recommended   **d.** argued against

   8. _____c_____

9. Philip likes to *haggle* with car dealers over their prices.
   a. bargain   **b.** bemoan   **c.** joke   **d.** juggle

   9. _____a_____

10. Ellen's plans for *refurbishing* the old trunk were unrealistic.
    a. selling   **b.** repainting   **c.** dismantling   **d.** renewing

    10. _____d_____

11. Before pursuing a *vocation*, Patrick interviewed people in a variety of professions.
    a. residence   **b.** tutor   **c.** occupation   **d.** trip

    11. _____c_____

12. If preseason exhibitions can be considered *skirmishes*, postseason tournaments must be viewed as wars.
    a. tests of skill   **c.** peaceful confrontations
    b. minor battles   **d.** demonstrations of courage

    12. _____b_____

13. A university should be considered a *sanctuary* for knowledge.
    a. training camp   **b.** safe place   **c.** distributor   **d.** supporter

    13. _____b_____

14. Mrs. George will *vouch* that I deliver her newspaper on time.
    a. claim   **b.** verify   **c.** complain   **d.** explain

    14. _____b_____

15. City officials reached a *stalemate* in their negotiations.
    a. deadlock   **b.** agreement   **c.** limitation   **d.** awkward stage

    15. _____a_____

Test: Lessons 13, 14, and 15

Part B   Identifying Synonyms

On the answer line, write the letter of the word or phrase that has the meaning that is the same as that of the capitalized vocabulary word.

16. CONTROVERSY :
    a. limitation   **b.** agreement   **c.** dispute   **d.** instrument

16. _____c_____

17. ABET :
    a. hinder   **b.** aid   **c.** promise   **d.** protect

17. _____b_____

18. CLAMOR :
    a. silence   **b.** friction   **c.** innocence   **d.** noise

18. _____d_____

19. ADVERSARY :
    a. enemy   **b.** partner   **c.** habit   **d.** relative

19. _____a_____

20. ENNOBLE :
    a. degrade   **b.** disguise   **c.** decide   **d.** promote

20. _____d_____

21. CLAIMANT :
    a. one who asserts a right   **c.** suspicious participant
    b. one who searches for gold   **d.** artful producer

21. _____a_____

22. CONTRADICT :
    a. explain   **b.** oppose   **c.** inform   **d.** believe

22. _____b_____

23. EXPEDITE :
    a. hasten   **b.** decide   **c.** improve   **d.** prevent

23. _____a_____

24. DECLAIM :
    a. give up   **c.** announce calmly
    b. prohibit   **d.** speak forcefully

24. _____d_____

25. DISCORD :
    a. extension   **b.** harmony   **c.** disagreement   **d.** formation

25. _____c_____

26. PACIFY :
    a. dampen   **b.** agitate   **c.** calm   **d.** alter

26. _____c_____

27. RECLAIM :
    a. enhance   **b.** recover   **c.** permit   **d.** lose

27. _____b_____

28. STRIFE :
    a. humor   **b.** conflict   **c.** virtue   **d.** peace

28. _____b_____

29. REINFORCE :
    a. ascend   **b.** support   **c.** weaken   **d.** calculate

29. _____b_____

30. REVOKE :
    a. summon   **b.** operate   **c.** validate   **d.** cancel

30. _____d_____

HOUGHTON MIFFLIN VOCABULARY FOR ACHIEVEMENT, SECOND COURSE

Test-Taking Skills

Synonym Tests

Many vocabulary tests, including some standardized tests, contain sections on identifying synonyms. A **synonym** is a word close in meaning to another word. (*Synonym* is derived from a Greek term meaning "similar name.") *Sly, tricky, cunning,* and *crafty* are all synonyms.

A synonym test item asks you to identify from several choices the word or phrase *closest* in meaning to the given word. Here are four strategies for answering such test items.

STRATEGIES

1. *Read all of the choices before selecting an answer.* Do not make the mistake of choosing an answer before you have considered all of the possibilities.

2. *Do not be misled by antonym choices.* An **antonym** (a word meaning the opposite of another word) is sometimes given as a choice in synonym items. In the following example, *injure* is an antonym of *protect. Guard* is a synonym, and the correct answer is (E).

    PROTECT :
    (A) rebel   (B) handle   (C) injure   (D) lose   (E) guard

3. *Watch for other deceptive choices.* The following example has misleading choices that test your ability to distinguish differences in word meanings.

    REFUGE :
    (F) immigrant   (G) heaven   (H) shelter   (J) park   (K) denial

    The correct answer is *shelter.* An *immigrant* is sometimes a *refugee,* which is a word related to *refuge. Heaven* looks similar to *haven,* a synonym for *refuge.* If you misread the given word as *refuse,* you might choose *denial* as your answer. Finally, *park* could suggest *wildlife refuge.*

4. *Pay attention to roots, prefixes, and suffixes.* By increasing your knowledge of these word parts, you will often be able to define words that you do not know. This ability can be very important when you take vocabulary tests.

Please turn to the next page.

Exercise Identifying Synonyms

Select the one word or phrase whose meaning is closest to the word given in capital letters. Write the letter of your choice on the answer line. Use your dictionary as needed.

1. EXPEND :
   (A) rely   (B) stretch   (C) use up   (D) give off   (E) purchase

   1. _____C_____

2. SERENE :
   (F) hot   (G) boring   (H) lazy   (J) peaceful   (K) humid

   2. _____J_____

3. IRRELEVANT :
   (A) disrespectful   (B) sorrowful   (C) not applicable
   (D) unauthorized   (E) unjust

   3. _____C_____

4. WANE :
   (F) tell   (G) warn   (H) surprise   (J) encourage
   (K) decrease

   4. _____K_____

5. INTRACTABLE :
   (A) hard to control   (B) evil   (C) poisonous   (D) complicated
   (E) untraceable

   5. _____A_____

6. WAFT :
   (F) airship   (G) crash   (H) float   (J) refuse   (K) wade

   6. _____H_____

7. INDOLENT :
   (A) lazy   (B) guiltless   (C) painful   (D) romantic
   (E) suffering

   7. _____A_____

8. SERF :
   (F) wave   (G) shrub   (H) tribe   (J) angle   (K) slave

   8. _____K_____

9. JUDICIOUS :
   (A) hasty   (B) healthful   (C) justifiable   (D) ambitious
   (E) sensible

   9. _____E_____

10. IMPUGN :
    (F) fall   (G) condemn   (H) stifle   (J) linger   (K) kiss

    10. _____G_____

11. BREADTH :
    (A) width   (B) height   (C) weight   (D) break
    (E) respiration

    11. _____A_____

12. RAMBLE :
    (F) propel   (G) wander   (H) hasten   (J) whisper
    (K) perplex

    12. _____G_____

13. UNANIMOUS :
    (A) differing   (B) in opposition   (C) in agreement   (D) varied
    (E) outstanding

    13. _____C_____

14. DRAB :
    (F) stylish   (G) dedicated   (H) noisy   (J) uninteresting
    (K) stubborn

    14. _____J_____

15. SARCASM :
    (A) harmony   (B) monotony   (C) fright   (D) complaint
    (E) scorn

    15. _____E_____

Government and Control

When people think of government, they generally think of national, state, and local organizations that control public affairs. The term *government* has a much broader application, however. Whenever people attempt to work together, a form of government arises. Groups and organizations cannot operate without some structure to make decisions, carry out tasks, and regulate change. Families, businesses, and schools are only a few of the groups that use different forms of government.

Each of the words in this lesson is related to government. Studying these vocabulary words will increase your understanding of how governments developed, why they are necessary, and how they function.

WORD LIST
anarchy
authoritarian
conservative
delegate
dominion
impeach
inaugurate
liberal
Spartan
tyrant

DEFINITIONS

After you have studied the definitions and example for each vocabulary word, write the word on the line to the right.

1. **anarchy** (ăn′ər-kē) *noun*   **a.** Political and social disorder resulting from an absence of governmental control. **b.** Chaos; confusion. (From the Greek *an-*, meaning "without," and *arkhos*, meaning "ruler")

   RELATED WORD   **anarchist** *noun*

   EXAMPLE   The country was in a state of *anarchy* after its ruler died.

   1. _____

2. **authoritarian** (ə-thôr′ĭ-târ′ē-ən) *adjective*   Requiring complete obedience to the rule of one person or group.   *noun*   A person who believes in authoritarian policies.

   RELATED WORDS   **authoritarianism** *noun;* **authority** *noun*

   EXAMPLE   Under an *authoritarian* government, individual freedom is greatly limited.

   2. _____

   MEMORY CUE An *authoritarian* leader wields absolute *authority.*

3. **conservative** (kən-sûr′və-tĭv) *adjective*   **a.** Favoring traditional values and existing conditions; tending to oppose change. **b.** Traditional in style or manners.   *noun*   A person who is moderate, cautious, and restrained. (From the Latin word *conservare*, meaning "to preserve")

   RELATED WORDS   **conservatism** *noun;* **conservatively** *adverb*

   EXAMPLE   The *conservative* politician did not support hasty revisions in the income-tax code.

   3. _____

4. **delegate** (dĕl′ĭ-gĭt) *noun* A person chosen to speak and act as the representative of another person or of a group. *verb* (dĕl′ĭ-gāt′) To commit or entrust to another: *to delegate tasks.* (From the Latin word *delegatus,* meaning "dispatched")

RELATED WORD **delegation** *noun*

EXAMPLE Sonya was delighted to be her school's *delegate* to the international conference.

4. _____

5. **dominion** (də-mĭn′yən) *noun* **a.** Control or power, particularly of one country over another. **b.** A territory or area of control; domain; realm. (From the Latin word *dominus,* meaning "lord")

EXAMPLE Some parts of Africa were once under French *dominion.*

5. _____

6. **impeach** (ĭm-pēch′) *verb* To accuse a public official of unacceptable conduct in office. (From the Latin word *impedicare,* meaning "to entangle")

RELATED WORD **impeachment** *noun*

EXAMPLE Andrew Johnson was *impeached* by the House of Representatives in 1868, but the Senate did not find him guilty.

6. _____

USAGE NOTE To *impeach* is to accuse. An *impeached* official must then stand trial.

7. **inaugurate** (ĭn-ô′gyə-rāt′) *verb* **a.** To install in office by formal ceremony. **b.** To initiate or make a formal beginning.

RELATED WORDS **inaugural** *adjective;* **inauguration** *noun*

EXAMPLE The new officers were *inaugurated* at a banquet.

7. _____

8. **liberal** (lĭb′ər-əl) *adjective* **a.** Having political views that favor individual rights, social and economic progress, and the protection of civil liberties. **b.** Tolerant of others; broad-minded. **c.** Tending to give generously. **d.** Generous in amount: *a liberal allowance.* *noun* A person with liberal opinions. (From the Latin word *liber,* meaning "free")

RELATED WORDS **liberalism** *noun;* **liberalize** *verb;* **liberally** *adverb*

EXAMPLE The senator supports *liberal* health-care policies.

8. _____

9. **Spartan** (spär′tn) *adjective* Resembling the Spartans of ancient Greece by living in a simple and self-disciplined way.

EXAMPLE The athlete followed a *Spartan* routine of training.

9. _____

10. **tyrant** (tī′rənt) *noun* A ruler who exercises power in a harsh, cruel manner; an oppressor.

RELATED WORDS **tyrannical** *adjective;* **tyrannize** *verb;* **tyranny** *noun*

EXAMPLE The *tyrant* forbade all subjects to leave the country without his permission.

10. _____

Name _____ Date _____

Exercise 1   Writing Correct Words

On the answer line, write the word from the vocabulary list that fits each definition.

1. Favoring traditional values; a moderate and cautious person
2. Disorder resulting from an absence of governmental control
3. To accuse a public official of unacceptable conduct in office
4. Requiring complete obedience
5. Living in a simple and disciplined way
6. To install a public official by formal ceremony
7. Having political views that favor individual rights, progress, and the protection of civil liberties; broad-minded
8. A harsh ruler
9. A person who represents others
10. Control or power; an area of control

1. _____conservative_____
2. _____anarchy_____
3. _____impeach_____
4. _____authoritarian_____
5. _____Spartan_____
6. _____inaugurate_____
7. _____liberal_____
8. _____tyrant_____
9. _____delegate_____
10. _____dominion_____

Exercise 2   Using Words Correctly

Each of the following questions contains an italicized vocabulary word. Decide the answer to the question, and write *Yes* or *No* on the answer line.

1. Is a *tyrant* a ruler who grants citizens a variety of liberties?
2. Would a *conservative* dresser be likely to choose colorful plaids?
3. Does *anarchy* consist of confusion caused by the absence of government?
4. Is a *delegate* a presidential candidate?
5. If you *inaugurate* a new activity, do you begin it?
6. Is a *liberal* person narrow-minded?
7. If public officials are *impeached*, are they placed in office?
8. Does a *Spartan* lifestyle lack luxuries?
9. Would an *authoritarian* person favor independent decision-making by people under him or her?
10. When the thirteen American colonies were ruled by Britain, did they have *dominion* over Britain?

1. _____No_____
2. _____No_____
3. _____Yes_____
4. _____No_____
5. _____Yes_____
6. _____No_____
7. _____No_____
8. _____Yes_____
9. _____No_____
10. _____No_____

Exercise 3   Choosing the Best Definition

For each italicized vocabulary word in the following sentences, write the letter of the best definition on the answer line.

1. England once held *dominion* over a quarter of the world's people.
   a. fear   **b.** confusion   **c.** control   **d.** discipline

1. _____c_____

2. To prevent *anarchy,* the Constitution of the United States provides for the orderly transfer of power if a President dies.
   a. disorder   **b.** ambition   **c.** dictatorship   **d.** jealousy

2. _____a_____

3. The *authoritarian* ruler jailed several political opponents.
   a. demanding complete obedience
   b. inspiring disobedience
   c. demanding sincere opinions
   d. widely respected

3. _____a_____

4. During the 1930s President Franklin Roosevelt *inaugurated* several social welfare programs.
   a. stopped   **b.** designed   **c.** increased   **d.** began

4. _____d_____

5. Our waitress was so efficient that we left her a *liberal* tip.
   a. light   **b.** generous   **c.** traditional   **d.** wrong

5. _____b_____

6. The convention *delegates* cheered when the nominee was introduced.
   a. supporters   **b.** workers   **c.** opponents   **d.** representatives

6. _____d_____

7. The builder gave us a *conservative* estimate for building an addition to our house.
   a. brief   **b.** expensive   **c.** cautious   **d.** incomplete

7. _____c_____

8. Angry citizens demanded that the governor be *impeached.*
   a. informed of their objections   **c.** supported
   b. accused of wrong-doing   **d.** encouraged

8. _____b_____

9. The king was a *tyrant* who cared nothing about the rights of his subjects.
   a. harsh ruler   **c.** ineffective ruler
   b. weak ruler   **d.** kind ruler

9. _____a_____

10. The campers followed a *Spartan* schedule that began at 5:00 A.M.
    a. healthy   **b.** entertaining   **c.** disciplined   **d.** Greek

10. _____c_____

Exercise 4   Using Different Forms of Words

Decide which form of the vocabulary word in parentheses best completes the sentence. The form given may be correct. Write your answer on the answer line.

1. Some tourists avoid traveling in countries that have __?__ governments. *(authoritarian)*

1. _____authoritarian_____

2. Three articles of __?__ had been proposed against President Nixon before he resigned in 1974. *(impeach)*

2. _____impeachment_____

3. The President's __?__ takes place on January 20. *(inaugurate)*

3. _____inauguration_____

4. Pamela tries to __?__ her younger brother. *(tyrant)*

4. _____tyrannize_____

5. During the children's play period, the room seems to be in a state of __?__ . *(anarchy)*

5. _____anarchy_____

6. Hortense, who now dresses __?__ , used to wear ribbons or feathers with every outfit. *(conservative)*

6. _____conservatively_____

7. Grant's room took on a __?__ appearance after he moved his furniture out. *(Spartan)*

7. _____Spartan_____

8. Our school sent a __?__ of five students to the city council meeting. *(delegate)*

    8. ___delegation___

9. Britain once considered its __?__ over the seas to be its best defense. *(dominion)*

    9. ___dominion___

10. Max sprinkled his salad __?__ with lemon juice. *(liberal)*

    10. ___liberally___

Reading Comprehension

Each numbered sentence in the following passage contains an italicized vocabulary word. After you read the passage, you will complete an exercise.

Two Ancient Governments: Athens and Sparta

Ancient Greece was for a long time made up of loosely organized tribes of people. **(1)** Each tribe was governed by a chieftain whose ***dominion*** included the army and the priesthood. Once warfare among tribes stopped and trade began to develop, the tribes united to form city-states.

Athens and Sparta were two of the largest and most important city-states. At first, both were governed by aristocrats who were concerned primarily with their own wealth and power. These wealthy landowners believed that the majority of people were not able to make good decisions and should not participate in government. This view led to the development of two very different forms of government in Athens and Sparta.

In Athens supporters of citizen participation in government finally overthrew the aristocrats. **(2)** Athenians called their new leaders ***tyrants*** because they had seized political power unlawfully. The tyrants, however, were capable individuals who actually improved conditions in Athens.

(3) By 600 B.C. Athenians had removed the tyrants from office and ***inaugurated*** constitutional government. The constitution established nine rulers, ten generals, a council divided into separate committees, and a citizen assembly. **(4)** The rulers and the ***delegates*** to the council were chosen annually by drawing lots; the generals were the only elected officials. **(5)** Built into the constitution was a provision for ***impeaching*** ineffective leaders. If the majority of citizens voted against an official, he was banished from Athens for ten years.

The citizen assembly, which passed laws, consisted of five hundred citizens. However, the Athenian idea of citizenship was narrowly defined. Only free male Athenians had rights and privileges; non-Athenians, women, and slaves could neither vote nor participate in government.

Unlike Athens, Sparta never developed a democracy. **(6)** Under the ***authoritarian*** rule of two kings, Spartans did not participate in government. Citizenship was based on the ability to

pay high taxes. Because most people could not pay the taxes, they were slaves. **(7)** The aristocratic rulers of Sparta tightly controlled the lives of the people because they feared that ***anarchy*** would occur if the slaves revolted. From age twenty to thirty, each free male served as a cadet and policed the countryside, maintaining the obedience of the slaves. **(8)** The ***Spartan*** lifestyle developed and was reinforced to serve the government of the city-state.

Because other Greek city-states copied the Athenian form of democracy, Sparta felt called upon to defend its position as the strongest city-state. Several decades of war among the city-states resulted, weakening Greece as a whole and making the country easy prey for the Romans. **(9)** ***Conservative*** Sparta, having concentrated on developing military strength and personal endurance, made few contributions to culture. **(10)** ***Liberal*** Athens, though, with its devotion to democracy and its openness to new ideas, made important advances in the arts and sciences.

Please turn to the next page.

Reading Comprehension Exercise

Each of the following statements corresponds to a numbered sentence in the passage. Each statement contains a blank and is followed by four answer choices. Decide which choice fits best in the blank. The word or phrase that you choose must express roughly the same meaning as the italicized word in the passage. Write the letter of your choice on the answer line.

1. The ___?___ of the chieftain included the army and the priesthood.
   a. area of popularity   **c.** usefulness
   b. area of control   **d.** changes

   1. _____ b

2. The Greek leaders who had seized power unlawfully were regarded as ___?___ .
   a. oppressors   **b.** giants   **c.** gods   **d.** weaklings

   2. _____ a

3. Constitutional government had ___?___ by 600 B.C.
   a. begun   **b.** been destroyed   **c.** changed   **d.** been discussed

   3. _____ a

4. Council ___?___ were chosen by drawing lots.
   a. witnesses   **b.** directions   **c.** visitors   **d.** representatives

   4. _____ d

5. The constitution had a provision for ___?___ ineffective leaders.
   a. predicting   **b.** accusing   **c.** supporting   **d.** rewarding

   5. _____ b

6. Under the ___?___ rule of two kings, Spartans did not take part in government.
   a. weak   **b.** undemocratic   **c.** conflicting   **d.** liberal

   6. _____ b

7. The rulers were afraid that ___?___ would occur if the slaves revolted.
   a. applause   **b.** hunger   **c.** disorder   **d.** anger

   7. _____ c

8. The ___?___ lifestyle served the government of the city-state.
   a. superior   **b.** luxurious   **c.** pleasant   **d.** disciplined

   8. _____ d

9. ___?___ Sparta had little to leave behind.
   a. Cautious   **b.** Military   **c.** Ancient   **d.** Democratic

   9. _____ a

10. ___?___ Athens left us many important contributions.
    a. Fearful   **b.** Creative   **c.** Tolerant   **d.** Peaceful

    10. _____ c

Writing Assignment

Imagine that a group of teachers, students, and administrators has met to discuss the need for student government at your school. The members have asked you to write a proposal in which you describe a form of student government that would be fair and effective. They want you to explain why a student government is necessary, how decisions would be made in the form of government you propose, and how student representatives would be selected. Include at least five of the vocabulary words from this lesson in your proposal and underline them.

Bonus: Lessons 15 and 16

(pages 93–98, 101–106)

Choose a vocabulary word from the box to complete each of the following sentences. You may need to change the form of some of the words to fit correctly in the sentence. Use each word only once, and write your answer on the answer line to the right.

anarchy	declaim	impeach	revoke
authoritarian	delegate	inaugurate	Spartan
claimant	disclaim	invoke	tyrant
clamor	dominion	liberal	vocation
conservative	evocative	reclaim	vouch

1. The __?__ of the crowd increased as the home team scored a touchdown.

2. After working as a volunteer at the health clinic, Alice decided that medicine was her true __?__.

3. The __?__ politicians were unwilling to support hasty changes in the law.

4. After the leader of the government died, the country experienced a temporary state of __?__.

5. The new president of the small nation was __?__ at a special ceremony.

6. During the California Gold Rush, there were many __?__ for the same piece of land.

7. The early Romans often __?__ Jupiter to assure victory against their enemies.

8. Before the marathon the athlete maintained a(n) __?__ routine of practice and rest.

9. Tarcher is a(n) __?__ coach who allows no violations of his training rules.

10. President Andrew Johnson suffered disgrace when he was __?__ by the House of Representatives in 1868.

11. The suspect __?__ any connection with the robbery.

12. Eating homemade bread like his grandmother's was a(n) __?__ experience for Ned.

13. Mohandas Gandhi __?__ for the independence of India.

14. The __?__ forbade all storekeepers to conduct business without his permission.

15. The __?__ to the United Nations delivered a stirring address about world hunger.

1. clamor
2. vocation
3. conservative
4. anarchy
5. inaugurated
6. claimants
7. invoked
8. Spartan
9. authoritarian
10. impeached
11. disclaimed
12. evocative
13. declaimed
14. tyrant
15. delegate

Notes

The following lists of words are from the preceding two lessons. You may wish to use these lists to pinpoint words for ongoing review or for midterm or final exams.

Lesson 15

claimant	invoke
clamor	reclaim
declaim	revoke
disclaim	vocation
evocative	vouch

Lesson 16

anarchy	impeach
authoritarian	inaugurate
conservative	liberal
delegate	Spartan
dominion	tyrant

Lesson 17

Crime and Justice

For years, crime and justice have been popular topics for writers. In the 1940s radios broadcast the adventures of such intriguing crime fighters as The Phantom. Where the radio left off, television programmers began with decades of justice seekers. There were private detectives, like Mike Hammer, and lawyer-investigators, such as Perry Mason.

Mystery novels still are very popular, with characters like Agatha Christie's Miss Jane Marple solving crimes in her own English village and halfway around the world. Many of the words in this lesson are used by mystery writers. Understanding these terms should increase your enjoyment of their work.

WORD LIST
acquit
arson
corrupt
counterfeit
culprit
felony
hijack
incriminate
repent
swindle

DEFINITIONS

After you have studied the definitions and example for each vocabulary word, write the word on the line to the right.

1. **acquit** (ə-kwĭt′) *verb* **a.** To free from a formal accusation of wrongdoing; find innocent. **b.** To release from a duty.

   RELATED WORD **acquittal** *noun*

   EXAMPLE The defendant was *acquitted* of the crime and released.

   1. _____

2. **arson** (är′sən) *noun* The crime of deliberately setting fire to buildings or other property. (From the Latin word *ardere*, meaning "to burn")

   RELATED WORD **arsonist** *noun*

   EXAMPLE The detective investigated the remains of the burned building for evidence of *arson*.

   2. _____

3. **corrupt** (kə-rŭpt′) *adjective* Immoral; dishonest; open to bribery.   *verb* To destroy someone's honesty or integrity. (From the Latin word *corrumpere*, meaning "to destroy")

   RELATED WORDS **corruptible** *adjective;* **corruption** *noun;* **corruptly** *adverb*

   EXAMPLE The *corrupt* politician awarded city contracts to people who gave him money secretly.

   3. _____

4. **counterfeit** (koun′tər-fĭt′) *verb* **a.** To make a copy of something, such as money, for a dishonest purpose. **b.** To make a pretense of. *noun* Something counterfeited. *adjective* Made in imitation of what is genuine in order to deceive. (From the Latin *contra-*, meaning "opposite," and *facere*, meaning "to make")

RELATED WORD **counterfeiter** *noun*

EXAMPLE The criminal *counterfeited* twenty-dollar bills on a special printing machine in the basement.

4. _____

5. **culprit** (kŭl′prĭt) *noun* A person guilty or accused of being guilty of a crime or offense.

EXAMPLE The store detective believed she knew who was the *culprit* in the theft.

5. _____

6. **felony** (fĕl′ə-nē) *noun* A serious crime such as murder or arson. (From the Medieval Latin word *fello*, meaning "villain")

RELATED WORD **felon** *noun*

EXAMPLE The thief received a ten-year prison sentence for the *felony*.

6. _____

7. **hijack** (hī′jăk′) *verb* To seize or take control of a vehicle or aircraft; steal goods from a vehicle.

RELATED WORD **hijacker** *noun*

EXAMPLE The outlaws *hijacked* the stagecoach and robbed the passengers.

7. _____

8. **incriminate** (ĭn-krĭm′ə-nāt′) *verb* To charge with or involve in a crime or other wrongful act. (From the Latin *in-*, meaning "in," and *crimen*, meaning "crime")

RELATED WORD **incrimination** *noun*

EXAMPLE The testimony of three witnesses *incriminated* the embezzler.

8. _____

9. **repent** (rĭ-pĕnt′) *verb* To feel or show regret for what one has done or failed to do.

RELATED WORDS **repentance** *noun;* **repentant** *adjective*

EXAMPLE Tom *repented* of bragging so much about his skill in football.

9. _____

10. **swindle** (swĭn′dl) *verb* **a.** To cheat or defraud someone of money or property. **b.** To obtain by practicing fraud. *noun* A dishonest act or scheme; a fraud. (From the Old High German word *swintan*, meaning "to vanish")

RELATED WORD **swindler** *noun*

EXAMPLE The bookkeeper *swindled* the firm out of thousands of dollars.

10. _____

Exercise 1   Writing Correct Words

On the answer line, write the word from the vocabulary list that fits each definition.

1. Deliberate burning of property

2. To cheat out of money or property

3. To accuse of or blame for a crime

4. Open to bribery; immoral

5. To make an imitation of something

6. To feel sorry for a wrongdoing

7. A serious crime

8. To capture a vehicle or aircraft

9. A person accused or guilty of a crime

10. To find innocent

1. _____ arson _____

2. _____ swindle _____

3. _____ incriminate _____

4. _____ corrupt _____

5. _____ counterfeit _____

6. _____ repent _____

7. _____ felony _____

8. _____ hijack _____

9. _____ culprit _____

10. _____ acquit _____

Exercise 2   Using Words Correctly

Decide whether the italicized vocabulary word or related form has been used correctly in the sentence. On the answer line, write *Correct* for correct use and *Incorrect* for incorrect use.

1. The *culprit* found the defendant guilty after a two-day trial.

2. An empty gasoline can led the police to suspect *arson*.

3. A salesperson *swindled* customers by selling empty lots in a swamp.

4. The *corrupt* manager took the company's funds and sailed to Australia.

5. The *repentant* criminal robbed a bank after leaving prison.

6. The jury *acquitted* the defendant because of a lack of evidence.

7. Airport security measures in the United States have made it difficult to *hijack* airplanes.

8. A person can be arrested if he or she *incriminates* someone else.

9. The dishonest artist misused his talent to *counterfeit* paintings.

10. Because the crime was only a *felony*, the judge dismissed the defendant with a warning.

1. _____ Incorrect _____

2. _____ Correct _____

3. _____ Correct _____

4. _____ Correct _____

5. _____ Incorrect _____

6. _____ Correct _____

7. _____ Correct _____

8. _____ Incorrect _____

9. _____ Correct _____

10. _____ Incorrect _____

Exercise 3   Choosing the Best Definition

For each italicized vocabulary word or related form in the following sentences, write the letter of the best definition on the answer line.

1. The defendant hoped that her alibi would fully *acquit* her.
   a. save   **b.** free   **c.** relax   **d.** harm

1. _____ b _____

2. A confidence game is the *swindle* of an unsuspecting person. **2.** _____c_____
   a. observation **b.** flattery **c.** cheating **d.** rewarding

3. Criminals often leave *incriminating* evidence at the scene of a crime. **3.** _____d_____
   a. very little **c.** designed to mislead others
   b. embarrassing **d.** telltale

4. The gangsters *hijacked* a large truck. **4.** _____b_____
   a. repaired **b.** robbed **c.** surprised **d.** detoured

5. The *culprit* in the mystery of the missing bananas was my
   five-year-old cousin. **5.** _____c_____
   a. hero **b.** detective **c.** guilty person **d.** victim

6. *Arson* is sometimes suspected as the cause of forest fires. **6.** _____a_____
   a. The crime of deliberately setting fire
   b. The stealing of property
   c. The invasion of tourists
   d. The falsification of documents

7. Edmund Burke wrote, "Among a people generally *corrupt*, liberty
   cannot long exist." **7.** _____d_____
   a. joyous **b.** unhappy **c.** lazy **d.** dishonest

8. Joel's unhappiness was obvious even though he tried to *counterfeit* a
   smile. **8.** _____c_____
   a. hide **b.** remember **c.** fake **d.** hold back

9. By burglarizing a house, the criminal committed a *felony*. **9.** _____a_____
   a. serious crime **c.** irrational act
   b. mild offense **d.** accidental crime

10. The *repentant* employee apologized for making a serious mistake. **10.** _____c_____
    a. sobbing **b.** shivering **c.** regretful **d.** happy

Exercise 4   Using Different Forms of Words

Decide which form of the vocabulary word in parentheses best completes the sentence. The form given may be correct. Write your answer on the answer line.

1. "Marry in haste, __?__ at leisure," wrote eighteenth-century English
   playwright William Congreve. *(repent)* **1.** _____repent_____

2. Convicted __?__ face heavy prison sentences. *(felony)* **2.** _____felons_____

3. Despite the defendant's __?__, many people still thought that he was
   guilty. *(acquit)* **3.** _____acquittal_____

4. The three __?__ moved to take control of the airplane. *(hijack)* **4.** _____hijackers_____

5. The mayor was indicted on charges of operating the city government
   __?__. *(corrupt)* **5.** _____corruptly_____

6. In a play entitled *The Firebugs*, Max Frisch wrote about two __?__.
   (arson) **6.** _____arsonists_____

7. __?__ were severely punished under old English law. *(counterfeit)* **7.** _____Counterfeiters_____

8. The __?__ was easy to find. *(culprit)* **8.** _____culprit_____

9. The lawyer read the __?__ letter to the jury. *(incriminate)* **9.** _____incriminating_____

10. In the Old West, __?__ were dealt with severely. *(swindle)* **10.** _____swindlers_____

Reading Comprehension

Each numbered sentence in the following passage contains an italicized vocabulary word or related form. After you read the passage, you will complete an exercise.

The Case of the Counterfeit Paintings

NARRATOR: The weekend guests of Lady Agatha Herringbone gather in the library to await the arrival of the world-famous detective, Hercules Parrot. (1) Everyone is shocked when Lady Agatha reveals that her priceless paintings are *counterfeits.* She believes that the counterfeit paintings were exchanged for the authentic ones during the weekend. (2) She also believes that one of the guests is the *culprit.* All look up anxiously as Parrot enters.

LADY AGATHA: Ah, Monsieur Parrot, I trust that your seven-course lunch was satisfactory. (3) Have you discovered any *incriminating* evidence about my guests?

PARROT: The answer to both questions is yes. You, Madame, are a poor judge of character. (4) The men and women in this room have committed *felonies.* They are perfect suspects.

LADY AGATHA: This is totally shocking! These people are my sister Emma's dearest friends. I'm only thankful that Emma is safely at the health spa in Germany. What proof do you have to make such accusations?

PARROT: Take Monsieur Jack, for example. (5) He is well known to Scotland Yard as an *arsonist.*

LADY AGATHA: Shocking news! Emma trusted you, Jack.

JACK: I'd burn those paintings, not steal them. That's all behind me now. I'm a reformed man.

PARROT: Sitting on the couch is Mademoiselle Louise. (6) She looks innocent enough, but Scotland Yard could tell you all about the time she *swindled* an elderly companion out of a great deal of money.

LADY AGATHA: Emma trusted you, Louise.

LOUISE: (7) If you'll remember, Monsieur, I was *acquitted* of that false accusation.

PARROT: There is one more case in point — that of Monsieur André. (8) Perhaps monsieur would like to tell about the time he attempted to *hijack* a plane and take it to Tahiti.

ANDRÉ: I apologized for the inconvenience.

LADY AGATHA: (9) Monsieur Parrot, which one of these *corrupt* villains took my paintings?

PARROT: None of them, Madame. (10) I believe them when they say they have *repented* of their crimes. What I do not believe is that your sister is at a health spa.

LADY AGATHA: Why . . . where is she, then?

PARROT: Making arrangements to sell the real paintings. You, Madame, have invited a roomful of reformed criminals, hoping to blame them for a crime that you yourself have planned from the beginning. Otherwise, why would you invite your sister's friends for a weekend when she is out of the country?

LADY AGATHA: Outrageous! Why would I steal my own paintings?

PARROT: For the insurance money, Madame, and also for the money received from the sale of the real paintings. Your ill-gotten funds will allow you to pay back taxes. I was expected to accuse the wrong suspect, but you have foolishly underestimated the cleverness of Hercules Parrot. Now, if you will excuse me, I must call Scotland Yard and prepare for my afternoon tea.

Please turn to the next page.

Reading Comprehension Exercise

Each of the following statements corresponds to a numbered sentence in the passage. Each statement contains a blank and is followed by four answer choices. Decide which choice fits best in the blank. The word or phrase that you choose must express roughly the same meaning as the italicized word in the passage. Write the letter of your choice on the answer line.

1. Lady Agatha discovered that her paintings were __?__ .
   a. masterpieces   **b.** imitations   **c.** lost   **d.** expensive

1. ___b___

2. She thought that one of the guests was the __?__ .
   a. detective   **b.** murderer   **c.** hijacker   **d.** wrongdoer

2. ___d___

3. Lady Agatha asked whether any evidence __?__ had been discovered.
   a. that proved guilt   **c.** that was permanent
   b. that was visible   **d.** that showed innocence

3. ___a___

4. Hercules Parrot pointed out that all the guests had committed __?__ .
   a. pranks   **b.** major crimes   **c.** bad deeds   **d.** minor crimes

4. ___b___

5. For example, Monsieur Jack had been __?__ .
   a. an enjoyer of life   **c.** a setter of fires
   b. a thief   **d.** a borrower of paintings

5. ___c___

6. Mademoiselle Louise had __?__ an elderly companion.
   a. supported   **b.** injured   **c.** abandoned   **d.** cheated

6. ___d___

7. Mademoiselle Louise reminded Parrot that she had been __?__ .
   a. accused   **b.** punished   **c.** cleared   **d.** imprisoned

7. ___c___

8. Hercules Parrot then revealed that Monsieur André had tried to __?__ a plane.
   a. catch   **b.** fly in   **c.** disable   **d.** seize

8. ___d___

9. Lady Agatha asked which __?__ guest took her paintings.
   a. dishonest   **b.** desperate   **c.** foolish   **d.** carefree

9. ___a___

10. Hercules Parrot felt that the suspects __?__ about their crimes.
    a. were glad   **c.** were relieved
    b. were sorry   **d.** were indifferent

10. ___b___

Writing Assignment

Imagine that you are a successful television scriptwriter. Your assignment is to create a story that deals with crime and justice. Write a summary that briefly explains the main characters, settings, and plot of your story. Include five words from this lesson and underline each one.

Lesson 18

Error and Confusion

Alexander Pope, an eighteenth-century writer, commented in one of his poems that "to err is human." Certainly, people try to do their best, but everybody makes mistakes. Some errors are minor and are corrected easily, such as a misspelled word. Other errors may be more serious but may still have positive results. For example, Alexander Fleming made the mistake of exposing to the air a bacteria culture that he was studying. The mistake, though, led to his discovery of penicillin.

Each of the words in this lesson deals with some form of error or confusion. You will find these words useful in describing behavior typical of all of us at various times.

WORD LIST
amiss
bewilder
blunder
erroneous
fallible
faux pas
fluster
miscalculate
misinterpret
overestimate

DEFINITIONS

After you have studied the definitions and example for each vocabulary word, write the word on the line to the right.

1. **amiss** (ə-mĭs′) *adjective* Out of proper order; wrong; faulty. *adverb* In an improper or defective way.

   EXAMPLE   Lucinda knew immediately that something in the room was *amiss;* on closer examination she saw that the furniture had been rearranged.

1. _____

USAGE NOTE *To take amiss* is an idiom that means "to misunderstand" or "to feel offended by."

2. **bewilder** (bĭ-wĭl′dər) *verb* To confuse or befuddle, especially with numerous conflicting situations, objects, or statements.

   RELATED WORD   **bewilderment** *noun*

   EXAMPLE   The noise and traffic of the busy street *bewildered* the tourist.

2. _____

3. **blunder** (blŭn′dər) *noun* A serious mistake, usually caused by ignorance or confusion.   *verb* **a.** To botch or bungle; say stupidly or thoughtlessly. **b.** To move awkwardly or clumsily; stumble. (From the Middle English word *blunderen,* meaning "to go blindly")

   EXAMPLE   Buying the worthless automobile was a *blunder* that cost Malcolm several thousand dollars.

3. _____

4. **erroneous** (ĭ-rō′nē-əs) *adjective* Wrong; mistaken; false. (From the Latin word *errare,* meaning "to wander")

   RELATED WORD   **erroneously** *adverb*

   EXAMPLE   There were several *erroneous* conclusions in the detective's report.

4. _____

SEE *fallible.*

Error and Confusion   **113**

5. fallible (făl′ə-bəl) *adjective* Likely to be wrong; capable of making an error. (From the Latin word *fallere*, meaning "to cause to fall" or "to deceive")

RELATED WORD **fallibility** *noun*

EXAMPLE All human beings are *fallible;* no one is perfect.

5. _____

USAGE NOTE *Erroneous* means that something is definitely wrong, whereas *fallible* means that someone or something is capable of being wrong.

6. faux pas (fō-pä′) *noun* A minor social error that may cause embarrassment. (From the French phrase *faux pas,* meaning "false step")

EXAMPLE Selma made a *faux pas* when she ate her salad with her dinner fork.

6. _____

7. fluster (flŭs′tər) *verb* To make nervous, excited, or confused. *noun* A state of agitation or confusion.

EXAMPLE Simon *flustered* Lila when he complimented her on her haircut.

7. _____

8. miscalculate (mĭs-kăl′kyə-lāt′) *verb* **a.** To make a wrong estimate of; make an error in judgment. **b.** To compute numbers incorrectly. (From the Latin *mis-,* meaning "wrong," and *calculus,* meaning "a stone used for counting")

RELATED WORD **miscalculation** *noun*

EXAMPLE The television producer *miscalculated* the appeal of the new program.

8. _____

9. misinterpret (mĭs′ĭn-tûr′prĭt) *verb* To draw a wrong conclusion from; understand incorrectly.

RELATED WORD **misinterpretation** *noun*

EXAMPLE Lionel *misinterpreted* Ms. Nelson's message and drove to the airport at the wrong time to pick her up.

9. _____

10. overestimate (ō′vər-ĕs′tə-māt′) *verb* To rate, value, or esteem too highly.

RELATED WORD **overestimation** *noun*

EXAMPLE Erica often feels that her coach *overestimates* her ability to make the Olympic team.

10. _____

Exercise 1 Completing Definitions

On the answer line, write the word from the vocabulary list that best completes each definition.

1. If you value or rate something too highly, you __?__ it.

2. If you compute numbers incorrectly or if you make an error in judgment, you __?__ .

3. If you understand something incorrectly, you __?__ it.

4. To make nervous, upset, or confused is to __?__ .

5. Something out of proper order is __?__ .

6. An embarrassing social error is a __?__ .

7. To confuse or befuddle is to __?__ .

8. If someone is capable of error or likely to be wrong, the person is __?__ .

9. A serious mistake caused by ignorance or confusion is a __?__ .

10. If something is wrong, mistaken, or false, it is __?__ .

1. overestimate
2. miscalculate
3. misinterpret
4. fluster
5. amiss
6. faux pas
7. bewilder
8. fallible
9. blunder
10. erroneous

Exercise 2 Using Words Correctly

Each of the following questions contains an italicized vocabulary word. Decide the answer to the question, and write *Yes* or *No* on the answer line.

1. Is a *faux pas* a serious mistake?

2. Is an *erroneous* answer incorrect?

3. Is a *fallible* person perfect?

4. If you compute numbers incorrectly, do you necessarily *overestimate?*

5. If you *misinterpret* a statement, do you misunderstand it?

6. If something is *amiss,* is it in its proper place?

7. Is a *blunder* a minor error in mathematics?

8. If you are *bewildered* by something, are you confused?

9. If you make an error in judgment, do you *miscalculate?*

10. If you *fluster* someone, do you make that person nervous or upset?

1. No
2. Yes
3. No
4. No
5. Yes
6. No
7. No
8. Yes
9. Yes
10. Yes

Exercise 3 Choosing the Best Word

Decide which vocabulary word or related form best completes the sentence, and write the letter of your choice on the answer line.

1. The police searched the room carefully but found nothing __?__ .
   a. fallible   **b.** flustered   **c.** bewildered   **d.** amiss

   1. d

2. People's use of erasers shows that they are __?__ .
   a. flustered   **b.** fallible   **c.** amiss   **d.** bewildered

   2. b

Error and Confusion   **115**

3. Michael made a __?__ by forgetting to introduce his mother to his friends.
   a. miscalculation **b.** fluster **c.** faux pas **d.** overestimation

3. _____c_____

4. Michael then exaggerated his error, saying "Oh, what a __?__ !"
   a. miscalculation **b.** blunder **c.** faux pas **d.** overestimation

4. _____b_____

5. Helga was __?__ when she forgot her lines.
   a. flustered **c.** overestimated
   b. erroneous **d.** miscalculated

5. _____a_____

6. The highways in and around Los Angeles can __?__ many a visitor.
   a. miscalculate **b.** misinterpret **c.** bewilder **d.** blunder

6. _____c_____

7. Before the time of Copernicus, most people held the __?__ view that Earth was the center of the solar system.
   a. erroneous **b.** overestimated **c.** bewildered **d.** flustered

7. _____a_____

8. David __?__ the amount of time that remained for finishing the test.
   a. bewildered **b.** flustered **c.** blundered **d.** miscalculated

8. _____d_____

9. Researchers who __?__ their information may draw conclusions that are false.
   a. blunder **b.** misinterpret **c.** bewilder **d.** fluster

9. _____b_____

10. Jessica __?__ her strength when she attempted to carry both bags of groceries at once.
    a. bewildered **b.** flustered **c.** overestimated **d.** blundered

10. _____c_____

Exercise 4 Using Different Forms of Words

Decide which form of the vocabulary word in parentheses best completes the sentence. The form given may be correct. Write your answer on the answer line.

1. Written sentences without punctuation are often open to __?__ . *(misinterpret)*

1. _____misinterpretation_____

2. The student took __?__ the teacher's well-intentioned criticism. *(amiss)*

2. _____amiss_____

3. A person who __?__ is frequently compared to a bull in a china shop. *(blunder)*

3. _____blunders_____

4. During an election campaign, a __?__ can cost a candidate hundreds of votes. *(faux pas)*

4. _____faux pas_____

5. Many animals try to __?__ their enemies by making threatening gestures before an attack. *(fluster)*

5. _____fluster_____

6. In 1948 some newspapers __?__ reported that Thomas Dewey had defeated Harry Truman for the presidency. *(erroneous)*

6. _____erroneously_____

7. Instant replays of sporting events sometimes show the __?__ of the officials. *(fallible)*

7. _____fallibility_____

8. To untrained people, Morse code is a __?__ collection of dots and dashes. *(bewilder)*

8. _____bewildering_____

9. We definitely __?__ the intelligence of our dog, who could not even learn to fetch the newspaper. *(overestimate)*

9. _____overestimated_____

10. __?__ of timing and distance can cause a trapeze artist to fall into the safety net. *(Miscalculate)*

10. _____Miscalculation_____

Reading Comprehension

Each numbered sentence in the following passage contains an italicized vocabulary word or related form. After you read the passage, you will complete an exercise.

Tulipomania

It is difficult to believe that the tulip, one of the most popular and beautiful spring flowers, was once the cause of a national scandal and an economic disaster. *Tulpenwoede,* or tulipomania, overtook Holland between 1633 and 1637.

The Viennese ambassador to Turkey introduced the onionlike bulbs, which actually belong to the lily family, to the Western world. In 1562 the arrival at Antwerp, Belgium, of a cargo of the bulbs marked the beginning of a new flower-cultivation industry. Soon the tulip, whose name comes from the Turkish word for turban, became the most fashionable flower in Europe.

The demand for new varieties of tulips gradually exceeded the supply. Unusual flowers were particularly costly. **(1)** One tulip fancier in Holland **erroneously** paid too high a price for a spectacular specimen. **(2)** News of his costly **blunder** spread quickly to bulb sellers, and within weeks nearly everyone in Holland was trading in tulips. Special markets sprang up just for buying and selling bulbs. A single bulb of a new variety became acceptable as the dowry for a bride. One person traded a flourishing factory for a tulip bulb. **(3)** The financial **miscalculation** that started this tulip madness caused homes and industries to be mortgaged so that more

flower bulbs could be purchased and resold at increasingly higher prices. The expectation that there was always someone willing to pay more for tulip bulbs supported tulipomania.

A story about a sailor and a shopkeeper illustrates what happened during the five years of tulip madness. One morning a sailor purchased a herring for his breakfast. Left alone while the shopkeeper went into his storeroom, the sailor noticed a delicious-looking onion, which was actually a tulip bulb. He took it and sliced it

to eat with his herring. **(4)** The merchant returned and noticed something was **amiss,** for his rare tulip bulb was gone. **(5)** Extremely **flustered,** he got the police and rushed after the sailor. **(6)** Imagine how **bewildered** the sailor was when he learned that his breakfast had cost him more than a thousand dollars!

People sold and resold tulip bulbs many times without the bulbs leaving the ground or the flowers being seen by their buyers. When a single bulb reached the astounding price of three thousand florins — a sum large enough to feed an entire family for a year — the tulip market crashed. **(7)** Suddenly, people realized that they had **overestimated** the value of the flower. Everyone began to sell tulips, and prices fell faster than they had risen.

(8) When it was all over, many people had lost fortunes by **misinterpreting** the trends in prices. **(9)** The few who had made money kept quiet about their good fortune, for it was considered a **faux pas** even to mention tulips.

(10) The story of tulipomania reminds us that human beings are **fallible.** No person has good judgment all the time. The Dutch continue to grow tulips and to export them, but no one since 1637 has paid a thousand dollars for one bulb.

Please turn to the next page.

Reading Comprehension Exercise

Each of the following statements corresponds to a numbered sentence in the passage. Each statement contains a blank and is followed by four answer choices. Decide which choice fits best in the blank. The word or phrase that you choose must express roughly the same meaning as the italicized word in the passage. Write the letter of your choice on the answer line.

1. One tulip buyer __?__ paid a high price for a spectacular bulb.
   a. thoughtlessly   **b.** ridiculously   **c.** quickly   **d.** mistakenly

1. _____d_____

2. News of his costly __?__ spread quickly.
   a. mistake   **b.** plan   **c.** bulbs   **d.** trick

2. _____a_____

3. A financial __?__ started tulip madness.
   a. greediness   **c.** panic
   b. error in judgment   **d.** need for flowers

3. _____b_____

4. The merchant realized something was __?__ when he saw that his rare bulb was gone.
   a. wrong   **b.** right   **c.** clear   **d.** moved

4. _____a_____

5. Feeling very __?__ , he got the police and went after the sailor.
   a. serious   **b.** wrong   **c.** upset   **d.** hungry

5. _____c_____

6. The sailor was __?__ when he learned about his expensive breakfast.
   a. angry   **b.** confused   **c.** incorrect   **d.** sorry

6. _____b_____

7. People realized that they had __?__ tulips.
   a. underpriced   **c.** overrated
   b. forgotten   **d.** found the right market for

7. _____c_____

8. People had __?__ the trends in tulip prices.
   a. wrongly judged   **c.** changed
   b. destroyed   **d.** accurately explained

8. _____a_____

9. After tulipomania, it was a __?__ even to mention the subject of tulips.
   a. serious mistake   **c.** bad judgment
   b. social error   **d.** financial loss

9. _____b_____

10. The story of tulipomania illustrates that people are __?__ .
    a. capable of perfection   **c.** funny
    b. able to make money   **d.** capable of error

10. _____d_____

Practice with Analogies

DIRECTIONS On the answer line, write the vocabulary word that completes each analogy.

See page 119 for some strategies to use with analogies.

1. Right is to wrong as correct is to __?__ .

1. _____erroneous_____

2. Naive is to gullible as imperfect is to __?__ .

2. _____fallible_____

3. Save is to spend as underrate is to __?__ .

3. _____overestimate_____

4. Enlighten is to bewilder as calm is to __?__ .

4. _____fluster_____

5. Minor is to faux pas as serious is to __?__ .

5. _____blunder_____

6. Miscalculate is to error as __?__ is to misunderstanding.

6. _____misinterpret_____

Use the clues to spell out the words on the answer blanks. Then identify
the mystery person at the bottom of the page by writing the numbered
letters on the lines with the corresponding numbers.

1. $\underset{3}{A}$ R S O N comes from a Latin word meaning "to burn."

2. Criminals try to $\underset{1}{C}$ O U N T E R F E I T money.

3. In French, a "false step" is a(n) F A U $\underset{14}{X}$ P A S .

4. Murder or burglary is considered a(n) F E L $\underset{7}{O}$ N Y .

5. Leaving her wallet at home was a(n) B L U $\underset{11}{N}$ D E R that Hannah never
made again.

6. To REPENT is to show R E G R E $\underset{6}{T}$ for what one has done.

7. Airlines have taken precautions to prevent planes from being seized by

$\underset{2}{H}$ I J A C K E R S .

8. Fingerprints may $\underset{4}{I}$ N C R I M I N A T E a suspect.

9. To value too highly is to O V E $\underset{9}{R}$ E S T I M A T E .

10. A politician who takes bribes is C O R R U $\underset{8}{P}$ T .

11. A large audience may F $\underset{10}{L}$ U S T E R an inexperienced speaker.

12. If you $\underset{12}{M}$ I S I N T E R P R E T a statement, you draw wrong
conclusions about it.

13. C O N F U $\underset{5}{S}$ E is a synonym for BEWILDER.

14. F A L L I $\underset{13}{B}$ L E means "capable of making errors."

$\underset{1}{C}$ $\underset{2}{H}$ $\underset{3}{R}$ $\underset{4}{I}$ $\underset{5}{S}$ $\underset{6}{T}$ $\underset{7}{O}$ $\underset{8}{P}$ $\underset{2}{H}$ $\underset{9}{E}$ $\underset{3}{R}$ $\underset{1}{C}$ $\underset{7}{O}$ $\underset{10}{L}$ $\underset{11}{U}$ $\underset{12}{M}$ $\underset{13}{B}$ $\underset{11}{U}$ $\underset{5}{S}$,

$\underset{9}{E}$ $\underset{14}{X}$ $\underset{8}{P}$ $\underset{10}{L}$ $\underset{7}{O}$ $\underset{3}{R}$ $\underset{9}{E}$ $\underset{3}{R}$

BONUS

Lessons 17 and 18

Notes

The following lists of words are from the preceding two lessons. You may wish to use these lists to pinpoint words for ongoing review or for mid-term or final exams.

Lesson 17

acquit	felony
arson	hijack
corrupt	incriminate
counterfeit	repent
culprit	swindle

Lesson 18

amiss	faux pas
bewilder	fluster
blunder	miscalculate
erroneous	misinterpret
fallible	overestimate

Test: Lessons 16, 17, and 18

(pages 101–118)

Part A   Completing the Definition

On the answer line, write the letter of the word or phrase that correctly completes each sentence.

1. If a moving vehicle has been *hijacked*, it has been __?__ .
   a. damaged   b. seized   c. rented   d. towed

   1. ____b____

2. To *misinterpret* something is to __?__ it.
   a. translate   b. comply with   c. misunderstand   d. simplify

   2. ____c____

3. A *conservative* attitude is __?__ .
   a. traditional   b. silly   c. generous   d. modest

   3. ____a____

4. Someone who has committed a *felony* is responsible for __?__ .
   a. an act of devotion   c. charitable contributions
   b. a minor offense   d. a serious crime

   4. ____d____

5. If you __?__ someone, you have *flustered* him or her.
   a. confuse   b. amuse   c. ignore   d. laugh at

   5. ____a____

6. *Anarchy* is a state of __?__ .
   a. happiness   b. disorder   c. indecision   d. harmony

   6. ____b____

7. One who *swindles* others __?__ them.
   a. entertains   b. compliments   c. cheats   d. interacts with

   7. ____c____

8. If you are guilty of a *faux pas,* you have made a(n) __?__ .
   a. investment   b. social error   c. close friend   d. change

   8. ____b____

9. To have *dominion* over something is to __?__ it.
   a. be nervous about   b. have power over   c. ignore   d. deny

   9. ____b____

10. When you *repent* you __?__ .
    a. show regret   b. protect others   c. hurry   d. argue

    10. ____a____

11. If you *miscalculate* something, you __?__ it.
    a. comprehend   c. voluntarily donate
    b. locate   d. incorrectly estimate

    11. ____d____

12. An *authoritarian* person __?__ .
    a. is an expert   c. expects strict obedience
    b. charms others   d. is a talented performer

    12. ____c____

13. To *incriminate* someone is to __?__ .
    a. clear the person's reputation
    b. recommend the person for promotion
    c. involve the person in a crime
    d. shock the person

    13. ____c____

14. If you *overestimate* something, you __?__ .
    a. rate it too highly   b. notice it   c. waste it   d. lose it

    14. ____a____

15. A *delegate* is a(n) __?__ .
    a. wanderer   b. official   c. philosopher   d. representative

    15. ____d____

HOUGHTON MIFFLIN VOCABULARY FOR ACHIEVEMENT, SECOND COURSE

Test: Lessons 16, 17, and 18

Part B Choosing the Best Word

On the answer line, write the letter of the word that best expresses the meaning of the italicized word or phrase.

16. The poem "The Charge of the Light Brigade" tells of men who suffered because someone had *made a serious mistake.*
    a. repented   **b.** flustered   **c.** misinterpreted   **d.** blundered

16. _____ d

17. The cause of the blaze was *the crime of deliberately setting fires.*
    a. a faux pas   **b.** a felony   **c.** arson   **d.** anarchy

17. _____ c

18. Private Johnson adjusted to the *simple and self-disciplined* existence of boot camp.
    a. Spartan   **b.** conservative   **c.** corrupt   **d.** authoritarian

18. _____ a

19. The lawyer proved that the testimony was *false.*
    a. erroneous   **c.** bewildering
    b. misinterpreted   **d.** conservative

19. _____ a

20. Uriah Heep, the *immoral* acquaintance of David Copperfield, was imprisoned.
    a. Spartan   **b.** tyrannical   **c.** corrupt   **d.** fallible

20. _____ c

21. The senate agreed not to *accuse of unacceptable conduct in office* the governor.
    a. impeach   **b.** acquit   **c.** incriminate   **d.** bewilder

21. _____ a

22. The engineers admitted that they were *capable of making an error.*
    a. corrupt   **b.** fallible   **c.** amiss   **d.** counterfeit

22. _____ b

23. The defendant was *freed from formal accusation of wrongdoing.*
    a. bewildered   **b.** impeached   **c.** incriminated   **d.** acquitted

23. _____ d

24. Anne sprinkled her cereal with a *generous in amount* helping of raisins.
    a. fallible   **b.** liberal   **c.** conservative   **d.** Spartan

24. _____ b

25. Nico realized that something was *out of proper order.*
    a. amiss   **b.** authoritarian   **c.** liberal   **d.** corrupt

25. _____ a

26. "Who is the *person guilty of an offense* who ate all the popcorn?" asked Dad.
    a. delegate   **b.** culprit   **c.** Spartan   **d.** tyrant

26. _____ b

27. Pisistratus was an *oppressor* who controlled Athens during the sixth century B.C.
    a. culprit   **b.** delegate   **c.** tyrant   **d.** Spartan

27. _____ c

28. Alice was *befuddled* by the actions of the White Rabbit.
    a. conservative   **b.** bewildered   **c.** flustered   **d.** corrupt

28. _____ b

29. The police discovered two rooms of *dishonestly copied* designer clothes.
    a. fallible   **b.** corrupt   **c.** hijacked   **d.** counterfeit

29. _____ d

30. The alliance between the countries *initiated* an era of prosperity.
    a. incriminated   **b.** bewildered   **c.** inaugurated   **d.** impeached

30. _____ c

Test-Taking Skills

Analogy Tests

Analogy items on vocabulary tests and standardized examinations measure your ability to understand relationships between words. An **analogy** is a similarity between things that are otherwise dissimilar. A word analogy is usually given in this form: Word A is to Word B as Word C is to Word D. The following strategies will help you answer analogy test items.

STRATEGIES

1. *Determine the relationship between the given words.* In the following example, you must understand the relationship between *school* and *fish* before you can answer the item.

   School is to fish as
   (A) calf is to cow   (B) pork is to pig
   (C) herd is to elephant   (D) house is to brick
   (E) dog is to pack

   A school is a group of fish. The relationship between the two words is that of a group to a single member of the group. You must look for the answer choice that expresses the same or a similar relationship. The correct answer is (C). A herd is a group of a single kind of animal, either domesticated or wild.

2. *Watch for reversed elements in answer choices.* In the example above, *dog is to pack* is similar to *school is to fish* because a pack is a group of dogs. However, the school-fish relationship is group to a single member of the group. It is not single member (dog) to group (pack). Thus, the only correct answer is herd (group) to elephant (single member).

3. *Examine all answer choices to make sure that you have selected the best one.* The following example shows you the importance of reading all answer choices.

   Bread is to sandwich as carrot is to
   (F) garden   (G) root   (H) dinner   (J) vegetable   (K) stew

   Dinner might seem to be the correct choice. Bread is an ingredient in a sandwich, and a carrot can be an ingredient in a dinner. Dinner, however, is an entire meal, while a sandwich is a kind of food. Stew is a kind of food, and a carrot is an ingredient. Carrot—stew expresses a closer relationship to bread—sandwich and is therefore the correct choice.

   Please turn to the next page.

Exercise **Identifying Analogies**

Find the relationship between the words in the first part of each sentence, and choose the answer that shows the same relationship or a similar one. Write the letter of your choice on the answer line. Use your dictionary as needed.

1. May is to spring as
   (A) warm is to rainy
   (B) January is to cold
   (C) October is to fall
   (D) August is to September
   (E) fall is to winter

   1. _____ C _____

2. Fierce is to lion as
   (F) cow is to docile
   (G) red is to fox
   (H) pack is to wolf
   (J) burrow is to prairie dog
   (K) loyal is to dog

   2. _____ K _____

3. Nose is to smell as
   (A) ear is to hearing
   (B) taste is to tongue
   (C) nerve is to body
   (D) face is to limb
   (E) sense is to organ

   3. _____ A _____

4. Iris is to flower as gull is to
   (F) fish   (G) ocean   (H) flight   (J) bird   (K) water

   4. _____ J _____

5. Lamb is to ram as
   (A) fry is to trout
   (B) chick is to rooster
   (C) calf is to cow
   (D) cub is to scout
   (E) child is to parent

   5. _____ B _____

6. Newspaper is to information as
   (F) book is to print
   (G) television is to electronics
   (H) ink is to paper
   (J) recording is to music
   (K) editor is to writer

   6. _____ J _____

7. Carpenter is to saw as
   (A) hammer is to nails
   (B) professor is to student
   (C) music is to note
   (D) secretary is to typewriter
   (E) easel is to artist

   7. _____ D _____

8. Graduation is to school as
   (F) party is to work
   (G) summer is to classes
   (H) retirement is to work
   (J) end is to beginning
   (K) report card is to grades

   8. _____ H _____

9. Grammar is to language as
   (A) talking is to writing
   (B) rules are to sports
   (C) minutes are to hour
   (D) fun is to play
   (E) work is to leisure

   9. _____ B _____

10. Joy is to elation as
    (F) sadness is to misery
    (G) happiness is to completeness
    (H) despair is to bliss
    (J) delight is to displeasure
    (K) temper is to anger

   10. _____ F _____

Lesson 19

Abundance and Extravagance

At times everyone overdoes things. Which of the following extravagances can you plead guilty to?

Seeing the same movie seven times
Overeating at a holiday dinner
Monopolizing the telephone for two hours straight
Spending all your hard-earned money on an outfit that you'll wear only once
Listening to a favorite record two hundred times

In this lesson you will study words that will help you understand and explain the tendency that people have to overdo things.

WORD LIST
embellish
exceed
glut
immoderate
intense
lavish
luxurious
outrageous
profuse
spendthrift

DEFINITIONS

After you have studied the definitions and example for each vocabulary word, write the word on the line to the right.

1. **embellish** (ĕm-bĕl′ĭsh) *verb* **a.** To make beautiful by decoration. **b.** To add fanciful or fictitious details to; exaggerate. (From the Latin *in-*, meaning "in," and *bellus*, meaning "beautiful")
   RELATED WORD **embellishment** *noun*
   EXAMPLE The students *embellished* the bulletin board by adding artwork.

1. _____

2. **exceed** (ĭk-sēd′) *verb* **a.** To go beyond reasonable limits; do more than. **b.** To be greater than. (From the Latin *ex-*, meaning "out," and *cedere*, meaning "to go")
   RELATED WORD **exceedingly** *adverb*
   EXAMPLE Cynthia's dreams greatly *exceeded* the realities of her life.

2. _____
SEE *immoderate.*

3. **glut** (glŭt) *verb* **a.** To fill, feed, or eat beyond capacity; stuff. **b.** To oversupply a market with goods. *noun* An oversupply. (From the Latin word *gluttire*, meaning "to eat greedily")
   RELATED WORDS **glutton** *noun;* **gluttonous** *adjective;* **gluttony** *noun*
   EXAMPLE The guests *glutted* themselves with food at Thanksgiving dinner.

3. _____

4. immoderate (ĭ-mŏd′ər-ĭt) *adjective* Done to an extreme; not within reasonable limits; excessive. (From the Latin *in-*, meaning "not," and *moderatus*, meaning "moderate")

RELATED WORD **immoderately** *adverb*

EXAMPLE "Ten hours of straight television watching is an *immoderate* amount," Mrs. Wilson said sharply to Stanley.

5. intense (ĭn-tĕns′) *adjective* **a.** Deeply felt: *an intense emotion.* **b.** Very deep, strong, forceful, or concentrated: *an intense color or odor.* (From the Latin *in-*, meaning "into," and *tendere*, meaning "to stretch")

RELATED WORDS **intensify** *verb;* **intensity** *noun;* **intensive** *adjective*

EXAMPLE Linda's tormented expression revealed her *intense* feelings about finishing last in the race.

6. lavish (lăv′ĭsh) *adjective* **a.** Extravagantly plentiful: *lavish refreshments.* **b.** Generous or free in giving or using: *lavish praise.* *verb* To give or spend to excess. (From the Old French word *lavasse*, meaning "downpour")

RELATED WORDS **lavishly** *adverb;* **lavishness** *noun*

EXAMPLE Bob was embarrassed by his friend's *lavish* compliments.

7. luxurious (lŭg-zhŏŏr′ē-əs) *adjective* Marked by luxury or showy, expensive magnificence. (From the Latin word *luxus*, meaning "overindulgence")

RELATED WORDS **luxuriantly** *adverb;* **luxuriate** *verb;* **luxury** *noun*

EXAMPLE Helen enjoyed the *luxurious* texture of her new angora sweater.

8. outrageous (out-rā′jəs) *adjective* Going beyond all limits of what is right or proper; shocking; monstrous. (From the Old French word *outre*, meaning "beyond")

RELATED WORDS **outrage** *noun;* **outrageously** *adverb*

EXAMPLE The audience laughed uproariously at the comic actor's *outrageous* stunts in the film.

9. profuse (prə-fyōōs′) *adjective* **a.** Large in quantity; abundant. **b.** Giving or given generously. (From the Latin *pro-*, meaning "forward," and *fundere*, meaning "to pour")

RELATED WORDS **profusely** *adverb;* **profusion** *noun*

EXAMPLE For the head table at the banquet, the florist created a *profuse* flower arrangement.

10. spendthrift (spĕnd′thrĭft′) *noun* A person who spends money wastefully or foolishly. *adjective* Wasteful; extravagant.

EXAMPLE The *spendthrift* found it impossible to save money.

Name _____ Date _____

Exercise 1 Writing Correct Words

On the answer line, write the word from the vocabulary list that fits each definition.

1. Concentrated or strong; deeply felt

2. One who wastes money

3. Magnificent in a showy way

4. To make beautiful with decoration

5. Excessive; extreme

6. Shocking; going beyond the limit of what is proper

7. Extravagantly plentiful

8. To go beyond reasonable limits

9. Large in quantity; abundant

10. To fill, feed, or eat beyond capacity

1. _____ intense _____

2. _____ spendthrift _____

3. _____ luxurious _____

4. _____ embellish _____

5. _____ immoderate _____

6. _____ outrageous _____

7. _____ lavish _____

8. _____ exceed _____

9. _____ profuse _____

10. _____ glut _____

Exercise 2 Using Words Correctly

Decide whether the italicized vocabulary word has been used correctly in the sentence. On the answer line, write *Correct* for correct use and *Incorrect* for incorrect use.

1. Showing bare legs in public was *outrageous* behavior in the nineteenth century.

2. Claude ate an *immoderate* amount for dinner because he wasn't very hungry.

3. The patient's *profuse* bleeding greatly concerned the doctor.

4. Jennifer *embellished* the walls by putting up several paintings.

5. Because the game was so difficult, Ken played it with *intense* concentration.

6. The hotel seemed very *luxurious* to the people who had been camping by the lake.

7. If someone *exceeds* the speed limit, he or she is driving too slowly.

8. The *spendthrift* found it easy to save money.

9. A trickle of water *glutted* the pipes.

10. A seven-course meal might be described as *lavish*.

1. _____ Correct _____

2. _____ Incorrect _____

3. _____ Correct _____

4. _____ Correct _____

5. _____ Correct _____

6. _____ Correct _____

7. _____ Incorrect _____

8. _____ Incorrect _____

9. _____ Incorrect _____

10. _____ Correct _____

Exercise 3 Choosing the Best Definition

For each italicized vocabulary word or related form in the following sentences, write the letter of the best definition on the answer line.

1. The movie star was uncomfortable under the *intense* studio lights.
   a. pale   **b.** irritating   **c.** gloomy   **d.** strong

1. _____ d _____

Abundance and Extravagance **123**

2. Julia's *outrageous* remarks embarrassed her mother.
   a. loud   **b.** serious   **c.** shocking   **d.** humorous

   2. _____c_____

3. Tom *embellished* the details of his simple vacation.
   a. invented   **b.** remembered   **c.** described   **d.** exaggerated

   3. _____d_____

4. *Profuse* recommendations from past employers helped Doug to find a new job.
   a. Generous   **b.** Sincere   **c.** Written   **d.** Personal

   4. _____a_____

5. The prices of computers fell because too many products *glutted* the market.
   a. emptied   **b.** oversupplied   **c.** broke   **d.** missed

   5. _____b_____

6. Esther received *luxurious* accommodations at the inn.
   a. shabby   **b.** ancient   **c.** magnificent   **d.** cramped

   6. _____c_____

7. Carl drives his new sports car at an *immoderate* speed.
   a. experimental   **b.** extreme   **c.** suitable   **d.** controlled

   7. _____b_____

8. Jack promised to stop being a *spendthrift*.
   a. money saver   **b.** banker   **c.** consumer   **d.** money waster

   8. _____d_____

9. The O'Neals held a *lavish* party that included a live band.
   a. extravagant   **b.** fun-filled   **c.** amusing   **d.** routine

   9. _____a_____

10. Tenderhearted Rebecca is *exceedingly* kind to her pets.
    a. never   **b.** occasionally   **c.** extremely   **d.** sometimes

    10. _____c_____

Exercise 4   Using Different Forms of Words

Decide which form of the vocabulary word in parentheses best completes the sentence. The form given may be correct. Write your answer on the answer line.

1. The __?__ of the heat caused the campers to back away from the fire. *(intense)*

   1. _____intensity_____

2. "This is an __?__ !" exclaimed Mr. Franz as he looked at his plumbing bill. *(outrageous)*

   2. _____outrage_____

3. Friends called Henry a __?__ after he ordered a third dessert. *(glut)*

   3. _____glutton_____

4. Patricia, who is usually sensible, becomes a __?__ in her favorite record store. *(spendthrift)*

   4. _____spendthrift_____

5. "You have __?__ my wildest expectations," Mary's piano teacher told her. *(exceed)*

   5. _____exceeded_____

6. The __?__ of the decorations impressed the Tuttles. *(lavish)*

   6. _____lavishness_____

7. The interior decorator hoped to add many __?__ to the expensive mansion. *(embellish)*

   7. _____embellishments_____

8. Keeping fresh flowers in the house was Joanna's only __?__ . *(luxurious)*

   8. _____luxury_____

9. Sylvia was perspiring __?__ after running ten miles. *(profuse)*

   9. _____profusely_____

10. Eating __?__ caused Jonathan to gain ten pounds in two weeks. *(immoderate)*

    10. _____immoderately_____

Reading Comprehension

Each numbered sentence in the following passage contains an italicized vocabulary word or related form. After you read the passage, you will complete an exercise.

The Royal Spendthrifts

King Louis XVI and Queen Marie Antoinette ruled France from 1774 to 1789, a time when the country was fighting bankruptcy. **(1)** The royal couple did not let France's insecure financial situation limit their **immoderate** spending, however. Even though the minister of finance repeatedly warned the king and queen against wasting money, they continued to spend great fortunes on their personal pleasure. **(2)** This **lavish** spending greatly enraged the people of France. **(3)** They felt that the royal couple bought its **luxurious** lifestyle at the poor people's expense.

(4) Marie Antoinette, the beautiful but **exceedingly** impractical queen, seemed uncaring about her subjects' misery. **(5)** While French citizens begged for lower taxes, the queen **embellished** her palace with extravagant works of art. **(6)** She also surrounded herself with artists, writers, and musicians, who encouraged the queen to spend money even more **profusely.**

(7) While the queen's favorites **glutted** themselves on huge feasts at the royal table, many people in France were starving. **(8)** The French government taxed the citizens **outrageously.** These high taxes paid for the entertainments the queen and her court so enjoyed. **(9)** When the minister of finance tried to stop these royal **spendthrifts,** the queen replaced him.

(10) The **intense** hatred that the people felt for Louis XVI and Marie Antoinette kept building until it led to the French Revolution. During this time of struggle and violence (1789–1799), thousands of aristocrats, as well as the king and queen themselves, lost their lives at the guillotine. Perhaps if Louis XVI and Marie Antoinette had reined in their extravagant spending, the events that rocked France would not have occurred.

Please turn to the next page.

Reading Comprehension Exercise

Each of the following statements corresponds to a numbered sentence in the passage. Each statement contains a blank and is followed by four answer choices. Decide which choice fits best in the blank. The word or phrase that you choose must express roughly the same meaning as the italicized word in the passage. Write the letter of your choice on the answer line.

1. King Louis XVI and Queen Marie Antoinette were warned against spending __?__ .
   a. for war   **b.** for charity   **c.** too much   **d.** too little

   1. _____c_____

2. This __?__ spending angered the people of France.
   a. extravagant   **b.** important   **c.** necessary   **d.** visible

   2. _____a_____

3. The people resented the royal couple's __?__ way of life.
   a. simple   **b.** enthusiastic   **c.** unhappy   **d.** expensive

   3. _____d_____

4. Marie Antoinette was __?__ impractical.
   a. moderately   **b.** extremely   **c.** understandably   **d.** never

   4. _____b_____

5. She __?__ her palace with expensive works of art.
   a. changed   **b.** decorated   **c.** destroyed   **d.** transformed

   5. _____b_____

6. The people surrounding the queen encouraged her to spend money __?__ .
   a. abundantly   **b.** happily   **c.** carefully   **d.** wisely

   6. _____a_____

7. Marie Antoinette's favorites __?__ at large banquets.
   a. stayed on diets   **c.** danced and sang
   b. talked freely   **d.** stuffed themselves

   7. _____d_____

8. Meanwhile, the poor people were taxed __?__ .
   a. carefully   **b.** yearly   **c.** shockingly   **d.** officially

   8. _____c_____

9. The minister of finance tried to curb these royal __?__ .
   a. money wasters   **b.** friends   **c.** enemies   **d.** aristocrats

   9. _____a_____

10. The people of France felt __?__ hatred for the king and queen.
    a. average   **b.** deep   **c.** little   **d.** fleeting

    10. _____b_____

Writing Assignment

Think back to a time in your life when you were in danger of overdoing something. You might have eaten too much of one type of food or collected too many of one type of record or book. Create a brief humorous incident of several paragraphs that tells about this experience in an exaggerated way. Write the incident from the first-person point of view, and begin by making clear what the problem is. By the time the story ends, you should have found an answer or resolution to this conflict. Include five words from this lesson and underline them.

Lesson 20

Importance

Every day, people make decisions based on how important they think an action is. You may, for example, write yourself a reminder to make an important phone call. Your history teacher may ask you to rank in order of importance the causes of the Civil War. You probably remember important occasions like a friend's birthday and forget unimportant occurrences like yesterday's breakfast. Sometimes you have to decide which of two events — a dance or a concert, for example — is more important to you. The words in this lesson will help you to express the different degrees of importance that you assign to various situations.

WORD LIST
eminent
indispensable
momentous
paramount
petty
prestige
priority
prominence
superficial
trivial

DEFINITIONS

After you have studied the definitions and example for each vocabulary word, write the word on the line to the right.

1. **eminent** (ĕm′ə-nənt) *adjective*   **a.** Outstanding or superior in performance or character; remarkable; noteworthy.   **b.** Well-known and respected. (From the Latin word *eminens,* meaning "standing out")

   RELATED WORDS   **eminence** *noun;* **eminently** *adverb*

   EXAMPLE   The *eminent* scientist was often asked to speak at conferences.

   1. _____

   USAGE NOTE   Don't confuse *eminent* with *imminent,* which means "about to occur." SEE   *prominence.*

2. **indispensable** (ĭn′dĭ-spĕn′sə-bəl) *adjective*   Required; essential; necessary.

   RELATED WORD   **indispensability** *noun*

   EXAMPLE   The typewriter was *indispensable* to the secretary.

   2. _____

3. **momentous** (mō-mĕn′təs) *adjective*   Of great importance or outstanding significance. (From the Latin word *momentum,* meaning "movement" or "influence")

   RELATED WORD   **momentousness** *noun*

   EXAMPLE   Receiving her first paycheck was a *momentous* experience for Germaine.

   3. _____

4. **paramount** (păr′ə-mount′) *adjective*   Of chief concern; foremost; primary. (From the Old French words *par,* meaning "by," and *amont,* meaning "above")

   EXAMPLE   The *paramount* aim of the colonists was winning their independence from England.

   4. _____

5. petty (pĕt'ē) *adjective*   **a.** Small or insignificant in quantity or quality.   **b.** Narrow-minded; selfish.   **c.** Mean and spiteful. (From the French word *petit*, meaning "small")

RELATED WORD   **pettiness** *noun*

EXAMPLE   The shopper made a *petty* complaint about the speed of the store's elevator.

5. _____

6. prestige (prĕ-stēzh') *noun*   High regard or status in the eyes of others. (From the Latin word *praestringere*, meaning "to dazzle")

RELATED WORD   **prestigious** *adjective*

EXAMPLE   Because of his *prestige* as a diplomat, the ambassador was often consulted about negotiating treaties.

6. _____

7. priority (prī-ôr'ĭ-tē) *noun*   **a.** Order of importance or urgency. **b.** Something more important than other considerations. (From the Latin word *prior*, meaning "previous" or "former")

RELATED WORD   **prior** *adjective*

EXAMPLE   In its list of improvements for the school, the committee gave *priority* to a new science laboratory.

7. _____

8. prominence (prŏm'ə-nəns) *noun*   The condition of being immediately noticeable or widely known. (From the Latin word *prominere*, meaning "to jut out")

RELATED WORDS   **prominent** *adjective;* **prominently** *adverb*

EXAMPLE   Ben's *prominence* in the community resulted from his participation in volunteer activities.

8. _____

USAGE NOTE   *Prominent* and *eminent* are synonyms, but *prominent* can also mean "immediately noticeable; conspicuous": *a prominent nose.*

9. superficial (sōō'pər-fĭsh'əl) *adjective*   **a.** On or near the surface: *a superficial wound.*   **b.** Concerned only with what is apparent or obvious; shallow; not deeply penetrating. (From the Latin *super-*, meaning "above," and *facies*, meaning "face")

RELATED WORDS   **superficiality** *noun;* **superficially** *adverb*

EXAMPLE   We did a *superficial* cleaning before our guests arrived.

9. _____

10. trivial (trĭv'ē-əl) *adjective*   **a.** Of little importance or significance.   **b.** Ordinary; commonplace. (From the Latin *tri-*, meaning "three," and *via*, meaning "road")

RELATED WORDS   **trivia** *noun;* **triviality** *noun;* **trivialize** *verb*

EXAMPLE   The topics for discussion seemed so *trivial* to Pam that she left the conference.

10. _____

Exercise 1 Writing Correct Words

On the answer line, write the word from the vocabulary list that fits each definition.

1. The condition of being favorably known or immediately noticeable

2. Small or insignificant; narrow-minded

3. Great status or favorable regard

4. Outstanding in performance or character; well-known and respected

5. Order of importance or urgency

6. Of greatest concern; supreme in rank or authority

7. Of or near the surface; concerned with what is apparent or obvious

8. Of little importance; ordinary

9. Required; necessary; essential

10. Of great importance

1. _____ prominence _____

2. _____ petty _____

3. _____ prestige _____

4. _____ eminent _____

5. _____ priority _____

6. _____ paramount _____

7. _____ superficial _____

8. _____ trivial _____

9. _____ indispensable _____

10. _____ momentous _____

Exercise 2 Using Words Correctly

Each of the following statements contains an italicized vocabulary word. Decide whether the sentence is true or false, and write *True* or *False* on the answer line.

1. No one pays attention to a person of *prominence*.

2. A *trivial* comment deserves a thoughtful, intelligent response.

3. Armstrong and Aldrin's landing on the moon in 1969 was a *momentous* achievement.

4. A bat and ball are *indispensable* to anyone who wants to play baseball.

5. A sincere person is likely to wear a *superficial* smile.

6. The president of a large corporation has a position of *prestige*.

7. Those who have been waiting in line for a long time usually have *priority* over newcomers.

8. Using reflectors is *paramount* when bicycling after dark.

9. An expert would be expected to make *petty* accusations on a television talk show.

10. *Eminent* people have poor reputations in their fields.

1. _____ False _____

2. _____ False _____

3. _____ True _____

4. _____ True _____

5. _____ False _____

6. _____ True _____

7. _____ True _____

8. _____ True _____

9. _____ False _____

10. _____ False _____

Exercise 3 Choosing the Best Definition

For each italicized word or related form in the following sentences, write the letter of the best definition on the answer line.

1. Color is a *trivial* consideration in the purchase of a lawnmower.
   a. important **b.** required **c.** realistic **d.** unimportant

1. _____ d _____

2. Dr. Bless had earned her *prestige* by writing numerous articles for scientific journals.
   a. salary   **b.** esteem   **c.** promotion   **d.** dislike

   2. _____b_____

3. Mr. O'Sullivan explained that his daughter's work was *indispensable* to his business.
   a. active   **b.** harmful   **c.** necessary   **d.** serious

   3. _____c_____

4. The directors made the *momentous* decision to sell the company.
   a. foolish   **b.** quick   **c.** certain   **d.** important

   4. _____d_____

5. Walter became an *eminent* chef when he began to write a weekly food column for the magazine.
   a. well-known   **b.** creative   **c.** clumsy   **d.** powerful

   5. _____a_____

6. Smoke detectors are the safety devices that have the highest *priority* in skyscrapers.
   a. order of importance   **c.** superiority
   b. level of failure   **d.** power

   6. _____a_____

7. The seriously ill woman has an appointment with a *prominent* doctor.
   a. wise   **b.** widely known   **c.** philosophical   **d.** prize-winning

   7. _____b_____

8. Will and Josephine made *superficial* conversation while they waited for the bus.
   a. brief   **b.** enjoyable   **c.** unintelligent   **d.** shallow

   8. _____d_____

9. The cartoonist's *petty* comments about the students' drawings brought groans from the class.
   a. humorous   **b.** positive   **c.** mean   **d.** kind

   9. _____c_____

10. Saving lives is *paramount* to firefighters.
    a. unimportant   **b.** most important   **c.** enjoyable   **d.** normal

    10. _____b_____

Exercise 4   Using Different Forms of Words

Decide which form of the vocabulary word in parentheses best completes the sentence. The form given may be correct. Write your answer on the answer line.

1. Because of her __?__, the artist received numerous requests to paint portraits of wealthy people. *(eminent)*

   1. _____eminence_____

2. The headwaiter suggested that next time we call for reservations __?__ to arriving at the restaurant. *(priority)*

   2. _____prior_____

3. Arguments often reveal the __?__ of the people involved. *(petty)*

   3. _____pettiness_____

4. Daily brushing is __?__ in keeping teeth healthy. *(paramount)*

   4. _____paramount_____

5. The __?__ of our new neighbor's friendliness was apparent to all of us. *(superficial)*

   5. _____superficiality_____

6. People sometimes __?__ important subjects by making jokes about them. *(trivial)*

   6. _____trivialize_____

7. Carl's announcement added to the __?__ of the occasion. *(momentous)*

   7. _____momentousness_____

8. The giraffe's most __?__ feature is its long neck. *(prominence)*

   8. _____prominent_____

9. Finding his pockets empty, Tom moaned about the __?__ of money. *(indispensable)*

   9. _____indispensability_____

10. Cecelia won the __?__ writing contest. *(prestige)*

    10. _____prestigious_____

Reading Comprehension

Each numbered sentence in the following passage contains an italicized vocabulary word or related form. At the end of the passage, you will complete an exercise.

Alfred Nobel: The Man and the Prize

(1) Alfred Nobel (1833–1896) was an *eminent* Swedish chemist, inventor, and industrialist. His experiments with explosives led to his invention of dynamite in 1866 and to the development of devices that make the dynamite explode. (2) After an accidental explosion killed his brother, Nobel's *paramount* concern was to make the dangerous substance nitroglycerin, from which dynamite is made, into a safe and useful explosive. (3) In fact, the results of his work became *indispensable* in mining, building roads, blasting tunnels, and carrying out other types of construction.

Nobel was talented in many areas. He held 355 patents for such developments as synthetic rubber and leather, artificial silk, and torpedoes. He even wrote novels and plays. (4) His literary efforts never gained *prominence,* however. (5) Swedish critics regarded his writing as *superficial.*

Nobel's health was not good, and in his later years, he became increasingly concerned about the future. (6) It was not a *trivial* matter to him that the substance he had created was used for warfare rather than for peace. Wanting to make a contribution to the future of humanity, Nobel left his nine-million-dollar fortune in trust. He specified that the interest earned from the trust be used to award five annual prizes to people whose achievements further the welfare of humanity. (7) *Petty* concerns such as nationality, race, or political beliefs were to play no part in the selection process. (8) Instead, he intended the selections to be based solely on *momentous* contributions in physics, chemistry, physiology or medicine, literature, and international peace. Since 1969, a sixth award, in economics, has also been granted.

(9) The *prestigious* Nobel Prizes are presented annually at ceremonies in Stockholm, Sweden, and Oslo, Norway, on December 10, which is the anniversary of Nobel's death. Each Nobel laureate, as a winner is called, receives a diploma and a gold medal in addition to the cash award, which now totals more than one hundred thousand dollars for each recipient. Each laureate delivers a lecture at some time during the year on his or her field.

(10) We can best understand Alfred Nobel's *priority* of encouraging and rewarding worthwhile contributions by remembering some of the most famous winners. Pierre and Marie Curie, Albert Schweitzer, Rudyard Kipling, Pearl Buck, Albert Einstein, Martin Luther King, Jr., and Mother Teresa are but a few of the Nobel laureates chosen since the prizes were first awarded in 1901.

Reading Comprehension Exercise

Each of the following statements corresponds to a numbered sentence in the passage. Each statement contains a blank and is followed by four answer choices. Decide which choice fits best in the blank. The word or phrase that you choose must express roughly the same meaning as the italicized word in the passage. Write the letter of your choice on the answer line.

1. Alfred Nobel was a(n) __?__ Swedish inventor and industrialist.
   a. well-known   **b.** creative   **c.** reserved   **d.** intelligent

   1. ___a___

2. Nobel's __?__ concern was to make nitroglycerin safe and useful.
   a. equal   **b.** present   **c.** secondary   **d.** primary

   2. ___d___

3. Nobel's invention was __?__ for many types of construction.
   a. useless   **b.** costly   **c.** necessary   **d.** extended

3. _____c_____

4. Nobel's literary efforts never gained __?__ .
   a. importance   **b.** quality   **c.** good reviews   **d.** prizes

4. _____a_____

5. Swedish critics said that Nobel's writing was __?__ .
   a. difficult   **b.** shallow   **c.** important   **d.** confusing

5. _____b_____

6. To Nobel, it was not a(n) __?__ matter that he had created a substance used for warfare.
   a. awful   **b.** practical   **c.** realistic   **d.** unimportant

6. _____d_____

7. __?__ concerns were to play no part in selecting Nobel Prize winners.
   a. Monetary   **b.** National   **c.** Major   **d.** Unimportant

7. _____d_____

8. Prizes would be awarded for __?__ contributions.
   a. outstanding   **b.** small   **c.** glamorous   **d.** timely

8. _____a_____

9. The __?__ prizes are presented annually in Sweden and Norway.
   a. large   **b.** secret   **c.** esteemed   **d.** exciting

9. _____c_____

10. Nobel's __?__ was to encourage and reward worthwhile contributions.
    a. first concern   **b.** secret expectation   **c.** wish   **d.** demand

10. _____a_____

Writing Assignment

You have been asked to introduce a famous person who will speak to an all-school assembly. Choose a prominent person, such as a scientist, a doctor, or an entertainer, who has made an important contribution to humanity. Write a short speech of introduction that provides background information about the person and stresses his or her achievements. Use at least five of the vocabulary words from this lesson in your introduction and underline them.

Vocabulary Enrichment

Trivial, one of the words in this lesson, has an interesting history. The word derives from the Latin *tri-*, meaning "three," and *via*, meaning "road." At first glance, it would appear that *trivial* and its definition, "unimportant" or "ordinary," have little to do with three roads. In ancient Rome, however, the intersection of three roads became a public square, or a *trivium*. In these squares, travelers and residents gathered to exchange gossip and information about everyday matters. Because a *trivium* was the site of ordinary conversation, *trivial* has evolved to mean "ordinary" or "unimportant."

ACTIVITY Other words have indirect connections with their original meanings. In a high school or college dictionary, look up each of the following words, and write its Latin root and the meaning of that root. Then write a brief explanation of the connection between the root and the most common definition of the English word.

1. visa   2. voyage   3. itinerary   4. journey

Name ________________________________ Date ____________

Bonus: Lessons 19 and 20

(pages 121–132)

Use the clues to complete the crossword puzzle.

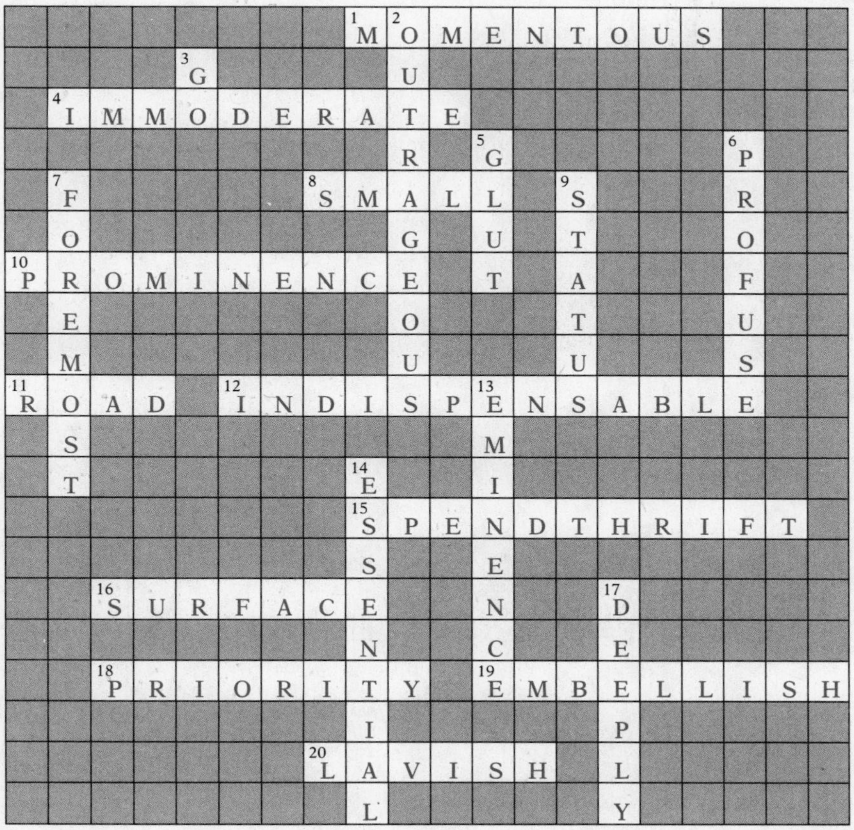
1 MOMENTOUS
2 OUTRAGEOUS
3 G
4 IMMODERATE
5 GLUT
6 PROFUSE
7 FOREMOST
8 SMALL
9 STATUS
10 PROMINENCE
11 ROAD
12 INDISPENSABLE
13 EMINENCE
14 ESSENTIAL
15 SPENDTHRIFT
16 SURFACE
17 DEEPLY
18 PRIORITY
19 EMBELLISH
20 LAVISH

Across

1. Graduation is this kind of an occasion.
4. Done to an extreme
8. A PETTY complaint is a(n) __?__ grievance.
10. The condition of being widely known
11. TRIVIAL comes from the Latin word *via*, meaning "__?__."
12. Opposite of unnecessary
15. One who spends money foolishly
16. A SUPERFICIAL wound exists only on the __?__.
18. Primary importance
19. To make beautiful with decoration
20. From the Old French word *lavasse*, meaning "downpour"

Down

2. Shocking
3. To EXCEED is to __?__ beyond reasonable limits.
5. An excess of goods may __?__ the market.
6. Abundant
7. A PARAMOUNT idea is of __?__ importance.
9. To have PRESTIGE is to possess great __?__.
13. The condition of being outstanding in performance or character
14. LUXURIOUS items give pleasure but are not __?__.
17. INTENSE emotions are __?__ felt.

Notes

The following lists of words are from the preceding two lessons. You may wish to use these lists to pinpoint words for ongoing review or for midterm or final exams.

Lesson 19

embellish	lavish
exceed	luxurious
glut	outrageous
immoderate	profuse
intense	spendthrift

Lesson 20

eminent	prestige
indispensable	priority
momentous	prominence
paramount	superficial
petty	trivial

Lesson 21

Fairness and Unfairness

Most basketball players would agree that they do not care how many fouls referees call, as long as those fouls are called fairly against all players. This desire for fairness holds true in every area of life, whether it be school, work, or friendship.

The words in this lesson refer to fair and unfair situations. Learning them may help you to understand and deal more effectively with the experiences in your own life that seem unfair.

DEFINITIONS

After you have studied the definitions and example for each vocabulary word, write the word on the line to the right.

1. **abide** (ə-bīd′) *verb* **a.** To put up with; bear; tolerate. **b.** To remain; stay. **c.** To live; reside. **d.** To wait patiently for; await. **e.** To live up to; comply with: *abide by an agreement.* (From the Old English word *abidare,* meaning "to wait")

   EXAMPLE   Robert could not *abide* his friend's annoying practical jokes.

   1. _____

2. **amenable** (ə-mē′nə-bəl) *adjective* Willing to cooperate; agreeable. (From the Latin word *minari,* meaning "to threaten")

   EXAMPLE   Therese was *amenable* to her parents' change of plans.

   2. _____
   ETYMOLOGY NOTE   *Amenable,* "not threatening" in Latin, is related to *menacing.*

3. **bias** (bī′əs) *noun* An inclination for or against something or someone that affects the fairness of one's judgment.
   verb To cause to have a prejudiced view; influence unfairly.

   EXAMPLE   Henry had a *bias* against foreign films because he hated reading subtitles.

   3. _____

4. **discrimination** (dĭ-skrĭm′ə-nā′shən) *noun* **a.** One or more acts based on unfairness or injustice toward a particular group of persons. **b.** The ability to distinguish, especially to recognize small differences or to make fine distinctions. (From the Latin *dis-,* meaning "apart," and *cernere,* meaning "to sift")

   RELATED WORDS   **discriminate** *verb;* **discriminatory** *adjective*

   EXAMPLE   Federal laws forbid *discrimination* on the basis of race, creed, color, sex, or age.

   4. _____

5. **forbearance** (fôr-bâr′əns) *noun* Patience, tolerance, or restraint.

   RELATED WORD   **forbear** *verb*

   EXAMPLE   Clifford showed great *forbearance* toward Sally, even after she made critical remarks about his cat, Claws.

5. ——————
SEE *tolerance.*

6. **objective** (əb-jěk′tĭv) *adjective* **a.** Not influenced by emotion or personal opinion. **b.** Real or actual: *objective facts.*

   RELATED WORDS   **objectively** *adverb;* **objectivity** *noun*

   EXAMPLE   Paul had trouble remaining *objective* when his favorite team was playing baseball.

6. ——————

7. **partisan** (pär′tĭ-zən) *noun* A strong supporter of a party, cause, team, or person.   *adjective* Having or showing a strong preference. (From the Italian word *partigiano,* meaning "supporter")

   RELATED WORD   **partisanship** *noun*

   EXAMPLE   Paul Revere was a *partisan* of the early independence movement in Colonial times.

7. ——————

8. **preconceived** (prē′kən-sēvd′) *adjective* Formed in the mind before full or adequate knowledge is acquired. (From the Latin *prae-,* meaning "before," and *concipere,* meaning "to take hold of")

   RELATED WORD   **preconception** *noun*

   EXAMPLE   Terence had a *preconceived* opinion about the issue before the committee.

8. ——————

9. **prejudice** (prěj′ə-dĭs) *noun* **a.** A strong feeling or opinion that is formed before one knows the facts. **b.** Hostility toward members of other races, religions, nationalities, or other groups.   *verb* To cause someone to judge before having complete information. (From the Latin *prae-,* meaning "before," and *judicium,* meaning "judgment")

   EXAMPLE   In the debate neither candidate showed any indications of *prejudice* on the topic.

9. ——————

10. **tolerance** (tŏl′ər-əns) *noun* **a.** Respect for the opinions, practices, and behavior of others. **b.** The capacity to endure hardship or pain. (From the Latin word *tolerare,* meaning "to bear")

    RELATED WORDS   **tolerant** *adjective;* **tolerate** *verb;* **toleration** *noun*

    EXAMPLE   My father's *tolerance* for rock music improved after he listened more closely to my records.

10. ——————
USAGE NOTE *Tolerance* refers to the acceptance of others. *Forbearance* suggests resigned acceptance.

Exercise 1   Writing Correct Words

On the answer line, write the word from the vocabulary list that fits each definition.

1. An opinion held without knowledge of the facts

2. Patience and restraint, even when one does not like a situation

3. A preference that leads to an unfair judgment

4. Formed in the mind before the facts are known

5. To tolerate or await patiently

6. One or more actions based on unfair, unjust attitudes toward a group

7. Respect for the attitudes of others

8. Agreeable; willing to cooperate

9. A supporter of a particular group or cause

10. Not influenced by emotion or personal opinion

1. _____ prejudice _____

2. _____ forbearance _____

3. _____ bias _____

4. _____ preconceived _____

5. _____ abide _____

6. _____ discrimination _____

7. _____ tolerance _____

8. _____ amenable _____

9. _____ partisan _____

10. _____ objective _____

Exercise 2   Using Words Correctly

Each of the following questions contains an italicized vocabulary word. Decide the answer to the question, and write *Yes* or *No* on the answer line.

1. Does an *amenable* person argue constantly with people?

2. Would an *objective* employer hire only friends?

3. Do you show *tolerance* if you listen receptively to people's opinions?

4. Would a *partisan* of democracy support the right to vote?

5. Would a librarian *abide* loud talking by a group of library users?

6. Would you be showing *forbearance* if you reacted calmly to an insult?

7. Are *preconceived* ideas always correct?

8. Does *prejudice* result from studying all sides of an issue?

9. If one treats members of all groups equally, is one guilty of *discrimination?*

10. Does a *bias* against young people mean an unfair attitude toward them?

1. _____ No _____

2. _____ No _____

3. _____ Yes _____

4. _____ Yes _____

5. _____ No _____

6. _____ Yes _____

7. _____ No _____

8. _____ No _____

9. _____ No _____

10. _____ Yes _____

Exercise 3   Choosing the Best Word

Decide which vocabulary word or related form best expresses the meaning of the italicized word or phrase in the sentence. On the answer line, write the letter of the correct choice.

1. Mark distinguished himself by his *ability to make fine distinctions.*
   a. partisanship   b. discrimination   c. bias   d. forbearance

1. _____ b _____

2. Monica had a *fixed idea* against outdoor weddings.
   a. tolerance   **b.** bias   **c.** discrimination   **d.** objectivity

2. _____b_____

3. Blair had several *prematurely developed* ideas about the city.
   a. preconceived   **b.** partisan   **c.** tolerant   **d.** forbearing

3. _____a_____

4. *Respect for the beliefs of others* is a requirement for effective student government.
   a. Partisanship   **b.** Prejudice   **c.** Preconception   **d.** Tolerance

4. _____d_____

5. Janet was *agreeable* to her parents' plans to relocate in another city.
   a. amenable   **b.** objective   **c.** discriminating   **d.** biased

5. _____a_____

6. The judges of the essay contest were *uninfluenced by personal opinion*.
   a. prejudiced   **b.** partisan   **c.** objective   **d.** tolerant

6. _____c_____

7. "I will *comply with* your decision," Simon told his mother.
   a. prejudice   **b.** abide by   **c.** discriminate   **d.** bias

7. _____b_____

8. The sportswriter admitted to having a *fixed opinion made without consideration of the facts* against hockey.
   a. forbearance   **b.** partisanship   **c.** objectivity   **d.** prejudice

8. _____d_____

9. Amanda showed great *restraint and patience* with her younger brother.
   a. partisanship   **b.** discrimination   **c.** objectivity   **d.** forbearance

9. _____d_____

10. The *supporters* of wildlife preservation will meet tomorrow afternoon.
    a. biases   **b.** discriminations   **c.** partisans   **d.** tolerance

10. _____c_____

Exercise 4   Using Different Forms of Words

Decide which form of the vocabulary word in parentheses best completes the sentence. The form given may be correct. Write your answer on the answer line.

1. Cathy had many __?__ about the new season's television shows. *(preconceived)*

1. _____preconceptions_____

2. Robert claims that the condominium rules __?__ against owners of pets. *(discrimination)*

2. _____discriminate_____

3. The instructor always evaluated the students' work __?__ . *(objective)*

3. _____objectively_____

4. A good driver, Mrs. Beck __?__ by the rules of the road. *(abide)*

4. _____abides_____

5. A __?__ opinion usually has no basis in fact. *(prejudice)*

5. _____prejudiced_____

6. Are you able to __?__ when teased by an older brother or sister? *(forbearance)*

6. _____forbear_____

7. "I can no longer __?__ your bad manners," Chuck told his younger brother. *(tolerance)*

7. _____tolerate_____

8. Everyone was __?__ to the idea of leaving early. *(amenable)*

8. _____amenable_____

9. Alan was a __?__ of the popular politician. *(partisan)*

9. _____partisan_____

10. The car dealer was __?__ against plans for improving mass transportation. *(bias)*

10. _____biased_____

Reading Comprehension

Each numbered sentence in the following passage contains an italicized vocabulary word. After you read the passage, you will complete an exercise.

The New Girl

The cafeteria line moved slowly, and I was in a hurry to join my friends. We always ate lunch together in a special section reserved for ninth graders. (1) The younger students accused us of **discrimination,** but ninth grade seating privileges were a time-honored tradition at Elmwood Junior High School. (2) It wasn't that we didn't have **tolerance** for the other students; it's just that they weren't ninth graders.

"Hi, Jennifer," Alicia said shyly. I hadn't noticed that she was behind me.

Alicia was new to the school. She seemed to have so much to say, only no one wanted to listen. It was usually like that when you were new. (3) People seemed to have a **bias** against you.

I knew how Alicia felt. It had been like that for me last year. (4) I didn't like thinking about it — the mornings when I could barely **abide** getting up, dreading another lonely day at school. That was all before I had found friends or, rather, Cindy and the other girls had found me. I knew how lonely Alicia was. I decided to smile back at her.

(5) "How do you have the **forbearance** to wait in these long cafeteria lines?" Alicia asked.

"Oh, you get used to it."

"I'm glad Mr. Fitzgibbons read your essay aloud in English class," Alicia told me. (6) "I'm also a **partisan** of the great outdoors. Last summer, my parents and I camped throughout most of Europe."

"You did! How was it? I wish I could do something like that."

"It was wonderful!" She smiled at the memory. "Of course, camping can be difficult. (7) You have to be very **amenable** to the unexpected. Would you like to see a few pictures of our trip? We could have lunch and I could show you — "

"Oh, I'd like to, but — " I interrupted quickly.

"Sure, some other time." Alicia's enthusiasm died.

Cindy and the other girls in our group were busy dissecting what they considered to be the major event of the morning when I finally joined them. Alicia was sitting at the outskirts of the ninth grade section, dangerously near some seventh graders. She read a book while she ate. I wondered if she ever turned a page. I hadn't when I'd sat alone in the cafeteria.

"Oh, I was talking to Alicia," I began, aware of five pairs of disapproving eyes turned in my direction. "Maybe we should ask her to eat lunch with us."

They all laughed, which was worse than an argument.

"I think Alicia's nice," I dared to say. "No one gives her a chance."

"Alicia talks funny. She doesn't dress in style, and it's obvious that she doesn't care about anything that's really important," Cindy pointed out.

(8) I was silent. If I said anything to contradict the girls' **preconceived** ideas about Alicia, they might change their minds about including me in their group. It was unfair. (9) They weren't being **objective** about Alicia, but there wasn't anything I could do to change their opinion.

I didn't see Alicia in the cafeteria for the rest of the week. I felt guilty and relieved at the same time. Finally, on a rainy Friday, Alicia ventured cautiously in. All of the tables were filled in the ninth grade section. Alicia hesitated and then sat down at the end of a table with some noisy seventh graders.

Cindy turned to me. "Looks like Alicia finally found some friends."

All the girls laughed.

"Leave her alone!" I said, surprising myself.

They looked at me in shocked disbelief. I had dared to contradict Cindy. I held my ground.

"If you're so worried about Alicia, why don't you sit with her?" Cindy challenged.

"Maybe I will." (10) I gathered up my things and walked away from their table, glad that I had finally had the courage to let the girls know how unfair and **prejudiced** I thought they were. Still, I'd be dishonest if I pretended that the loud laughter at their table didn't bother me.

Please turn to the next page.

Reading Comprehension Exercise

Each of the following statements corresponds to a numbered sentence in the passage. Each statement contains a blank and is followed by four answer choices. Decide which choice fits best in the blank. The word or phrase that you choose must express roughly the same meaning as the italicized word in the passage. Write the letter of your choice on the answer line.

1. The younger students accused the ninth graders of __?__ .
   a. cheating   b. ignorance   c. unfairness   d. cruelty

   1. ___c___

2. It wasn't true, Jennifer jokingly said, that ninth graders lacked __?__ the younger students.
   a. acceptance of   c. anger toward
   b. dislike for   d. mistreatment of

   2. ___a___

3. Jennifer pointed out the __?__ new students.
   a. friendliness toward   c. competition against
   b. unfair opinion of   d. jealousy of

   3. ___b___

4. Jennifer remembered that she could barely __?__ getting ready for school each day.
   a. endure   b. avoid   c. remember   d. stop

   4. ___a___

5. Alicia asked Jennifer how she had the __?__ to wait in the cafeteria lines.
   a. nerve   b. ability   c. strength   d. patience

   5. ___d___

6. Alicia described herself as __?__ outdoor activities.
   a. afraid of   c. a supporter of
   b. ready for   d. experienced in

   6. ___c___

7. She explained that it is necessary to be __?__ in the face of unexpected events.
   a. healthy   b. flexible   c. active   d. emotional

   7. ___b___

8. Jennifer was afraid that she would be left out if she contradicted her friends' opinions, which were __?__ .
   a. formed prematurely   c. lacking in intelligence
   b. fair   d. negative

   8. ___a___

9. Jennifer knew that the girls were not __?__ in their view of Alicia.
   a. daring   b. critical   c. fair   d. kind

   9. ___c___

10. Finally, Jennifer was able to let the girls know how __?__ she thought they were.
    a. critical   b. right   c. logical   d. unfair

    10. ___d___

Writing Assignment

Think of a time when you were judged unfairly or when you were guilty of misjudging someone else. Choose an experience that you would like to share with a friend. Tell about this experience, explaining how you handled the problem. Include five words from this lesson and underline each one.

Test: Lessons 19, 20, and 21

(pages 121–138)

Part A Choosing the Best Definition

On the answer line, write the letter of the best definition of the italicized word.

1. An *eminent* physician will represent our town at the state convention.
   a. outstanding   **b.** reliable   **c.** kindly   **d.** generous

   1. ____a____

2. Success in the stock market depends on the proper *discrimination* between risk and sound investment.
   a. relationship   **c.** ability to distinguish
   b. understanding   **d.** ability to guess

   2. ____c____

3. Robert Browning wrote that "a man's reach should *exceed* his grasp."
   a. be less than   **c.** be greater than
   b. come before   **d.** come after

   3. ____c____

4. Surviving the first winter was the Pilgrims' *paramount* concern.
   a. wishful   **b.** deliberate   **c.** chief   **d.** ever present

   4. ____c____

5. Jeremy cannot *abide* noise while he studies.
   a. sacrifice   **b.** tolerate   **c.** prevent   **d.** avoid

   5. ____b____

6. The fans displayed *immoderate* anger over the defeat.
   a. senseless   **b.** little   **c.** contagious   **d.** excessive

   6. ____d____

7. Mike's *preconceived* notions about sports changed dramatically.
   a. ridiculous   **c.** firm
   b. formed without evidence   **d.** limited in experience

   7. ____b____

8. The monarch of Lilliput was a *partisan* of the Small-Endians.
   a. supporter   **b.** opponent   **c.** ruler   **d.** founder

   8. ____a____

9. Annie *embellished* her story about the zucchini cake disaster.
   a. published   **b.** wrote   **c.** forgot   **d.** exaggerated

   9. ____d____

10. The team's *priority* is to stop Number 24 from getting the ball.
    a. job   **b.** responsibility   **c.** main consideration   **d.** strategy

    10. ____c____

11. Alice did not want to *prejudice* Armando against the movie.
    a. cause someone to be upset   **c.** restrain
    b. cause someone to judge prematurely   **d.** cause someone to miss

    11. ____b____

12. Dr. Blau's *prestige* increased after the publication of her book.
    a. status   **b.** patients   **c.** finances   **d.** publicity

    12. ____a____

13. Luke was surprised about the *prominence* of his role in the school play.
    a. naturalness   **b.** limits   **c.** difficulty   **d.** conspicuousness

    13. ____d____

14. Professor Walker is known for her *tolerance* of experimental theories.
    a. encouragement   **c.** acceptance
    b. agreement   **d.** understanding

    14. ____c____

15. The film critic gave *lavish* praise to the new adventure film.
    a. undeserved   **b.** little   **c.** generous   **d.** satisfying

    15. ____c____

HOUGHTON MIFFLIN VOCABULARY FOR ACHIEVEMENT, SECOND COURSE

Test: Lessons 19, 20, and 21

Part B Identifying Synonyms

On the answer line, write the letter of the word or phrase that has the same meaning as that of the capitalized word.

16. BIAS :
    a. tape   **b.** partiality   **c.** intensity   **d.** neutrality

17. INDISPENSABLE :
    a. necessary   **b.** insulting   **c.** inadequate   **d.** solid

18. GLUT :
    a. bother   **b.** harvest   **c.** reduction   **d.** oversupply

19. SUPERFICIAL :
    a. rough   **b.** obvious   **c.** superb   **d.** shallow

20. MOMENTOUS :
    a. huge   **b.** negligible   **c.** important   **d.** timely

21. SPENDTHRIFT :
    a. wasteful   **b.** precise   **c.** inexpensive   **d.** miserly

22. OBJECTIVE :
    a. photographic   **b.** emotional   **c.** false   **d.** neutral

23. TRIVIAL :
    a. insensitive   **b.** ordinary   **c.** profound   **d.** three-tiered

24. LUXURIOUS :
    a. expensively magnificent   **c.** uncomfortable
    b. essentially wholesome   **d.** worshipful

25. AMENABLE :
    a. agreeable   **b.** uncooperative   **c.** stubborn   **d.** friendly

26. PETTY :
    a. unattractive   **b.** unmistakable   **c.** minor   **d.** confused

27. INTENSE :
    a. subdued   **b.** forceful   **c.** lazy   **d.** musical

28. FORBEARANCE :
    a. descendants   **b.** apology   **c.** patience   **d.** accuracy

29. OUTRAGEOUS :
    a. shocking   **b.** hasty   **c.** angry   **d.** privileged

30. PROFUSE :
    a. threatening   **b.** abundant   **c.** supreme   **d.** proper

16. ___b___
17. ___a___
18. ___d___
19. ___d___
20. ___c___
21. ___a___
22. ___d___
23. ___b___
24. ___a___
25. ___a___
26. ___c___
27. ___b___
28. ___c___
29. ___a___
30. ___b___

HOUGHTON MIFFLIN VOCABULARY FOR ACHIEVEMENT, SECOND COURSE

Reading Skills

Context Clues: Synonyms

Sometimes you may be puzzled by an unfamiliar word in your reading. If you study the sentence containing the word, you may find clues to the meaning of the word. A sentence will often include a synonym of the unfamiliar word. (A synonym is a word similar in meaning to another word.) Suppose that you do not know the meaning of the italicized word in this sentence:

> Three exhausted *raconteurs* left the party, but the fourth storyteller stayed to entertain us.

In the sentence, *storyteller* is a synonym of *raconteurs*. It is a context clue that suggests the meaning of the italicized word. The following strategies will help you use synonyms as context clues.

STRATEGIES

1. *Look for a word in the sentence that is the same part of speech as the unfamiliar word.* An unfamiliar word and its synonym will usually be the same part of speech. In the example above, both *raconteur* and *storyteller* are nouns.

2. *Examine the structure of the sentence.* The unfamiliar word and its synonym will often function in the same way in the sentence. Both *raconteur* and *storyteller* function as the subjects of independent clauses in the example above.

3. *Look for other words in the sentence that can serve as clues.* Both the unfamiliar word and its synonym will frequently be preceded or followed by words that are the same part of speech. For instance, *raconteurs* and *storyteller* are each preceded by an adjective (*three* and *fourth*).

4. *Check the meaning of the word in a dictionary.* Definitions based on context clues are approximate. Whenever possible, look up the unfamiliar word in the dictionary.

Exercise   Using Synonyms as Context Clues

Each of the sentences on the following page contains a synonym of the italicized word. *Step 1:* Write the synonym of the italicized word. *Step 2:* Write the appropriate dictionary definition of the italicized word. *Step 3:* Write a sentence of your own in which you use the word with the same meaning as the dictionary definition.

Please turn to the next page.

1. The *stipend* was enough to live on, but the payment allowed no luxuries.

SYNONYM ___payment___

DICTIONARY DEFINITION ___A fixed and regular payment___

SENTENCE ___My brother's scholarship stipend covers tuition, room, and board.___

2. The other meeting was dull, but our *symposium* was interesting.

SYNONYM ___meeting___

DICTIONARY DEFINITION ___A meeting or conference for discussing a topic___

SENTENCE ___The topic of our Geography Day symposium was "Rivers of South America."___

3. Having promised not to *divulge* Anna's secret, Tim never did reveal it.

SYNONYM ___reveal___

DICTIONARY DEFINITION ___To make known; reveal; tell___

SENTENCE ___The witness refused to divulge the contents of the letter at the trial.___

4. The team's *exuberance* was matched by the liveliness of the spectators.

SYNONYM ___liveliness___

DICTIONARY DEFINITION ___The condition of being lively and joyous; high spirits___

SENTENCE ___The exuberance of the cheerleaders spread to everyone at the rally.___

5. Some thought his trite compliments and *banal* remarks brilliant.

SYNONYM ___trite___

DICTIONARY DEFINITION ___Lacking originality; meaningless and dull; trite___

SENTENCE ___Our entire family laughed at the unbelievably banal dialogue in the movie.___

6. "You are *tenacious*," Bob told Sarah, "and I like persistent people."

SYNONYM ___persistent___

DICTIONARY DEFINITION ___Holding or tending to hold firmly; persistent___

SENTENCE ___The collie was tenacious in her refusal to let the sheep cross the highway.___

7. Calvin's *duplicity* is no worse than the deception that Simone practices.

SYNONYM ___deception___

DICTIONARY DEFINITION ___Deliberate deception; double-dealing___

SENTENCE ___Cora's incorruptible honesty ruled out duplicity of any kind.___

8. Sam managed to control the conversation and thus *monopolize* our discussion.

SYNONYM ___control___

DICTIONARY DEFINITION ___To gain exclusive control___

SENTENCE ___As usual, the baby sitter monopolized the television all evening long.___

Planning and Action

Have you ever planned an action and carried it out? For example, suppose you are working on a science project. You wonder whether there is any scientific truth in the idea that house plants respond well when people talk nicely to them. In order to put this idea into action, you need to set up an experiment that tests the scientific accuracy of your idea. For example, you could give two plants equal amounts of sunlight, water, and fertilizer. However, you would talk encouragingly to one of the plants but not to the other. Then you would observe the plants to see whether one thrives more than the other.

In this lesson you will learn words that refer to many kinds of plans and activities.

WORD LIST
administer
animate
concoct
devise
endeavor
execute
implement
reactivate
render
undertaking

DEFINITIONS

After you have studied the definitions and example for each vocabulary word, write the word on the line to the right.

1. **administer** (ăd-mĭn′ĭ-stər) *verb* **a.** To direct or manage: *to administer a business.* **b.** To carry out: *to administer laws.* **c.** To give as a remedy. (From the Latin *ad-*, meaning "to," and *ministrare*, meaning "to manage")

   RELATED WORDS **administration** *noun;* **administrator** *noun*

   EXAMPLE Personnel managers sometimes *administer* the training program of a company.

   1. _____

2. **animate** (ăn′ə-māt′) *verb* **a.** To give life to; fill with life; enliven. **b.** To design so as to create the illusion of motion: *to animate a cartoon.*   *adjective* (ăn′ə-mĭt) Possessing life; living. (From the Latin word *anima*, meaning "soul")

   RELATED WORD **animation** *noun*

   EXAMPLE The hilarious comedian *animated* the party.

   2. _____

3. **concoct** (kən-kŏkt′) *verb* **a.** To make up or invent, such as a plan or an excuse. **b.** To make by mixing or combining ingredients. (From the Latin *com-*, meaning "together," and *coquere*, meaning "to cook")

   RELATED WORD **concoction** *noun*

   EXAMPLE The mystery writer *concocted* an exciting plot for her new book.

   3. _____

4. **devise** (dĭ-vīz′) *verb* To form or arrange in the mind; plan or invent, as a solution to a problem.

EXAMPLE Margaret *devised* an excellent advertising campaign for the new product.

4. —————

5. **endeavor** (ĕn-dĕv′ər) *noun* A major effort or attempt to accomplish something. *verb* To make an effort or attempt. (From the French word *devoir*, meaning "duty")

EXAMPLE "I wish you luck in your new business *endeavor*," Mr. Chan told his former employee.

5. —————

6. **execute** (ĕk′sĭ-kyōōt′) *verb* **a.** To perform: *to execute a difficult gymnastic routine.* **b.** To carry out what is required. **c.** To put to death. (From the Latin *ex-*, meaning "out," and *sequi*, meaning "to follow")

RELATED WORDS **execution** *noun;* **executive** *noun;* **executive** *adjective*

EXAMPLE The dolphin *executed* an impressive series of tricks.

6. —————

7. **implement** (ĭm′plə-mĕnt′) *verb* To put into effect; carry out: *to implement a plan.* *noun* (ĭm′plə-mənt) A tool, utensil, or instrument. (From the Latin word *implere*, meaning "to fill up")

RELATED WORD **implementation** *noun*

EXAMPLE The librarian plans to *implement* a new system for checking out books.

7. —————

8. **reactivate** (rē-ăk′tə-vāt′) *verb* To make active again; restore the ability to function.

RELATED WORD **reactivation** *noun*

EXAMPLE The warm weather *reactivated* the children's interest in swimming.

8. —————

9. **render** (rĕn′dər) *verb* **a.** To give or make available: *to render service.* **b.** To cause to become: *The hailstorm rendered the crop worthless.* (From the Latin *re-*, meaning "back," and *dare*, meaning "to give")

EXAMPLE The volunteers *rendered* assistance to those who had lost their homes in the flood.

9. —————

10. **undertaking** (ŭn′dər-tā′kĭng) *noun* A task, assignment, or project.

RELATED WORD **undertake** *verb*

EXAMPLE The construction of the fifty-story building was an expensive *undertaking*.

10. —————

USAGE NOTE Although the related noun *undertaker* also means "one who undertakes a task," it is more commonly used to mean "mortician."

Exercise 1   Completing Definitions

On the answer line, write the word from the vocabulary list that best completes each definition.

1. To make something by combining ingredients is to __?__ it.

2. A venture or task is a(n) __?__ .

3. If you put a plan into effect, you __?__ it.

4. A person who knows how to manage an organization knows how to __?__ .

5. When you perform a task, you __?__ it.

6. If you enliven something, you __?__ it.

7. To __?__ a solution is to plan or invent one.

8. To give or provide something, such as a service, is to __?__ it.

9. A major attempt or effort is a(n) __?__ .

10. To restore something to action is to __?__ it.

1. _____ concoct _____

2. _____ undertaking _____

3. _____ implement _____

4. _____ administer _____

5. _____ execute _____

6. _____ animate _____

7. _____ devise _____

8. _____ render _____

9. _____ endeavor _____

10. _____ reactivate _____

Exercise 2   Using Words Correctly

Each of the following questions contains an italicized vocabulary word. Decide the answer to the question, and write *Yes* or *No* on the answer line.

1. Would a three-month-old puppy probably be *animated*?

2. Would the writing of a novel be a small *undertaking*?

3. Should a university president know how to *administer* a large organization?

4. Could a professional ice skater *execute* a difficult routine?

5. Is dialing a telephone an *endeavor* for most people?

6. Does a doctor *render* treatment to his or her patients?

7. Should a person *devise* a plan before tackling a difficult problem?

8. When you *implement* a plan, are you rejecting it?

9. Might a person *concoct* a new recipe?

10. If you *reactivate* an engine, do you turn it off?

1. _____ Yes _____

2. _____ No _____

3. _____ Yes _____

4. _____ Yes _____

5. _____ No _____

6. _____ Yes _____

7. _____ Yes _____

8. _____ No _____

9. _____ Yes _____

10. _____ No _____

Exercise 3   Choosing the Best Definition

For each italicized vocabulary word in the following sentences, write the letter of the best definition on the answer line.

1. In the story the sorcerer *concocts* a sleeping potion.
   a. labels   **b.** drinks   **c.** boils   **d.** mixes

1. _____ d _____

2. Studying to become a doctor is an *endeavor*.
   a. amusing game   c. good idea
   b. worthwhile pastime   d. major effort

2. ___d___

3. The general contractor will *administer* the construction of the skyscraper.
   a. assist   b. direct   c. eliminate   d. describe

3. ___b___

4. The aircraft company hoped to *reactivate* several old airplanes.
   a. destroy immediately   c. find unexpectedly
   b. change radically   d. restore to service

4. ___d___

5. Mort will *implement* a new exercise program tomorrow.
   a. put into effect   c. seriously record
   b. try to invent   d. hope to finish

5. ___a___

6. The climbing of Mount Everest is a serious *undertaking*.
   a. hike   b. project   c. mistake   d. crime

6. ___b___

7. Several pedestrians *rendered* assistance to the motorist who was stuck in the snow.
   a. gave   b. withheld   c. promised   d. called for

7. ___a___

8. Andrea was *animated* by an unexpected phone call.
   a. pleased   b. bored   c. enlivened   d. bothered

8. ___c___

9. Sammy *devised* a more efficient way to wash dishes.
   a. borrowed   b. enjoyed   c. invented   d. ignored

9. ___c___

10. In the last seconds, the quarterback *executed* a difficult play.
    a. invented   b. performed   c. botched   d. stopped

10. ___b___

Exercise 4   Using Different Forms of Words

Decide which form of the vocabulary word in parentheses best completes the sentence. The form given may be correct. Write your answer on the answer line.

1. The league has strict rules for the __?__ of injured players. (*reactivate*)

1. ___reactivation___

2. Bertha will soon __?__ the swimming of the English Channel. (*undertaking*)

2. ___undertake___

3. John's serve effectively __?__ Larry's backhand useless. (*render*)

3. ___rendered___

4. The __?__ was admired for her strong leadership abilities. (*execute*)

4. ___executive___

5. Student records are usually kept in the college __?__ building. (*administer*)

5. ___administration___

6. Parents were happy to hear about the __?__ of a new reading program in the city schools. (*implement*)

6. ___implementation___

7. The architect __?__ to design unusual houses. (*endeavor*)

7. ___endeavored___

8. The children enjoyed watching the __?__ cartoons. (*animate*)

8. ___animated___

9. Margaret invited everyone to taste her __?__ of fresh fruit. (*concoct*)

9. ___concoction___

10. Sid has __?__ a way to do his homework faster. (*devise*)

10. ___devised___

Reading Comprehension

Each numbered sentence in the following passage contains an italicized vocabulary word or related form. After you read the passage, you will complete an exercise.

The Mammalian Diving Reflex: Fact or Fiction?

Could someone be submerged in freezing cold water for twenty minutes and survive? Four-year-old Jimmy Tontlewicz did. Here is his story.

(1) On a cold January day in 1984, Jimmy's father **concocted** a plan to take Jimmy sledding on a frozen section of Lake Michigan in Chicago. (2) This pleasant **undertaking** soon turned into a disaster when the ice broke and Jimmy slipped into the freezing lake.

(3) For twenty minutes Jimmy remained underwater until scuba divers from the fire department **executed** a daring rescue mission. An ambulance then rushed Jimmy to the hospital, where he lay in a deathlike state. (4) Doctors surrounded Jimmy, trying to **devise** a treatment, but the case seemed hopeless. Jimmy's heart had stopped beating. His lungs were not functioning, and his temperature had dropped to eighty-five degrees.

(5) To start Jimmy's heart beating, the doctors **administered** electric shock treatment. Nothing happened. (6) They then **implemented** artificial respiration through the use of a respirator, hoping this would restore Jimmy's breathing. The respirator kept Jimmy's lungs inflated and his blood oxygenated, but there was still no sign of life. (7) All of the doctors' **endeavors** to save Jimmy appeared to have failed.

Suddenly, there was a beep on the screen of the heart monitor. Jimmy's heart had started. He was still alive! (8) His parents reacted to the news with great **animation.**

How could Jimmy have survived after his heart had stopped beating? Scientists explained that the shock of the cold water had put Jimmy into a state of hypothermia, a condition of abnormally low body temperature. The hypothermia had triggered what is known as the "mammalian diving reflex."

(9) This reflex **renders** marine mammals, such as whales and seals, able to remain underwater for long periods of time without breathing. The "mammalian diving reflex" takes place as blood is forced near the heart and the brain. These organs then function very slowly while the mammal remains underwater. (10) Once the mammal emerges from the water, normal heart and brain functions are **reactivated.**

It is rare that human beings exhibit the mammalian diving reflex. Luckily, Jimmy Tontlewicz is one of these people.

Please turn to the next page.

Reading Comprehension Exercise

Each of the following statements corresponds to a numbered sentence in the passage. Each statement contains a blank and is followed by four answer choices. Decide which choice fits best in the blank. The word or phrase that you choose must express roughly the same meaning as the italicized word in the passage. Write the letter of your choice on the answer line.

1. Jimmy's father __?__ a way to take his son sledding.
   a. thought of   **b.** imagined   **c.** obeyed   **d.** ignored

2. The __?__ turned into disaster when Jimmy slipped into the freezing water.
   a. holiday   **b.** venture   **c.** exercise   **d.** detour

3. Scuba divers __?__ a rescue mission that brought Jimmy to the surface.
   a. called   **b.** failed   **c.** planned   **d.** performed

4. Doctors tried to __?__ a treatment to save Jimmy's life.
   a. plan   **b.** remember   **c.** imitate   **d.** read about

5. They __?__ electric shock to Jimmy's heart.
   a. rejected   **b.** suggested   **c.** applied   **d.** questioned

6. Doctors then __?__ artificial respiration.
   a. invented   **b.** hoped for   **c.** rejected   **d.** carried out

7. However, their __?__ seemed to have failed.
   a. research   **b.** instruments   **c.** practice   **d.** attempts

8. Jimmy's parents experienced great __?__ at the change in their son's condition.
   a. puzzlement   **b.** depression   **c.** elation   **d.** uncertainty

9. Jimmy's recovery was due, in part, to the mammalian diving reflex, which __?__ the ability to remain underwater without breathing.
   a. tricks   **b.** provides   **c.** prevents   **d.** resembles

10. When the mammal leaves the water, the actions of the heart and brain are __?__ .
    a. dead   **b.** numbed   **c.** restored   **d.** forgotten

1. _____a_____
2. _____b_____
3. _____d_____
4. _____a_____
5. _____c_____
6. _____d_____
7. _____d_____
8. _____c_____
9. _____b_____
10. _____c_____

Practice with Analogies

DIRECTIONS   On the answer line, write the vocabulary word that completes each analogy.

See page 119 for some strategies to use with analogies.

1. Aid is to assist as enliven is to __?__ .
2. Occupation is to job as task is to __?__ .
3. Succeed is to accomplish as try is to __?__ .
4. Planner is to conceive as manager is to __?__ .
5. Solution is to devise as excuse is to __?__ .
6. Hatbox is to container as pen is to __?__ .

1. _____ animate _____
2. _____ undertaking _____
3. _____ endeavor _____
4. _____ administer _____
5. _____ concoct _____
6. _____ implement _____

Bonus: Lessons 21 and 22

(pages 133–138, 141–146)

Use the following clues to identify the words, and write the words on the lines to the right. Then circle each word in the word-search box below. The words may overlap and may read in any direction.

1. TOLERANCE involves __?__ for the opinions of others. (7 letters)

2. Synonym for ADMINISTER (6 letters)

3. CONCOCT comes from the Latin word meaning "to __?__." (4 letters)

4. Synonym for RENDER (4 letters)

5. An undertaking is a(n) __?__. (4 letters)

6. You can expect an AMENABLE person to __?__. (9 letters)

7. PRECONCEIVED opinions are formed __?__ knowing the facts. (6 letters)

9. Synonym for FORBEARANCE (8 letters)

9. To REACTIVATE is to make active __?__. (5 letters)

10. An attempt to accomplish something (8 letters)

11. ANIMATE comes from a Latin word meaning "__?__." (4 letters)

12. Federal laws prevent __?__ on the basis of race, creed, age, or sex. (14 letters)

13. To form or arrange in the mind (6 letters)

14. This prevents one from judging situations fairly. (4 letters)

15. A strong supporter of a party or cause (8 letters)

1. ___respect___
2. ___direct___
3. ___cook___
4. ___give___
5. ___task___
6. ___cooperate___
7. ___before___
8. ___patience___
9. ___again___
10. ___endeavor___
11. ___soul___
12. ___discrimination___
13. ___devise___
14. ___bias___
15. ___partisan___

```
A D M I N A N I M A C O N C O D E V I
T C E R I D I S C R I M I N A T I O N
E O S N D E A V O K E C I D U J E R P
X O I O M P L E O M E T N R E A C L U
E P R E U N D O E R U N A D B E R T A
C E K I N L C G A B I B S I A I C I R
S R O B J E C T I V E C I R I M A N O
A A C I M P L E M E N T M A T I S V
F T R B E A R R O X B J R E C T I E A
O E P A R T O L E S K S A T A A N S E
R P C O N F E C I V E D P J G U D I N
E G I V E D U A M E D I B A I N I V N
T L R B C T C E P S E R I S T E R E
O W A N E O B J E E C N E I T A P D T
```

CHALLENGE
Locate and circle the five additional vocabulary words in the word-search box.

abide
execute
implement
objective
prejudice

HOUGHTON MIFFLIN VOCABULARY FOR ACHIEVEMENT, SECOND COURSE

Notes

The following lists of words are from the preceding two lessons. You may wish to use these lists to pinpoint words for ongoing review or for mid-term or final exams.

Lesson 21

		Lesson 22	
abide	objective	administer	execute
amenable	partisan	animate	implement
bias	preconceived	concoct	reactivate
discrimination	prejudice	devise	render
forbearance	tolerance	endeavor	undertaking

Lesson 23

The Root -*port*-

The Latin root -*port*- is the basis of many of our English words. This root comes from the Latin word *portare*, which means "to carry." Therefore, *import* means to carry products into a location, and *export* means to carry products out of a location. *Transportation* is the means for carrying people from place to place. An *important* event carries weight. The words in this lesson come from the root -*port*- and refer in some way to the idea or action of carrying.

DEFINITIONS

After you have studied the definitions and example for each vocabulary word, write the word on the line to the right.

1. **comport** (kəm-pôrt') *verb*   To behave or conduct oneself in a particular way. (From the Latin *com-*, meaning "together," and *portare*, meaning "to carry")

   RELATED WORD   **comportment** *noun*

   EXAMPLE   The ambassadors *comported* themselves with dignity at the queen's garden party.

1. —————————

USAGE NOTE   Although the verbs *comport* and *deport* mean the same thing, *deport* is more often used for its other meaning, "to expel from a country."

2. **deportment** (dĭ-pôrt'mənt) *noun*   Conduct or behavior. (From the Latin *de-*, meaning "away," and *portare*)

   EXAMPLE   The speaker praised the polite *deportment* of the audience.

2. —————————

SEE   *comport.*

3. **disport** (dĭ-spôrt') *verb*   To entertain or occupy oneself; play. (From the Latin *dis-*, meaning "apart," and *portare*)

   EXAMPLE   At recess the children *disported* themselves on the playground.

3. —————————

4. **insupportable** (ĭn'sə-pôr'tə-bəl) *adjective*   **a.** Unbearable or intolerable.   **b.** Lacking grounds or defense; unjustifiable: *an insupportable argument.*

   EXAMPLE   In the Middle Ages, living conditions for many people were almost *insupportable.*

4. —————————

The Root -*port*-   **147**

5. **portable** (pôr′tə-bəl) *adjective* Easily carried; conveniently moved.   *noun* Something that is portable. (From the Latin word *portabilis*, meaning "able to be carried")

   RELATED WORD **portability** *noun*

   EXAMPLE I store my *portable* dishwasher in the corner of the kitchen.

5. _____

6. **portage** (pôr′tĭj) *noun* The carrying of a boat and supplies overland between two waterways.   *verb* To transport a boat and supplies. (From the Latin word *portare*)

   EXAMPLE We planned to learn *portage* on our canoe trip.

6. _____

7. **porter** (pôr′tər) *noun* **a.** A person employed to carry luggage for travelers. **b.** An attendant who waits on passengers in a railroad car. (From the Latin word *portare*)

   EXAMPLE The *porter* put our luggage on a rack and wheeled it to the elevator.

7. _____

8. **portfolio** (pôrt-fō′lē-ō′) *noun* **a.** A carrying case for loose papers, photographs, or drawings. **b.** The materials collected in a carrying case, especially when they are samples of a person's work: *a photographer's portfolio.* **c.** An itemized list of stocks, bonds, or other securities held by an investor or financial institution. (From the Latin words *folium*, meaning "leaf," and *portare*)

   EXAMPLE Janice's *portfolio* contained examples of her work in water colors.

8. _____

9. **purport** (pər-pôrt′) *verb* To give the impression, often falsely, of being or intending; to profess.   *noun* (pûr′pôrt′) The presented, intended, or implied meaning of something, such as a story. (From the Latin *pro-*, meaning "forth," and *portare*)

   RELATED WORD **purportedly** *adverb*

   EXAMPLE Kevin *purported* to be an excellent ice skater but fell flat on his face when he ventured onto the ice.

9. _____

10. **sportive** (spôr′tĭv) *adjective* Playful; frolicsome. (From the English word *disport*, meaning "to play" or "to amuse oneself")

   RELATED WORDS **sportively** *adverb*; **sportiveness** *noun*

   EXAMPLE The *sportive* puppies got tangled in each other's legs.

10. _____

Exercise 1 Writing Correct Words

On the answer line, write the word from the vocabulary list that fits each definition.

1. Easily carried; conveniently moved

1. _____portable_____

2. A folder or carrying case for drawings or documents; the samples of a person's work that are collected in the carrying case

2. _____portfolio_____

3. Frolicsome; playful

3. _____sportive_____

4. To conduct or behave oneself in a particular way

4. _____comport_____

5. Unbearable or intolerable; lacking grounds or defense

5. _____insupportable_____

6. The carrying of a boat and supplies overland between waterways

6. _____portage_____

7. A person who carries baggage for travelers; an attendant in a railroad car

7. _____porter_____

8. Conduct or behavior

8. _____deportment_____

9. To entertain oneself; play

9. _____disport_____

10. To give an impression of being or intending; the implied meaning

10. _____purport_____

Exercise 2 Using Words Correctly

Each of the following statements contains an italicized vocabulary word. Decide whether the sentence is true or false, and write *True* or *False* on the answer line.

1. If Nathan has a job as a *porter*, he is employed to sell clothing.

1. _____False_____

2. People who *disport* themselves never have anything to do.

2. _____False_____

3. If Jeanine *comports* herself with sophistication, she acts silly.

3. _____False_____

4. An *insupportable* excuse is one that cannot be defended.

4. _____True_____

5. You can carry a *portable* computer onto an airplane.

5. _____True_____

6. Twelve-year-old dogs are usually more *sportive* than puppies.

6. _____False_____

7. If Hans *purports* to be studying hard, he may be pretending to study.

7. _____True_____

8. Orchestras frequently perform lengthy *deportments*.

8. _____False_____

9. If Lily and Sylvester cannot learn *portage*, they cannot learn to carry their boat and supplies overland.

9. _____True_____

10. Max may use a *portfolio* to take his sketches to job interviews.

10. _____True_____

Exercise 3 Choosing the Best Word

Decide which vocabulary word or related form best expresses the meaning of the italicized word or phrase in the sentence. On the answer line, write the letter of the correct choice.

1. Mrs. Barrett always chooses a *playful* horse when she goes riding.
   a. sportive   **b.** disported   **c.** portable   **d.** insupportable

1. _____a_____

2. Before meeting the king and queen of Spain, Franklin read a book telling him how to *conduct* himself with royalty.
   a. portage   **b.** disport   **c.** comport   **d.** purport

2. _____ c

3. Giselle placed her manuscript in a *carrying case* and started for the publishing house.
   a. portage   **b.** portfolio   **c.** porter   **d.** deportment

3. _____ b

4. When Jenny broke her toes, she suffered *unbearable* pain for several days.
   a. sportive   **b.** insupportable   **c.** portable   **d.** purported

4. _____ b

5. A canal constructed through an isthmus saves boaters from having to *carry their boats across land.*
   a. disport   **b.** comport   **c.** purport   **d.** portage

5. _____ d

6. We enjoy watching Tom's kitten *play* with a ball of yarn.
   a. comport   **b.** portage   **c.** purport   **d.** disport

6. _____ d

7. The medical researchers *pretended* to have found a cure for the common cold.
   a. purported   **b.** comported   **c.** disported   **d.** portaged

7. _____ a

8. During the interview Ms. Runyon studied the *conduct* of each job applicant.
   a. deportment   **b.** porter   **c.** portage   **d.** portfolio

8. _____ a

9. Colin worked his way through college as a *luggage carrier* at an airport.
   a. portfolio   **b.** portage   **c.** comportment   **d.** porter

9. _____ d

10. Jan liked the first radio that the salesperson showed her because it was *easily carried.*
    a. insupportable   **b.** sportive   **c.** portable   **d.** purported

10. _____ c

Exercise 4 Using Different Forms of Words

Decide which form of the vocabulary word in parentheses best completes the sentence. The form given may be correct. Write your answer on the answer line.

1. The only way to get across the sandbar spanning the lake is to __?__ one's boat. *(portage)*

1. _____ portage

2. During the graduation parade at West Point, General Saxon studied the __?__ of the cadets. *(comport)*

2. _____ comportment

3. Although Kevin liked the features of the television, he wondered about its __?__ . *(portable)*

3. _____ portability

4. Mrs. O'Leary __?__ contributed ten thousand dollars to the firefighters' fund. *(purport)*

4. _____ purportedly

5. Tommy ran __?__ through the cornfield. *(sportive)*

5. _____ sportively

6. Proper __?__ is essential to Harry Higgins. *(deportment)*

6. _____ deportment

7. The witness's __?__ testimony weakened the prosecutor's case. *(insupportable)*

7. _____ insupportable

8. While Margaret was running to the bus, her __?__ opened, spilling her drawings into the snow. *(portfolio)*

8. _____ portfolio

9. Mr. Peters is an experienced ___?___ . *(porter)*

10. When she has a spare moment, the busy bank president always enjoys ___?___ with her grandchildren. *(disport)*

9. _____ porter _____

10. _____ disporting _____

Reading Comprehension

Each numbered sentence in the following passage contains an italicized vocabulary word. After you read the passage, you will complete an exercise.

Professional Modeling: Hard Work or Glamour?

(1) Some professional photographic models **purport** to lead glamorous and exciting lives. (2) Their **deportment** as celebrities is envied and copied. (3) Magazine and television advertisements show models **disporting** at the seashore, dining at elegant restaurants, or sitting at the wheel of the latest luxury car. Models who reach the top of their profession make large salaries, wear beautiful clothes, and enjoy varied assignments that take them all over the world.

This typical image of professional modeling is misleading, however. The work of a photographic model is harder and more demanding than it appears. Hours are long, and competition is fierce. Although the career attracts thousands of men, women, and children, only a small percentage become celebrities.

(4) Models begin their careers by assembling a **portfolio** of photographs that show them in a variety of poses with different facial expressions. (5) Advertisers select their models on the basis of how the models **comport** themselves in front of the camera. They must be well-groomed, physically attractive, and quite thin, be-

cause photographs give the illusion of adding extra pounds. Models must also possess the special "look" that the advertiser wants, whether it be innocence or elegance. The ability to create the image that the client requires depends on the model's acting ability. (6) He or she may have to portray a college student in one picture or a **porter** in an airport in another.

The nature of assignments varies tremendously. (7) **Portable** cameras have enabled producers to shoot commercials in unusual places, such as deserts and mountain peaks. (8) One day models may find themselves **portaging** canoes up a stream for a blue-jeans sales promotion. (9) The next day they may have to participate **sportively** in an exercise

class for the filming of a commercial. (10) They must hold uncomfortable poses that can seem almost **insupportable** under hot lights. Large amounts of patience, energy, and flexibility are necessary. Because advertisers plan far in advance, models may find themselves wearing bathing suits in winter or heavy coats in summer.

Careers in modeling are usually short-lived. Although there are exceptions, the average length of a photographic model's career is about five years. "New faces" are always trying to break into the business, and modeling agencies and advertisers are looking constantly for fresh replacements. Photographic modeling is an exciting career, but also one that is demanding.

Please turn to the next page.

Reading Comprehension Exercise

Each of the following statements corresponds to a numbered sentence in the passage. Each statement contains a blank and is followed by four answer choices. Decide which choice fits best in the blank. The word or phrase that you choose must express roughly the same meaning as the italicized word in the passage. Write the letter of your choice on the answer line.

1. Some professional models __?__ to lead glamorous and exciting lives.
   a. try   **b.** wish   **c.** practice   **d.** profess

   1. ____d____

2. People envy and copy the __?__ of models.
   a. poses   **b.** behavior   **c.** careers   **d.** families

   2. ____b____

3. Advertisements show models eating in elegant restaurants or __?__ at the beach.
   a. swimming   **c.** enjoying themselves
   b. looking glamorous   **d.** posing

   3. ____c____

4. Models first must assemble __?__ .
   a. samples of their work   **c.** an autobiography
   b. a client list   **d.** a group of friends

   4. ____a____

5. Advertisers are interested in the way models __?__ in front of the camera.
   a. appear beautiful   **c.** conduct themselves
   b. smile   **d.** are nervous

   5. ____c____

6. A model may have to portray a college student or a __?__ .
   a. professor   **b.** luggage carrier   **c.** rower   **d.** writer

   6. ____b____

7. __?__ cameras allow producers to shoot commercials in unusual locations.
   a. Advanced   **b.** Large   **c.** Highly technical   **d.** Easily carried

   7. ____d____

8. Models may have to __?__ canoes for a sales promotion.
   a. carry   **b.** paddle   **c.** fall out of   **d.** pose in

   8. ____a____

9. The following day they may have to participate __?__ in an exercise class.
   a. athletically   **b.** playfully   **c.** seriously   **d.** silently

   9. ____b____

10. Models must hold poses that can be almost __?__ under hot lights.
    a. historical   **b.** artistic   **c.** easy   **d.** unbearable

    10. ____d____

Writing Assignment

Imagine that you are a photographer hired by a sports magazine to take pictures of a canoe race for the magazine's next issue. To accompany your photographs, write a brief report that tells what you saw and photographed. You may want to include details about the contestants, the canoes, the setting, and the spectators. Use at least five of the vocabulary words from this lesson to describe your day's work and underline each word that you use.

Lesson 24

Activity and Inactivity

What does being active mean to you? Listed below are some different ways to spend time. Which pastimes require a high degree of activity? Which ones indicate inactivity?

Reading a book
Swimming
Solving a math problem
Debating a controversial issue
Writing a poem
Planning a fund-raising project
Jogging two miles

All of the above items show a high degree of activity. Some of the activities are physical, such as jogging two miles, while some of them are intellectual, such as writing a poem. To function well, however, the body and the mind also require periods of inactivity or rest. The words in this lesson will help you to distinguish further between the states of activity and inactivity.

WORD LIST

boisterous
chaos
complacent
dynamic
monotonous
restive
static
steadfast
tranquil
velocity

DEFINITIONS

After you have studied the definitions and example for each vocabulary word, write the word on the line to the right.

1. **boisterous** (boi′stər-əs) *adjective* **a.** Noisy and lacking restraint or discipline. **b.** Rough and stormy; violent. (From the Middle English word *boistres*, meaning "rude")

   RELATED WORDS **boisterously** *adverb;* **boisterousness** *noun*

   EXAMPLE The *boisterous* football fans tore down a goal post.

   1. _____

2. **chaos** (kā′ŏs′) *noun* Great disorder or confusion. (From the Greek word *khaos,* meaning "a state of formlessness")

   RELATED WORDS **chaotic** *adjective;* **chaotically** *adverb*

   EXAMPLE A small group of four-year-olds created *chaos* at their friend's birthday party.

   2. _____

3. **complacent** (kəm-plā′sənt) *adjective* Pleased or contented with oneself in an untroubled manner; self-satisfied; smug. (From the Latin word *complacere,* meaning "to please")

   RELATED WORDS **complacency** *noun;* **complacently** *adverb*

   EXAMPLE *Complacent* students sometimes do not study enough to do well in their classes.

   3. _____

4. **dynamic** (dī-năm′ĭk) *adjective* **a.** Forceful; energetic; vigorous. **b.** Characterized by change, action, or movement. (From the Greek word *dunamikos,* meaning "powerful")

RELATED WORD **dynamically** *adverb*

EXAMPLE The class applauded enthusiastically after Gerard's *dynamic* presentation.

4. _____

5. **monotonous** (mə-nŏt′n-əs) *adjective* **a.** Never varied or enlivened; repetitiously dull. **b.** Uttered or sounded in one repeated tone; unvarying in pitch. (From the Greek words *monos,* meaning "one," and *tonos,* meaning "tone")

RELATED WORDS **monotonously** *adverb;* **monotony** *noun*

EXAMPLE The office workers objected strongly to their *monotonous* routine.

5. _____

6. **restive** (rĕs′tĭv) *adjective* **a.** Impatient; restless; nervous because of restrictions, pressures, or delays. **b.** Hard to handle. (From the Latin word *restare,* meaning "to keep back")

RELATED WORDS **restively** *adverb;* **restiveness** *noun*

EXAMPLE The *restive* commuters waited an extra half-hour for the delayed bus.

6. _____

USAGE NOTE *Restive* is correctly used in place of *restless. Restive,* however, also suggests resistance to restraint.

7. **static** (stăt′ĭk) *adjective* **a.** Having no motion; at rest. **b.** Of or producing stationary electric charges; electrostatic. *noun* Random noise such as crackling in a radio receiver or specks on a television screen. (From the Greek word *statos,* meaning "standing")

RELATED WORD **statically** *adverb*

EXAMPLE A plot in a novel seems *static* when nothing important happens to the characters.

7. _____

8. **steadfast** (stĕd′făst′) *adjective* **a.** Fixed or unchanging; steady. **b.** Firmly loyal.

RELATED WORDS **steadfastly** *adverb;* **steadfastness** *noun*

EXAMPLE Mrs. Alvarez was *steadfast* in her dedication to abandoned animals.

8. _____

9. **tranquil** (trăng′kwəl) *adjective* Peaceful; calm; undisturbed; free from anxiety. (From the Latin word *tranquillus,* meaning "calm")

RELATED WORDS **tranquilize** *verb;* **tranquillity** *noun*

EXAMPLE Barry spent a *tranquil* vacation at the uncrowded mountain resort.

9. _____

10. **velocity** (və-lŏs′ĭ-tē) *noun* **a.** Speed. **b.** In science, the rate per unit of time at which an object moves in a specified direction. (From the Latin word *velox,* meaning "quick")

EXAMPLE Wind often travels at a high *velocity.*

10. _____

Name _____ Date _____

Exercise 1   Completing Definitions

On the answer line, write the word from the vocabulary list that best completes each definition.

1. When an activity is repetitive and boring, it is __?__ .

2. A person who is self-satisfied is __?__ .

3. To be rude and noisy is to be __?__ .

4. The rate of speed at which something travels is its __?__ .

5. To be energetic or forceful is to be __?__ .

6. When someone is firmly loyal, he or she is __?__ .

7. If something is calm and peaceful, it is __?__ .

8. Anything that is without motion or at rest is __?__ .

9. To be restless and impatient is to be __?__ .

10. A state of great confusion is called __?__ .

1. _____monotonous_____

2. _____complacent_____

3. _____boisterous_____

4. _____velocity_____

5. _____dynamic_____

6. _____steadfast_____

7. _____tranquil_____

8. _____static_____

9. _____restive_____

10. _____chaos_____

Exercise 2   Using Words Correctly

Each of the following statements contains an italicized vocabulary word. Decide whether the sentence is true or false, and write *True* or *False* on the answer line.

1. A library is an appropriate place for *boisterous* behavior.

2. A rock resting on the ground has no *velocity*.

3. If you try to improve something, you have a *complacent* attitude about it.

4. A *monotonous* speaker is likely to be popular with an audience.

5. A *restive* dog lies calmly in one place all day.

6. Quietly reading a book is a *tranquil* activity.

7. A cat who sits as still as a statue is in a *static* position.

8. Professional entertainers often have *dynamic* personalities onstage.

9. A good organizer aims for *chaos* in a project.

10. Someone with a *steadfast* opinion is quick to change his or her mind.

1. _____False_____

2. _____True_____

3. _____False_____

4. _____False_____

5. _____False_____

6. _____True_____

7. _____True_____

8. _____True_____

9. _____False_____

10. _____False_____

Exercise 3   Choosing the Best Word

Decide which vocabulary word or related form best expresses the meaning of the italicized word or phrase in the sentence. On the answer line, write the letter of the correct choice.

1. There was total *confusion* after the fox entered the hen house.
   a. restiveness   **b.** chaos   **c.** tranquillity   **d.** velocity

1. _____b_____

2. Lulu became *impatient* after waiting an hour in the dentist's chair.
   a. static   **b.** complacent   **c.** monotonous   **d.** restive

2. _____d_____

3. For Jim early morning is the most *peaceful* part of the day.
   a. tranquil   **b.** dynamic   **c.** steadfast   **d.** boisterous

3. _____a_____

4. Because of the friction caused by their high *rate of speed*, meteors burn up in the atmosphere.
   a. chaos   **b.** steadfastness   **c.** tranquillity   **d.** velocity

4. _____d_____

5. Margaret studied her *motionless* reflection in the still water of the lake.
   a. restive   **b.** dynamic   **c.** static   **d.** complacent

5. _____c_____

6. Reggie was *smug* about his high position in the company.
   a. monotonous   **b.** dynamic   **c.** static   **d.** complacent

6. _____d_____

7. Luther was so bored by the *repetitive* landscape that he fell asleep.
   a. monotonous   **b.** chaotic   **c.** restive   **d.** boisterous

7. _____a_____

8. Tammy's *energetic* personality helped her to win the election.
   a. tranquil   **b.** dynamic   **c.** complacent   **d.** monotonous

8. _____b_____

9. The soldiers pledged their *unchanging* allegiance to their country.
   a. restive   **b.** steadfast   **c.** boisterous   **d.** complacent

9. _____b_____

10. The angry residents became *noisy and undisciplined* during the community meeting.
    a. restive   **b.** steadfast   **c.** boisterous   **d.** dynamic

10. _____c_____

Exercise 4   Using Different Forms of Words

Decide which form of the vocabulary word in parentheses best completes the sentence. The form given may be correct. Write your answer on the answer line.

1. Loren could not be stirred out of his __?__ . *(complacent)*

1. _____complacency_____

2. The hockey team __?__ protested their disqualification from the tournament. *(boisterous)*

2. _____boisterously_____

3. Alicia works __?__ to preserve island wildlife. *(dynamic)*

3. _____dynamically_____

4. Brad could not explain his own __?__ . *(restive)*

4. _____restiveness_____

5. The sudden snowstorm had a __?__ effect on the region. *(chaos)*

5. _____chaotic_____

6. Sophia broke the __?__ of waiting for the bus by reading a book. *(monotonous)*

6. _____monotony_____

7. For a rocket to escape the earth's gravity, it must travel at a high __?__ . *(velocity)*

7. _____velocity_____

8. The __?__ of the forest setting attracted many tourists to the lodge. *(tranquil)*

8. _____tranquillity_____

9. The hunting dog remained in a __?__ position. *(static)*

9. _____static_____

10. __?__ is an admirable quality in a friend. *(steadfast)*

10. _____Steadfastness_____

Reading Comprehension

Each numbered sentence in the following passage contains an italicized vocabulary word or related form. After you read the passage, you will complete an exercise.

Home Run!

I was mad at Mom and didn't care if everyone in the Little League ballpark knew about it. Instead of watching my game, she had spent the whole afternoon reading a book.

"Did you at least see my home run?" I asked. (1) I had had the good luck to make the one and only run in what so far had been a very *monotonous* baseball game.

"Oh, you made a home run, Pam? (2) That must have been what all the *chaos* was about," Mom joked.

"Why did you bother to come to the game if you're not going to watch what goes on?" I ignored her conscience-stricken look. "You can read your book anytime. This is my last season in the league. It would be nice to have my own mother watch me play."

With that dramatic statement, I returned to left field, thinking that there were ways of striking out that had nothing to do with baseball. Mom just wasn't your typical Little League mother. (3) She was the *tranquil* type, always reading a book or thinking some deep thought. (4) She was just the opposite of some of the other mothers, who became *boisterous* every time their kids were up at bat. They watched their kids like hawks and bawled them out whenever they made a mistake. (5) That was bad too, but at least they were watch-ing the game, not *complacently* reading a book. Mom had better be watching now, I thought, as I took my place in left field.

It was now the sixth and final inning, with the score still 1 to 0. (6) If Lenny, our *dynamic* pitcher, could keep the Broncos from scoring, we'd win the game. With only one runner on third base and two batters out for the Broncos, it looked pretty good for us. It looked good, that is, until Lenny began holding his right arm and Coach Jones had to take him out of the game. Out of the dugout walked our worst pitcher, Billy Hargrove. Up to the plate stepped Tim Richards, one of the best batters in the league.

(7) Looking from Mom to Tim, I had never felt so *restive.* I wanted to yell at Mom to keep her eye on the game and, at the same time, I had to keep my eye on the ball. (8) Any second now, there might be a thunderous crack, and the ball would come sailing out at such a *velocity* that even Willie Mays would not be able to catch it.

I heard the hit, and before I knew it, the ball was in my glove. Then I dropped it! In that instant the Bronco on third base came across home plate, and Tim, with the whole team cheering him on, was running bases as if his life depended on it.

Quickly I looked at the grandstand. Mom was watching. I looked back down but couldn't find the ball. Finally I located it and made as strong a throw as I could toward home plate. My throw was right on target, but Tim beat the ball by an instant, sliding in for a home run. The score was now 2 to 1 in favor of the Broncos, and the team and the fans were wild. You would have thought they had won the league cham-pionship instead of only one game. The Broncos' coach huddled briefly with Coach Jones, and they decided not to finish out the inning since we were running very late.

I knew Mom had seen the whole thing. Embarrassed, I walked slowly toward the grandstand. (9) Mom was no longer sitting in a *static* position on a bench. She was walking quickly toward me. "Well," I said, "I guess you chose the wrong time to watch the game."

Mom put her arm around my shoulder. "You know, Pam," she said, "anyone can make a mistake, as you did when you dropped the ball. (10) But what pleased me was the way you remained *steadfast* and didn't panic. Then you made that good throw to home plate. I'll tell you something else, too — that game was really excit-ing. From now on, I won't miss a pitch!"

I smiled. As far as I was concerned, Mom had just hit a home run.

Please turn to the next page.

Reading Comprehension Exercise

Each of the following statements corresponds to a numbered sentence in the passage. Each statement contains a blank and is followed by four answer choices. Decide which choice fits best in the blank. The word that you choose must express roughly the same meaning as the italicized word in the passage. Write the letter of your choice on the answer line.

1. Pam called the baseball game __?__ .
   a. dull   **b.** fast-paced   **c.** tiring   **d.** action-packed

   1. _____ a _____

2. Mom suggested that Pam's home run created __?__ .
   a. a win   **b.** disorder   **c.** hilarity   **d.** a tie

   2. _____ b _____

3. Mom was a __?__ type of person.
   a. calm   **b.** rude   **c.** undisciplined   **d.** loud

   3. _____ a _____

4. Some of the other mothers were __?__ .
   a. talkative   **b.** quiet   **c.** moody   **d.** noisy

   4. _____ d _____

5. Instead of watching the game, Mom read __?__ .
   a. quickly   **b.** thoroughly   **c.** contentedly   **d.** nervously

   5. _____ c _____

6. The pitcher, Lenny, is described as __?__ .
   a. ambitious   **b.** lazy   **c.** motivated   **d.** forceful

   6. _____ d _____

7. Looking from Mom to Tim, Pam felt __?__ .
   a. uncertain   **b.** rested   **c.** impatient   **d.** renewed

   7. _____ c _____

8. Pam worried about the __?__ of a well-hit baseball.
   a. speed   **b.** outcome   **c.** direction   **d.** impact

   8. _____ a _____

9. Mom abandoned her __?__ position on the bench.
   a. quiet   **b.** motionless   **c.** uncomfortable   **d.** solitary

   9. _____ b _____

10. Mom praised Pam for being __?__ .
    a. calm   **b.** athletic   **c.** alert   **d.** dependable

    10. _____ d _____

Practice with Analogies

DIRECTIONS On the answer line, write the letter of the phrase that best completes the analogy.

See page 119 for some strategies to use with analogies.

1. Boisterous is to noisy as
   (A) restive is to restless   (B) dynamic is to static   (C) tranquil is to anxious
   (D) complacent is to restless

   1. _____ A _____

2. Chaos is to order as
   (A) upset is to pacify   (B) rigid is to strict   (C) confusion is to clarity
   (D) war is to conflict

   2. _____ C _____

3. Loyal is to steadfast as
   (A) friend is to acquaintance   (B) real is to genuine
   (C) steady is to wavering   (D) pledge is to promise

   3. _____ B _____

4. Speed is to velocity as
   (A) length is to capacity   (B) height is to altitude
   (C) kilometer is to distance   (D) falsehood is to veracity

   4. _____ B _____

5. Drone is to monotonous as
   (A) mumble is to inarticulate   (B) boring is to whine   (C) wail is to groan
   (D) stutter is to precise

   5. _____ A _____

Bonus: Lessons 23 and 24

(pages 147–158)

Use the clues to complete the crossword puzzle.

							¹P	O	R	T	A	B	L	E			
							L										
				²P	O	R	T	A	G	E							
³I						Y											
N						F											
S			⁴F			U		⁵C	H	A	O	S	⁶S			⁷S
U		⁸P	E	A	C	E	F	U	L			P				T
P			L									E				E
P		⁹D	I	S	¹⁰P	O	R	T		¹¹P	O	R	T	E	R	A
O		Y		E		N				O			D			D
R		N		L		E		¹²C	A	R	R	Y		¹³C		F
T		A		Y						T				O		A
A		M								F				M		S
¹⁴B	O	I	S	T	E	R	O	U	¹⁵S		O		¹⁶C	O	M	P	O	R	T
L		C							T		L		O		L	
E				¹⁷I	M	P	A	T	I	E	N	T		A	
								T		O		D		C	
								I		U		E	
								C		C		N	
								T			T		

Across

1. Conveniently moved
2. Necessary when land separates two waterways
5. Great confusion
8. Synonym for TRANQUIL
9. To entertain oneself
11. A person employed to carry luggage for travelers
12. The meaning of the Latin root *-port-*
14. Noisy and lacking discipline
16. To __?__ oneself in a particular way
17. Synonym for RESTIVE

Down

1. A SPORTIVE mood is __?__.
3. Intolerable
4. To PURPORT is to give the impression, often __?__, of being or intending.
6. Synonym for VELOCITY
7. Fixed or unchanging
9. From a Greek word meaning "powerful"
10. The meaning of the prefix in MONOTONOUS
11. A carrying case for papers or photographs
13. Smug
15. Having no motion
16. Synonym for DEPORTMENT

HOUGHTON MIFFLIN VOCABULARY FOR ACHIEVEMENT, SECOND COURSE

Notes

The following lists of words are from the preceding two lessons. You may wish to use these lists to pinpoint words for ongoing review or for mid-term or final exams.

Lesson 23

comport
deportment
disport
insupportable
portable

portage
porter
portfolio
purport
sportive

Lesson 24

boisterous
chaos
complacent
dynamic
monotonous

restive
static
steadfast
tranquil
velocity

Test: Lessons 22, 23, and 24

(pages 141–158)

Part A Completing the Definition

On the answer line, write the letter of the word or phrase that correctly completes each sentence.

1. *Executing* one's duties involves __?__ them.
   a. forgetting   **b.** performing   **c.** ignoring   **d.** enduring

   1. _____ b

2. A *restive* person is __?__ .
   a. silent   **b.** sleepy   **c.** cheerful   **d.** impatient

   2. _____ d

3. The carrying of __?__ is called *portage*.
   a. heavy objects by animals   **c.** manufactured articles
   b. a boat and supplies over land   **d.** luggage

   3. _____ b

4. To *reactivate* something is to restore its __?__ .
   a. reputation   **b.** value   **c.** glamor   **d.** ability to function

   4. _____ d

5. Anything that is __?__ is *static*.
   a. horrifying   **b.** electrical   **c.** exact   **d.** motionless

   5. _____ d

6. A *porter* __?__ .
   a. tastes food for a chef   **c.** carries baggage for travelers
   b. moves heavy furniture   **d.** writes articles for newspapers

   6. _____ c

7. To *implement* something is to __?__ .
   a. divide it equally   **c.** put it into effect
   b. store it carefully   **d.** reduce it to rubble

   7. _____ c

8. Someone can be described as *steadfast* when he or she is __?__ .
   a. loyal   **b.** snobbish   **c.** clever   **d.** poor

   8. _____ a

9. A *portfolio* is a(n) __?__ .
   a. stage set   **b.** advertisement   **c.** carrying case   **d.** vehicle

   9. _____ c

10. An *undertaking* is a __?__ .
    a. tool   **b.** discovery   **c.** substitute   **d.** task

    10. _____ d

11. A *tranquil* person feels __?__ .
    a. agitated   **b.** unhappy   **c.** calm   **d.** seasick

    11. _____ c

12. *Sportive* applies to something that is __?__ .
    a. playful   **b.** colorful   **c.** competitive   **d.** repetitive

    12. _____ a

13. When you *render* aid, you __?__ assistance.
    a. question the need for   **b.** provide   **c.** promise   **d.** schedule

    13. _____ b

14. The *velocity* of an object is its __?__ .
    a. uniqueness   **b.** speed   **c.** physical dimensions   **d.** sound

    14. _____ b

15. To *purport* to be something is to __?__ having that identity.
    a. profess   **b.** deny   **c.** question   **d.** prefer

    15. _____ a

HOUGHTON MIFFLIN VOCABULARY FOR ACHIEVEMENT, SECOND COURSE

Test: Lessons 22, 23, and 24

Part B Choosing the Best Word

On the answer line, write the letter of the word that best completes the sentence.

16. The advice columnist was unable to __?__ a solution to her reader's problem.
    a. execute **b.** undertake **c.** implement **d.** devise

    16. ___d___

17. Kevin quit his job after his working conditions had become __?__ .
    a. insupportable **b.** animated **c.** sportive **d.** restive

    17. ___a___

18. Insecure people may see confident individuals as __?__ .
    a. boisterous **b.** dynamic **c.** complacent **d.** sportive

    18. ___c___

19. Shirley made a valiant __?__ to save the old theater from demolition.
    a. portage **b.** undertaking **c.** endeavor **d.** deportment

    19. ___c___

20. Cafeteria monitors will not tolerate rowdy __?__ .
    a. concoctions **b.** velocity **c.** deportment **d.** chaos

    20. ___c___

21. Ruth was lulled to sleep by the __?__ drone of the lawnmower.
    a. static **b.** monotonous **c.** complacent **d.** dynamic

    21. ___b___

22. Quiz show contestants are expected to be intelligent and __?__ .
    a. animated **b.** reactivated **c.** restive **d.** monotonous

    22. ___a___

23. If the children promise to __?__ themselves well while we're out, we'll bring them a surprise.
    a. concoct **b.** comport **c.** animate **d.** purport

    23. ___b___

24. The rules make it clear that no __?__ activities are permitted during study hours.
    a. monotonous **b.** boisterous **c.** insupportable **d.** tranquil

    24. ___b___

25. This medication must be __?__ to the patient at four-hour intervals.
    a. administered **b.** reactiviated **c.** executed **d.** concocted

    25. ___a___

26. Chelsea picked up the __?__ television and carried it into the den.
    a. portable **b.** dynamic **c.** static **d.** monotonous

    26. ___a___

27. Robert is a powerful salesman because he has such a __?__ personality.
    a. restive **b.** monotonous **c.** tranquil **d.** dynamic

    27. ___d___

28. The secret agent __?__ an alibi for her absence from the country.
    a. executed **b.** disported **c.** concocted **d.** purported

    28. ___c___

29. If young children have the right kind of toys, they can learn to __?__ themselves at a very early age.
    a. reactivate **b.** animate **c.** render **d.** disport

    29. ___d___

30. The appearance of the cat created __?__ among the dogs in the veterinarian's waiting room.
    a. deportment **b.** static **c.** chaos **d.** velocity

    30. ___c___

Reading Skills

The Prefix *pre-*

A **prefix** is a letter or group of letters that is added to the beginning of a root. (A root is the part of a word that contains its basic meaning. A root also can be a complete word. Many different words can be formed from a single root.) Like all prefixes, *pre-* changes the meaning of the roots to which it is added. If you know the meaning of the prefix, you can determine the meanings of unfamiliar words. The prefix *pre-* has one common meaning.

PREFIX MEANING	WORD	DEFINITION
before; in advance	precaution	care taken before
	prefabricated	made in advance

Use the following procedure to determine the meaning of words that begin with the prefix *pre-*.

PROCEDURE

1. *Substitute the meaning of the prefix for the prefix itself.* Suppose that you do not know the meaning of the word *preconceptions*. Substituting the meaning of *pre-* gives you "before" or "in advance of" *conceptions*.

2. *Think of possible definitions for the entire word.* If you know that *conceptions* means "ideas," you can combine the meanings of both prefix and root. This will give you the rough definition "ideas formed before" or "ideas formed in advance."

3. *Check your definition of the word in the dictionary.* The dictionary defines *preconceptions* as "ideas or opinions formed before full knowledge is available." This is close to your definition.

Exercise   Using the Prefix *pre-*

Step 1: Write your definition of the italicized word in each of the following sentences. *Step 2:* Write the dictionary definition of the word. Choose the definition that best fits the way the word is used in the sentence. *Step 3:* Write a sentence in which you use the word correctly.

1. There is a *prepaid* delivery charge on all orders from this catalogue.

   YOUR DEFINITION Paid in advance

   DICTIONARY DEFINITION Paid in advance

   SENTENCE Our railroad tickets are prepaid.

Please turn to the next page.

2. Alan and I went to the *preview* of Veronica's exhibit at the art gallery.

YOUR DEFINITION ___An advance viewing___

DICTIONARY DEFINITION ___A private showing before presentation to the general public___

SENTENCE ___Constance took her two best friends to the sneak preview of the movie.___

3. Annie is excited about starting *preschool* this fall.

YOUR DEFINITION ___A school before regular school___

DICTIONARY DEFINITION ___A nursery school___

SENTENCE ___Sally's favorite activity in preschool is painting.___

4. The child was afraid of the models of *prehistoric* animals at the museum.

YOUR DEFINITION ___From a time before history___

DICTIONARY DEFINITION ___Of or belonging to the time before recorded history___

SENTENCE ___Cave drawings tell us much about the lives of prehistoric human beings.___

5. Katie is thinking about taking *premedical* courses at college.

YOUR DEFINITION ___In advance of medical school___

DICTIONARY DEFINITION ___Courses taken in preparation for the study of medicine___

SENTENCE ___Arthur's premedical training included chemistry and biology.___

6. I think your suggestion that we begin writing our report is *premature*.

YOUR DEFINITION ___Before the proper time; too soon___

DICTIONARY DEFINITION ___Done or happening too soon; too hasty___

SENTENCE ___Since the plumber hadn't even arrived, Anne's estimate of the damage was premature.___

7. I had a *premonition* that something might go wrong. (Clue: *-mon-* is a Latin root meaning "to warn.")

YOUR DEFINITION ___Advance warning___

DICTIONARY DEFINITION ___A feeling that something is going to happen___

SENTENCE ___Manny's premonition that the plane would be late turned out to be correct.___

8. Heavy snow and strong winds *precluded* a trip into the mountains. (Clue: *-clud-* is a Latin root meaning "to close.")

YOUR DEFINITION ___Closed off in advance___

DICTIONARY DEFINITION ___To make impossible by consequence___

SENTENCE ___This year heavy spring rains precluded early plowing of the fields.___

Lesson 25

Forms and Boundaries

Geographers study the physical features of the earth — where mountains are located, for example, and how they were formed. Of particular interest to geographers are the surface and boundary changes that take place continually. These scientists study the effects of natural forces, such as ocean currents that alter a coastline. They are concerned also with the ways in which people have altered the environment. Recently, for instance, there has been considerable research into how overgrazing by livestock has contributed to the expansion of the Sahara Desert.

The words in this lesson will help you to describe the forms and boundaries of the landscape. In addition, studying these words may provide insight into the kinds of environmental changes that interest geographers.

WORD LIST
confines
delineate
demarcation
distend
distinct
embody
marginal
omnipresent
penetration
substantial

DEFINITIONS

After you have studied the definitions and example for each vocabulary word, write the word on the line to the right.

1. **confines** (kŏn'fīnz') *noun* The limits of a space or area; borders; boundaries. (From the Latin *com-*, meaning "with," and *fines*, meaning "limits")

   RELATED WORD **confine** *verb*

   EXAMPLE Snow-capped mountains mark the northern *confines* of the state.

   1. _____
   USAGE NOTE The noun *confines* is plural and therefore takes a plural verb.

2. **delineate** (dǐ-lǐn'ē-āt') *verb* **a.** To draw or trace the outline of. **b.** To establish the exact limits or extent of: *delineate duties.* **c.** To describe in great detail. (From the Latin *de-*, meaning "from," and *linea*, meaning "line")

   RELATED WORD **delineation** *noun*

   EXAMPLE The architect *delineated* the slant of the roof and the placement of the columns.

   2. _____

3. **demarcation** (dē'mär-kā'shən) *noun* **a.** The process of determining and marking off the boundaries of something. **b.** A separation.

   RELATED WORD **demarcate** *verb*

   EXAMPLE The surveyor's map showed the lines of *demarcation* of our land.

   3. _____
   MEMORY CUE The *demarcation* between countries is clearly *marked* on a map.

4. **distend** (dĭ-stĕnd′) *verb* **a.** To swell or stretch, as if by internal pressure; expand or increase. **b.** To cause to expand. (From the Latin *dis-*, meaning "apart," and *tendere*, meaning "to stretch")

RELATED WORD **distention** *noun*

EXAMPLE The child's boil was badly *distended*.

5. **distinct** (dĭ-stĭngkt′) *adjective* **a.** Different in nature or quality; individual. **b.** Easily perceived by the senses or intellect; plain; clear; unmistakable. (From the Latin word *distinguere*, meaning "to separate")

RELATED WORDS **distinctly** *adverb;* **distinctness** *noun*

EXAMPLE Each of their five cats has a *distinct* personality.

MEMORY CUE Something is *distinct* if it can be *distinguished* easily from other similar objects.

6. **embody** (ĕm-bŏd′ē) *verb* **a.** To give concrete form to an idea; personify. **b.** To make or include as part of a united whole; organize; incorporate.

RELATED WORD **embodiment** *noun*

EXAMPLE The Olympic athletes *embody* the vigor of youth.

7. **marginal** (mär′jə-nəl) *adjective* **a.** Located at the border or edge; geographically adjacent. **b.** Minimal for requirements; barely acceptable. **c.** Written in the margin of a book.

RELATED WORDS **margin** *noun;* **marginally** *adverb*

EXAMPLE The states of Vermont and New Hampshire are *marginal* to Canada.

8. **omnipresent** (ŏm′nĭ-prĕz′ənt) *adjective* Existing everywhere at the same time. (From the Latin words *omnis,* meaning "all," and *praesens,* meaning "present")

RELATED WORD **omnipresence** *noun*

EXAMPLE Although we tend to forget about it, air is *omnipresent* in our atmosphere.

9. **penetration** (pĕn′ĭ-trā′shən) *noun* **a.** The process of piercing, entering, or forcing a way into. **b.** The ability to understand; insight. (From the Latin word *penitrare,* meaning "to penetrate")

RELATED WORD **penetrate** *verb*

EXAMPLE *Penetration* of the forest was nearly impossible because of dense thorn bushes.

10. **substantial** (səb-stăn′shəl) *adjective* **a.** Considerable in amount, importance, value, or extent. **b.** Strong; firm; solidly built. (From the Latin *sub-,* meaning "under," and *stare,* meaning "to stand")

RELATED WORD **substantially** *adverb*

EXAMPLE The volunteers donated a *substantial* portion of their time to the hospital.

4. _____

5. _____

6. _____

7. _____

8. _____

9. _____

10. _____

Exercise 1 Completing Definitions

On the answer line, write the word from the vocabulary list that fits each definition.

1. Different in nature or quality; easily perceived by the senses or intellect

2. Existing everywhere at the same time

3. To draw the outline of; establish the limits of

4. Considerable; strong and solidly built

5. To swell or stretch; cause to expand

6. The limits of a space; boundaries

7. To give concrete form to an idea; include as part of a united whole

8. The process of piercing, entering, or forcing a way into; the ability to understand

9. Situated at the border or edge; minimal for requirements

10. The process of determining and marking off boundaries; a separation

1. _____ distinct _____

2. _____ omnipresent _____

3. _____ delineate _____

4. _____ substantial _____

5. _____ distend _____

6. _____ confines _____

7. _____ embody _____

8. _____ penetration _____

9. _____ marginal _____

10. _____ demarcation _____

Exercise 2 Using Words Correctly

Decide whether the italicized vocabulary word has been used correctly in the sentence. On the answer line, write *Correct* for correct use and *Incorrect* for incorrect use.

1. During our snorkeling trip, we stayed within the *confines* of the coral reef surrounding the island.

2. The port of *demarcation* for the cruise is Miami.

3. Gerald showed only *marginal* interest in the speech.

4. The *substantial* tree house was not damaged by the storm.

5. The snow sculpture *distended* in the sun to half its original size.

6. During the meeting Mr. Manfredo was at a *distinct* disadvantage because he had not received the report.

7. Ardis wanted to have her hair *delineated* by a professional hairdresser.

8. The children attempted to *embody* the basket of apples, but it was much too heavy for them.

9. The *penetration* of moonlight through the branches of the tree created strange shadows.

10. Most people are *omnipresent* because they eat both animal and vegetable substances.

1. _____ Correct _____

2. _____ Incorrect _____

3. _____ Correct _____

4. _____ Correct _____

5. _____ Incorrect _____

6. _____ Correct _____

7. _____ Incorrect _____

8. _____ Incorrect _____

9. _____ Correct _____

10. _____ Incorrect _____

Exercise 3   Choosing the Best Definition

For each italicized vocabulary word or related form in the following sentences, write the letter of the best definition on the answer line.

1. Kyle's handwriting is so *distinct* that I can always recognize it.
   a. messy   **b.** unmistakable   **c.** elegant   **d.** complex

1. _____b_____

2. The spring floods destroyed a *substantial* portion of our corn crop.
   a. small   **b.** considerable   **c.** reserved   **d.** technical

2. _____b_____

3. If the ball passes beyond the *confines* of the playing floor, the referee calls "Out of bounds."
   a. limits   **b.** bleachers   **c.** wood   **d.** center

3. _____a_____

4. Mr. Hall will *delineate* the procedure for welding sheet metal.
   a. forget   **c.** memorize and use
   b. test   **d.** describe in detail

4. _____d_____

5. Classical Greek architecture *embodies* the principles of proportion and beauty.
   a. contradicts   **c.** gives concrete form to
   b. begins   **d.** prevents understanding of

5. _____c_____

6. The archaeologist made careful plans for *penetrating* the walls of the tomb.
   a. piercing   **b.** studying   **c.** walking by   **d.** uncovering

6. _____a_____

7. The homeowners argued about the line of *demarcation* between their properties.
   a. resemblance   **b.** difference   **c.** appearance   **d.** separation

7. _____d_____

8. The senator's new plan received *marginal* support.
   a. unanimous   **b.** local   **c.** minimal   **d.** great

8. _____c_____

9. The small child was frightened by the *distended* throat of the croaking bullfrog.
   a. colorful   **b.** exposed   **c.** swollen   **d.** ordinary

9. _____c_____

10. I have never played softball in the summer without being bothered by gnats; they seem to be *omnipresent*.
    a. everywhere   **b.** nuisances   **c.** hungry   **d.** multiplying

10. _____a_____

Exercise 4   Using Different Forms of Words

Decide which form of the vocabulary word in parentheses best completes the sentence. The form given may be correct. Write your answer on the answer line.

1. Elaine's teacher praised her __?__ of the Adirondack Mountain range on her map. *(delineate)*

1. _____delineation_____

2. The club's money-raising project was __?__ successful. *(marginal)*

2. _____marginally_____

3. Abraham Lincoln is considered by many to be the __?__ of honor and virtue. *(embody)*

3. _____embodiment_____

4. To score points in soccer, you must __?__ your opponents' defense and kick the ball into their goal. *(penetration)*

4. _____penetrate_____

5. I __?__ heard Mother tell us not to be late. *(distinct)*

5. _____distinctly_____

6. The students noted the __?__ of chaperones at the dance. *(omnipresent)*

7. After living in Italy for three months, Ella __?__ improved her ability to speak Italian. *(substantial)*

8. The __?__ of the juice cans indicated that their contents had been contaminated. *(distended)*

9. This map __?__ all the national parks in the southwestern United States. *(demarcation)*

10. Before being __?__ to quarters, Lieutenant Bragg surrendered his weekend pass. *(confines)*

6. _____*omnipresence*_____

7. _____*substantially*_____

8. _____*distention*_____

9. _____*demarcates*_____

10. _____*confined*_____

Reading Comprehension

Each numbered sentence in the following passage contains an italicized vocabulary word or related form. After you read the passage, you will complete an exercise.

Nature's Artistry: The Grand Canyon

My brother's desire to see the Grand Canyon during our family's trip to Arizona met with less than overwhelming enthusiasm. My parents believed that we would have enough sightseeing in our visits to American Indian reservations and desert museums. My sister and I could not imagine what appeal a deep gorge could have. Alexander was persuasive, though. He convinced all of us that we should not miss the Grand Canyon.

Alexander was right. The Grand Canyon was one of the most awe-inspiring spectacles we had ever seen. After only a brief glimpse, however, Alexander insisted that we go to the visitors' center, where we would learn about the canyon's geological history. From the exhibits in the center, we learned that the Grand Canyon is the world's most complex system of rock formations. **(1)** It owes its spectacular appearance to the powerful Colorado River, which cuts and shapes the canyon's **confines.** **(2)** Scientists believe that six million years ago the river was only a narrow stream moving across the Colorado Plateau, which forms a **substantial** portion of northwestern Arizona. Geologists have discovered a series of geological changes that forced the plateau above sea level. As the land rose, the slope along which the river ran became steeper. **(3)** The waters moved more rapidly and picked up sand and silt, which **distended** the river and cut a course through the rock. **(4)** Over thousands of years, water **penetrated** the rock to create the extraordinary peaks and valleys.

After our tour of the visitors' center, we returned to the south rim of the canyon. **(5)** Behind us and across the canyon, blue spruce and aspen trees served to **demarcate** the rims. **(6)** Below, the **margins** of the rock layers glistened in the sun. **(7)** Each rock layer was **delineated** by a different color. **(8)** **Distinct** shades of pink, green, violet, brown, and beige turned the canyon into a rainbow.

(9) We stood watching the shifting patterns of color and shadow and the seemingly **omnipresent** Colorado River churning its way toward the Gulf of Mexico. **(10)** Thanks to Alexander's stubbornness, we had the pleasure of learning about the Grand Canyon, a unique **embodiment** of nature's artistry.

Please turn to the next page.

Reading Comprehension Exercise

Each of the following statements corresponds to a numbered sentence in the passage. Each statement contains a blank and is followed by four answer choices. Decide which choice fits best in the blank. The word or phrase that you choose must express roughly the same meaning as the italicized word in the passage. Write the letter of your choice on the answer line.

1. The Grand Canyon owes its appearance to the Colorado River, which cuts and shapes the canyon's __?__ .
   a. rocks   **b.** limits   **c.** depth   **d.** height

   1. _____b_____

2. The river was once only a stream that crossed the Colorado Plateau, a __?__ portion of northwestern Arizona.
   a. rocky   **b.** flat   **c.** small   **d.** considerable

   2. _____d_____

3. Sand and silt __?__ the river and helped it cut a course through the rock.
   a. moved   **b.** stopped   **c.** expanded   **d.** slowed

   3. _____c_____

4. Water __?__ the rock to form the canyon's peaks and valleys.
   a. forced its way through   **c.** poured over
   b. bounced off   **d.** covered

   4. _____a_____

5. Blue spruce and aspen trees served to __?__ the canyon rims.
   a. set the boundaries of   **c.** protect the fragility of
   b. shade   **d.** cross over

   5. _____a_____

6. The __?__ of the rock layers glistened in the sun.
   a. colors   **b.** roughness   **c.** center   **d.** edges

   6. _____d_____

7. Each rock layer __?__ a different color.
   a. was covered over by   **c.** was outlined in
   b. was created by   **d.** was decorated with

   7. _____c_____

8. __?__ shades of pink, green, violet, brown, and beige turned the Canyon into a rainbow.
   a. Pale   **b.** Different   **c.** Intense   **d.** Blended

   8. _____b_____

9. The Colorado River seems __?__ .
   a. all-powerful   **c.** friendly
   b. to be everywhere   **d.** to stop suddenly

   9. _____b_____

10. The Grand Canyon is a unique __?__ of nature's artistry.
    a. example   **b.** tourist site   **c.** rejection   **d.** history

    10. _____a_____

Writing Assignment

Write a descriptive paragraph about a scene that you find attractive or interesting. For example, you might describe a park in autumn or a skyline at sunset. Write the paragraph for a real or imaginary friend. Use at least five of the vocabulary words from this lesson in your description and underline them.

The Root *-pel-*

The Latin words *pellere*, meaning "to drive out, beat, or strike," and *appellare*, meaning "to summon or speak to," have both contributed the root *-pel-* to the English language. A large number of words come from this root. For example, if you are *expelled* from school, you are forced to leave. If a friend *dispels* your doubts about something, those doubts are driven from your mind. An *appeal* is an earnest or urgent request, while one's *appellation* is one's name or title.

Although their etymologies are different, all of the words in this lesson come from the root *-pel-*. As you study each word, pay close attention to its etymology.

DEFINITIONS

After you have studied the definitions and example for each vocabulary word, write the word on the line to the right.

1. **compel** (kəm-pĕl′) *verb* **a.** To force to do something by using power or influence. **b.** To make necessary: *compels careful money management.* (From the Latin *com-*, meaning "together," and *pellere*, meaning "to drive")

   RELATED WORD **compelling** *adjective*

   EXAMPLE High prices may *compel* people to save fuel.

   1. _____
   SEE *impel.*

2. **compulsion** (kəm-pŭl′shən) *noun* **a.** An urge, often unreasonable, that is nearly impossible to control: *a compulsion to eat.* **b.** The force or influence that makes it necessary for someone to do something. (From the Latin word *compulsus*, meaning "driven together" or "compelled")

   RELATED WORDS **compulsive** *adjective;* **compulsory** *adjective*

   EXAMPLE Eric's *compulsion* for neatness and organization pleases his parents.

   2. _____

3. **impel** (ĭm-pĕl′) *verb* **a.** To urge to action; spur. **b.** To drive forward; propel. (From the Latin *in-*, meaning "in," and *pellere*, meaning "to drive")

   EXAMPLE Speaking in a soft, coaxing voice, Veronica *impelled* her horse to go faster.

   3. _____
   USAGE NOTE *Compel* and *impel* share the sense of using physical or other force. *Compel* suggests more actual force, whereas *impel* suggests inner drive.

4. **impulsive** (ĭm-pŭl′sĭv) *adjective* Likely to act suddenly without thinking; uncalculated. (From the Latin word *impulsus*, meaning "driven into" or "impelled")

RELATED WORDS **impulse** *noun;* **impulsively** *adverb;* **impulsiveness** *noun*

EXAMPLE The *impulsive* driver made a left turn without signaling and nearly caused an accident.

5. **peal** (pēl) *noun* **a.** The ringing of a set of bells. **b.** A loud burst of noise or series of noises: *peals of laughter.* *verb* To sound loudly; ring. (From the Latin word *appellare*, meaning "to call upon")

EXAMPLE The hourly *peal* of the church bells helped Candace learn to tell time.

6. **propulsion** (prə-pŭl′shən) *noun* The act or process of driving, moving, or pushing forward. (From the Latin *pro-*, meaning "forward," and *pulsus*, meaning "a beat" or "a stroke")

RELATED WORD **propel** *verb*

EXAMPLE Jet *propulsion* radically changed the nature of air travel.

7. **pulsate** (pŭl′sāt′) *verb* **a.** To expand and contract rhythmically, as the heart does; throb; beat. **b.** To move or occur in a regular, rhythmical way. (From the Latin word *pulsare*, meaning "to strike" or "to beat")

RELATED WORD **pulsation** *noun*

EXAMPLE Luke could feel the bird's heart *pulsate* in fear.

8. **repeal** (rĭ-pēl′) *verb* To withdraw or cancel, especially by formal or official act; revoke. *noun* The act or process of repealing. (From the Old French *re-*, meaning "back," and *apeler*, meaning "to appeal")

EXAMPLE The commission *repealed* the ban on watering lawns.

9. **repellent** (rĭ-pĕl′ənt) *adjective* **a.** Acting or tending to drive off, force back, or keep away. **b.** Causing dislike or disgust. **c.** Resistant to a specified substance or influence: *water-repellent cloth.* *noun* Something that repels. (From the Latin *re-*, meaning "back," and *pellere*, meaning "to drive")

RELATED WORDS **repel** *verb;* **repellence** *noun*

EXAMPLE The odor from the paper mill was *repellent.*

10. **repulse** (rĭ-pŭls′) *verb* **a.** To drive back. **b.** To reject or refuse firmly or suddenly. (From the Latin word *repulsus*, meaning "driven away" or "repelled")

RELATED WORDS **repulsion** *noun;* **repulsive** *adjective*

EXAMPLE The odor of Limburger cheese *repulses* Anna.

4. _____

5. _____

6. _____

7. _____

8. _____

9. _____

SEE *repulse.*

10. _____

USAGE NOTE *Repel* and *repulse* share the sense of physically driving back or off. *Repulse* can also mean "to rebuff with rudeness," but *repel* connotes strong distaste or aversion.

Exercise 1   Writing Correct Words

On the answer line, write the word from the vocabulary list that fits each definition.

1. An unreasonable urge
2. The act or process of driving, moving, or pushing forward
3. Tending to drive off or keep away; causing disgust
4. To make someone do something by using force or influence
5. To urge to action; drive forward
6. To drive back; reject
7. To expand and contract rhythmically
8. Likely to act suddenly without thinking
9. To withdraw or cancel
10. The ringing of a set of bells; a loud burst of noise

1. _____compulsion_____
2. _____propulsion_____
3. _____repellent_____
4. _____compel_____
5. _____impel_____
6. _____repulse_____
7. _____pulsate_____
8. _____impulsive_____
9. _____repeal_____
10. _____peal_____

Exercise 2   Using Words Correctly

Decide whether the italicized vocabulary word has been used correctly in the sentence. On the answer line, write *Correct* for correct use and *Incorrect* for incorrect use.

1. An *impulsive* reply may be more truthful than one that has been carefully thought out.
2. Although the citizens disliked the new policy, the legislators would not *repeal* it.
3. Larry felt a *compulsion* to explore the cave.
4. A *peal* of leaves fell from the oak tree.
5. The doctor decided immediately to *repulse* my appendix.
6. The film showed blood vessels *pulsating* as blood ran through them.
7. The *propulsion* to operate a television set comes from electricity.
8. More than anything else, curiosity *impels* the research scientist.
9. Barney *compelled* the rock down the hill.
10. Researchers attracted the coyote to the enclosure with a *repellent* mixture of food.

1. _____Correct_____
2. _____Correct_____
3. _____Correct_____
4. _____Incorrect_____
5. _____Incorrect_____
6. _____Correct_____
7. _____Incorrect_____
8. _____Correct_____
9. _____Incorrect_____
10. _____Incorrect_____

Exercise 3   Choosing the Best Word

Decide which vocabulary word or related form best expresses the meaning of the italicized word or phrase in the sentence. On the answer line, write the letter of the correct choice.

1. Brian experienced an *unreasonable urge* to dive into the icy water.
   a. repellent   **b.** peal   **c.** propulsion   **d.** compulsion

1. _____d_____

The Root *-pel-*   **169**

2. *Loud bursts* of laughter filled the classroom when Lou's hamster escaped. 2. _____c_____
   a. Propulsions **b.** Repeals **c.** Peals **d.** Repellents

3. The odor of a skunk is certainly *disgusting*. 3. _____a_____
   a. repellent **b.** repealing **c.** impulsive **d.** compulsive

4. A longing to be alone *pushed* Sally to drive to the mountains. 4. _____d_____
   a. pulsated **b.** repealed **c.** repulsed **d.** impelled

5. The committee *canceled* the funding for plant research. 5. _____b_____
   a. impelled **b.** repealed **c.** compelled **d.** pulsated

6. The engine provided no *force pushing forward* and needed repair. 6. _____a_____
   a. propulsion **b.** compulsion **c.** repellent **d.** peal

7. Dwight's parents *force* him to do well in school. 7. _____c_____
   a. repeal **b.** repel **c.** compel **d.** pulsate

8. Daniel is so *likely to act without thinking* that he often invites friends for dinner without having any food in the house. 8. _____b_____
   a. repealed **b.** impulsive **c.** repellent **d.** impelled

9. The twins *rejected* Lee's efforts to be friendly. 9. _____c_____
   a. pulsated **b.** repealed **c.** repulsed **d.** compelled

10. Cesar could feel his heart *beat rhythmically* as he raced out of the burning house. 10. _____d_____
    a. compel **b.** repeal **c.** impel **d.** pulsate

Exercise 4 Using Different Forms of Words

Decide which form of the vocabulary word in parentheses best completes the sentence. The form given may be correct. Write your answer on the answer line.

1. A __?__ of thunder broke the silence. *(peal)* 1. _____peal_____

2. Laws make it __?__ to wear seat belts while driving in certain states. *(compulsion)* 2. _____compulsory_____

3. An effective lieutenant __?__ troops to fight bravely. *(impel)* 3. _____impels_____

4. The naturalist used a homemade lotion to __?__ insects. *(repellent)* 4. _____repel_____

5. Larry studied the __?__ of ships by steam turbines. *(propulsion)* 5. _____propulsion_____

6. The litter laws could not be __?__ for at least two years. *(repeal)* 6. _____repealed_____

7. Agatha Christie's novels are __?__ mysteries. *(compel)* 7. _____compelling_____

8. The __?__ beat of the music soon had the crowd tapping their toes. *(pulsate)* 8. _____pulsating_____

9. My first efforts in cooking were __?__ . *(repulse)* 9. _____repulsive_____

10. Christopher's father worried that his son's __?__ would lead him to make poor decisions. *(impulsive)* 10. _____impulsiveness_____

Reading Comprehension

Each numbered sentence in the following passage contains an italicized vocabulary word or related form. After you read the passage, you will complete an exercise.

The Wright Brothers: Fathers of Aviation

Many great inventions are greeted with ridicule and disbelief. The invention of the airplane was no exception. **(1)** Although many people who heard about the first powered flight on December 17, 1903, were excited and impressed, others reacted with **peals** of laughter. **(2)** The idea of flying an aircraft was **repulsive** to some people. **(3)** Such people called Wilbur and Orville Wright, the inventors of the first flying machine, **impulsive** fools. Negative reactions, however, did not stop the Wrights. **(4)** **Impelled** by their desire to succeed, they continued their experiments in aviation.

(5) Orville and Wilbur Wright had always had a **compelling** interest in aeronautics and mechanics. As young boys they earned money by making and selling kites and mechanical toys. Later, they designed a newspaper-folding machine, built a printing press, and operated a bicycle-repair shop. **(6)** In 1896, when they read about the death of Otto Lilienthal, the brothers' interest in flight grew into a **compulsion.**

Lilienthal, a pioneer in hang-gliding, had controlled his gliders by shifting his body in the desired direction. **(7)** This idea was **repellent** to the Wright brothers, however, and they searched for more efficient methods to control the balance of airborne vehicles. In 1900 and 1901, the Wrights tested numerous gliders and developed control techniques. The brothers' inability to obtain enough lift power for the gliders almost led them to abandon their efforts.

After further study, the Wright brothers concluded that the published tables of air pressure on curved surfaces must be wrong. They set up a wind tunnel and began a series of experiments with model wings. **(8)** Because of their efforts, the old tables were **repealed** in time and replaced by the first reliable figures for air pressure on curved surfaces. This work, in turn, made it possible for them to design a machine that would fly.

In 1903 the Wrights built their first airplane, which cost less than one thousand dollars. **(9)** They even designed and built their own source of **propulsion** — a lightweight gasoline engine. **(10)** When they started the engine on December 17, the airplane **pulsated** wildly before taking off. The plane managed to stay aloft for twelve seconds, however, and it flew one hundred twenty feet.

By 1905 the Wrights had perfected the first airplane that could turn, circle, and remain airborne for half an hour at a time. Others had flown in balloons or in hang gliders, but the Wright brothers were the first to build a full-size machine that could fly under its own power. As the contributors of one of the most outstanding engineering achievements in history, the Wright brothers are accurately called the fathers of aviation.

Please turn to the next page.

Reading Comprehension Exercise

Each of the following statements corresponds to a numbered sentence in the passage. Each statement contains a blank and is followed by four answer choices. Decide which choice fits best in the blank. The word or phrase that you choose must express roughly the same meaning as the italicized word in the passage. Write the letter of your choice on the answer line.

1. Some of the people who heard about the first airplane flight reacted with __?__ of laughter.
   a. bursts   **b.** a lack   **c.** cheers   **d.** reports

   1. _____a_____

2. The idea of flying an aircraft was __?__ to some people.
   a. boring   **b.** distasteful   **c.** encouraging   **d.** exciting

   2. _____b_____

3. People thought that the Wright brothers had __?__ .
   a. acted without thinking
   b. thought without acting
   c. been too cautious
   d. been negatively influenced

   3. _____a_____

4. The Wright brothers were __?__ by their desire to succeed.
   a. stopped   **b.** exhausted   **c.** defeated   **d.** spurred on

   4. _____d_____

5. The Wrights had always had a __?__ interest in aeronautics and mechanics.
   a. powerful   **b.** slight   **c.** financial   **d.** lively

   5. _____a_____

6. The Wrights' interest in flight grew into a __?__ .
   a. financial empire   **b.** fear   **c.** need to act   **d.** plan

   6. _____c_____

7. Lilienthal's idea about controlling airborne vehicles was __?__ the Wrights.
   a. proven wrong by   **c.** opposite to the ideas of
   b. researched by   **d.** disliked by

   7. _____d_____

8. The old tables were __?__ and replaced by the first reliable figures for air pressure on curved surfaces.
   a. destroyed   **b.** canceled   **c.** decreased   **d.** multiplied

   8. _____b_____

9. The Wrights designed and built their own source of __?__ .
   a. force for moving forward   **c.** turning
   b. stopping   **d.** force for turning around

   9. _____a_____

10. As the engine started, the airplane __?__ wildly.
    a. vibrated   **b.** stalled   **c.** skipped   **d.** ran

    10. _____a_____

Writing Assignment

In your science class, suppose that you are about to begin a unit on famous inventors. Your teacher has asked you to choose an invention that interests you and to do library research on the inventor. Write a paragraph that summarizes the inventor's life and include an explanation of some of the influences that led to his or her achievements. In your paragraph use at least four of the vocabulary words from this lesson and underline them.

Bonus: Lessons 25 and 26

(pages 161–172)

Unscramble the letters of each italicized vocabulary word, and write the word on the answer line to the right.

1. Nobel scientists *mybdoe* the spirit of dedication and hard work.

2. Each of the puppies has a(n) *nitcsdti* personality.

3. The American colonists fought to *eaeprl* England's harsh and restrictive laws.

4. The insect *npllreeet* had little effect on the ravenous mosquitoes.

5. Finishing the race, the runner could feel her heart *stlpaue*.

6. We sometimes forget that the change of seasons is *pmerintenos*.

7. Because of the dense vegetation, *eettnpnrioa* of the jungle was difficult.

8. The students spent a(n) *ttlbsaiusan* portion of their time studying.

9. The townspeople were accustomed to the hourly *lpae* of the church bells.

10. Louise was not a(n) *luievmpsi* shopper, but she could not resist buying another hat.

11. The patient's *nsmooiplcu* to exercise worried the doctor.

12. The countries of Switzerland and Italy are *cjndtaae* to southern France.

13. Bob's sprained hand was definitely *dsedidten*.

14. The odor of the polluted pond *eueldspr* the hikers.

15. In a gentle tone, the child *lldpemei* the cat to jump down from the closet shelf.

16. The burning desert marked the eastern *esiocfnn* of the country.

17. The racing car's incredible speed was due to jet *sluoiopprn*.

18. The artist *eeeatddlni* the arches and columns of the amphitheater in the sketch.

19. The lines of *rcmtneaaoid* showed up clearly on the surveyor's map.

20. A shortage of gasoline *ldploeecm* people to drive less.

1.	embody
2.	distinct
3.	repeal
4.	repellent
5.	pulsate
6.	omnipresent
7.	penetration
8.	substantial
9.	peal
10.	impulsive
11.	compulsion
12.	adjacent
13.	distended
14.	repulsed
15.	impelled
16.	confines
17.	propulsion
18.	delineated
19.	demarcation
20.	compelled

BONUS Lessons 25 and 26

HOUGHTON MIFFLIN VOCABULARY FOR ACHIEVEMENT, SECOND COURSE

Notes

The following lists of words are from the preceding two lessons. You may wish to use these lists to pinpoint words for ongoing review or for mid-term or final exams.

Lesson 25

confines
delineate
demarcation
distend
distinct

embody
marginal
omnipresent
penetration
substantial

Lesson 26

compel
compulsion
impel
impulsive
peal

propulsion
pulsate
repeal
repellent
repulse

Lesson 27

Secrecy and Openness

Things may be hidden from view or open for everyone to see. Questions on a test are kept secret so that no one taking the test will have an unfair advantage. Governments also conceal certain information for security reasons. Top-level information on defense is kept secret.

Much information, though, is readily available. Government officials must reveal information about their financial status. Companies must make certain information available about the products they sell.

Each word in this lesson relates to the concept of secrecy or to the concept of openness. The words will help you to understand the concepts and to write about or discuss them.

DEFINITIONS

After you have studied the definitions and example for each vocabulary word, write the word on the line to the right.

1. **accessible** (ăk-sĕs′ə-bəl) *adjective* **a.** Easily obtained, approached, or reached. **b.** Easy to communicate with.

   RELATED WORDS **access** *noun;* **accessibility** *noun*

   EXAMPLE The company library is *accessible* to all employees.

   1. _____

2. **cache** (kăsh) *noun* **a.** A stockpile, reserve, or supply, usually hidden; a store of goods in a hiding place. **b.** Such a hiding place itself. (From the French word *cacher*, meaning "to hide")

   EXAMPLE The secret panel in the library concealed a *cache* of jewels and stock certificates.

   2. _____

3. **conspicuous** (kən-spĭk′yōō-əs) *adjective* Noticeable; obvious. (From the Latin word *conspicere*, meaning "to observe")

   RELATED WORDS **conspicuously** *adverb;* **conspicuousness** *noun*

   EXAMPLE Maurice made himself *conspicuous* by wearing funny hats.

   3. _____

4. **disclosure** (dĭ-sklō′zhər) *noun* **a.** The act or process of making known; a revelation. **b.** Something that is made known.

   RELATED WORD **disclose** *verb*

   EXAMPLE The museum intends to make a *disclosure* to the press of the amount paid for the Goya portrait.

   4. _____

5. **inter** (ĭn-tûr′) *verb* To bury; place in a grave or tomb. (From the Latin *in-*, meaning "in," and *terra*, meaning "earth")

RELATED WORD **interment** *noun*

EXAMPLE Some pharaohs of ancient Egypt were *interred* in pyramids.

5. _____

6. **intrigue** (ĭn′trēg′) *noun* A scheme or secret plot.   *verb* (ĭn-trēg′) **a.** To devise a plot; scheme. **b.** To fascinate; arouse the interest of. (From the Latin word *intricare*, meaning "to entangle")

EXAMPLE At least three people were involved in the *intrigue* to steal the crown jewels.

6. _____

7. **obscure** (ŏb-skyо̄o͞r′) *adjective* **a.** Not easily seen or found; remote. **b.** Not well known; uncommon. **c.** Difficult to understand.   *verb* To make unclear; darken. (From the Latin word *obscurare*, meaning "to darken")

RELATED WORDS **obscurely** *adverb;* **obscurity** *noun*

EXAMPLE At the end of the garden, there was an *obscure* doorway leading to a secret passage.

7. _____

8. **secluded** (sĭ-klо̄o͞′dĭd) *adjective* Isolated; set apart from others. (From the Latin word *secludere*, meaning "to shut away")

RELATED WORDS **seclude** *verb;* **seclusion** *noun*

EXAMPLE No roads passed near the *secluded* house.

8. _____

9. **unavailable** (ŭn′ə-vā′lə-bəl) *adjective* Not obtainable; not at hand; inaccessible.

RELATED WORD **unavailability** *noun*

EXAMPLE My ophthalmologist was *unavailable* for appointments on Tuesdays because he taught courses at the university.

9. _____

10. **unearth** (ŭn-ûrth′) *verb* To dig up; bring up out of the ground.

EXAMPLE Sometimes farmers *unearth* fossils while plowing their fields.

10. _____

Name _____ Date _____

Exercise 1 Matching Words and Definitions

Match the definition in Column B with the word in Column A. Write the letter of the correct definition on the answer line.

Column A	Column B
1. unearth	a. a store of goods hidden away
2. disclosure	b. a secret scheme
3. inter	c. easily obtained
4. secluded	d. to dig up
5. cache	e. not obvious
6. unavailable	f. to bury in a grave
7. accessible	g. a revelation
8. obscure	h. noticeable
9. conspicuous	i. not at hand
10. intrigue	j. isolated

1. _____ d _____
2. _____ g _____
3. _____ f _____
4. _____ j _____
5. _____ a _____
6. _____ i _____
7. _____ c _____
8. _____ e _____
9. _____ h _____
10. _____ b _____

Exercise 2 Using Words Correctly

Decide whether the italicized vocabulary word has been used correctly in the sentence. On the answer line, write *Correct* for correct use and *Incorrect* for incorrect use.

1. I walked right past my friend because she was so *conspicuous*.

2. Shoes in Sheila's unusual size were *unavailable* at the discount store.

3. The meaning of the poem was so *obscure* that Sally found it easy to understand.

4. Harold swiftly *unearthed* the bone that Rover had buried.

5. The professor is so *accessible* to students that it is impossible to find him between classes.

6. Gently Wendy *interred* the flower arrangement on top of the dining room table.

7. "*Disclosure* the door, and let in some fresh air," said Tom.

8. Mrs. Kasarda needed *cache* to buy the groceries.

9. Melvin found a *secluded* spot in the park where he could read without being disturbed.

10. The police force conducted a public *intrigue* in order to locate the missing jewels.

1. _____ Incorrect _____
2. _____ Correct _____
3. _____ Incorrect _____
4. _____ Correct _____
5. _____ Incorrect _____
6. _____ Incorrect _____
7. _____ Incorrect _____
8. _____ Incorrect _____
9. _____ Correct _____
10. _____ Incorrect _____

Exercise 3 Choosing the Best Definition

For each italicized vocabulary word in the following sentences, write the letter of the best definition on the answer line.

1. The airport is easily *accessible* from the city.
   a. detoured   **b.** within reach   **c.** visible   **d.** crowded

1. _____ b _____

2. Katherine is familiar with many *obscure* varieties of plants.　　2. ____d____
   a. colorful　**b.** poisonous　**c.** isolated　**d.** uncommon

3. In his haste the pirate *unearthed* many worms with the treasure　　3. ____a____
   chest.
   a. dug up　**b.** lifted　**c.** buried　**d.** found

4. Ariadne was *conspicuous* because of her orange clothes.　　4. ____b____
   a. fashionable　**b.** noticeable　**c.** rich　**d.** avoided

5. Sylvia did not like the beach because it was so *secluded*.　　5. ____c____
   a. polluted　**b.** warm　**c.** isolated　**d.** crowded

6. It was a difficult task to *inter* the elephant.　　6. ____b____
   a. feed　**b.** bury　**c.** transport　**d.** hide

7. My younger brother enjoys movies that involve complex *intrigues*.　　7. ____a____
   a. schemes　**b.** characters　**c.** magic　**d.** confusion

8. The reporter's *disclosure* was a shock to everyone.　　8. ____d____
   a. message　**b.** secret　**c.** story　**d.** revelation

9. Lars had a *cache* of marbles in his jacket pocket.　　9. ____c____
   a. bag　**b.** slab　**c.** supply　**d.** display

10. An English translation of the Italian poetry was *unavailable*.　　10. ____a____
    a. unobtainable　**b.** unknown　**c.** undiscovered　**d.** unwritten

Exercise 4　**Using Different Forms of Words**

Decide which form of the vocabulary word in parentheses best completes the sentence. The form given may be correct. Write your answer on the answer line.

1. Spies avoid behaving __?__ . *(conspicuous)*　　1. ____conspicuously____

2. Coral and Stephen found the puzzle __?__ . *(intrigue)*　　2. ____intriguing____

3. Rescued miners joined the struggle to __?__ those still trapped underground. *(unearth)*　　3. ____unearth____

4. The brilliant young student spends hours every day in __?__ in the library. *(secluded)*　　4. ____seclusion____

5. The emperor's __?__ was a solemn affair. *(inter)*　　5. ____interment____

6. Only students in the photography class are allowed __?__ to the darkroom. *(accessible)*　　6. ____access____

7. The investors waited for the chairman to __?__ the results of last year's financial performance. *(disclosure)*　　7. ____disclose____

8. Rodney congratulated Jean for her discovery of the __?__ of birthday presents. *(cache)*　　8. ____cache____

9. Merchants expected that the __?__ of pineapple would continue for several days. *(unavailable)*　　9. ____unavailability____

10. The meaning of my friend's remark was cloaked in __?__ . *(obscure)*　　10. ____obscurity____

Reading Comprehension

Each numbered sentence in the following passage contains an italicized vocabulary word. After you read the passage, you will complete an exercise.

A Rare Cache

Fourteen-year-old Martha Henderson had always dreamed of finding buried treasure. One day, to her amazement, her dream came true.

(1) As Martha walked along a *secluded* stretch of Las Tortugas Beach, which was near her house, she immediately noticed and picked up a coin that she assumed to be a quarter. (2) However, this *conspicuous* piece of metal turned out to be a very old Spanish coin.

Martha could not read the writing on the coin. She showed it to her best friend, Consuela Aguilar, who told her that it was Spanish. (3) Furthermore, Consuela knew that it was from seventeenth-century Spain because of the *obscure* image of King Philip V stamped upon it.

(4) The discovery *intrigued* the two girls, and they decided to return to the beach the following day to see if they could find any more "pieces of eight." They set off, along with Martha's dog, Prince, down a long narrow path. (5) The path led to the part of the beach that was least *accessible* to the public and passed through a thick grove of palm trees where the girls decided to stop for a while.

Prince, after doing some exploring on his own, drank from a nearby water hole. (6) Noticing the dog, Consuela remarked that fresh water was usually *unavailable* so close to the ocean. She suggested that perhaps a well had been dug there long ago.

Martha agreed and ventured further into the palm grove to explore it, inching her way through the thick, matted beach grass. Suddenly she yelled to Consuela to join her. The tangled grasses concealed the ruins of a Spanish camp. Nothing significant appeared on the surface: some large stones, an old metal cup, and a piece of what seemed to have once been a candlestick.

(7) Modest as it was, the find encouraged the two girls to try to *unearth* other objects. With great effort they moved some of the large stones and uncovered a deep stone-lined pit. Their anticipation building, Martha and Consuela explored the pit by raking the bottom with long sticks of driftwood from the beach.

Unexpectedly, the girls heard the clattering of what sounded like a great many coins. Martha scrambled to the bottom of the pit. (8) To her amazement she discovered hundreds of coins that had been *interred* there. (9) The girls realized that the rare *cache* must have been hidden there more than two centuries before.

Amazed at their good fortune, Martha and Consuela filled their pockets with as many coins as they could carry, covered over the pit, and returned home with Prince. (10) That very afternoon the girls decided to make a *disclosure* of their discovery and turned over the treasure of Las Tortugas to the local museum.

Please turn to the next page.

Reading Comprehension Exercise

Each of the following statements corresponds to a numbered sentence in the passage. Each statement contains a blank and is followed by four answer choices. Decide which choice fits best in the blank. The word or phrase that you choose must express roughly the same meaning as the italicized word in the passage. Write the letter of your choice on the answer line.

1. Martha walked along a(n) __?__ stretch of beach.
   a. central   **b.** pretty   **c.** isolated   **d.** sparkling

2. The __?__ piece of metal was actually an old Spanish coin.
   a. noticeable   **b.** colorful   **c.** valuable   **d.** dull

3. An __?__ image of King Philip V was stamped on the coin.
   a. unusual   **b.** apparent   **c.** indistinct   **d.** imperial

4. The discovery __?__ the two girls.
   a. fascinated   **b.** bored   **c.** pleased   **d.** scared

5. A part of the beach could not be __?__ by the public.
   a. used frequently   **c.** occupied
   b. considered safe   **d.** easily reached

6. Fresh water was usually __?__ so close to the ocean.
   a. not pure   **c.** not obtainable
   b. expensive   **d.** refreshing

7. The two girls tried to __?__ other objects.
   a. bury   **b.** find   **c.** stake out   **d.** dig up

8. Coins had been __?__ in the pit.
   a. buried   **b.** found   **c.** hidden   **d.** placed

9. The __?__ had been placed there two hundred years before.
   a. Spanish camp   **c.** hidden stockpile
   b. stones for the pit   **d.** tangled grass covering

10. The girls made an immediate __?__ of their find.
    a. revelation   **b.** secret   **c.** claim   **d.** controversy

1. _____ c
2. _____ a
3. _____ c
4. _____ a
5. _____ d
6. _____ c
7. _____ d
8. _____ a
9. _____ c
10. _____ a

Practice with Analogies

DIRECTIONS On the answer line, write the vocabulary word that completes each analogy.

1. Expose is to exposure as disclose is to __?__ .

2. Common is to accessible as rare is to __?__ .

3. Willing is to eager as visible is to __?__ .

4. Audible is to muted as visible is to __?__ .

5. Obstetrician is to deliver as mortician is to __?__ .

6. Planner is to design as plotter is to __?__ .

7. Explorer is to discover as archeologist is to __?__ .

8. Alliance is to conspiracy as stockpile is to __?__ .

See page 119 for some strategies to use with analogies.

1. _____ disclosure
2. _____ unavailable
3. _____ conspicuous
4. _____ obscure
5. _____ inter
6. _____ intrigue
7. _____ unearth
8. _____ cache

Test: Lessons 25, 26, and 27

(pages 161–178)

Part A   Choosing the Best Definition

On the answer line, write the letter of the best definition of the italicized word.

1. The *demarcation* of the two properties had never been recorded.
   a. map   **b.** history   **c.** geography   **d.** separation

   1. _____ d

2. Diane is motivated by a *compulsion* to be the best at whatever she does.
   a. attempt   **b.** reward   **c.** code   **d.** urge

   2. _____ d

3. Ethan followed the squirrel to its *cache* of nuts.
   a. nest   **b.** gift   **c.** wealth   **d.** hidden supply

   3. _____ d

4. I got the *distinct* impression that something was bothering Darcie.
   a. unmistakable   **b.** logical   **c.** undefined   **d.** uncomfortable

   4. _____ a

5. The rhythm of Poe's poem "The Bells" imitates the *peal* of its subject matter.
   a. color   **b.** attractiveness   **c.** ringing   **d.** shape

   5. _____ c

6. A famous quotation from *Julius Caesar* is "The evil that men do lives after them, /The good is oft *interred* with their bones."
   a. buried   **b.** consumed   **c.** forgotten   **d.** destroyed

   6. _____ a

7. George Orwell's *1984* describes a society in which there is no privacy, even within the *confines* of one's house.
   a. rooms   **b.** limits   **c.** secrecy   **d.** foundations

   7. _____ b

8. Rose *impelled* her friends to join her crusade for a litter-free city.
   a. forced   **b.** selected   **c.** honored   **d.** urged

   8. _____ d

9. The architects made the building *accessible* for the disabled.
   a. illegal   **b.** necessary   **c.** useless   **d.** approachable

   9. _____ d

10. A balloon *distends* when it is blown up.
    a. breaks   **b.** is destroyed   **c.** expands   **d.** becomes rigid

    10. _____ c

11. *Billy Budd*, a story by Herman Melville, relates the tragic consequences of a young man's *impulsive* actions.
    a. illegal   **b.** uncalculated   **c.** physical   **d.** ridiculous

    11. _____ b

12. Paula felt uncomfortably *conspicuous* at the formal dance.
    a. noticeable   **b.** overdressed   **c.** anxious   **d.** ignored

    12. _____ a

13. The captain of the debate team *delineated* the group's strategy.
    a. described in detail   **c.** improved the quality of
    b. restructured   **d.** eliminated

    13. _____ a

14. Nothing would *compel* the dog to let go of its bone.
    a. allow   **b.** coax   **c.** force   **d.** exhaust

    14. _____ c

15. The committee discovered several inaccuracies in the candidates' financial *disclosures*.
    a. records   **c.** business dealings
    b. revelations   **d.** campaign promises

    15. _____ b

HOUGHTON MIFFLIN VOCABULARY FOR ACHIEVEMENT, SECOND COURSE

Test: Lessons 25, 26, and 27

Part B Choosing the Best Word

On the answer line, write the letter of the word that best expresses the meaning of the italicized word or phrase.

16. No one recognized the speaker's *uncommon* reference to Robert Frost's poem "Once by the Pacific."
    a. obscure   **b.** marginal   **c.** impulsive   **d.** omnipresent

16. ___a___

17. The town council voted to *withdraw officially* certain useless bylaws.
    a. inter   **b.** repulse   **c.** repeal   **d.** delineate

17. ___c___

18. Roger's qualifications for the job are *barely acceptable.*
    a. obscure   **b.** marginal   **c.** substantial   **d.** unavailable

18. ___b___

19. Erik just read a mystery novel about international *secret plots.*
    a. penetration   **b.** intrigue   **c.** compulsion   **d.** disclosure

19. ___b___

20. Technicians checked the *process of pushing forward* system of the space shuttle for today's lift off.
    a. repellent   **b.** demarcation   **c.** compulsion   **d.** propulsion

20. ___d___

21. A *considerable* portion of Wendy's first paycheck went to taxes.
    a. substantial   **b.** conspicuous   **c.** distinct   **d.** marginal

21. ___a___

22. During excavation for the office building, a construction worker *dug up* an old chest.
    a. embodied   **b.** unearthed   **c.** interred   **d.** delineated

22. ___b___

23. Alana could feel the blood *throb* at her temples.
    a. pulsate   **b.** penetrate   **c.** distend   **d.** impel

23. ___a___

24. Greek sculpture *gives concrete form to* the classical concepts of balance and proportion.
    a. repulses   **b.** compels   **c.** delineates   **d.** embodies

24. ___d___

25. The barber will be *not at hand* for appointments next week.
    a. unavailable   **b.** omnipresent   **c.** conspicuous   **d.** marginal

25. ___a___

26. Bigotry is *causing disgust* to most people.
    a. substantial   **b.** obscure   **c.** repellent   **d.** marginal

26. ___c___

27. A camera crew recorded the scientist's *act of entering* of the ancient crypt.
    a. disclosure   **b.** intrigue   **c.** penetration   **d.** demarcation

27. ___c___

28. Jan found her brother studying in an *isolated* corner of the library.
    a. marginal   **b.** obscure   **c.** secluded   **d.** conspicuous

28. ___c___

29. "If we're to win this game, we must *drive back* the next goal-line surge," the coach emphasized.
    a. repeal   **b.** repulse   **c.** penetrate   **d.** pulsate

29. ___b___

30. At the carnival the feeling of excitement was *in existence everywhere at the same time.*
    a. omnipresent   **b.** substantial   **c.** distinct   **d.** repellent

30. ___a___

Reading Skills

The Prefix *in-*

The prefix *in-* meaning "not" is one of a pair of homographs—separate words that are spelled alike but differ in origin and meaning. (The other prefix *in-* means "in.") The prefix *in-* meaning "not" has three alternative forms that are used according to the first letter of the root. The form *il-* is used before *l;* the form *im-* is used before *b, m,* and *p;* and the form *ir-* is used before *r.* The basic form *in-* is used before all other letters.

PREFIX MEANING	WORD	DEFINITION
not	incorrect	not correct
	illogical	not logical
	immature	not mature
	irreversible	not reversible

To determine the meaning of an unfamiliar word beginning with *in-*, use the following procedure. First, substitute the meaning of the prefix for the prefix itself. Then think of possible definitions for the entire word. Remember that *in-* may mean "in" rather than "not," so be sure that your definition makes sense in the context. Finally, check your definition in the dictionary.

Exercise   Using the Prefix *in-*

Each sentence in this exercise contains an italicized word with the prefix *in-* or one of its alternative forms. *Step 1:* Write your definition of the word. *Step 2:* Write the dictionary definition of the word. Choose the definition that best fits the way the word is used in the sentence. *Step 3:* Write a sentence of your own in which you use the word correctly.

1. The telegram read, "We regret the *inexplicable* actions of our representative in Great Falls."

   YOUR DEFINITION Not explainable

   DICTIONARY DEFINITION Not capable of being explained

   SENTENCE When all the facts were in, his disappearance was still inexplicable.

2. The driving instructor told Darlene that a left turn from the right lane was *illegal*.

   YOUR DEFINITION Not legal

   DICTIONARY DEFINITION Prohibited by law

   SENTENCE Right turns on red lights are not illegal in some states.

Please turn to the next page.

3. The teacher asked the student to recopy the *illegible* paper.

YOUR DEFINITION ___Not legible___

DICTIONARY DEFINITION ___Not capable of being deciphered; not readable___

SENTENCE ___I misread his note because several words were illegible.___

4. The detective's methods were *irregular,* but he always solved his cases.

YOUR DEFINITION ___Not regular___

DICTIONARY DEFINITION ___Not standard or uniform, as in shape, size, length, or arrangement___

SENTENCE ___Their family eats at irregular times.___

5. "Bad manners are *inexcusable,*" said Aunt Sophie.

YOUR DEFINITION ___Not excusable___

DICTIONARY DEFINITION ___Impossible to excuse, pardon, or justify___

SENTENCE ___I don't agree that Wes's remark was inexcusable.___

6. The large oak cabinet was *immovable.*

YOUR DEFINITION ___Not movable___

DICTIONARY DEFINITION ___Not capable of being moved___

SENTENCE ___The baby soon learned to crawl around immovable objects.___

7. Jim used to have an *irrational* fear of cats.

YOUR DEFINITION ___Not rational___

DICTIONARY DEFINITION ___Not based on or guided by reason___

SENTENCE ___Mike's decisions are usually irrational and impulsive—but never wrong.___

8. Ben has an unfortunate tendency to drive at *immoderate* speeds; someday he will get into an accident.

YOUR DEFINITION ___Not moderate___

DICTIONARY DEFINITION ___Exceeding normal or appropriate bounds; extreme___

SENTENCE ___Dina denies that she has an immoderate desire to be elected class president.___

9. Just before construction began, the engineer discovered that her calculations were *inaccurate.*

YOUR DEFINITION ___Not accurate___

DICTIONARY DEFINITION ___Not accurate; containing errors___

SENTENCE ___We were late because Lila's watch was inaccurate.___

10. The dense foliage and vines made the rain forest practically *impenetrable.*

YOUR DEFINITION ___Not able to be penetrated___

DICTIONARY DEFINITION ___Not capable of being entered or penetrated___

SENTENCE ___The wilderness area is impenetrable without a four-wheel-drive vehicle.___

Lesson 28

The Roots -*rupt*- and -*fract*-

The Latin words *ruptus*, meaning "broken," and *fractus*, meaning "shattered," have given us the roots -*rupt*- and -*fract*-, which form the basis of many of our English words. If you *interrupt* a conversation, for example, you break into it. A *fracture*, on the other hand, is a break in bone or cartilage, and something that is *fragile* is easily shattered. All of the words in this lesson are from the roots -*rupt*- and -*fract*-, and they all have something to do with breaking.

WORD LIST
abrupt
disrupt
eruption
fractious
fragment
infraction
infringe
refractory
rout
rupture

DEFINITIONS

After you have studied the definitions and example for each vocabulary word, write the word on the line to the right.

1. **abrupt** (ə-brŭpt′) *adjective*   **a.** Unexpected; sudden.   **b.** Brief to the point of rudeness; curt; brusque.   **c.** Very steep: *an abrupt hill*. (From the Latin *ab-*, meaning "off," and *ruptus*, meaning "broken")

   RELATED WORDS   **abruptly** *adverb;* **abruptness** *noun*

   EXAMPLE   The turn in the road was so *abrupt* that we almost missed the driveway.

   1. _____

2. **disrupt** (dĭs-rŭpt′) *verb*   **a.** To upset the order of; throw into confusion or disorder.   **b.** To interrupt or block progress. (From the Latin *dis-*, meaning "apart," and *ruptus*)

   RELATED WORDS   **disruption** *noun;* **disruptive** *adjective*

   EXAMPLE   Alice's laughter *disrupted* the other students' concentration.

   2. _____

3. **eruption** (ĭ-rŭp′shən) *noun*   **a.** A violent emergence from limits or restraint; an explosion or outburst.   **b.** The forcing out or release of a substance, such as lava from a volcano or steam from a geyser. (From the Latin *ex-*, meaning "out," and *ruptus*)

   RELATED WORD   **erupt** *verb*

   EXAMPLE   In the climax of the play, the main character reacts with an *eruption* of anger.

   3. _____
   SEE *rupture*.

The Roots -*rupt*- and -*fract*-   **181**

4. **fractious** (frăk′shəs) *adjective*   **a.** Inclined to make trouble; unruly.   **b.** Irritable; cranky. (From the Latin word *fractus*, meaning "shattered")

RELATED WORD   **fractiousness** *noun*

EXAMPLE   The inexperienced rider could not control the *fractious* horse.

5. **fragment** (frăg′mĕnt′) *verb*   To break apart into pieces; separate.   *noun* (frăg′mənt)   **a.** A part broken off or detached.   **b.** Something incomplete. (From the Latin word *fragmentum*, meaning "a piece broken off")

RELATED WORDS   **fragmentary** *adjective;* **fragmentation** *noun*

EXAMPLE   The glass bowl was *fragmented* by rough handling in the mail.

6. **infraction** (ĭn-frăk′shən) *noun*   A violation of a law or rule. (From the Latin word *infractus*, meaning "destroyed")

EXAMPLE   The sergeant would not tolerate even minor *infractions* of the uniform code.

7. **infringe** (ĭn-frĭnj′) *verb*   **a.** To trespass or encroach on.   **b.** To violate or go beyond the limits of (a law, for example). (From the Latin word *infringere*, meaning "to break off" or "to shatter")

RELATED WORD   **infringement** *noun*

EXAMPLE   By building the fence, the Flanagans accidentally *infringed* on their neighbor's property.

8. **refractory** (rĭ-frăk′tə-rē) *adjective*   **a.** Stubborn; obstinate; unmanageable.   **b.** Difficult to melt, shape, or work with.   **c.** Not responsive to medical treatment. (From the Latin word *refractus*, meaning "broken up")

RELATED WORD   **refractorily** *adverb*

EXAMPLE   Mules have the reputation of being *refractory* animals.

9. **rout** (rout) *verb*   **a.** To drive or force out.   **b.** To defeat overwhelmingly.   *noun*   A defeat or disorderly retreat. (From the Latin word *ruptio*, meaning "the act of breaking")

EXAMPLE   Jason had the pleasure of seeing his opponent *routed* at the polls.

10. **rupture** (rŭp′chər) *noun*   A break or split.   *verb*   **a.** To break open; burst.   **b.** To break off.   **c.** To undergo or suffer a break. (From the Latin word *ruptus*)

EXAMPLE   The *rupture* in the water line caused a minor flood.

4. _____
SEE *refractory.*

5. _____

6. _____
SEE   *infringe.*

7. _____
USAGE NOTE   *Infringement* and *infraction* can be used interchangeably, but *infringement* can also suggest the *gradual* intrusion on someone's property or rights.

8. _____
USAGE NOTE A *refractory* person is stubborn. A *fractious* person is one likely to make trouble.

9. _____

10. _____
MEMORY CUE An *eruption* of lava might follow a *rupture* in a volcano.

Name _____ Date _____

Exercise 1   **Completing Definitions**

On the answer line, write the word from the vocabulary list that best completes each definition.

1. Someone who causes trouble or tends to be irritable is __?__ .   1. _____ fractious _____
2. To trespass on or go beyond limits is to __?__ .   2. _____ infringe _____
3. A statement that is sudden or curt is __?__ .   3. _____ abrupt _____
4. To drive out or to defeat is to __?__ .   4. _____ rout _____
5. To be stubborn is to be __?__ .   5. _____ refractory _____
6. To break apart into pieces is to __?__ .   6. _____ fragment _____
7. The breaking of a rule is a(n) __?__ .   7. _____ infraction _____
8. A violent outburst or explosion is a(n) __?__ .   8. _____ eruption _____
9. To upset the order of something is to __?__ it.   9. _____ disrupt _____
10. A break or split is a(n) __?__ .   10. _____ rupture _____

Exercise 2   **Using Words Correctly**

Decide whether the italicized vocabulary word has been used correctly in the sentence. On the answer line, write *Correct* for correct use and *Incorrect* for incorrect use.

1. Medical research has succeeded in *routing* many infectious diseases such as smallpox.   1. _____ Correct _____
2. The doctor set Ted's *fractious* arm and placed it in a cast.   2. _____ Incorrect _____
3. Mary *infringed* the hem of her skirt with green thread.   3. _____ Incorrect _____
4. The pottery vase was *fragmented* in the dishwasher.   4. _____ Correct _____
5. With an *abrupt* nod, the professor ended our conversation.   5. _____ Correct _____
6. Oil leaked slowly from a hidden *rupture* in the tank.   6. _____ Correct _____
7. The principal rewarded Barney for his *infraction* of school rules.   7. _____ Incorrect _____
8. Jennifer wished to *disrupt* the band during her favorite song.   8. _____ Incorrect _____
9. The *refractory* dog was increasingly difficult to control.   9. _____ Correct _____
10. The children hid the *eruption* of the plate in the cupboard.   10. _____ Incorrect _____

Exercise 3   **Choosing the Best Word**

Decide which vocabulary word or related form best completes the sentence, and write the letter of your choice on the answer line.

1. Brian __?__ the quiet classroom with a loud sneeze.   1. _____ c _____
   a. routed   **b.** infringed   **c.** disrupted   **d.** erupted

2. Carlo hit the brakes when the car ahead made a(n) __?__ stop.   2. _____ a _____
   a. abrupt   **b.** fragmented   **c.** refractory   **d.** fractious

     The Roots *-rupt-* and *-fract-*   **183**

3. Do not allow aggressive people to __?__ on your rights.
   a. rout   **b.** rupture   **c.** disrupt   **d.** infringe

3. _____d_____

4. Engineers searched furiously for the __?__ in the oil pipeline.
   a. infringement   **b.** infraction   **c.** rupture   **d.** rout

4. _____c_____

5. Not wishing to go to bed, the toddler became __?__ .
   a. routed   **b.** refractory   **c.** fragmented   **d.** abrupt

5. _____b_____

6. The china doll __?__ into tiny pieces when it hit the floor.
   a. fragmented   **b.** fractious   **c.** infringed   **d.** disrupted

6. _____a_____

7. The explosion caused a(n) __?__ of water.
   a. infraction   **b.** eruption   **c.** fragment   **d.** infringement

7. _____b_____

8. The __?__ youths were asked to leave the theater.
   a. fragmented   **b.** routed   **c.** abrupt   **d.** fractious

8. _____d_____

9. The fire __?__ shoppers from the store.
   a. routed   **b.** fragmented   **c.** ruptured   **d.** infringed

9. _____a_____

10. Although Johnny was guilty of a(n) __?__ of camp rules, he was not punished because he saved his friend's life in the process.
   a. eruption   **b.** refractory   **c.** infraction   **d.** rupture

10. _____c_____

Exercise 4   Using Different Forms of Words

Decide which form of the vocabulary word in parentheses best completes the sentence. The form given may be correct. Write your answer on the answer line.

1. Small annoyances occasionally cause Chris to __?__ in anger. *(eruption)*

1. _____erupt_____

2. Greta never realized that reading Felice's diary was an __?__ on her privacy. *(infringe)*

2. _____infringement_____

3. Fortunately, Dana's parents rushed him to the hospital before his appendix __?__ . *(rupture)*

3. _____ruptured_____

4. For her __?__ of the dormitory rules, Sharon had to appear before the student court. *(infraction)*

4. _____infraction_____

5. The song ended so __?__ that Michelle thought her tape player was broken. *(abrupt)*

5. _____abruptly_____

6. Marjorie's friends had not expected such __?__ from her. *(fractious)*

6. _____fractiousness_____

7. In a surprising victory, the home team __?__ the visiting team, which had been heavily favored. *(rout)*

7. _____routed_____

8. Archaeologists put together the pieces of the __?__ tablet and attempted to read it. *(fragment)*

8. _____fragmented_____

9. Four-year-old Jeremy was a __?__ influence on the other children. *(disrupt)*

9. _____disruptive_____

10. Jane insisted __?__ that she sit in the front seat. *(refractory)*

10. _____refractorily_____

Reading Comprehension

Each numbered sentence in the following passage contains an italicized vocabulary word or related form. After you read the passage, you will complete an exercise.

Nellie Bly: Daring Woman Journalist

Elizabeth Cochrane Seaman (1867–1922), the first American woman reporter to achieve international fame, was a pioneer in opening doors for women journalists. The only daughter of a judge, Elizabeth was encouraged to study law — a career not generally open to women at that time. **(1)** Judge Cochrane's death in 1884 brought an **abrupt** end to her career plans, however. **(2)** Her older brothers refused to allow her to **disrupt** their lives with what they considered to be ridiculous ideas.

Instead of law, Elizabeth began a career in journalism at the age of eighteen. **(3)** One day, as she was reading the *Pittsburgh Dispatch,* she **erupted** in anger over an editorial about women in the workplace. **(4)** Furious with the editor for his **infringement** on the right of women to be employed, she wrote him an indignant letter. The editor was so impressed with her writing style that he wanted to hire her as a reporter. **(5)** Elizabeth knew that her **refractory,** old-fashioned brothers would not approve of her working as a journalist. When the editor suggested that she use a pen name to protect her identity, Elizabeth chose "Nellie Bly," the familiar Stephen Foster song title.

(6) Nellie Bly concentrated first on exposing the terrible conditions under which

people worked — the long hours, the **fragmentation** of families, and the starvation wages. Although her articles did not make cheerful reading, circulation of the newspaper boomed.

After two years of working, Nellie Bly was less inclined to allow her brothers to dictate her life. She decided to move to New York. **(7)** Although the **rupture** with her family was painful, she was ready for a change.

New York newspaper editors were totally against hiring women as reporters. Nellie could not even get an interview. Finally she decided that she would not leave the office of Joseph Pulitzer, owner of *The World,* until she had spoken to him. **(8)** Told repeatedly of the crazy woman camped out all day in the reception

area, Pulitzer, in a **fractious** mood, finally agreed to see her. He gave her three minutes to prove to him that she was a reporter with original ideas. Recalling that people had referred to her all day as "the crazy lady," she told Pulitzer that she wanted to get herself committed to the city mental asylum in order to write the inside story of conditions there. Pulitzer hired her immediately.

As a result of her exposé, "Behind Asylum Bars," Nellie Bly became famous overnight. **(9)** She unfolded tales of inhuman treatment and countless **infractions** of sound medical practice. Because of her efforts, conditions for the inmates were improved.

In 1889 Nellie Bly decided to break the record of Jules Verne's imaginary hero Phileas Fogg in *Around the World in Eighty Days.* The editor and staff of *The World* refused to support her plan at first because they worried about what could happen to an unchaperoned woman on such a trip. **(10)** By threatening to make the trip anyway and write about it for a rival paper, Nellie completely **routed** their resistance. She became the best-known and most-loved newspaper reporter when she outdid Fogg's fictional time by setting a record of seventy-two days, six hours, and eleven minutes.

Please turn to the next page.

The Roots *-rupt-* and *-fract-*   **185**

Reading Comprehension Exercise

Each of the following statements corresponds to a numbered sentence in the passage. Each statement contains a blank and is followed by four answer choices. Decide which choice fits best in the blank. The word or phrase that you choose must express roughly the same meaning as the italicized word in the passage. Write the letter of your choice on the answer line.

1. Her father's death brought a(n) __?__ end to her career plans.
   a. sudden **b.** unhappy **c.** favorable **d.** independent

   1. _____ a _____

2. Elizabeth's older brothers refused to allow her to __?__ their lives.
   a. ruin **c.** upset the order of
   b. manipulate **d.** take advantage of

   2. _____ c _____

3. Elizabeth __?__ in anger about an editorial in the *Pittsburgh Dispatch*.
   a. wrote **b.** exploded **c.** restrained herself **d.** acted

   3. _____ b _____

4. Elizabeth was furious with the editor for his __?__ the rights of women.
   a. encroachment on **c.** attitudes toward
   b. decisions about **d.** goals for

   4. _____ a _____

5. Elizabeth knew that a newspaper job would cause problems with her __?__ brothers.
   a. younger **b.** dreadful **c.** practical **d.** stubborn

   5. _____ d _____

6. Nellie Bly exposed the terrible conditions of workers, such as the __?__ of families and low wages.
   a. employment **b.** abuse **c.** breakdown **d.** intolerance

   6. _____ c _____

7. Nellie decided to move to New York even though the __?__ with her family was painful.
   a. relationship **b.** break **c.** argument **d.** obligation

   7. _____ b _____

8. Joseph Pulitzer was in a(n) __?__ mood when he agreed to see her.
   a. irritable **b.** famous **c.** curious **d.** innocent

   8. _____ a _____

9. Nellie unfolded tales of countless __?__ medical practice.
   a. horrors of **b.** mistakes in **c.** experiments in **d.** violations of

   9. _____ d _____

10. She __?__ the staff's resistance by threatening to make the trip anyway.
    a. encouraged **b.** defeated **c.** ignored **d.** predicted

    10. _____ b _____

Writing Assignment

Suppose you have a creative idea for a disaster movie that you want to sell to a movie studio. Write a plot outline that describes a catastrophe, such as a hurricane or an earthquake. Invent the characters, explaining what happens to them and how they cope with the disaster. Use five of the vocabulary words from this lesson and underline them.

Bonus: Lessons 27 and 28

(pages 173–178, 181–186)

Use the clues to complete the crossword puzzle.

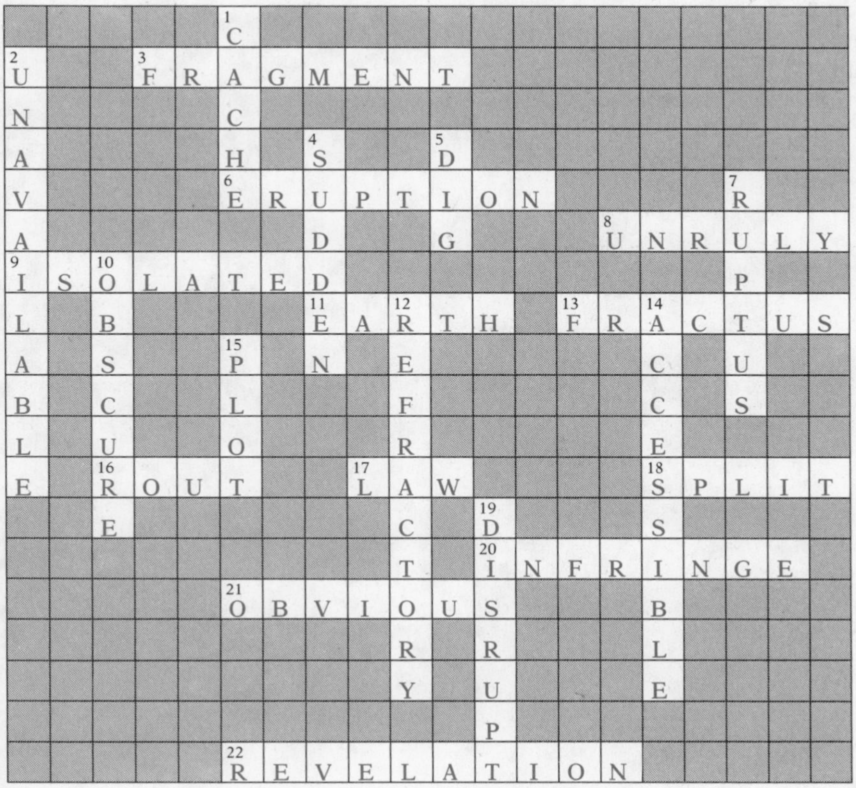

The crossword grid contains the following answers:

- 1 Down / across: **C** (CACHE vertical)
- 2 Down: **UNAVAILABLE**
- 3 Across / Down: **FRAGMENT**
- 4 Down: **SUDDEN**
- 5 Down: **DIG**
- 6 Across: **ERUPTION**
- 7 Down: **RUPTUS**
- 8 Across: **UNRULY**
- 9 Across: **ISOLATED**
- 10 Down: **OBSCURE**
- 11 Across: **EARTH**
- 12 Down: **INFRACT**
- 13 Across: **FR**
- 14 Down: **ACCUS** / **FRACTUS**
- 15 Down: **PLOT**
- 16 Across: **ROUT**
- 17 Across: **LAW**
- 18 Down: **SPLIT** / **SBLE**
- 19 Down: **DISRUP**
- 20 Across: **INFRINGE**
- 21 Across: **OBVIOUS**
- 22 Across: **REVELATION**

Across

3. An incomplete part
6. A volcanic ___?___
8. Synonym for FRACTIOUS
9. A SECLUDED location is ___?___.
11. INTER comes from the Latin word *terra*, meaning "___?___."
13. Latin word meaning "shattered"
16. To drive out or force out
17. An INFRACTION is a violation of the ___?___.
18. Synonym for RUPTURE
20. A person should not ___?___ upon the rights of others.
21. Synonym for CONSPICUOUS
22. A DISCLOSURE is a(n) ___?___.

Down

1. A hidden supply or reserve
2. Not at hand
4. An ABRUPT ending is a(n) ___?___ conclusion.
5. To UNEARTH is to ___?___ up from underground.
7. Latin word meaning "broken"
10. Not well known or not easily found
12. Stubborn or unmanageable
14. Easily approached, obtained, or reached
15. An INTRIGUE is a scheme or secret ___?___.
19. To throw into confusion or disorder

HOUGHTON MIFFLIN VOCABULARY FOR ACHIEVEMENT, SECOND COURSE

Notes

The following lists of words are from the preceding two lessons. You may wish to use these lists to pinpoint words for ongoing review or for mid-term or final exams.

Lesson 27

accessible	intrigue
cache	obscure
conspicuous	secluded
disclosure	unavailable
inter	unearth

Lesson 28

abrupt	infraction
disrupt	infringe
eruption	refractory
fractious	rout
fragment	rupture

Lesson 29

Harm and Criticism

At first glance the words *harm* and *criticism* may seem rather negative. These words, however, can also be viewed in a positive light. Positive criticism can lead a person to correct a fault. An effective tennis instructor, for example, constructively criticizes a student's playing techniques. In addition, people must understand why something is harmful if they are to protect themselves from it. To warn a child about fire can certainly protect that child from harm. In this lesson you will learn how to use words about harm and criticism to your advantage.

DEFINITIONS

After you have studied the definitions and example for each vocabulary word, write the word on the line to the right.

1. **admonish** (ăd-mŏn′ĭsh) *verb* **a.** To criticize for a fault in a kind but serious way. **b.** To advise, warn, urge, or caution. (From the Latin words *ad*, meaning "to," and *monere*, meaning "to warn")

   RELATED WORD **admonition** *noun*

   EXAMPLE Mrs. Robbins *admonished* her son for riding his tricycle in the street.

   1. _____
   SEE *denounce.*

2. **alienate** (āl′yə-nāt′) *verb* **a.** To cause to become unfriendly or indifferent. **b.** To remove or disassociate oneself from other people. (From the Latin word *alius*, meaning "other")

   RELATED WORD **alienation** *noun*

   EXAMPLE Jack's constant arguing *alienated* him from his friends.

   2. _____

3. **censure** (sĕn′shər) *noun* An expression of blame or disapproval.   *verb* To criticize severely or blame. (From the Latin word *censura*, meaning "severe judgment")

   EXAMPLE Linda *censured* her younger brother for breaking her camera.

   3. _____

4. **denounce** (dĭ-nouns′) *verb* **a.** To express very strong disapproval of; condemn openly. **b.** To accuse formally. (From the Latin word *denuntiare*, meaning "to announce" or "to warn")

   RELATED WORD **denunciation** *noun*

   EXAMPLE The politician *denounced* her opponent's tax proposal.

   4. _____
   USAGE NOTE To *denounce* is to criticize in a way that implies rejection. To *admonish* is to criticize in a kindly way.

5. **detriment** (dĕt′rə-mənt) *noun*　**a.** Damage, harm, or loss.　**b.** Something that causes damage, harm, or loss. (From the Latin *de-*, meaning "away," and *terere*, meaning "to rub")

RELATED WORD　**detrimental** *adjective*

EXAMPLE　Little or no rainfall can be a serious *detriment* to a farm community.

5. _____

6. **imperil** (ĭm-pĕr′əl) *verb*　To put in danger.

EXAMPLE　The frequent use of pesticides *imperiled* the fresh-water supply.

6. _____

7. **incapacitate** (ĭn′kə-păs′ĭ-tāt′) *verb*　To deprive of power, strength, or ability; disable.

RELATED WORDS　**incapacitation** *noun;* **incapacity** *noun*

EXAMPLE　The ice skater's sprained ankle *incapacitated* him for several weeks.

7. _____

8. **injurious** (ĭn-jŏŏr′ē-əs) *adjective*　**a.** Causing injury or damage; harmful.　**b.** Slanderous; libelous.

RELATED WORDS　**injuriousness** *noun;* **injury** *noun*

EXAMPLE　Parents teach their children not to eat or drink anything that is *injurious* to their health.

8. _____

9. **malign** (mə-līn′) *verb*　To speak evil of; tell lies about. *adjective*　Evil in nature or influence. (From the Latin word *malus*, meaning "bad")

EXAMPLE　Carrie *maligned* her former best friend to anyone who would listen.

9. _____
SEE *scoff.*

10. **scoff** (skŏf) *verb*　To make fun of or mock.　*noun*　An expression of mockery or scorn. (From the Middle English word *scof*, meaning "mockery")

RELATED WORD　**scoffingly** *adverb*

EXAMPLE　Years ago people *scoffed* at "horseless carriages," or early automobiles.

10. _____
USAGE NOTE To *scoff* is to make fun of mildly. To *malign* is to criticize in an evil way.

Exercise 1   Completing Definitions

On the answer line, write the word from the vocabulary list that best completes each definition.

1. To __?__ a person is to show disapproval of him or her.

2. Something that causes injury or damage is __?__ .

3. If you __?__ at someone, you mock that person.

4. An action that causes harm can be a __?__ .

5. To disable or deprive of strength is to __?__ .

6. If you criticize someone gently, you __?__ that person.

7. To speak evil of or to lie about is to __?__ .

8. When you place yourself in danger, you __?__ yourself.

9. To cause someone to become unfriendly toward you is to __?__ that person.

10. To condemn openly or express strong disapproval of is to __?__ .

1. _____ censure _____

2. _____ injurious _____

3. _____ scoff _____

4. _____ detriment _____

5. _____ incapacitate _____

6. _____ admonish _____

7. _____ malign _____

8. _____ imperil _____

9. _____ alienate _____

10. _____ denounce _____

Exercise 2   Using Words Correctly

Decide whether the italicized vocabulary word has been used correctly in the sentence. On the answer line, write *Correct* for correct use and *Incorrect* for incorrect use.

1. Carl *scoffed* at his younger brother's frightened reaction to thunder.

2. Because Brigetta was *incapacitated*, she was able to go skiing.

3. Hank *maligned* the bowling pins, forcing Ralph to reset them.

4. Reading in a dimly lit room can be a *detriment* to your eyesight.

5. The more people you *alienate*, the more friends you will have.

6. When the plant outgrew its pot, Laura *censured* it.

7. Swimming in freezing water can be *injurious* to your health.

8. Smiling, the theater usher *admonished* the girls to stop talking.

9. Charles *denounced* the club for inviting only athletes to become members.

10. Charlene *imperiled* her dog Hector by walking him on a leash.

1. _____ Correct _____

2. _____ Incorrect _____

3. _____ Incorrect _____

4. _____ Correct _____

5. _____ Incorrect _____

6. _____ Incorrect _____

7. _____ Correct _____

8. _____ Correct _____

9. _____ Correct _____

10. _____ Incorrect _____

Exercise 3   Choosing the Best Definition

For each italicized vocabulary word or related form in the following sentences, write the letter of the best definition on the answer line.

1. Joyce *censured* the hotel management for the burned dinner.
   a. complimented   **b.** blamed   **c.** forgave   **d.** sued

2. A severe headache *incapacitated* Joseph for the morning.
   a. disabled   **b.** annoyed   **c.** cheered   **d.** soothed

1. _____ b _____

2. _____ a _____

3. Rudi *admonished* his sister for wandering away from the campsite.
   a. encouraged   **b.** laughed at   **c.** praised   **d.** criticized

3. _____d_____

4. The sewage is *detrimental* to the quality of the water in the river.
   a. measurable   **b.** necessary   **c.** harmful   **d.** explainable

4. _____c_____

5. Janet *scoffed* at her friend's idea for a science project.
   a. made fun of   **c.** complimented
   b. identified with   **d.** tuned out

5. _____a_____

6. The sea captain refused to *imperil* the lives of her passengers by taking the dangerous route.
   a. add excitement to   **c.** endanger
   b. identify with   **d.** save

6. _____c_____

7. Doreen *alienated* many of her classmates when she bragged about her trip to Europe.
   a. pleased   **c.** brought closer
   b. made unfriendly   **d.** cheered up

7. _____b_____

8. A medical treatment that helped some patients was *injurious* to others.
   a. unpleasant   **b.** fair   **c.** soothing   **d.** harmful

8. _____d_____

9. Gilbert *denounced* the class president's suggestion.
   a. approved   **b.** waited for   **c.** reversed   **d.** condemned

9. _____d_____

10. The former follower *maligned* the unpopular leader.
    a. said evil things about   **c.** willingly deserted
    b. plotted against   **d.** greatly assisted

10. _____a_____

Exercise 4   Using Different Forms of Words

Each sentence contains an italicized vocabulary word in a form that does not fit the sentence. On the answer line, write the form of that word that does fit the sentence.

1. The lifeguard said that swimmers going anywhere near the severe undertow were *imperil* their lives.

1. _____imperiling_____

2. Marlene risked the *alienate* of her friends by never listening to what they said.

2. _____alienation_____

3. Ricardo minimized the seriousness of his arm *injurious*.

3. _____injury_____

4. The manager had a bad habit of *censure* players in public.

4. _____censuring_____

5. Barry's fall down the icy steps resulted in a month's *incapacitate*.

5. _____incapacitation_____

6. A stern look was the only *admonish* Julie needed to clean up her room.

6. _____admonition_____

7. At last night's meeting, the town gossip *malign* just about everyone in the community.

7. _____maligned_____

8. Lenore's sudden *denounce* of the club shocked everyone.

8. _____denunciation_____

9. Rick pointed *scoff* at his brother's new haircut.

9. _____scoffingly_____

10. Not wearing seat belts could be *detriment* to your health.

10. _____detrimental_____

Reading Comprehension

Each numbered sentence in the following passage contains an italicized vocabulary word or related form. After you read the passage, you will complete an exercise.

Elizabeth Cady Stanton: Early Women's Rights Leader

During her long lifetime, Elizabeth Cady Stanton (1815–1902) had a distinguished career as a writer, campaigner, and speaker for the early women's rights movement. Although Mrs. Stanton did not live long enough to see the women's suffrage amendment pass, she helped greatly to stir public consciousness so that women were finally given the right to vote in 1920.

Her keen awareness of women's problems began early. As a child growing up in Johnstown, New York, Elizabeth spent time in her father's law office and was deeply influenced by the moving stories she happened to hear from women seeking legal help. (1) Desperate women described how their husbands had **maligned** them before taking away their property and their children. The current laws supported these unfair actions.

Elizabeth's father was by no means a champion of women's rights. After Elizabeth's only brother died, Daniel Cady turned sadly to the eleven-year-old Elizabeth and said, "Oh, my daughter, I wish you were a boy!" (2) This **admonition** was a challenge to Elizabeth, who already rebelled against the idea that women were mentally and legally inferior to men. (3) Elizabeth did not, however, let this statement **alienate** her from her father. Instead, she decided to prove to him that daughters were as valuable as sons.

As a student Elizabeth was intelligent and resourceful. (4) While her schoolmates **scoffed** at her determination to do well in subjects that were considered unfeminine, Elizabeth mastered mathematics and the classics.

After college Elizabeth took an active role in the antislavery movement. While attending antislavery meetings, Elizabeth met her future husband, Henry Brewster Stanton. (5) Stanton was a journalist and reformer who **denounced** the institution of slavery. Elizabeth and Stanton were married on May 10, 1840.

Immediately after the ceremony, Mrs. Stanton accompanied her husband to London, where he was a delegate to the World Anti-Slavery Convention. There she protested the exclusion of women delegates from the convention. (6) Convention leaders **censured** women who wished to participate with remarks like "Turn out the women!"

This experience strengthened Mrs. Stanton's motivation to improve the status of women. She and another protester, Lucretia Mott, a Quaker minister, promised themselves that they would organize and hold the very first women's rights convention. This dream did not become a reality until eight years later.

In the intervening years, Mrs. Stanton worked for women's rights by circulating petitions for a married women's property bill and speaking before the New York legislature on the subject. (7) Mrs. Stanton told her audiences that marriage often **incapacitated** women, causing them to submit to laws in which they had had no choice. (8) Marriage, she maintained, was financially **detrimental** to women, since their husbands owned and controlled all property and money. Because of Mrs. Stanton's efforts, the New York legislature in 1848 passed a law guaranteeing married women the right to hold real estate in their own name after marriage.

With this success in mind, Mrs. Stanton and Mrs. Mott organized and held the first women's rights convention, in Seneca Falls, New York, on July 19, 1848. (9) For the occasion Mrs. Stanton created a "Declaration of Sentiments," a strong written reaction to the **injurious** treatment that she felt women had suffered.

Mrs. Stanton surprised the convention delegates by introducing a resolution that stated women must gain the right to vote. (10) There were some who thought that Mrs. Stanton was going too far, that her "daring" demand to gain the vote might **imperil** the overall aims of the movement. However, Elizabeth Cady Stanton's unexpected resolution was to become the rallying point for generations of women as they later campaigned for the right to vote.

Please turn to the next page.

Reading Comprehension Exercise

Each of the following statements corresponds to a numbered sentence in the passage. Each statement contains a blank and is followed by four answer choices. Decide which choice fits best in the blank. The word or phrase that you choose must express roughly the same meaning as the italicized word in the passage. Write the letter of your choice on the answer line.

1. It was not unusual for husbands to __?__ their wives.
   a. tolerate   c. take action against
   b. speak ill of   d. question

   1. _____b_____

2. Elizabeth saw her father's __?__ as a challenge.
   a. cruel remark   c. supportive comment
   b. insightful statement   d. gentle criticism

   2. _____d_____

3. She did not become __?__ her father after his comment.
   a. indifferent to   c. impressed by
   b. informed by   d. obedient to

   3. _____a_____

4. The other students __?__ her desire to do well in school.
   a. praised   b. questioned   c. mocked   d. admired

   4. _____c_____

5. Henry Brewster Stanton __?__ the institution of slavery.
   a. struggled against   c. campaigned for
   b. openly supported   d. expressed strong disapproval of

   5. _____d_____

6. Antislavery convention leaders __?__ women who tried to participate.
   a. strongly endorsed   c. severely criticized
   b. gently scolded   d. reacted favorably to

   6. _____c_____

7. Mrs. Stanton felt that marriage could easily __?__ women.
   a. disable   b. benefit   c. demoralize   d. destroy

   7. _____a_____

8. She added that marriage could also prove financially __?__ to women.
   a. necessary   b. harmful   c. beneficial   d. boring

   8. _____b_____

9. Mrs. Stanton felt that many women had received __?__ treatment.
   a. illegal   b. fair   c. critical   d. harmful

   9. _____d_____

10. Some women hoped that Mrs. Stanton's resolution would not __?__ the goals of the movement.
   a. enrich   b. gamble with   c. endanger   d. protect

   10. _____c_____

Practice with Analogies

DIRECTIONS On the answer line, write the vocabulary word that completes each analogy.

See page 119 for some strategies to use with analogies.

1. Compliment is to praise as scold is to __?__ .

   1. _____admonish_____

2. Enable is to empower as disable is to __?__ .

   2. _____incapacitate_____

3. Please is to captivate as offend is to __?__ .

   3. _____alienate_____

4. Fresh is to stale as beneficial is to __?__ .

   4. _____injurious_____

5. Rescue is to save as endanger is to __?__ .

   5. _____imperil_____

6. Rainfall is to boon as drought is to __?__ .

   6. _____detriment_____

Lesson 30

Kindness

Whether we volunteer our time to an organization, contribute money to a favorite charity, or simply help a friend complete a task, we perform kind acts on a daily basis. Some people give help out of a sense of duty or obligation; others act kindly in the hope of reward. Regardless of the motive, the result of kindness is the same: the acceptance by others of needed support or assistance. The words in this lesson will enable you to express your thoughts and observations about kindness.

WORD LIST
altruistic
benefactor
beneficial
benevolent
benign
bountiful
gratify
humanitarian
indulge
philanthropic

DEFINITIONS

After you have studied the definitions and example for each vocabulary word, write the word on the line to the right.

1. **altruistic** (ăl′troo-ĭs′tĭk) *adjective*   Unselfishly concerned with or devoted to the welfare of others. (From the Latin word *alter,* meaning "other")

   RELATED WORDS   **altruism** *noun;* **altruistically** *adverb*

   EXAMPLE   Andrew Carnegie's *altruistic* beliefs inspired him to donate money for the libraries of the United States.

1. _____

2. **benefactor** (bĕn′ə-făk′tər) *noun*   One who helps another person in need; one who gives income or property to an institution. (From the Latin phrase *bene facere,* meaning "to do well")

   RELATED WORD   **benefaction** *noun*

   EXAMPLE   In the novel *Great Expectations,* Pip wonders who his *benefactor* is.

2. _____
   SEE *humanitarian.*

3. **beneficial** (bĕn′ə-fĭsh′əl) *adjective*   Helpful; advantageous; promoting a favorable result. (From the Latin phrase *bene facere,* meaning "to do well")

   RELATED WORDS   **beneficiary** *noun;* **benefit** *noun;* **benefit** *verb*

   EXAMPLE   Sunshine and rain are *beneficial* to crops.

3. _____

4. **benevolent** (bə-nĕv′ə-lənt) *adjective*   Characterized by or expressing good will or kindness. (From the Latin words *bene,* meaning "well," and *volens,* meaning "wishing")

   RELATED WORDS   **benevolence** *noun;* **benevolently** *adverb*

   EXAMPLE   The Red Cross is a *benevolent* organization that helps victims of fires, floods, and other disasters.

4. _____

5. **benign** (bǐ-nīn′) *adjective* **a.** Kind and gentle; mild and favorable. **b.** Not seriously harmful. (From the Latin word *benignus,* meaning "kind")

RELATED WORD **benignly** *adverb*

EXAMPLE Caroline's *benign* manner makes her an excellent dolphin trainer.

5. _____

6. **bountiful** (boun′tə-fəl) *adjective* **a.** Plentiful; abundant. **b.** Giving generously. (From the Latin word *bonitas,* meaning "goodness")

RELATED WORDS **bountifully** *adverb;* **bounty** *noun*

EXAMPLE The family's *bountiful* contribution was used to feed and clothe the refugees.

6. _____

7. **gratify** (grăt′ə-fī′) *verb* To please or satisfy. (From the Latin word *gratificari,* meaning "to do a favor")

RELATED WORD **gratification** *noun*

EXAMPLE The results of the canned-food drive *gratified* the entire committee.

7. _____

8. **humanitarian** (hyōō-măn′ĭ-târ′ē-ən) *noun* A person concerned with helping to improve human welfare and promote social reform. *adjective* Relating to the desire to promote human welfare and social reform: *humanitarian contributions.*

RELATED WORD **humanitarianism** *noun*

EXAMPLE Helen Keller is considered a great humanitarian because of her work in establishing educational programs for blind and deaf people.

8. _____

USAGE NOTE A *humanitarian* promotes the welfare of people in general. A *benefactor* helps one person or one institution.

9. **indulge** (ĭn-dŭlj′) *verb* **a.** To yield to the desires or wishes of; pamper. **b.** To allow oneself some special pleasure. **c.** To engage or take part in: *to indulge in a sport.* (From the Latin word *indulgere,* meaning "to be kind")

RELATED WORDS **indulgence** *noun;* **indulgent** *adjective*

EXAMPLE Mother *indulges* in afternoon naps on Sundays.

9. _____

10. **philanthropic** (fĭl′ən-thrŏp′ĭk) *adjective* Relating to the effort to help other people, such as by making donations of money, property, or work; charitable. (From the Greek words *philos,* meaning "loving," and *anthropos,* meaning "person")

RELATED WORDS **philanthropically** *adverb;* **philanthropist** *noun;* **philanthropy** *noun*

EXAMPLE Most people did not know of Mr. Johnson's *philanthropic* activity until after his death.

10. _____

Exercise 1 Writing Correct Words

On the answer line, write the word from the vocabulary list that fits each definition.

1. A person who improves human welfare and promotes social reform

2. To please or satisfy

3. Gentle; not seriously harmful

4. One who helps a person in need

5. Characterized by good will or kindness

6. To yield to the desires or wishes of; allow oneself some special pleasure

7. Relating to the effort to help other people through donations or work; charitable

8. Plentiful; giving generously

9. Helpful; promoting a favorable result

10. Unselfishly concerned with the welfare of others

1. _____humanitarian_____

2. _____gratify_____

3. _____benign_____

4. _____benefactor_____

5. _____benevolent_____

6. _____indulge_____

7. _____philanthropic_____

8. _____bountiful_____

9. _____beneficial_____

10. _____altruistic_____

Exercise 2 Using Words Correctly

Each of the following statements contains an italicized vocabulary word. Decide whether the sentence is true or false, and write *True* or *False* on the answer line.

1. A *humanitarian* treats others badly.

2. An action performed out of spite is *altruistic*.

3. A compliment on a hand-knitted sweater would *gratify* the knitter.

4. Someone who won a large amount of money in a lottery might *indulge* in a new camera.

5. Clear weather and brisk winds were *beneficial* to sailors on sailing ships.

6. Children would be likely to run in fear from a *benign* dog.

7. A *philanthropic* contribution is usually accepted with gratitude.

8. A *benevolent* person would be generous toward other people.

9. A nation with a *bountiful* supply of food would have food shortages.

10. A person's *benefactor* would take money away from him or her.

1. _____False_____

2. _____False_____

3. _____True_____

4. _____True_____

5. _____True_____

6. _____False_____

7. _____True_____

8. _____True_____

9. _____False_____

10. _____False_____

Exercise 3 Choosing the Best Word

Decide which vocabulary word or related form best completes the sentence, and write the letter of your choice on the answer line.

1. Christie is a __?__ child who tries to help all injured animals.
   a. gratifying   **b.** beneficial   **c.** benevolent   **d.** bountiful

1. _____c_____

2. Although the store has run out of shelled walnuts, it has a(n) __?__ supply of almonds.
   a. bountiful   **b.** indulged   **c.** philanthropic   **d.** altruistic

2. _____ a

3. In the winter I __?__ by sitting in front of the fireplace and watching old movies on television.
   a. am bountiful   **c.** am benign
   b. act philanthropically   **d.** indulge myself

3. _____ d

4. "I am __?__ by your request for my stew recipe," said the chef.
   a. gratified   **b.** indulged   **c.** benign   **d.** altruistic

4. _____ a

5. The weather was so __?__ when we left home that we did not consider taking umbrellas.
   a. bountiful   **b.** humanitarian   **c.** altruistic   **d.** benign

5. _____ d

6. The magazine article about Delores Smythe, a local __?__ , failed to describe her work with the community garden.
   a. benefit   **b.** humanitarian   **c.** bounty   **d.** benevolence

6. _____ b

7. Milk and milk products __?__ for both young children and the elderly.
   a. are benevolent   **c.** are beneficial
   b. seem altruistic   **d.** are bountiful

7. _____ c

8. __?__ is necessary to keep private colleges and universities operating.
   a. Philanthropy   **b.** Bounty   **c.** Gratification   **d.** Indulgence

8. _____ a

9. Their __?__ led the Morrisons to set aside several acres of their farm as a camp for disabled children.
   a. bounty   **b.** benefactor   **c.** indulgence   **d.** altruism

9. _____ d

10. For years Beth searched for the __?__ who had paid for her music lessons.
    a. altruism   **b.** bounty   **c.** benefactor   **d.** humanitarian

10. _____ c

Exercise 4 Using Different Forms of Words

Each sentence contains an italicized vocabulary word in a form that does not fit the sentence. On the answer line, write the form of the word that does fit the sentence.

1. Without the *benefactor* provided by the wealthy stranger, Lee could not have gone to medical school.

1. _____ benefaction

2. The Sammarcos' *humanitarian* was appreciated by the entire community.

2. _____ humanitarianism

3. The hungry travelers marveled at the *bountiful* in their hosts' kitchen.

3. _____ bounty

4. The parents were more *indulge* with their youngest child than with the others.

4. _____ indulgent

5. *Benevolent* brings rich rewards.

5. _____ Benevolence

6. The teacher smiled *benign* at the new student standing nervously at the door.

6. _____ benignly

7. The woman rewarded her nephew for his *altruistic*.

7. _____ altruism

8. The voice coach's praise brought Jane *gratify*.

8. _____ gratification

9. The famous *philanthropic* contributed a large sum of money for the new wing of the hospital.

9. _____philanthropist_____

10. The primary *beneficial* listed in Mr. McLeod's will was his wife.

10. _____beneficiary_____

Reading Comprehension

Each numbered sentence in the following passage contains an italicized vocabulary word or related form. After you read the passage, you will complete an exercise.

Albert Schweitzer: Doctor and Humanitarian

(1) Dr. Albert Schweitzer (1875–1965) was one of the most **altruistic** men of all time. (2) He is remembered and respected as an outstanding **humanitarian** who gave up promising careers in his native Germany to help the people who needed him.

Before he reached the age of thirty, Dr. Schweitzer was already a well-known philosopher, minister, musician, and writer. (3) His accomplishments in any one of these fields would have **gratified** most people. (4) Although he could have **indulged** himself with comfortable living, Dr. Schweitzer decided instead to serve humanity.

(5) After completing medical school, the **benign** doctor went to Africa in 1913. (6) As a medical missionary, he was ready to put his **philanthropic** dream into action. (7) In French Equatorial Africa, he became the **benefactor** of thousands of people who were without medical attention. Operating under primitive conditions, he fought leprosy, sleeping

sickness, and other tropical diseases. (8) He used the **bountiful** donations from his former parishioners, as well as money he had earned from his organ concerts in Germany and France, to finance a modern hospital at Lambaréné. (9) When this **benevolent** man won the Nobel Peace Prize in 1952, he even contributed his prize of thirty-three thousand dollars to the hospital fund.

(10) Dr. Albert Schweitzer is remembered not only for the **benefits** he brought to Africans but also as a symbol. Believing that all people deserve respect, he appreciated the preciousness of life and hated violence. His happiness made him feel a duty to help others. In doing so, he became an example to the world of what kindness in thought and action could accomplish.

Please turn to the next page.

Reading Comprehension Exercise

Each of the following statements corresponds to a numbered sentence in the passage. Each statement contains a blank and is followed by four answer choices. Decide which choice fits best in the blank. The word or phrase that you choose must express roughly the same meaning as the italicized word in the passage. Write the letter of your choice on the answer line.

1. Dr. Albert Schweitzer was one of the most __?__ men of all time.
   a. active
   b. unselfishly devoted
   c. clearly honest
   d. talented

   1. _____ b

2. He is remembered and respected as an outstanding __?__ .
   a. healer of the sick
   b. adviser to governments
   c. entertainer
   d. contributor to others' welfare

   2. _____ d

3. Schweitzer's accomplishments in any one of his careers would have __?__ most people.
   a. satisfied   b. annoyed   c. challenged   d. disappointed

   3. _____ a

4. Dr. Schweitzer could have __?__ comfortable living.
   a. taught himself   c. given up
   b. hoped for   d. pampered himself with

   4. _____ d

5. The __?__ doctor went to Africa in 1913.
   a. old   b. talented   c. kind   d. musical

   5. _____ c

6. Schweitzer wanted to put his __?__ dream into action.
   a. charitable   b. lifelong   c. impossible   d. realistic

   6. _____ a

7. He became the __?__ thousands of people in French Equatorial Africa.
   a. traveler to   c. consultant to
   b. helper of   d. organist for

   7. _____ b

8. He used the __?__ donations from his former parishioners to build a modern hospital.
   a. small   b. property   c. tax-free   d. generous

   8. _____ d

9. When this __?__ man won the Nobel Peace Prize, he contributed his prize money to the hospital fund.
   a. persistent   b. brilliant   c. kind   d. unusual

   9. _____ c

10. Dr. Schweitzer is remembered for the __?__ he brought to Africans.
    a. advantages   b. dramatic cures   c. knowledge   d. machinery

    10. _____ a

Writing Assignment

Think of a situation in which a person demonstrated kindness. The situation might have been one that you took part in, or it might have been an event that you witnessed or read about. Write a paragraph in which you narrate the incident, focusing on what happened and what the outcome was. Use at least five of the words from this lesson in your narrative paragraph and underline them.

Bonus: Lessons 29 and 30

(pages 187–198)

Use the clues to complete the crossword puzzle.

The completed crossword grid contains the following entries:

- 1 Down: HELPFUL
- 2 Down: ALTRUISTIC
- 3 Down: PLENTEOUS
- 4 Across: WELL
- 5 Down: DANGER
- 6 Down: SCOFF
- 7 Across: INCAPACITATE
- 8 Down: ALIENATE
- 9 Down: CENSURE
- 10 Down: INDULGE
- 11 Across: CRITICIZE
- 12 Across: BENIGN
- 13 Across: DISAPPROVAL
- 13 Down: DICTATE
- 14 Down: GRATIFY
- 15 Across: BENEFACTOR
- 15 Down: BENEFICIAL
- 16 Across: HUMANITARIAN
- 17 Across: HARMFUL
- 18 Across: DETRIMENT
- 19 Across: MALIGN

Across

4. BENEVOLENT comes from the Latin word *bene*, meaning "___?___."

7. What an ankle injury could do to you.

11. If you ADMONISH someone, you ___?___ that person in a kind, but serious, way.

12. Not especially harmful

13. To DENOUNCE is to express very strong ___?___.

15. One who helps another person in need

16. One who promotes social reform

17. Synonym for INJURIOUS

18. Something that causes damage, harm, or loss

19. To speak evil of

Down

1. PHILANTHROPIC pertains to the effort to ___?___ others.

2. From the Latin word *alter*, meaning "other"

3. Synonym for BOUNTIFUL

5. To IMPERIL involves putting something in ___?___.

6. To make fun of

8. To cause to become unfriendly

9. Disapproval or blame

10. To pamper

14. To please or satisfy

15. Something that promotes a favorable result is ___?___.

HOUGHTON MIFFLIN VOCABULARY FOR ACHIEVEMENT, SECOND COURSE

T33

BONUS Lessons 29 and 30

Notes

The following lists of words are from the preceding two lessons. You may wish to use these lists to pinpoint words for ongoing review or for mid-term or final exams.

Lesson 29

admonish	imperil
alienate	incapacitate
censure	injurious
denounce	malign
detriment	scoff

Lesson 30

altruistic	bountiful
benefactor	gratify
beneficial	humanitarian
benevolent	indulge
benign	philanthropic

Test: Lessons 28, 29, and 30
(pages 181–198)

Part A Completing the Definition

On the answer line, write the letter of the word or phrase that correctly completes each sentence.

1. When you *censure* someone, you __?__ him or her.
   a. pay **b.** trust **c.** voluntarily help **d.** severely criticize

   1. ____d____

2. An *incapacitated* person is __?__.
   a. disabled **b.** mistaken **c.** recommended **d.** successful

   2. ____a____

3. Anything that can __?__ is said to be *injurious*.
   a. be decided by a jury **c.** revive dying plants
   b. cause harm or damage **d.** make a person stronger

   3. ____b____

4. When you study *eruptions* in science, you learn about __?__.
   a. rocks **b.** the ocean **c.** climate **d.** explosions

   4. ____d____

5. A *benefactor* is one who __?__.
   a. helps others **b.** is friendly **c.** works hard **d.** complains

   5. ____a____

6. An *infraction* is a __?__.
   a. major argument **c.** minor concern
   b. violation of a law **d.** perceptive observation

   6. ____b____

7. If you *indulge* a child, you __?__ him or her.
   a. confuse **b.** punish **c.** teach **d.** pamper

   7. ____d____

8. A *fractious* person is __?__.
   a. practical **b.** shy **c.** irritable **d.** well liked

   8. ____c____

9. *Philanthropic* impulses are __?__.
   a. unobserved **b.** deceitful **c.** astonishing **d.** charitable

   9. ____d____

10. Drivers who *infringe* the traffic laws __?__ them.
    a. ignore **b.** depend on **c.** violate **d.** enforce

    10. ____c____

11. *Altruistic* people are __?__.
    a. habitually late **c.** unselfishly concerned about others
    b. dedicated **d.** entertaining

    11. ____c____

12. A *rout* is a __?__.
    a. defeat **b.** highway **c.** weakness **d.** refusal

    12. ____a____

13. If you *scoff* at something, you __?__ it.
    a. study **b.** mock **c.** ignore **d.** cherish

    13. ____b____

14. When a water or gas pipe *ruptures*, it __?__.
    a. freezes **b.** shrinks **c.** breaks **d.** becomes rusted

    14. ____c____

15. *Humanitarian* contributions __?__.
    a. help to improve human welfare **c.** develop hidden talents
    b. inform others **d.** prevent jealousy

    15. ____a____

HOUGHTON MIFFLIN VOCABULARY FOR ACHIEVEMENT, SECOND COURSE

Name _____ Date _____

Test: Lessons 28, 29, and 30

Part B   Identifying Synonyms

On the answer line, write the letter of the word or phrase that has the same meaning as that of the capitalized word.

16. BENEFICIAL :
    a. abnormal   **b.** harmful   **c.** advantageous   **d.** unnecessary

16. _____ c

17. ABRUPT :
    a. sudden   **b.** rude   **c.** gradual   **d.** upset

17. _____ a

18. DENOUNCE :
    a. arrive   **b.** combine   **c.** excel   **d.** condemn

18. _____ d

19. BENIGN :
    a. kind   **b.** harsh   **c.** ancient   **d.** direct

19. _____ a

20. MALIGN :
    a. praise moderately   **c.** speak evil of
    b. please   **d.** plan carefully

20. _____ c

21. ALIENATE :
    a. frighten   **b.** befriend   **c.** disassociate   **d.** measure

21. _____ c

22. BOUNTIFUL :
    a. large   **b.** scarce   **c.** festive   **d.** plentiful

22. _____ d

23. FRAGMENT :
    a. separate   **b.** unify   **c.** torment   **d.** reduce

23. _____ a

24. ADMONISH :
    a. baffle   **b.** warn   **c.** compliment   **d.** surprise

24. _____ b

25. GRATIFY :
    a. smooth   **b.** satisfy   **c.** accept   **d.** displease

25. _____ b

26. REFRACTORY :
    a. unresponsive   **b.** unmanageable   **c.** transparent   **d.** sloppy

26. _____ b

27. DETRIMENT :
    a. damage   **b.** condiment   **c.** benefit   **d.** necessity

27. _____ a

28. BENEVOLENT :
    a. lazy   **b.** kind   **c.** mean   **d.** dishonest

28. _____ b

29. DISRUPT :
    a. hasten   **b.** organize   **c.** demand   **d.** hinder

29. _____ d

30. IMPERIL :
    a. decorate   **b.** protect   **c.** endanger   **d.** neglect

30. _____ c

HOUGHTON MIFFLIN VOCABULARY FOR ACHIEVEMENT, SECOND COURSE

Reading Skills

The Suffixes *-ion* and *-ness*

A **suffix** is a group of letters added to the end of a root. (A root is the part of a word that contains its basic meaning. A root can also be a complete word.) Some of the words in this book, such as *dissection* and *momentousness*, end with the suffixes *-ion* and *-ness*. The suffix *-ion* changes a verb or adjective into a noun. The suffix *-ness* changes an adjective into a noun. Each of these suffixes has one meaning.

SUFFIX MEANING	WORD	DEFINITION
-ion: action, process, or state	correction (correct + *-ion*)	act or process of correcting
	confusion (confuse + *-ion*)	state of being confused
-ness: state or condition	gloominess (gloomy + *-ness*)	state of being gloomy
	softness (soft + *-ness*)	condition of being soft

The spelling of the roots to which *-ion* and *-ness* are added sometimes changes. In the examples above, the final *e* of *confuse* is dropped when *-ion* is added. When *-ness* is added to *gloomy*, the *y* changes to *i*.

To determine the meanings of words ending with *-ion* or *-ness*, follow these steps. First, substitute the meaning of the suffix for the suffix itself. Second, think of possible definitions for the entire word. Third, check each definition in a dictionary.

Exercise   Using the Suffixes *-ion* and *-ness*

Each sentence in this exercise contains an italicized verb or adjective. *Step 1:* Form a noun by adding *-ion* or *-ness* to the italicized word. Write the resulting word. *Step 2:* Write your definition of the noun. Use a dictionary to check your definition and spelling of the word. *Step 3:* Write a sentence of your own in which you use the noun correctly.

1. The police officer had to stay *alert* during night duty.

   NOUN FORM   alertness

   DEFINITION   The state of being attentive or aware

   SENTENCE   Your alertness affects your performance on tests

Please turn to the next page.

2. Wash your knee so that dirt won't *infect* the bruise.

NOUN FORM   infection

DEFINITION   The state of being contaminated with germs

SENTENCE   Enrique's ear infection cleared up within a week.

3. Our city *possesses* the finest public library in the state.

NOUN FORM   possession

DEFINITION   The state of having or owning

SENTENCE   The thieves were arrested for the possession of stolen goods.

4. A pilot light *ignites* the gas burner in the water heater.

NOUN FORM   ignition

DEFINITION   The act or process of starting a fire

SENTENCE   Ignition of the rocket engines is done by an automatic system.

5. Liz claims that my room is *sloppy,* but I say it just looks lived in.

NOUN FORM   sloppiness

DEFINITION   A messy condition

SENTENCE   The sergeant would not tolerate sloppiness in her barracks.

6. His *meek* appearance belied his crafty mind.

NOUN FORM   meekness

DEFINITION   The state of being patient, humble, or mild

SENTENCE   He endured his brother's bullying with great meekness.

7. The author *revised* his book to bring it up to date.

NOUN FORM   revision

DEFINITION   The act of revising

SENTENCE   Revision is an important part of the process of writing.

8. The old shack by the railroad station is *mean* and shabby.

NOUN FORM   meanness

DEFINITION   The state or condition of being poor, common, or low in quality

SENTENCE   The meanness of the houses was outweighed by the warmth of the people who lived in them.

9. The *harsh* north wind caused Monica's nose to turn bright red.

NOUN FORM   harshness

DEFINITION   The condition of being severe

SENTENCE   The harshness of the desert did not stop the prospectors.